Facing the Monarch

Harvard East Asian Monographs 359

Facing the Monarch

Modes of Advice in the Early Chinese Court

Garret P. S. Olberding, Editor

Published by the Harvard University Asia Center
Distributed by Harvard University Press
Cambridge (Massachusetts) and London 2013

Printed in the United States of America

The Harvard University Asia Center publishes a monograph series and, in coordination with the Fairbank Center for Chinese Studies, the Korea Institute, the Reischauer Institute of Japanese Studies, and other faculties and institutes, administers research projects designed to further scholarly understanding of China, Japan, Vietnam, Korea, and other Asian countries. The Center also sponsors projects addressing multidisciplinary and regional issues in Asia.

Library of Congress Cataloging-in-Publication Data

Facing the monarch : modes of advice in the early Chinese court / Garret P. S. Olberding, editor.
pages cm. — (Harvard East Asian monographs ; 359)
Includes bibliographical references and index.
Summary: "Focused on the era between the Spring and Autumn period and the latter Han dynasty, this volume investigates the dynamics between early Chinese ministers and monarchs at a time when ministers employed manifold innovative rhetorical tactics by analyzing discrete excerpts from classical Chinese works"—Provided by publisher.
ISBN 978-0-674-72671-0 (hardcover : alk. paper)
1. China—History—Han dynasty, 202 B.C.-220 A.D. 2. China—Social life and customs—221 B.C.-960 A.D. 3. Rhetoric—China—History. I. Olberding, Garret P. S.
DS748.13.F33 2013
931'.04—dc23

2013007733

Index by David Prout.

♾ Printed on acid-free paper

Last figure below indicates year of this printing
22 21 20 19 18 17 16 15 14 13

For Mike Olberding

Acknowledgments

This volume arose out of a workshop, "Addressing the Autocrat: The Drama of Early Chinese Court Discourse," held at the University of Oklahoma, March 21–22, 2009. Its publication would not have been possible without generous assistance from a number of quarters. First, I must offer my most profound gratitude to the workshop participants, many of whom are contributors to this volume, for their thought-provoking papers and congenial yet provocative discussions, as well as for their enduring patience and encouragement for their junior colleague in his efforts to put together the workshop and this volume. I sincerely appreciate their willingness to commit to these projects, in spite of everything else they had to do. Special thanks must go to Michael Nylan, who not only very generously agreed to attend the workshop, lending it the imprimatur of her significant stature, but who also urged I contact several others with her recommendation to attend. These extraordinary gestures made it possible for me to meet and confer with other giants of the field. The Chiang Ching-Kuo Foundation for International Scholarly Exchange deserves great recognition for its sponsorship of this workshop, but equal recognition needs to be paid to Dean Paul Bell of the College of Arts and Sciences at the University of Oklahoma for his astounding magnanimity, a magnanimity that extended even into the economic tempest of the autumn of 2008. He is the stalwart foundation of this whole endeavor. Additional aid for the workshop, both logistic and financial, was also kindly provided by my chair, Dr. Robert Griswold. His gracious leadership continually reinforces the warm, collegial place that the University of Oklahoma's History Department is. William Hammell, Kristen Wanner, and Deborah Del Gais of the Harvard University Asia Center Publications Program gave careful, professional guidance in bringing this project to publication. I am very grateful for their assistance, as well as for the remarks, corrections, and suggestions offered by our copyeditor, Maura High. Finally I must acknowledge a profound personal debt to a true gentleman and doting grandfather, Mike Olberding, whose unwavering encouragement and love helps put everything I do in proper perspective. It is to him that this volume is humbly dedicated.

A version of my essay entitled "How Did Ministers Err?" is published in *Dubious Facts: The Evidence of Early Chinese Historiography* (Albany, New York: State University of New York Press, 2012).

G.P.S.O.

Contents

Contributors

Su-ching Chang, *National Taiwan University*

Wai-yee Li, *Harvard University*

Michael Nylan, *University of California, Berkeley*

Garret P. S. Olberding, *University of Oklahoma*

Yuri Pines, *Hebrew University of Jerusalem*

Sarah A. Queen, *Connecticut College*

David Schaberg, *University of California, Los Angeles*

Griet Vankeerberghen, *McGill University*

Abbreviations

CQFL	*Chunqiu fanlu*
HNZ	*Huainanzi*
HS	*Hanshu*
HSBZ	*Hanshu buzhu*
HHS	*Hou Hanshu*
SJ	*Shiji*
TPYL	*Taiping yulan*
Zuo	*Zuozhuan*

Facing the Monarch

Introduction

Political Address: General Issues

The power of the monarch proves an enduring topic, and with good reason, for in matters of state the crucial moment is the executive decision, when a deliberative body ceases counsel and sets upon its course. Within monarchical government, the essential task is thus to win the executive ear, even if with falsity and deception. The dangers of such influence, for both actors and state, are heavily emphasized in world literature. Myriad moralizing critiques forewarn of woes inflicted by the devious and viper-tongued seeking appeal with the monarch. Too often, however, such woes are blamed more directly on the perils of eloquence itself, of the ability of well-wrought language to entrance and confuse. The sole hope for the artlessly honest, as with Shakespeare's credulous Othello, is for the virtues of truth and faithful service to overcome, by dint of their very virtue, the shams of mendacity—for virtue to "out-tongue" false complaints. Yet this hope, as Othello's example poignantly illustrates, is most often misplaced.

Given the perils of rhetoric, of its daunting power to cunningly manipulate the auditor, there is a tendency in studies of politicized discourse to emphasize the ornate characteristics that could possibly influence the listener, to conflate eloquence with manipulation, and prevarication. This volume attempts to correct for such by accentuating the necessary interaction between content and style that informs all compromised speech and thus, by extension, politicized historiography. Our interest is not only in the analysis of Chinese court politics but also in questions pertaining to the means and aims of early Chinese historiography. We wish to better articulate how politics was "voiced," how the early Chinese circumstance shaped and phrased—and prohibited—certain types of expression. Through such investigations, we not only endeavor to speak to any seeming "Chinese" mode of discourse (if there is such) but also to offer hypotheses about the expressions permitted in classical political formations, touching on subjects of censorship, humilifics, irony, and dissidence. These issues are far from limited to the early Chinese circumstance.

The examination of the modes and structures of political discourse is naturally not a new enterprise. The study of ancient Greek and Roman oratory was, at least until the mid-nineteenth century, a staple of Western higher education. In the United States, the study of political oratory began systematically to decline among university students only after President Eliot of Harvard declared a new program of electives in 1869. Even then, the mark of the gentleman through much of the early twentieth century was his ability to quote and mimic the styles of the ancient public speakers. Indeed, the current political debate clubs at U.S. universities are the remnants of the once central mission of any educated man to become expert in public speaking and debate.[1] But these exercises were aimed to hone the minds of those preparing to engage in debate among relative equals,

---

1. Originally used for the discussion of classroom issues in a Latinate syllogistic form, by 1809 the practice of oratory was abandoned in the colonial chartered colleges, for various reasons, including the surge of secular questions around the time of the American Revolution "which could not be adequately debated in the restrictive Latin syllogistic manner." (Potter, *Debating in the Colonial Chartered Colleges*, 121.) Forensic disputation took its place, having first appeared in classrooms and commencement exercises in the middle of the eighteenth century. Less restricted in form and presentation, "the forensic disputation offered the collegian a more flexible form of debate as suitable for discussing political and literary questions as for moral and metaphysical issues, and as useful in preparing for the law and the legislature as for the clergy" (ibid.) By the mid-nineteenth century, forensic disputation, too, suffered a decline, as literary societies allowed more informal participation; and the liberalization and increased professionalization of the curriculum, promoted by the land grant state institutions, made acquiring sophisticated argu-

or in a controlled classroom setting, not those who were, as was the case for the centuries before the Enlightenment, readying themselves for the precarious, deferential stance of the monarch's supplicant. How to engage with one's opponent in an inequitable environment, in spite of the incessant need, even in our era, is still relatively little understood. These dichotomous alternatives are typically described in highly jaundiced terms, often leading to the latter's denigration and rejection: the political intercourse between relative equals is characterized as permitting an open, confrontational engagement, captured ideally in democratic fora, that of "honest debate," in which the intelligence and reason of both parties is appealed to; and the intercourse of supplicant and monarch, as sycophantic manipulation of master by servant, that of "rhetorical" persuasion, in which conniving trickery, empty flourishes, and clever diversions are employed to mesmerize and confuse. As the classical rhetor Gorgias argued on behalf of Helen of Troy, audiences need beware of the power of *logoi*, of speech itself, for its power can be so mesmerizing as to exonerate one from all its effects, however wrong: "To be persuaded by them [i.e., by *logoi*] is tantamount to being *forced* to do what you do."[2] G. E. R. Lloyd characterizes these two alternatives as those that, grossly framed, distinguish the modes of argumentative interface in ancient Greece and China. In *Adversaries and Authorities*, he states that "in one respect, at least, Greek dialectic leaves more room for acceptable face-to-face argument with partners and opponents than is usually the case in China. This was in that the Greeks eventually came to formalise rules of procedure—for example concerning the roles of questioner and answerer—that allowed dialectic, as a joint endeavor, to be clearly distinguished, in principle at least, from eristic" or showy disputation, as was the norm among popular Greek rhetors such as Gorgias.[3] When the adherents of the various Greek philosophical and medical traditions were locked in dialectical disputes with one another, their chief means for expressing their views was "both lectures (public and private) and open, often public, debates,

---

mentative techniques seem less essential for undergraduates. See also Brubacher and Rudy, *Higher Education in Transition*, 93.

2. Lloyd, *Adversaries and Authorities*, 82.

3. Ibid., 34.

sometimes modeled directly on the adversarial exchanges so familiar in Greek law-courts and political assemblies. The audiences they were aiming to persuade were *first, a general public*, and then more particularly their own immediate rivals and colleagues and potential adherents or pupils." By contrast, in China, as Lloyd states, the preferred audience in such disputes was almost inevitably the ruler.[4]

For Plato and Aristotle, the greatest of ancient Greek political thinkers, unfettered eloquence was a dangerous distraction from the matters of truth at hand. Truth was to *inform* eloquence; uninformed eloquence was merely manipulative. As Aristotle argues, "The arousing of prejudice, pity, anger, and similar emotions has nothing to do with the essential facts, but is merely a personal appeal to the man who is judging the case."[5] To play on the emotions was to not allow the truth itself to speak. If one is allowed to speak truthfully, if truth is the only issue, both Plato and Aristotle would maintain, there is no real need to hone one's abilities in manipulative sycophancy. Rhetoric is in the service to truth, and because truth is more convincing than falsehood, one should castigate the rhetor if, in arguing for the truth, he fails to convince. Aristotle's epistemological optimism is explicit: "[T]hings that are true and things that are better are, by their nature, practically always easier to prove and more persuasive."[6] In essence, it is the truth itself, not the formulation, that lies at the root of the force of the persuasion. Naturally, both Plato and Aristotle realized that in most, if not all, persuasive dialogue, one must be circumspect in how one says what one says. Nevertheless, in the democratic fora at least, it is assumed that one need not, and should not, twist the content, that content is supreme. One cannot just ignore the "facts."

But speaking truthfully should not be equated with speaking aggressively, or even directly. In political discourse, one must often use indirect means, whether it be metaphor, heavily veiled allusion, or riddle. Indeed, within the charged political setting of early Chinese discourse, in which an erudite ministerial subordinate addressed a

---

4. Ibid., 39. Italics mine.

5. Aristotle, *Rhetoric* 1354a16–19; trans. Barnes, *The Complete Works of Aristotle*, 2152.

6. Ibid., 1354a37–8; 2154.

perhaps intellectually inferior executive, the difference in their status, and the associated norms of etiquette, were frequently vulnerable to irreverent contestation. Though the essence of political persuasion ideally is the argument, an element of drama is almost unavoidable. The political address must embrace both reasonable argument and unreasonable bias; certainly, it is sometimes difficult to separate one from the other. Because of this, analyzing the effectiveness of a political appeal requires parsing its various contextualizing, dramatic aspects, which reside outside any merely summary account of its content. How an addressor delivered his remarks—in oral or written form, as monologue or in dialogue with others, employing established rhetorical forms or innovating—provides rubrics for assessing the way dissent and truthful representation were conveyed and received. With this volume, any effort to present merely the unvarnished "truth" in a political setting—thus, in almost any setting—is shown to be at bottom impossible, unproductive, and, in all honesty, not actually wished for. The essays focus on a time in ancient China, a society without the political optimism of Greece, when political address, and theoretical discussions of its exercise, reached a high art: from the Warring States (453–221 BCE) through the early imperial period, the Qin (221–207 BCE) and Han (206 BCE–220 CE) dynasties. Of course, it is not our aim to deny that varnished speech can obscure the grain of truth; instead, we hope to augment previous studies of politicized, "rhetorical" speech by analyzing the unavoidable constraints—institutional and intellectual—that necessarily guide and form political address. The topics covered in this volume may readily speak to a wider audience, not only those interested in the vagaries of court politics but also in their recording and, indeed, in the composition of historiography in general, for early Chinese historiography was, if anything, supremely political.

Early Chinese historiographers, since at least the late Spring and Autumn (Chunqiu) period, were lesser nobles employed as the retainers and stewards of their more prominent relations. As David Schaberg reveals in his essay, "Functionary Speech: On the Work of *Shi* 使 and *Shi* 史," the roots of early Chinese historiography are found in the negotiations of decision and action by the diplomatic corps, the *shi* 使. Their "occasional speeches," made at pivotal Chunqiu summits, are, as Su-ching Chang notes, the precursors of the hortatory addresses of the ministerial *shi* 士 of later eras. From the late Chunqiu through the early imperial period, these diplomats and ministerial *shi* were a primary source of advice and critique for their monarchs, and thus a continuous source of friction. Indeed, we see over the course of the Chunqiu and Warring States eras a heightening in tension and increasingly acerbic critique, a trend that was to culminate in the late Warring States monarch's reassertion of his prerogative over the terms of political discourse. These long-standing tensions between minister and monarch were in part possibly the residue of the sublimated acrimony between the enfranchised superior lineages of the Chunqiu period and their lesser relations, but they were also due to a ceaseless struggle over the control of historiographical representation, and thus of scriptural immortality. This struggle resulted in what David Schaberg has aptly described as a display of Nietzschean *ressentiment*, with an accompanying transformation of value: "In recounting the events of the Spring and Autumn period as a series of ritual aberrations and corrections," Chunqiu historiographers, as indeed their later peers, very self-consciously depicted themselves as "steadfastly conservative, prescient, and eloquent," thereby wresting normative legitimacy away from their political superiors.[7]

Certainly the *shi* ministerial class was not the only source of advice. Griet Vankeerberghen's analysis of the Han period underscores the continuing advisory role of the *zhuhou* 諸侯, the "many lords" (see her essay "Kinship and Kingship in Han China" in this volume). As members of the imperial family, they were presumed ready to assist the emperor and yet, as Vankeerberghen makes poignantly clear, their ultimate aims were often at odds with the emperor's, obliging him to remind his kin of their familial bond and filial duties to the throne, reminders that more than occasionally failed, as the case of Liu Pi 劉濞, king of Wu 吳, so abundantly proved.[8] Thus, whether the source was a close relation, as Vankeerberghen demonstrates with Liu Chang 劉萇; an indirect relation, as with Huo Guang 霍光; or with any number of the *shi* ministerial class, from the illustri-

7. Schaberg, *A Patterned Past*, 259.
8. Liu Pi 劉濞 instigated the infamous Seven Kingdoms Rebellion in 154 BCE.

ous Dong Zhongshu 董仲舒 to the myriad anonymous advisors, tensions were ubiquitous between the monarch and his advisor-attendants.

Despite the obvious wealth of material concerning politicized interaction to be found in premodern China, scholars have only begun to assay what it can offer. Much of the contemporary scholarship that is centered on the early Chinese circumstance speaks to the subject of rhetoric and of the problems of persuasion in general, rather than focusing more narrowly on specific exchanges or period issues. Many of the most imaginative and insightful works, such as François Jullien's *Detour and Access*, are highly abstract, while others, such as as Christoph Harbsmeier's volume for Needham's *Science and Civilisation in China* series or Mary Garrett's work, focus on the various philosophical responses posed by Chinese thinkers.[9] Scholarship from China, whether premodern or modern, typically consists of encyclopedias of rhetorical terminology, often containing later terminology anachronistically applied to documents written centuries, or even millenia, earlier.[10]

While acknowledging that the variety of our sources permits multiple approaches, we aspire to address a shared body of questions that principally concern the transmission of truth and the manner of critique. The essays in this volume broach a variety of questions, among them the following:

1. How precisely did the development of diplomatic activities inform the creation of historiographical archives?
2. What exactly does the desuetude of ritualized, polite speech over the course of the Chunqiu and Warring States periods really indicate? A new consensus, an arbitrary happenstance, or a pointed rejection, whether "legalist" or not, of the old? Were power relations transformed or just subtly modified, that is, did the power over discourse truly concentrate more fully into the hands of the monarch?
3. If the facts did matter, what was important in their representation? If not, what would have prevented their outright distortion?

---

9. For instance, see Harbsmeier, *Language and Logic*; Garrett, "Pathos Reconsidered"; and Levi, "L'art de la persuasion à l'époque des Royaumes Combattants."

10. For instance, see Huang Jianlin, *Hanyu xiucige jianshang cidian*; Wang Zhanfu, *Gudai hanyu xiucixue*; and Chen Wangdao, *Xiucixue fafan*.

Was the monarch's or central court's insistence that the ministers stand by their statements, do what they promised to do, sufficient to handle this rampant problem? If not, how else did the Chinese state prevent the channels of governance from being obstructed by insidious scheming?

4. What can riddled speech say to our understanding of early China? Was a riddle an effective means of persuasion or was it merely a literary artifice to allow for plausible deniability?
5. Was early China in any sense an autocracy? If not, what does this mean for our understanding of the assertion of executive power in early China, how executive directives came about and, more directly pertinent, how ministerial advice could show subtle shifts in articulation relating to who might actually have been controlling the levers of government?

Below I offer a brief encapsulation of some of the important points made in each essay.

Synopses

The volume begins with the question of historical representation rooted in the interposition of the scribe between the sometimes inconvenient truths of collective memory and the demands of institutionalized power. David Schaberg's essay, "Functionary Speech: On the Work of *Shi* 使 and *Shi* 史," links two official vocations of the Chunqiu period: the earlier office of "scribe" (*shi* 史) and the later office of "envoy" (*shi* 使). In asserting their connection, Schaberg suggests that the production of the historiographical narratives of *Zuozhuan* is rooted in the mediative diplomatic mission, posing a tight correlation between the mastery of official documentation (and, later, historical memory) and the envoy's management of the monarchal voice. Though the offices and responsibilities of the *shi* 史 and the *shi* 使 are not explicitly related in the primary sources or in the various secondary studies that Schaberg reviews, several investigations offer evidence for the hypothesis that certain classes of *shi* 史 were at times sent across the borders, apparently as emissaries. From Wolfgang Behr's and Axel Schuessler's analyses of various terms related to writing, the office of the *shi* 史 appears to have been conceptually tied to any number of duties involving official representation, including "being sent" on official business. These conceptual relationships, notes Behr, would have been effaced by the linguistic changes of the Warring States period. While it is not clear what was primary—writing or being sent out on official business—Schaberg argues that writing was not a central feature of the *shi* 史 office as represented in the records of *Zuozhuan* and *Guoyu*, nor was the oral reproduction of historical memory. Schaberg perceives that the duties of both the scribe (*shi* 史) and the envoy (*shi* 使) center upon their mastery of "occasional speech," both being appointed "to utter the right words in important religious and political ceremonies, whether routine or extraordinary, whether at home or abroad." By the Warring States period, if not long before, these occasional speeches became the material for the education of men preparing for positions of authority, men who wished to enter the public sphere, as the expert speeches of Greek and Roman orators became material for later Western politicians. Indeed, one of the main aims of *Zuozhuan*, Schaberg maintains, seems to be "to offer its readers versions of the speeches spoken by envoys on key diplomatic occasions," with historical citations frequently used to bolster the comprehension of the relevant political obligations.

In her essay in this volume, "Three Rhetorical Modes in Pre-Qin Court Remonstrances," Su-ching Chang argues that three general modes of advice emerged in succession between the Chunqiu period to the Qin dynasty: the "instructive," the "confrontational," and the "authoritarian." Drawing on numerous examples, Chang demonstrates that each mode marked a distinctive pattern of interaction between an advisor and his lord. In the instructive stance, a mode that held sway from the Western Zhou to Chunqiu periods, the advisor acted as tutor, delicately offering guidance using references to ancient precedents or citing normatively authoritative classical texts, such as the *Book of Odes* (*Shijing*) and *Book of Documents* (*Shujing*). Examples of "instructive" remonstrances are readily found in the *Zuozhuan* and *Guoyu*, in the "occasional speeches" presented by ministers to their lords at pivotal diplomatic summits and court debates, in which often a shift in power dynamic was being negotiated or threatened. These speeches, Chang makes clear, were exquisitely constructed, their weaving of argument and reference creating a musical effect akin to that of a court orchestra. In the instructive stance, the advisor's disposition remained mild and accommodating, avoiding challenge to the ruler's authority. His aim was not to berate but to cajole. Alas, more often than not, these instructive remonstrances failed to persuade. Without significant negative pressure, rulers revealed themselves unwilling to modify their behavior and plans. The second, "confrontational" mode, observable in the reproaches of Confucian and Mohist tutors, was dominant from the late Eastern Zhou to the end of the Warring States period, after which point the manipulative "authoritarian" mode preferred by legalist ministers such as Li Si became the rule. The confrontational approach emerged with the rise of the *shi* 士, or "scholar-official," who traveled among the various states urging their rulers to act in accord with certain general ideals. Because these *shi* were not permanently dependent on a ruler's patronage, the dynamic between advisor and ruler became more fluid, with cutting criticism more the norm. While still employing the references common in the remonstrances of the instructional mode, the advisor's loyalties in this confrontational era were to prescribed norms of rulership, not to the ruler himself, and an advisor felt a duty to speak when a course of action was deleterious to the future welfare of the state. In the final "authoritarian" disposition, the advisor desisted from attempts to cajole or challenge the ruler; instead, he depended on manipulations of the ruler's own predilections. In their promotion of instrumentalist policy, these advisors showed little regard for historical precedent. The speeches of this era aimed, in Chang's words, to augment the authority of the ruler in "inverse proportion to the diminished power of his subjects."

Yuri Pines, in his essay "From Teachers to Subjects: Ministers Speaking to the Rulers, from Yan Ying 晏嬰 to Li Si 李斯," further sharpens this diachronic shift. The evolution of advisory modes, Pines maintains, correspond to the shifting differential in the relative status of advisor and lord. These shifts are marked by an increasingly circumspect tone in the advisor's remarks, moving from one of self-confidence in the Chunqiu era to one of (at least pretended) subservience in the Qin. Yan Ying, Pines's exemplar for the Chunqiu, repeatedly oversteps the formal divide between advisor and ruler, caustically challenging, however indirectly, the ruler's legitimacy. It is notable not only that Yan Ying is forthright in his critiques but also that Lord Jing of Qi is self-denigrating in his acceptance of them. Indeed, Pines points out, in the records of *Zuozhuan*, such remonstrative transgressions were rarely punished: "Even in extreme cases, when a remonstrating official broke the rules of decorum and publicly humiliated or even threatened the ruler, punishment was far from inevitable." Rulers in this period were obliged to accept such impertinence, being sometimes only nominally superior to their advisors; thus punishing them was extremely risky. The decline of the regard for their lords reached such an extent that some advisors, such as Zichan of Zheng, seemed to consider that their lords hardly even merited admonition. In the succeeding Warring States period, with the concentration of power into the hands of the monarch, one would expect the *shi* 士, with their relative lack of power, to be more deferential. Instead, the *shi* were just as critical, and at times more audacious, in their remonstrations than their aristocratic predecessors. Mengzi (Mencius), Pines's exemplar for this trend, could reduce his lordly audience to the position of humble disciple, as he did King Hui of Wei (r. 369–318 BCE), at times contesting the ruler's fitness for office. Mengzi even brazenly proposed that failure to heed instructive remonstrance was reason enough for the monarch's removal. Pines suggests that the source of the *shi*'s audacity lay with their marketability. In a multistate world, a ruler could not afford to render his state hostile to these talented itinerant advisors. His power to punish them for any perceived slight, in consequence, was severely curtailed.

Toward the end of the Warring States period the ministerial voice became more diffident. In this period, although the hierarchical distinction between minister and monarch is pronounced, we nevertheless see the preservation of the ministerial prerogative for candid critique. In the one dialogue preserved in the *Xunzi*, an exchange between Xunzi and King Zhao of Qin (r. 306–250 BCE), Xunzi is clearly depicted as the ruler's inferior, his responses deferential to the ruler's queries. Nevertheless, at least in theory, the dialogue permits the moral and even political superiority of those who adhere to Ru 儒 norms. But more ominously, the text implicitly seems to anticipate a unified empire, in which advisors could no longer rely upon the open competition for their talents to protect them from punishment. And, in fact, such was to be. Consequently, the rhetorical flourishes in ministerial address begin to reveal a heightened awareness of the extent of the political, and personal, vulnerability of the now completely dependent minister, producing a rhetoric that was to become veiled in ritual references and gnomic metaphor.

The analysis of these metaphoric occlusions is detailed by Wai-yee Li in her essay, "Riddles, Concealment, and Rhetoric in Early China." Success in advising the ruler, regardless of period, required the minister to adapt to the demands of the moment and master what the *Xunzi* deems the art of the transformative composition, in Li's words to "command range without appearing far-fetched, adhere to practicality while rising above the pedestrian." The ideal persuader must remain pliant, but he also is obliged to conceal his ultimate aims, as well as his powers, for, following the *Hanfeizi*, persuasion is "a cat-and-mouse game that depends on the persuader's hiding the very qualities responsible for his success," surreptitiously exploiting the ruler's personal motivations. Once he gains the ruler's trust, the persuader will be able to openly avow his true views, to seduce the ruler into accepting notions he otherwise might not. Riddles are a common device to these ends, concealing behind symbols and metaphors the transformative message the persuader wishes to impart. Their allure is mesmerizing, an allure, Li observes, symbolically reinforced by anecdotes of women employing them. Although superficially a more frivolous medium than direct, earnest remonstrance, riddles, being simultaneously opaque and clear, can achieve an effect denied to remonstrance, for the riddle lightly coaxes the listener, attracted by the challenge of unraveling the riddle, into ameliorative self-examination. Offering the appearance of a merely facile, impish jest, the riddle permits the persuader to subtly remonstrate without fear of punitive retribution. Like the court poet, the jester approaches the emperor with "an unpredictable mix of intimacy, influence, and vulnerability." Both poet and jester blend a celebration of pleasure with the offering of corrective admonition, and for both, the possibility of correction retroactively condones such hedonistic celebration (a hedonism that, according to their historical critics, ultimately compromises their political efficacy). With female persuaders, the contradiction between pleasure and efficacy is almost unavoidable. Anecdotes from the chapter "Rhetorical Prowess" in *Lienü zhuan*, involving ugly female riddlers, play on this tension, with the attractions of the riddle compensating for the riddlers' lack of physical attractiveness.

Such tension reinforces the axiom, Li notes, that apparent attractions, whether of physique or riddle, are deceptive, founded on casual evaluation. The ugliness of the female persuader divests her of the easy power of physical seduction, a power that is only reendowed with the receipt of the riddle, and the concomitant acknowledgment of a hidden worth. As with the riddle, the true value of the physically repellent woman cannot immediately be appreciated. The riddle forces the listener "to rise above appearance," to seek a concealed excellence and thereby become transformed. The similarly mesmerizing powers of both riddle and woman speak broadly "to the fantasies and anxieties of persuaders: their *modus operandi* limited by the increasing power of the ruler, these stories imagine escape from the rigid hierarchy of ruler and subject by gaining the ruler's absolute trust, their authority becoming incontrovertible as their power and influence are enhanced by being invisible and indefinable." As in classical Greece, politics and aesthetics are inextricably interwoven.

Given all the emphasis on manipulative diversion, one might understandably wonder how substantive, how firmly grounded in verifiable reality, these ministerial remonstrations were, how much of their effect was based on the comprehension of concrete particulars bearing upon the matter at hand and whether these particulars were central, or even salient, for the success of the minister's case.[11] It is to such concerns that Garret Olberding's analysis turns. In his essay "How Did Ministers Err?" Olberding not only asks what the inclusion of facts actually could achieve but also offers a hypothesis for their apparent persuasive impotence. Much of recent analysis on the contents of ministerial addresses to the monarch centers on the minister's attention to and use of canonical sources, whether as an indication of the use of ritualized norms (*li* 禮) or a logic of signs. Olberding's essay takes a different tack in the study of ministerial address by evaluating how error was perceived by Han emperors with regard to the information they received. His analysis speaks specifically to the ways in which error or "fault" was discussed in the court setting and how these might point to the standards by which a

11. For a more extended discussion of these and other related issues, see Olberding, *Dubious Facts.*

minister's presented evidence could be taken to be flawed or mistaken. It is clear, from Olberding's examinations, that the monarch was very concerned with the quality and reliability of forwarded concrete information. Instead of viewing the lack of emphasis on the full and accurate representation of concrete matters in Han court debates as indicative of a general indifference toward accuracy, or concrete facts in general, as some scholars maintain, Olberding argues that reliance on concrete facts was deemphasized because of the very reasonable concern that the official sources of the facts were suspect. Given the widespread propensity among officials to misrepresent states of affairs, the monarch could not but be skeptical of all the information he received through official channels. Accordingly, error was thus not characterized as absolute error of perception but of representation, and representations were not evaluated as to their complete accuracy but to their general plausibility. Because of the unreliability of any representation of a state of affairs, the monarch was obliged to consider other types of "information" revealing the state of the empire, including natural signs and even the riddle-like peasant chants. Such chants, the content of which might objectively be deemed "rumor," were in fact means of conveying indirectly to those who would listen to the conditions the common people were experiencing, conditions that their local officials might wish to obscure. In consequence, in order to appraise the fidelity of his ministers and their efficient and honest supervision of political affairs, the monarch was better served not to try to evaluate the quality of the information he received but instead to evaluate the applied consequences and constructive uses of received policy proposals employing such information.

With Sarah Queen's investigation of addresses by Dong Zhongshu ("The Rhetoric of Dong Zhongshu's Imperial Communications") we introduce specific, detailed case studies from the Han dynasty. Queen explores three exemplars to illustrate the rhetorical variations among modes of addressing the monarch: the first directly to Emperor Wu himself; the second, indirectly via King Yi of Jiangdu, one of Emperor Wu's brothers; and the third indirectly through a letter sent with an emissary to Emperor Wu. Because these addresses were offered at different stages in Dong Zhongshu's career, they speak to his consistent use of rhetorical conventions. Through her examinations, Queen establishes that Dong Zhongshu adjusts his honorific rhetorical prefaces and postscripts to accord with the respect he believes his audience deserves. However, in spite of his audience's elevated station, Dong Zhongshu's honorifics and humilifics frequently are disingenuous, betraying an acid condescension and low regard of his audience's intellectual capabilities and ethical standards. Excerpts of his audience's responses reveal an irreverent impatience on their part as well, whether these responses come from the emperor himself or his brother, King Yi. Though Dong's patrons are sincerely requesting his perspectives on matters of state, and thus seem to believe them worth consideration, their responses are not without biting objections. In her detailed exposition of these episodes, Queen lays bare the rhetorical traces of the tensions in these minister-monarch relationships, with the monarch appearing both as impotent student and potent sovereign. As Queen remarks, the hierarchy of formal protocol conventions "stands in constant tension with the hierarchy of moral knowledge." Dong Zhongshu's repeated insistence on the priority of moral conduct thus inevitably leads to the rhetorical subversion of traditional power relations.

Griet Vankeerberghen, in her essay "Kinship and Kingship in Han China: The 120 CE Case of Liu Chang, King of Lecheng," demonstrates how historical narrative and political address are mutually, and crucially, informative, proffering a detailed treatment of a further significant structural facet of imperial address: the interaction between members of the imperial family, specifically between the *zhuhou* 諸侯 kingly lineages and the emperor. Much like the ministers on whom this volume is focused, the *zhuhou* were appointed to their official positions to aid the emperor in governing the realm, yet their sense of duty toward, and respect for, the emperor was consistently clouded by their personal relationship to the emperor and, more important, his familial competitors. The tone of their addresses thus naturally sometimes betrays caustic discontent with the emperor and his policies, revealing the many fissures in the putative bonds of kinship, fissures that were widened by the influence of the emperor's ministers. In the aftermath of the Great Rebellion of 154 BCE, court officials, probably with the emperor's sanction, worked assiduously to reduce the power, and potential threat, of the emperor's relatives, upbraiding the kings in memorials to the throne, attacks on familial bonds against which the kings railed. Compromising, the emperor permitted the kings to preserve their ritual status without retaining any real political power.

The politically weakened institution of kingship survived into the Eastern Han, with persistent struggles between the kings and the emperor's officials, who would act as proxies for the various factions of the imperial family. Vankeerberghen raises the case of Liu Chang, king of Lecheng, who was charged with impiety in 120 or 121 CE. Likely a member of the contingent brought to the capital as a child by Empress Dowager Deng to be educated, Liu Chang was appointed as king to Lecheng but after his arrival was almost immediately accused by officials in the employ of the previous king's widow of ignoring his ritual obligations toward her and his deceased predecessor, Liu Bin. As the Empress Dowager Deng had died in the very year of his accession, Liu Chang apparently had no imperial protection against the machinations of Liu Bin's widow. Thus we see in the charge of his impiety a struggle between the distaff members of the imperial family, rendered visible in possibly fraudulent attacks memorialized by officials against the hapless, if not innocent, king. The accusations of violence and ill behavior presented against Liu Chang were so extreme that one cannot but suspect their mendacity. Whether or not the emperor himself was aware of these machinations—and Vankeerberghen gives good reasons to believe he was—he reduced Liu Chang's capital punishment to a demotion of rank. But perhaps the most striking aspect of the exchanges revolving around Liu Chang's case is the explicit and implicit references to classic texts, particularly the *Zhouli* 周禮, by Cen Hong, an official offering a plea on behalf of Liu Chang, to justify the reduction of Liu Chang's penalty as an imperial relative. Reconstructing the emperor's decision-making process through an incisive comparative examination of the imperial annals and Cen Hong's plea, Vankeerberghen offers the hypothesis that Cen's plea, making perhaps somewhat tongue-in-cheek use of passages from the *Zhouli*, permits the emperor to reduce Liu Chang's charge without openly dismissing the charges brought by Liu Bin's widow. Vankeerberghen's investigation suggests an emperor embroiled in a political rivalry with his distaff relatives, in which Liu Chang was really something of a pawn.

The first seven essays in the volume elucidate the centrality of the culture of innuendo, insincere self-effacement, and evasion to early Chinese court address, but in the eighth and final essay, "Yang Xiong's 揚雄 Final *Fayan* 法言 Chapter: Rhetoric to What End and for Whom?," Michael Nylan shows that artful insinuation pervaded numerous other compositional formats as well. A Han-era literary giant, Yang Xiong—much like Dong Zhongshu, discussed in Sarah Queen's essay—critiqued imperial policy through an exposition of Ru 儒, or "classicist," norms, including, in the *Fayan*'s final chapter, the central Ru virtue of "filial piety" (*xiao* 孝), a virtue so basic to the Ru vision that one might have expected its exposition to be at the beginning, rather than the end, of the *Fayan*. Previous interpretations of the ultimate intent of the exposition were snarled by seeming praise of Wang Mang, the eventual usurper of the Han throne, in Yang Xiong's closing remarks about the fate of the Han house. But praise, implied or not, can be a double-edged sword, intended more as constructive critique than as flattery.

On Nylan's reading, the chapter is focused on the central matters of state: war and sacrifice. According to two insightful commentators, Yang discusses *xiao* to ground his vision of the ruler's obligations, with pointed reference to the Ru sage-rulers. Though Yang's chapter covers many topics, its central thesis is that the emperor's devotion to the welfare of the empire will result in the implementation of benevolent policies, which are only the proper compensation for his subjects' dutiful service. Like the requiting of the unseen presence of the spirits, it is the requiting of the "unseen" service of his subjects that renders the emperor most human. But if the emperor's policies are only for his own self-aggrandizement, to the detriment of his subjects, as aggressive plans for military expansion might seem to be, then, for Yang, they cannot be rationalized as paying homage to the ancestors. *Xiao* is manifested in the emperor's duty to his people, but it is also further reflected in the people's ability to perform cult obligations to their ancestral dead, and thus, by extension, to fulfill their own social duties. For both ruler and subject, it is worldly effort that is most pleasing to the spirits, not perfunctory prayers and incantations. *Xiao* then acts as a bridge between past and future, between the ancestors and the future prosperity of the empire. Similar critical exhortations also apply, as Nylan demonstrates, to Wang Mang himself. Yang Xiong's chapter is thus clearly not an unalloyed panegyric to Wang Mang, however its enigmatic last lines are interpreted. Indeed, the chapter is not, Nylan concludes, necessarily directed at any monarch specifically at all but at future generations, to espouse the adoption of a new classicism, to promote his new method of using the classics to speak to vital matters of state. As with the great Greek philosophers, Yang's ultimate aim was to persuade not just a particular audience but the general governing elite, both current and future, of the practical utility of an ethical disposition in governance.

CHAPTER 1

Functionary Speech: On the Work of *Shi* 使 and *Shi* 史

David Schaberg, University of California, Los Angeles

A curious feature of the *Zuozhuan* 左傳, and more generally of texts purporting to recount events of the Spring and Autumn period (770–453 BCE), is their emphasis on reported speech. A great majority of the discrete anecdotes concerning this period include or foreground some quoted exchange. It did not have to be this way, naturally. Other early historical works, including the founding works of Greek historiography and even prominent Chinese works like the *Shiji* 史記, tell more of their tales without quoted speech, ignoring or summarizing many of the remarks their characters might have made. The prominence of speech in the Spring and Autumn lore, then, bespeaks some strong predilection among the users of this narrative corpus, a preference for a mixed mode of mimesis in which the narrator alternates between narrating and impersonating. The remarks and speeches were evidently good for remembering, and perhaps also for imitating.

Among the most memorable speeches reproduced in this lore are addresses delivered by diplomatic travelers, that is, by envoys to or from the royal court, by visitors from one of the local courts to another, or by representatives of a local court at a meeting of allies or a confrontation with enemies. These speeches can be impressive not only for their language, which at times reaches into elevated and archaizing registers, but also for their rhetorical patterning and their mustering of historical data. Most important, they often show off a canny solution to some quandary of policy presented in the framing narrative: the good speaker might turn back an invading army, for example, or save his small state from an overlord's excessive demands, or continue or restore ties of amity, or even win the release of an imprisoned ruler. It should not surprise us that memories of such achievements were preserved and committed to writing, or that it was considered important to provide some account of the precise words spoken. Again, for the earliest known users of these materials, the speeches may have been useful models of rhetoric and oratorical skill rather than simple objects of historical contemplation.

Admiration for the eloquence of the envoy is well attested in Warring States texts. Confucius (551–479 BCE) is said to have regarded effectiveness in diplomatic speech as the intended result of studying the *Shijing*: "If one can recite the three hundred songs, but when one is entrusted with administrative duties one cannot succeed, and when one is sent on a mission to some distant place one cannot respond on one's own initiative, then as many songs as that may be, what is one to do with them?" 誦詩三百，授之以政，不達；使於四方，不能專對，雖多亦奚以爲.[1] When a visitor comes from Qu Boyu 蘧伯玉, an upright officer of Wei, and offers a well-chosen remark on his master's efforts at self-improvement, Confucius remarks with obvious approval: "What an envoy! What an envoy!" 使乎！使乎![2] Both of Confucius's comments are cited by Ban Gu 班固 (32–92 CE) in his introduction to the section of his bibliography that collects the works of the "criss-cross persuaders" (*zonghengjia* 縱橫家), whom he regards as professional and intellectual descendants of the envoys.[3] The enormous number of exemplary speeches attributed to these roving persuader figures—Su Qin 蘇秦, Zhang Yi 張儀, and many others—and collected in *zhuzi* 諸子 ("Masters") texts and, later, in the *Shiji* and *Zhanguoce* 戰國策, itself attests to the lasting interest in oratory's powers.

Taken with other materials that offer direct advice on the art of persuasion, both the Spring and Autumn lore and the vast corpus of persuader speeches suggest that, at least during and after the Warring

1. *Analects* 13.5.
2. Ibid., 14.25.
3. *HS* 30.1740.

States period (453–221 BCE), men of means were interested in educating themselves in, or receiving education from others in, oratorical techniques. For these centuries we have some sense, however vague, of the principles and exemplary texts that a teacher or autodidact would have used. By contrast, we have few clues as to the training given their predecessors, that is, the statesmen, envoys, and subjects who must have spoken with some degree of eloquence to one another during the Spring and Autumn period itself. If the accounts of *Zuozhuan*, *Guoyu* 國語, and similar works carry any weight at all, then good speaking was a skill prized as highly during the early Eastern Zhou (770–221 BCE) as it was later. Some information can be derived from the speeches represented in these texts, which may capture some of the words actually spoken in history—it is impossible to know—and likely do convey at least some of the rhetorical preferences of those earlier speakers. But as for the cultivation of young talent and instruction in the forms and registers of speech that would be required in official life, these are nearly invisible to us.

One promising approach is to consider who the envoys' forebears in Zhou court life might have been. Neither bronze inscriptions nor received texts have much to say about the bearers of words among courts, and the most familiar terms for "envoy"—*shi* 使, *shizhe* 使者, and the slightly different *xingren* 行人—do not appear as such in sources describing Western Zhou (ca. 1045–771 BCE) life. Nonetheless, in the duties of one key court official, the *shi* 史, we may have a precedent for the later carrying of words among states. Although narratives about the Spring and Autumn period draw a clear distinction between *shi* 史 and *shi* 使, both in respect of their duties and in respect of their status within court hierarchies, the two types of officers do have in common a responsibility for certain types of elevated, regulated, or sensitive speech. The *shi* 史 normally speak at court or in a court's home rituals, while the *shi* 使 normally carry rulers' messages to other courts, but there are exceptions to this distinction. Seen against the background of Zhou politics and the steady waning of royal prestige, the emergence of the *shi* 使 as significant actors in interstate relations would appear to be the result of a differentiation within the original office of the *shi* 史. The likely familial connection between lowly court functionary and higher-placed traveling spokesperson sheds light on the nature of speeches attributed to both sorts of officers, and ultimately on the linked origins of eloquence and historiography.

Duties and Speeches of the Shi 史

The office of the *shi* 史, its origins and earliest duties, and the significance of the graph chosen to represent the name of the office, have long been matters of scholarly concern. Especially energetic have been the many efforts to explain the graph and to identify the object it seems to show grasped in one hand: a writing brush, bamboo strips, fire-making materials, a torch, hunting nets, to name a few examples.[4] In the main these efforts have been animated by a drive to find in the earliest textual remains and in the writing system itself an ancestry for the most familiar senses of the term *shi* 史 in later times, "historian" and "history." Already for Xu Shen 許慎 (ca. 55–ca. 149 CE), the graph—which he saw as hands holding to the "central" (*zhong* 中) and thus the "correct" (*zheng* 正)—represented "the one who records affairs" (*jishizhe* 記事者).[5] Wang Guowei 王國維 (1877–1927 CE), citing an *Yili* 儀禮 passage, famously reinterpreted the element *zhong* 中 as a container for the bamboo slips used in scorekeeping in archery matches; he speculated that the same sort of container would have been used for the bamboo writing materials used by a scribe.[6] Xu Fuguan 徐復觀 (1902–83) more carefully set aside the later associations of *shi* 史 in order to consider what the duties of the *shi* 史 were at the time of the creation of the graph and to argue for a strong connection between the earliest *shi* 史 and such ritual specialists as the *ce* 冊 (recorder) and *zhu* 祝 (invocator). For Xu, the graph shows a mouth over a hand holding a writing brush; the *shi* 史 began as prayer masters whose addresses to the spirits involved both speech and writing.[7]

The question of the early duties of *shi* 史, and especially of the extent of their religious duties, persists in more recent investigations

4. Xu Zhaochang, *Xian Qin shiguan de zhidu yu wenhua*, 2–6.
5. Xu Shen, *Shuowen jiezi xinding*, 187.
6. Wang Guowei, *Guantang jilin*, 263–74.
7. "Yuan shi" 原史, in Xu Fuguan, *Liang Han sixiang shi*, 3:132–84.

of the subject. For Xu Zhaochang 許兆昌, the forerunners of the *shi* 史 were shamans (*wu* 巫) and blind reciters (*gu* 瞽), court personnel who in Xu's view were primarily responsible for astronomical observation and the marking of seasons.[8] Kai Vogelsang, reviewing the Western Zhou inscriptional evidence with a fastidious resistance to anything smacking of anachronistic interpretation, finds no evidence whatsoever for religious duties of the kind Xu Zhaochang has in mind, or for that matter of the kind attributed to the *shi* 史 of the Spring and Autumn period. Instead, Vogelsang emphasizes the *shi*'s 史 close connection with the *zuoce* 作冊 (makers of records), their responsibility for the articulation of commissions (*ming* 命) and the presentation of investiture gifts, and their involvement in the overseeing and documentation of legal cases. Tantalizingly, for the present investigation, Vogelsang notes the travels of *shi* 史 as envoys (*Gesandte*) and wonders if the *neishi* 內史 ("inner" or "court" *shi*) were perhaps so named in order to distinguish them from the *shi* 史 who traveled beyond court.[9]

In a recent study, Martin Kern confirms that neither inscriptions nor the oldest received texts ever portray the *shi* 史 of the Western Zhou as historians or archivists. Instead, they are "secretaries," highly placed officials responsible for writing as it is used in investiture ceremonies. In contrast to Vogelsang, Kern prefers not to differentiate the unmarked *shi* 史 from the various more specific titles that occasionally appear (such as *neishi*), and he allows that the term *zuoce* may designate the same office.[10] He also finds evidence that the *shi* 史 were engaged both in religious ceremonies, such as divination, and in the secular business of the court.[11] The secretary is "the main representative of the king. He goes on diplomatic and military mission [*sic*], he leads various kinds of rituals, and he announces the royal appointments."[12]

Also relevant to the early duties of the *shi* 史 and to their possible afterlife in the duties of *shi* 使 is the historical phonological analysis

8. Xu Zhaochang, *Xian Qin shiguan de zhidu yu wenhua*, 7–29.

9. Vogelsang, *Geschichte als Problem*, 38–43.

10. Kern, "The Performance of Writing in Western Zhou China," 109–76, 117.

11. Ibid., 121.

12. Ibid., 157.

of Wolfgang Behr, cited by both Vogelsang and Kern.[13] Behr connects *shi* 史, *shi* 使, *li* 理, *ji* 紀 and *ji* 記, *shi* 事, *li* 吏, *shi* 仕, and *shi* 士 as morphological derivations from the root *li* 理, "to divide, regulate, mark (of field divisions)." He theorizes on the basis of reconstructed morphological markers that the *shi* 史 was one who performed the act of *li* 理, "marking" or "scratching." The verbs *ji* 紀 and *ji* 記, both "to record," had a prefix signifying the definitive nature of the act. The *li* 吏 "clerk" was a "marker" or "regulator," and to *shi* 使 was to treat someone as a "clerk," that is, "to employ" or "to send" someone. To *shi* 事, "to serve for," would derive from *li* 吏 and suggest the willingness to serve; *shi* 仕 would be a "nondirectional" version of this verb, and *shi* 士 would be the one who served in this capacity. In short, around the original verb for marking—whether the marking of fields or the scratching out of signs on a surface—hovers a cloud of forms designating various aspects of official service and the sorts of personnel employed in it. Behr takes pains to note, as analysts of graphs seem rarely to have done, that by the Warring States period linguistic change would have rendered invisible many of the connections and distinctions implied by Old Chinese morphology.[14] Nonetheless, the root and its derivatives do suggest a shared institutional point of origin that may help explain connections between *shi* 史 and *shi* 使 even in much later settings.

Axel Schuessler treats these words somewhat differently. He provisionally distinguishes three homophonic words written with the graph *li* 理: one meaning "to divide," one meaning "to regulate, reason, administer," and one meaning "envoy." He acknowledges that in other reconstructions the three words are thought to be one. From *li* 理 in the sense of "envoy," Schuessler derives *li* 吏, "official," *shi* 使, "to send, employ, cause," *shi* 史, "a secretary, scribe," and finally the noun *shi* 使, "an ambassador." He calls into question the derivation of *shi* 史 and *shi* 使 from *li* 理, noting that the latter is never attested in the sense "to write," and cites James Matisoff's argument that both *shi* 史 and *shi* 使 were related to Proto-Lolo-Burmese and Written Burmese words for "send on business, employ."[15]

---

13. Behr, "Language Change in Premodern China," 13–51, 16–17.
14. Ibid., 16–17.
15. Schuessler, *ABC Etymological Dictionary of Old Chinese*, 349–50.

The question, then, is whether and to what extent the physical act of marking played a role in the institutional context that gave rise to the complex of words around *shi* 史 and *shi* 使. In that early moment, likely before the origin of writing proper, was official service characterized more by the ability to make marks, whether on the land or on some smaller surface, or by the ability of the ruler to "employ" proxies and "send" them out as his representatives? More broadly, is the core concept the moment-to-moment power and control of a large human organization, or is it instead the more permanent traces such an organization leaves in the landscape and in the human world? At the very least one may say that, in the Spring and Autumn period lore, the division of labor between *shi* 史 and *shi* 使 argues for a continuing connection between the two notions of control, with perhaps greater weight on the side of controlled representation.

The *shi* 史 of the *Zuozhuan*, the *Guoyu*, and other texts' many accounts of Spring and Autumn period life do in some cases write, but this activity does not seem to define their role. Nor does the oral transmission of historical memories account for very much of what they do, though in a few examples *shi* 史 do show a spectacular mastery of the past. Overall, these officials seem to carry on many of the duties Martin Kern describes for the secretaries of the Western Zhou, albeit it without the high status their predecessors enjoyed; they also have many duties that are unattested for the earlier period, either because the *shi* 史 had not yet taken them on or because the formulaic nature of bronze inscriptions made no place to mention them. What defines the role of the *shi* 史 in almost all of their manifold activities, both in the Western Zhou examples and in the later ones we are about to examine, is their mastery of occasional speech: they are the officials appointed to utter the right words in important religious and political ceremonies, whether routine or extraordinary, whether at home or abroad.

It is not entirely clear what might have distinguished simple *shi* 史 from the several special forms of *shi* 史 mentioned in the *Zuozhuan*.[16] The *neishi* 內史 appear only at the Zhou royal court or in service to

16. On these differentiations, see also Vogelsang, *Geschichte als Problem*, 50.

it.[17] That they sometimes travel beyond the royal domain is of interest in connection with Vogelsang's hypothesis on the meaning of *neishi* and in connection with our investigation of *shi* 使 origins.[18] A *waishi* 外史 ("external" *shi*) in Lu is summoned to craft the language of a covenant.[19] Perhaps supporting the notion of a division of labor between *shi* 史 in the Zhou court and *shi* 史 elsewhere, all the *taishi* 大史 ("grand" *shi*) except for two are employed in local courts rather than in the royal court;[20] the exceptions are one very early *taishi*, possibly legendary, and one very late *taishi*.[21] Three *zuoshi* 左史 (*shi* "of the left") are mentioned; one of them, in Chu, seems to be responsible for knowing ancient texts, while the others, one in Chu and one in Jin, have a special expertise in military matters.[22] The titles of the *shishi* 筮史 ("milfoil divination" *shi*) and the *jishi* 祭史 ("sacrifice" *shi*) are self-explanatory.[23] In sum, the specifying titles pick out, rather inconsistently, a few of the key functions attributed to *shi* 史 in general and discussed below.

Some of the various types of *shi* 史 mentioned in the *Zuozhuan* are anonymous, identified only by their office. Others are identified with a given name: "the *shi* 史 so-and-so," "the *neishi* so-and-so," or "the *taishi* so-and-so." *Taishi* are more likely to be nameless than *neishi*. The *jishi* and *shishi* are always unnamed, presumably because

---

17. *Zuo*, Huan 2.2 (Yang, 90), Zhuang 32.3 (Yang, 251–52), Xi 11.2 (Yang, 337–38), Xi 16.1 (Yang, 369), Xi 28.3h (Yang, 463), Wen 1.1 (Yang, 510), Wen 14.7 (Yang, 604), Xiang 10.2 (Yang, 978). Hereafter all references to the *Zuozhuan* will be marked, as in this note, by the ducal passage reference followed by the page number in Yang Bojun's translation.

18. *Zuo*, Xi 11.2 (Yang, 337–38), Xi 16.1 (Yang, 369), Xi 28.3h (Yang, 463), Wen 1.1 (Yang, 510), Xiang 10.2 (Yang, 978).

19. *Zuo*, Xiang 23.5 (Yang, 1083).

20. *Zuo*, Min 2.5 (Yang, 266), Wen 18.7a (Yang, 633–42), Xuan 2.3c (Yang, 662–63), Xiang 25.2 (Yang, 1099), Xiang 30.13 (Yang, 1180), Zhao 1.9 (Yang, 1215), Zhao 2.1 (Yang, 1226), Zhao 17.2 (Yang, 1384–85), Ai 11.3 (Yang, 1663), Ai 14.3 (Yang, 1685), Ai 24.1 (Yang, 1723).

21. For Xin Jia 辛甲, supposed to have been a Yin defector and subject of King Wen of Zhou (r. 1056–1050 BCE) see *Zuo*, Xiang 4.7 (Yang, 938); for a late Zhou *taishi*, see Ai 6.4 (Yang, 1635–36).

22. *Zuo*, Zhao 12.11 (Yang, 1340); Xiang 14.3a (Yang, 1009), Ai 17.4 (Yang, 1708).

23. *Zuo*, Xi 28.12 (Yang, 474), Zhao 17.4 (Yang, 1390).

they, like other anonymous *shi*, are of low rank and as individuals relatively forgettable. Among the more famous and influential *shi* figures are the obscure early Zhou *shi* Yi 佚 (in other texts sometimes Yi 逸, sometimes a *zuoce*), whose words several characters cite;[24] the *neishi* Guo 過, *neishi* Shuxing 叔興, and *neishi* Shufu 叔父 of Zhou;[25] *shi* Zhao 趙 of Jin;[26] and especially *shi* Mo 墨 from Cai, also known as *shi* An 黯, who appears to pass his career in the service of Zhao Yang 趙鞅 of Jin.[27] In the *Zuozhuan* only the Jin *shi* Dong Hu 董狐 (fl. ca. 607 BCE) has a known family name and a long pedigree of highly placed *shi* 史 to go with it.[28] Only Sima Qian's 司馬遷 (?146–?86 BCE) later account of his own family line suggests as long an ancestry for a line of *shi* 史.[29]

The official duties of the *shi* 史 revolved around the use of texts, written or unwritten, under special circumstances. To judge from a single episode, they retained their old role in the crafting and delivery of investiture documents (*ce* 策) from the Zhou king; another passage shows a Zheng *taishi* delivering an appointment document (*ce*) to a man newly elevated to the position of high minister (*qing* 卿).[30] They were entrusted with the drafting of covenant language and the writing up of covenant documents, a duty that would have required not only literacy but savvy in the scripting and management of the spoken word as well.[31]

Most common by far of the duties of the *shi* 史 who appear in *Zuozhuan* narratives are the duties relating to sacrifices, especially to nature spirits or in response to natural disasters. The *shi* 史 are

---

24. *Zuo*, Xi 15.4e (Yang, 359–60), Wen 15.4 (Yang, 611), Xuan 12.3 (Yang, 747), Cheng 4.4 (Yang, 818), Xiang 14.9 (Yang, 1019), Zhao 1.13 (Yang, 1224).

25. *Zuo*, Zhuang 32.3 (Yang, 251–52), Xi 11.2 (Yang, 337–38); Xi 16.1 (Yang, 369), Xi 28.3h (Yang, 463); Wen 1.1 (Yang, 510), Wen 14.7 (Yang, 604).

26. *Zuo*, Zhao 8.3 (Yang, 1302), Zhao 8.6 (Yang, 1305), Zhao 11.7 (Yang, 1326–27).

27. *Zuo*, Zhao 29.5 (Yang, 1504–5), Zhao 31.6 (Yang, 1513–14), Zhao 32.2 (Yang, 1516), Zhao 32.4 (Yang, 1519–20), Ai 20.3 (Yang, 1717).

28. *Zuo*, Xuan 2.3c (Yang, 662–63); at Zhao 15.7 (Yang, 1371–73), the Zhou king himself is made to remind a descendant of the Dong line of his forebears' migration from Zhou to Jin and of their long responsibility for written records.

29. *SJ* 130.3285–86.

30. *Zuo*, Xi 28.3h (Yang, 463); Xiang 30.13 (Yang, 1180).

31. *Zuo*, Cheng 11.9 (Yang, 854); Xiang 23.5 (Yang, 1083); Zhao 1.9 (Yang, 1215).

responsible for identifying and responding appropriately to unknown spirits and for conducting sacrifices at such sites as the Luo river.[32] Paired with *zhu* (invocators), they are involved in ancestral worship and make reports (in the form of *ci* 辭) to the spirits,[33] and they offer ritual responses to natural prodigies like eclipses, fires, and landslides, sometimes using *ci* 辭.[34] Perhaps due to this responsibility for sacrifices to natural powers, they also serve frequently as interpreters of divinations (usually by milfoil), omens, and dreams and more generally as prophets of good and ill fortune.[35]

At one end of the spectrum, the *shi* 史 merely displayed written texts that had come into their keeping; at the other end of the spectrum, they composed and performed new spoken texts adapted to the needs of a particular moment. A Zhou *shi* visiting Chen shows the lord of Chen a copy of the *Zhouyi*, and at the residence or office of an unnamed *taishi* in Lu, a Jin visitor "views" (*guan* 觀) the *Yi* 易 (probably the *Zhouyi* 周易), the *Xiang* 象 (perhaps some version of the "Images" commentary on the *Zhouyi*), and the Lu *Chunqiu*

32. *Zuo*, Zhuang 32.3 (Yang, 251–52), Zhao 1.12 (Yang, 1217), Zhao 17.4 (Yang, 1390).

33. *Zuo*, Xiang 27.4 (Yang, 1133), Zhao 20.6 (Yang, 1416).

34. *Zuo*, Cheng 5.4 (landslide) (Yang, 823); Zhao 17.2 and Zhao 26.10 (eclipses) (Yang, 1385, 1479–80). In Zhao 18.3 (Yang, 1396), during the Zheng fire, the *zhu* 祝 and *shi* 史 offer less ceremonial aid as they are deployed to move ancestral tablets and oversee the clearing of a space north of the city for an exorcism. *Zhu* 祝 and *shi* 史 are listed with *zong* 宗 (lineage priests) and *bu* 卜 (diviners) among the ritual personnel granted to the founder of Lu among the things necessary for the founding of the state; see the lengthy speech of invocator Tuo 佗 at Ding 4.1 (Yang, 1535–42). In one anomalous passage late in the *Zuozhuan*, a single named officer is called a *zhushi* 祝史, but the passage reveals little about his duties; see Ai 25.1 (Yang, 1726).

35. Divination: *Zuo*, Zhuang 22.1 (Yang, 222–24), Xi 15.4g (Yang, 363–65), Xi 28.12 (Yang, 474), Wen 13.3 (Yang, 597), Cheng 16.5 (Yang, 885), Xiang 9.3 (Yang, 964–66), Xiang 25.2 (Yang, 1096), Zhao 7.15 (Yang, 1298), Ai 9.6 (Yang, 1653). Omens: Huan 2.2 (Yang, 90), Zhao 8.6 (Yang, 1305), Zhao 31.6 (Yang, 1513–14), Ai 6.4 (Yang, 1635–36). Dreams: Zhao 7.15 (Yang, 1297–98), Zhao 31.6 (Yang, 1513–14). Good and ill fortune: Wen 1.1 (Yang, 510), Zhao 11.7 (Yang, 1326–27), Zhao 32.2 (Yang, 1516), Zhao 32.4 (Yang, 1519–20), Ding 13.3 (Yang, 1591–92). Descriptions of the duties of invocators in *Zhouli* emphasize speech, including the use of *ci* 辭; see *Zhouli zhengyi*, vol. 8, 2061.

春秋.[36] *Shi* 史 were reputed to use both their texts and their speeches to prevent and correct errors in their rulers.[37] In two famous episodes, the *taishi*'s manner of recording a historical event becomes an act of bravado, akin to certain *shi*'s 史 insistence on making true reports to the spirits.[38] The *shi* 史 who oversaw covenants would have chosen and committed crucial words to writing. The *ci* 辭 addressed to spirits may or may not have been closely scripted, but would have followed generic criteria that *shi* 史 would have had to learn. The learning of formulas and verbal routines was without question a prerequisite for service as a *shi* 史.

The few longer speeches attributed to *shi* 史 characters speaking *ex tempore* or for a particular end, that is, without a generic script, do show an intriguing preference for historical summary. The *taishi* Ke 克 of Lu, sent by Ji Wenzi 季文子 to explain the expulsion of a wealthy Ju 莒 refugee, offers a vast account of noble lines and exiled malefactors in the predynastic era.[39] The *shi* Mo 墨, asked by Zhao Yang about the reasons for the power of the Ji lineage in Lu, recounts the omens of the lineage founder's birth and the whole course of its rise.[40] The invocator Tuo of Wei, taken along to a meeting of Jin and the allies, defends Wei's precedence in the covenant ceremony with a virtuosic recitation of early Zhou investiture narratives. Interestingly, Tuo at first hesitates to accompany his ruler beyond the borders of Wei, noting that invocators traditionally do not go abroad and further expressing his fear that he will fail if he attempts to perform the duties of two offices at once.[41] It could well be that the second office he has in mind is that of the *shi* 史, here understood as the

36. *Zuo*, Zhuang 22.1 (Yang, 222); Zhao 2.1 (Yang, 1226). One might recall here *zuoshi* Yixiang 倚相 of Chu, who was supposed to be able to *du* 讀, either "to recite" or "to read out," four obscure early works; see again Zhao 12.11 (Yang, 1340).

37. *Zuo*, Xiang 4.7 (Yang, 938), Xiang 14.6 (Yang, 1017).

38. *Zuo*, Xuan 2.3c (Yang, 662–63), Xiang 25.2 (Yang, 1099). See also Xiang 29.11 (Yang, 1160), where *shi* 史 in Jin record regular visits from tributaries, and Xi 26.3 (Yang, 440), where Yang Bojun speculates that the *taishi* 大師 responsible for keeping the archived covenant between King Cheng (r. 1042/35–1006 BCE) and his ministers must have been a *taishi* 大史.

39. *Zuo*, Wen 18.7 (Yang, 633–42).

40. *Zuo*, Zhao 32.4 (Yang, 1519–20).

41. *Zuo*, Ding 4.1 (Yang, 1535).

right person to accompany a ruler to a covenant ceremony and to produce timely, historically informed speech.

As invocator Tuo's remarks may indicate, the *shi* 史 could and did travel beyond the borders of their home state. As in the preceding era, they made these trips as representatives of the ruler or nobleman who sent them and as bearers of his words. Along with the Shao Duke Wu 召武公, *neishi* Guo is "sent" or "employed" (*shi* 使) by the Zhou king in 649 BCE to bestow a command (*ming* 命) upon the new ruler of Jin. This command, which according to Western Zhou conventions would have been presented in writing and also pronounced aloud, would have represented the speech of the king himself appointing the Jin ruler to office.[42] A few years later, the *neishi* Shuxing makes an official visit (*pin* 聘)—that is, is sent—to Song, where he is asked about omens, stones falling from the sky and birds flying backward. He answers the question but later explains that these events were natural occurrences, not to be understood as omens; in both responses the envoy shows that he is also an expert in the natural world and the phenomena that might require sacrifice.[43] Another *neishi*, Shufu, goes to Lu for the funeral of Lord Xi, performing two physiognomic predictions while he is there.[44] When Qin and Jin make peace, the Qin *shi* Ke 顆 is sent to Jin to swear a covenant with the ruler of Jin, his visit being reciprocated by a Jin nobleman, Xi Chou 郤犨.[45]

Of all the many facets of the *shi*'s 史 vocation, two seem most relevant to the work of the *shi* 使. First, whether they travel abroad or perform their duties at home, they serve as surrogates for their lord. In the case of the *shi* 史 who must address the spirits on their lord's behalf, this effort can lead to derangement and death:

> Though the spirits grow angry and the people suffer, he does not repent in his heart. Should his invocators and scribes set forth the truth, this would amount to bringing an indictment against him. But should they cover up his failures and enumerate his better points, this would amount to falsehood. For advancing and withdrawing alike

---

42. *Zuo*, Xi 11.2 (Yang, 337).
43. *Zuo*, Xi 16.1 (Yang, 369).
44. *Zuo*, Wen 1.1 (Yang, 510).
45. *Zuo*, Cheng 11.9 (Yang, 854–55).

> they have no words of justification, and so with empty words they curry favor. For this reason the ghosts and spirits do not consume the domain's sacrifices, but bring calamity down upon it, and the invocators and scribes have their part in this. The reason that they die young, lose their wits, lose their loved ones, and suffer illness is that they are representatives of a cruel ruler, and their words are false and an insult to the ghosts and spirits.
>
> 神怒民痛，無悛於心。其祝、史薦信，是言罪也；其蓋失數美，是矯誣也。進退無辭，則虛以求媚。是以鬼神不饗其國以禍之，祝、史與焉。所以夭昏孤疾者，爲暴君使也，其言僭嫚於鬼神。[46]

Speaking truth to power is a hazardous occupation.

Second, as they represent the interests and aims of their masters, the *shi* 史 speak in learned languages, whether the formulas of the investiture and the covenant, or the prayers appropriate to a particular spirit or phenomenon, or the verses of divination. Under certain circumstances they produce elaborate accounts of history, these being explicable in part as the knowledge required for maintaining sacrifices owed to spirits and rulers who had been powerful in the past. The *shi* 使, who in the Spring and Autumn period differ from the *shi* 史 in so many respects, do share with them the problem of representing a superior and his aims in a ceremonial language and do on occasion employ an elevated historical discourse. For more on this complex of duties, we must consider narratives about the *shi* 使 themselves.

Duties and Speeches of the Shi 使

In many ways, the *shi* 使 barely amounts to an office in the strict sense of the term. The word is normally a verb, the person performing the duty holding the putative office only as long as he is the object of the verb, that is, during the period of his assignment or mission. Unnamed envoys may be referred to as *shizhe* 使者 or *shiren* 使人; the latter is the preferred term for noble envoys and the term they use in humble references to themselves during missions.[47]

---

46. *Zuo*, Zhao 20.6 (Yang, 1416–17).

47. E.g., *Zuo*, Yin 5.8 (Yang, 47), Wen 12.6 (Yang, 592); Xuan 13.5 (Yang, 752), Xiang 27.5 (Yang, 1134).

That the name of the office does not seem quite stable in the Spring and Autumn lore certainly does not mean that the duties themselves were new in that period. During the Western Zhou and throughout the history of the large-scale polities that preceded it, power holders would have needed trusted functionaries capable of conveying their commands and persuasions beyond court to the locales under their governance. Even with the invention of writing and the spread of literacy among governing elites, competent men would have been required to carry messages, to ensure their correct interpretation, to observe the disposition of local rulers, and to bring back responses and reports. Evidence in the Western Zhou bronze inscriptions and in the *Zuozhuan* suggests that these functions were sometimes performed by the *neishi* 內史. I will argue that the emergence of the *shi* 使 as a discrete office represents an inflection and specialization of the old role of the *shi* 史, and that even with this shift the two types of officers continue to share a part of their verbal repertoire.

The visits paid by *shi* 使 from state to state formed only a small part of the larger pattern of travel that connected courts. Besides their ritually scheduled visits and occasional trips for wedding preparations, funerals, and the recognition of newly acceding rulers, there were also journeys to meetings (*hui* 會), whether for covenants or for joint military action. Battlefield confrontations with enemies also brought states together and required sensitive communication through intermediaries. Prisoners taken in battle and hostages—sometimes envoys detained in the course of their missions—were yet another part of the web, as were noble brides and the retinues accompanying them to their new home. Largely invisible to us, at least in the Spring and Autumn lore, are the merchants who no doubt traveled across borders for commercial reasons.[48] All of these different travels and travelers would have served to reinforce elements of common knowledge and common culture, especially in courts, and would have kept open lines of communication.

---

48. Memorable is the episode in which a Zheng merchant on his way to Zhou encounters the Qin army marching to attack Zheng. Thinking as nimbly as any envoy, the merchant presents the army with cattle as a gift, making it seem that Zheng already knows of the danger. See Xi 33.1 (Yang, 495).

Although the *shi* 使 may not yet constitute a stable office in this period, one other office with duties for nonreligious official and ceremonial communication is well attested in the *Zuozhuan*. This is the *xingren* 行人, literally "the man who goes," the "itinerant" or "intermediary"; both a senior and a junior *xingren* are mentioned in the *Zhouli* 周禮, where the title is translated "messenger" by Hucker and "director"/"assistant to the director of the bureau of foreign affairs" by Broman.[49] The office has attracted a good deal of attention in recent years, especially among Chinese scholars.[50] In *Zuozhuan* narratives, the core of the *xingren*'s duties seems to be his service during court rituals honoring visiting dignitaries; he carries messages between the delegations of the two states, especially when things do not go as expected in the ceremony. If the host regards the guest's response to music as inappropriate, or if the guest wishes to explain his refusal of some aspect of the ritual, a *xingren* is sent.[51] The *xingren* is trusted with delicate missions, as when Zheng sends its famous *xingren* Ziyu 子羽 to convince Gongzi Wei 公子圍 of Chu that, contrary to regular practice, he cannot lodge in the Zheng capital, his military guard posing too great a threat to the city.[52] When the Jin *xingren* Zizhu 子朱 is passed over for the crucial task of managing Qin visitors, the explanation given him confirms the importance of speech and personal representation in the *xingren*'s duties: he is told that the Jin *xingren* summoned in his stead, Ziyun 子員, "conveys the words of the two states without private bias, while you always alter them." 子員道二國之言無私，子常易之.[53] When a noble

49. Hucker, *A Dictionary of Official Titles in Imperial China*, nos. 5957, 2401; Broman, "Studies on the *Chou li*," 51. For the *Zhouli* description of these offices, see *Zhouli zhengyi*, 12:2945–3009.

50. See, *inter alia*, Chen Zhihong, *Yuyongxue yu* Zuozhuan *waijiao ciling*, 37–61.

51. *Zuo*, Wen 4.7 (Yang, 535), Xiang 4.3 (Yang, 933), Zhao 6.4 (Yang, 1277).

52. *Zuo*, Zhao 1.1 (Yang, 1199). Ziyu is the most prominent *xingren* in the *Zuozhuan*, at times offering predictions and comments in the manner of noblemen and *shi* 史. See Xiang 24.12 (Yang, 1093–94), Xiang 29.3 (Yang, 1155), Xiang 31.10 (Yang, 1190–91), Zhao 1.1 (Yang, 1199, 1203) (where besides speaking to Gongzi Wei's delegation he also comments on the latter's unusual royal-style bodyguard), and Zhao 1.12 (Yang, 1221).

53. *Zuo*, Xiang 26.1 (Yang, 1111). See also Xiang 4.3 (Yang, 933), Xiang 8.7b (Yang, 959).

Jin exile is robbed in Zhou, a *xingren* carries his complaint to the royal court.[54]

In what appears to be an easy extension of their in-court duties, *xingren* cross battle lines during military confrontations between states, carrying words (*ci* 辭) to and from the leaders of opposing forces.[55] Most relevant for this study, they also travel beyond the borders of their home states, either on their own or as leaders of their own delegations, to carry out missions for their courts.[56] On these occasions, as when they serve in court, they are sometimes explicitly sent to carry words, as when Zheng sends *xingren* to the allies to report (*gao* 告) on its fires.[57] In one case, a *xingren* may become a permanent ambassador of one state in the other, as when Jin sends Huyong 狐庸, son of the Chu exile Wuchen 巫臣, to serve as *xingren* in Wu, there representing Jin's interests and helping to urge on Wu attacks against Chu.[58] The appointment looks like an early precedent for the Warring States institution of *keqing* 客卿 or "guest ministers."

Because *shi* 使 does not have all the properties of an official title, and because anecdotes do not necessarily specify the offices their characters hold, it is difficult to know how stable a distinction there was between *xingren*, especially the traveling sort, and the *shi* 使 and *shi* 史 who represented their states beyond the borders. It may well be that many of the men who were sent on missions could have been referred to as *xingren* by their contemporaries. Certainly the duties performed by *shi* 使 overlap considerably with those performed by *xingren*. Like the latter, *shi* 使 carry announcements (*gao*);[59] they are

---

54. *Zuo*, Xiang 21.5 (Yang, 1061–62).

55. *Zuo*, Wen 12.6 (Yang, 592), Xuan 12.2 (Yang, 734) ("the *xingren* misspoke" 行人失辭, says a Jin commander as he changes the message to the Chu army), Cheng 16.5 (Yang, 889).

56. *Zuo*, Huan 9.2 (Yang, 125), Xiang 11.5 (Yang, 991), Xiang 13.7 (Yang, 1003), Xiang 18.2 (Yang, 1035), Xiang 24.12 (Yang, 1093–94), Xiang 26.10 (Yang, 1122), Zhao 8.2 (Yang, 1302), Zhao 23.2 (Yang, 1442), Ai 12.4 (Yang, 1671).

57. *Zuo*, Zhao 18.3 (Yang, 1396–97). The case is more ambiguous at Xiang 8.7b (Yang, 959), where the *xingren* Ziyun may respond in Jin to a Zheng visitor or may actually travel to Zheng to make his response.

58. *Zuo*, Cheng 7.5 (Yang, 835), Ding 4.3 (Yang, 1542). It is possible that *xingren* refers primarily to Huyong's position in the Wu court rather than to his association with Jin. Nonetheless, it is clear that his presence in Wu serves Jin aims.

59. *Zuo*, Xi 11.1 (Yang, 337), Wen 1.5 (Yang, 513), Zhao 26.9 (Yang, 1475–79).

useful in the communication between states during wartime;[60] and they are treated, sometimes violently, as proxies for their rulers or their states.[61]

Episodes in the *Zuozhuan* suggest that the visits of *shi* 使 were, as we would expect, guided by ritual specifications. These specifications come into clearest view when some violation of them occurs. A Wei noble, paying an official visit (*pin* 聘) to Lu, fails to stay one step behind the Lu ruler as the two of them ascend the stairs during a covenant ceremony; the Lu noble who is acting as his ruler's assistant (*xiang* 相) in the ritual rushes forward to point out the error.[62] During the years when Jin, as overlord, comes to enforce a dense schedule of visits from representatives and rulers of allied states, speakers allude to older rules for diplomatic contact. According to Zitaishu 子大叔 of Zheng, speaking to his Jin hosts:

> In times past, when Lords Wen and Xiang were overlords, their endeavors did not overtax the great princes. By their command, the great princes sent envoys on formal visits every three years, and they themselves came to court every five years. Whenever there was some matter at hand they met, and when there was discord they swore a covenant. When a ruler expired, high officers paid visits of condolence and ministers participated in the burial. When the ruler's wife died, officers paid visits of condolence and high officers escorted the funeral cortège. This system sufficed for displaying ritual propriety, for giving commands about affairs, and for deliberating about shortcomings, and it stopped at that. No additional commands were given.
>
> 昔文、襄之霸也，其務不煩諸侯，令諸侯三歲而聘，五歲而朝，有事而會，不協而盟。君薨，大夫弔，卿共葬事；夫人，士弔，大夫送葬。足以昭禮、命事、謀闕而已，無加命矣。[63]

60. *Zuo*, Cheng 9.8 (Yang, 844).

61. *Zuo*, Xuan 14.3 (Yang, 755–56), Zhao 2.5 (Yang, 2130), Zhao 5.4 (Yang, 1267–69), Ding 6.6 (Yang, 1558–59), Ding 8.7 (Yang, 1567). At Ding 8.3 (Yang, 1564), when Yue Qi 樂祁 of Song is released after a long detention in Jin, the Jin leaders briefly contemplate having his son stay on in his place, a thought that perhaps looks forward to the formal practice of keeping hostages (*zhi* 質), common during the Warring States period.

62. *Zuo*, Xiang 7.7 (Yang, 952–53).

63. *Zuo*, Zhao 3.1 (Yang, 1232–33); see also Shuxiang's remarks at Zhao 13.3 (Yang, 1355–56).

Another outline of diplomatic practice comes when King Ling 靈 of Chu (r. 540–529 BCE)—always one to think outside the ritual box—proposes mutilating two noble Jin envoys and turning them into palace slaves. In a carefully worded argument against this plan, the Chu minister Wei Qiqiang 薳啓彊 explains and justifies the proper treatment of envoys:

> For this reason the sage kings devoted themselves to practicing ritual and did not seek to humiliate others. For rulers and envoys attending court or paying official visits there were jade tablets; for feasts and audiences there were jade plaques. For small domains there were visits to report on their official duties; for great domains there were excursions to inspect meritorious deeds. Armrests were set out, but no one leaned on them. Goblets were filled, but no one drank from them. At banquets there were choice gifts; for meals there were supplementary dishes; on the entry of a visitor there was a reward for his exertions on the outskirts of the city, and on his departure there was a presentation of gifts. This was the height of ritual propriety. The failure of a domain and its patrimonies comes when this way is lost and trouble and turmoil erupt in consequence.
>
> 是以聖王務行禮，不求恥人。朝聘有珪，享覜有璋，小有述職，大有巡功。設机而不倚，爵盈而不飲；宴有好貨，飧有陪鼎，入有郊勞，出有贈賄，禮之至也。國家之敗，失之道也，則禍亂興。[64]

In normal times, the *shi* 使, as proxies for their ruler, participate in rituals that allow the host state to display its respect and its determination to continue peaceful relations.[65]

One of the main aims of the *Zuozhuan* seems to be to offer its readers versions of the speeches spoken by envoys on key diplomatic occasions. So many fine speeches are attributed to envoys that they cannot be listed here.[66] One example might suffice to suggest the

---

64. *Zuo*, Zhao 5.4 (Yang, 1267–68).

65. Another interesting consideration of the specifications for visits comes in *Zuo*, Ai 15.2 (Yang, 1690–92), when an envoy from Chen dies en route to Wu.

66. Besides speeches discussed below, some other especially fine examples are to be found in: *Zuo*, Xi 4.1 (Yang, 289–91), Xi 26.3 (Yang, 439–40), Xuan 11.5 (Yang, 714–16), Xuan 12.2e (Yang, 730), 12.2f (Yang, 733), 12.2g (Yang, 736), Xuan 13.5 (Yang, 752), Xuan 15.1 (Yang, 759–60), Cheng 2.3 (Yang, 796–99), Cheng 2.9 (Yang, 809–10), Cheng 7.5 (Yang, 834–35), Cheng 12.3 (Yang, 857–58), Cheng 13.3 (Yang, 861–65), Cheng 16.5 (Yang, 887–88), Xiang 4.3 (Yang, 933–34), Xiang 8.7

problems envoys faced and the solutions they found. When King Ling of Chu completes his grand Zhanghua 章華 complex, he wishes to show it off to the lords of other states. Wei Qiqiang himself undertakes the mission:

> When the Master of Chu had completed the Zhanghua terrace, he hoped to have great princes in attendance as he dedicated it. The grand steward Wei Qiqiang said, "I can secure the Prince of Lu." Wei Qiqiang came to summon the lord, offering this explanation [*ci* 辭]: "In times past, your former ruler Lord Cheng gave a command to our former high officer Yingqi and said, 'We have not forgotten the amity of our former rulers, but will send Hengfu to shine over the domain of Chu and to steady its altars of earth and grain, in order to pacify your people.' Yingqi received this command at Shu. He carried it back with him, not daring to forget any part of it, and announced it at the ancestral temple. In days past our former ruler King Gong stretched his collar as he gazed northward, keeping hope alive from day to day and month to month, and this hope was passed down in order from one to another for four reigns now. The kind largess has not yet reached us; only Lord Xiang deigned to attend one of our funerals. The orphaned son and his closest men, in the bereavement saddening their hearts, erred in their planning. Even for the altars of earth and grain they did not have enough time, much less for being able to cherish in their thoughts the virtue of your ruler. If now you should put forward your jade foot and condescend to give our unworthy ruler an audience, favoring the domain of Chu with your sacred blessings in order to make good on the covenant made during the campaign at Shu and to present your kind largess, then this in itself our unworthy ruler would receive as a gift. How would he presume to hope for fulfillment of the promise made at Shu? Even the ghosts and spirits of our former rulers would endorse this with good will; how could it only be our unworthy ruler himself? If you, my lord, fail to come, I, a subject envoy, must ask a date for setting out; our unworthy ruler will bear gifts of silk and hold an audience with

---

(Yang, 858–59), Xiang 16.5 (Yang, 1031–32), Xiang 18.4 (Yang, 1041), Xiang 26.13 (Yang, 1124), Xiang 28.8 (Yang, 1143–44), Xiang 30.1 (Yang, 1170), Xiang 31.6 (Yang, 1186–88), Zhao 2.3 (Yang, 1229), Zhao 3.1 (Yang, 1232–33), Zhao 5.8 (Yang, 1271–72), Zhao 6.4 (Yang, 1277), Zhao 13.3 (Yang, 1358–59), Zhao 19.8 (Yang, 1403–4), Zhao 26.9 (Yang, 1475–79), Zhao 31.2 (Yang, 1510–11), Ai 7.3 (Yang, 1641), Ai 11.3 (Yang, 1662), Ai 12.3 (Yang, 1671), Ai 12.4 (Yang, 1671–72), Ai 15.4 (Yang, 1693–94).

> you at Shu in order to request the gift promised by your former ruler."
>
> 楚子成章華之臺，願與諸侯落之。大宰薳啓彊曰：「臣能得魯侯。」薳啓強來召公，辭曰：「昔先君成公命我先大夫嬰齊曰：『吾不忘先君之好，將使衡父照臨楚國，鎮撫其社稷，以輯寧爾民。』嬰齊受命于蜀。奉承以來，弗敢失隕，而致諸宗祧。日我先君共王引領北望，日月以冀，傳序相授，於今四王矣。嘉惠未至，唯襄公之辱臨我喪。孤與其二三臣悼心失圖，社稷之不皇，況能懷思君德？今君若步玉趾，辱見寡君，寵靈楚國，以信蜀之役，致君之嘉惠，是寡君既受貺矣，何蜀之敢望？其先君鬼神實嘉賴之，豈唯寡君？君若不來，使臣請問行期，寡君將承質幣而見于蜀，以請先君之貺。」[67]

After being defeated by Chu in 589 BCE, some fifty-four years before the present episode, Lu had promised to send Hengfu, a son of Lord Cheng 成 (r. 590–573), to Chu as a hostage, but had never followed through.[68] Wei Qiqiang reminds Lu of this promise and threatens a Chu attack if Lord Zhao (r. 542–517) does not attend the Zhanghua dedication. Lord Zhao immediately begins preparations for his trip.

Wei Qiqiang's speech is introduced with the verb *ci* 辭, which I have translated here as "to offer an explanation." The word often means "to decline politely," but as has been observed in connection with the speech of *shi* 史 and *xingren* 行人, it also refers to the special forms of language used in prayer and covenant. It likewise refers to the eloquence of envoys. When Zichan of Zheng tears down the walls of a guest lodge in Jin and then delivers to his Jin hosts a masterful justification of the action, Shuxiang praises Zichan: "Such is the case showing that eloquent words cannot be dispensed with! Zichan has eloquent words, and the princes benefited accordingly. How can we discard eloquent words?" 辭之不可以已也如是夫！子產有辭，諸侯賴之，若之何其釋辭也。[69] It is noted elsewhere that when Zichan was preparing for diplomatic missions, he sought the help of the *xingren* Ziyu, both for information about goings-on in the other states and for the preparation of speeches (*ciling* 辭令).[70] Wei Qiqiang's speech, with its elegant and somewhat archaic diction and its

67. *Zuo*, Zhao 7.3 (Yang, 1285–86).
68. *Zuo*, Cheng 2.8 (Yang, 806–9).
69. *Zuo*, Xiang 31.6 (Yang, 1189).
70. *Zuo*, Xiang 31.10 (Yang, 1191); cf. *Analects* 14.8.

citation of Lord Cheng's words, is a superb example of the elevated register that would have been expected on the ritual occasions of court visits.

As Ban Gu observes just after citing Confucius's remarks on diplomatic speech, Confucius implied that speakers "put in order what is appropriate at the moment of weighing the situation; when they receive their command they do not receive the precise words [*ci*] for it, and this is the area in which they excel." 當權事制宜，受命而不受辭，此其所長也.[71] Like the *shi* 史 who conduct prayers and compose covenant texts and draft investitures, the *shi* 使 of Confucius's remark and of Ban Gu's comment are masters of specialized speech (*ci*) and exercise some discretion in determining the appropriate speech to use on specific occasions. This speech will perhaps inevitably draw some of its authority from its connection with the past. If it is a prayer, it belongs to a learned formulaic tradition. If it is a diplomatic speech, like Zitaishu's or Wei Qiqiang's or the envoy *pro tem* Invocator Tuo's, it will be delivered in court or in a formal court-like setting and will make use of an elevated register that stresses its ties with the past. Further, its argument may be based wholly or in part upon knowledge of some past events and a judgment concerning their relevance to the diplomatic matter at hand. Zitaishu refers directly to past practice as precedent for interstate tribute visits, as does Wei Qiqiang in the first speech cited above. Invocator Tuo performs a more elaborate rehearsal of past precedent. In Wei Qiqiang's speech in Lu—a speech that is framed as a rhetorical challenge ("I can secure the Prince of Lu")—the speaker seizes upon a single detail of past relations between two states and makes it the basis of his claim. For envoys, as perhaps for the *shi* 史 involved in making and maintaining investitures, the past was a treasury of binding political obligations. Invoked appropriately and articulated in suitably authoritative language, this past could continue to inform the present by guiding political relations. In this respect, envoys from state to state were Spring and Autumn period successors to the *shi* 史 of the Western Zhou royal court, who would have established and continually reinforced the ties of fealty that bound the king and local rulers.

---

71. *HS* 13.1740.

Conclusion

As representatives of their rulers and their states, the *shi* 史, *xingren*, and *shi* 使 shared a common function and would presumably have received similar training. This training was in one or more aspects of the art of occasional speech, and it encompassed both ritual formulas and more substantial knowledge of history and official practice. In many respects, the *shi* 使 envoys were newly versatile and powerful successors to the *shi* 史 officials of an earlier era. While *shi* 史 were relatively low in status and exercised very little power in determining the precise policy that was to be pursued, the *shi* 使 envoys were themselves noble-born members of the policy-making circle around the ruler of a state and derived their authority as speakers and representatives both from their ties with the ruler and from their own familial wealth and power.[72] Since these traveling noblemen were the same men who participated in the ritual feasting and song recitations (*fu shi* 賦詩) that tied together the states of the Spring and Autumn period, and since these song recitations did frequently serve as occasions for expression of policy aims, it is possible to conceive of envoys' speech as an extension of the reaffirmations of Zhou cultural solidarity that feasting and recitations represented. Like recitation, diplomatic speech presumed a mastery of more or less antique language, invoking a shared past and reasserting its claims on the present.[73]

Without accepting at face value Ban Gu's sketch of the early history of diplomatic oratory in China, it is nonetheless possible to see a rough truth in it. The "criss-cross persuaders" (*zonghengjia*) do succeed to the talents and status of the envoys in that they act as diplomatic representatives for states and mould interstate relations through the force of persuasion. They do so without noble status and outside of the ritual occasions (such as banquets) and expectations that characterized Spring and Autumn period diplomatic speech. And the most representative among them—the likes of Su Qin and

72. One of the arguments Wei Qiqiang adduces against the Chu king's plan to mutilate the Jin envoys is the power and influence the envoys' families enjoy in Jin and the likelihood that any offense against the envoys would be avenged with force. See *Zuo*, Zhao 5.4 (Yang, 1268–69).

73. See Schaberg, *A Patterned Past*, 234–43.

Zhang Yi and the many others to whom speeches are attributed in *Zhanguoce* and similar texts—draw on different sorts of knowledge, generally invoking present strategic expedience rather than historical precedent or traditional authority. They rely on quick wit and adaptable rhetoric instead of the models of the past. But another sort of speaker, a roving persuader of the type Mencius was supposed to have been—and perhaps of the type Confucius was supposed to have been before him—approached rulers with a full repertoire of historical and legendary precedents, ready to assert their relevance for contemporary practice. Especially as thinkers of the Han dynasty began to collect and order the speeches and other passages of argumentation they knew from their predecessors, the various legacies of the *shi* 史 scribes and the *shi* 使 envoys would come together again, producing a form of historical knowledge informed both by a confidence in the value of precedent and by a flexible readiness to adapt it to present uses.

CHAPTER 2

Three Rhetorical Modes in Pre-Qin Court Remonstrances

Su-ching Chang, National Taiwan University

This essay discusses three major rhetorical modes employed in remonstrances that ministers submitted to their rulers, dating roughly from the Zhou to Qin dynasties (before 207 BCE). Customarily, remonstrators from this period would appeal to the ruler's emotions, reason with him, and attack his vulnerabilities, often simultaneously, but sometimes preferring one approach to others. Regardless of whether remonstrators would invoke past precedents or advance new suggestions in their arguments, pre-Qin remonstrances belonged to one or more of the following three categories: the instructive, confrontational, and authoritarian modes. These categories may not encompass all the various modes of rhetoric, but they may serve as useful rhetorical parallels to the Confucian, Mohist, and legalist strains of thought found in the period when the hundred masters rose in prominence.

Prevalent in records from the Western Zhou (1045–771 BCE) and Spring and Autumn (770–476 BCE) periods, the instructive mode places the minister and ruler in the roles of the tutor and student respectively: the minister uses indirect rhetorical means to exhort his charge, the ruler strives to fulfill his obligations to the best of his abilities. During the Warring States period (453–221 BCE), as the *shi* 士 class expanded, the intelligentsia of the Confucian and Mohist persuasions would rely on the force of reason to sway their rulers, displaying a confrontational stance vis-à-vis the ruler, refusing to surrender their self-dignity or downplay their self-importance. The legalists of the same period employed arguments that worked to protect and strengthen the ruler's central authority by keeping his ministers' influence at bay. In sum, the instructional mode places the ruler on favorable terms with the remonstrator while gently introducing the intended remonstrance; the confrontational mode appeals to higher values and principles even if the remonstrator's indelicacy ends up chafing the ruler; and the authoritarian mode upholds the ruler's authority at the cost of suppressing other voices. The following sections of this essay will examine these three general modes of rhetoric.

The Instructive Mode

Prior to the Spring and Autumn period, rulers and ministers sustained relationships with relatively well-defined roles whereby the minister, charged with the responsibility of assisting the ruler in matters of governance, would present arguments to the ruler. When the ruler proved to be corrupt or willful, and his conduct or policies faltered, the most the minister could do in most cases (short of rebellion) was to draw up remonstrances and hope for the best. Leaving aside ministers who might be the sources of trouble themselves, and speaking only in terms of the normative political system of that period, remonstrances form an arena where conflicting approaches and viewpoints between minister and ruler are worked out. When conflicts arose, the instructive remonstrator would either point the ruler's attention to ancient ways and customs, remind him of the virtues of former kings, or cite the *Book of Odes* (*Shijing* 詩經) and the *Book of Documents* (*Shujing* 書經), often adopting a modest attitude while steering the ruler onto the right path. Invoking past precedents, speaking to the ruler's heart and mind, and exhibiting a sincere and earnest attitude are all strategies defining the instructive mode of remonstrance, which for reasons beyond the scope of this essay to discuss fully, was most widely adopted in later ages as well.

In the *Guoyu* 國語 (*Discourses of the States*), examples of instructive remonstrances from the pre-Qin period abound. In the *Guoyu*'s first episode, Duke Moufu 謀父 of Zhai 祭公 (?–936 BCE), remonstrates against King Mu of Zhou's 周穆王 (r. 956–918 BCE) decision to conquer the Rong Di, a western tribe settled around the Jing-Wei 涇渭 river basin. Duke Zhai's main argument is that "former kings would (only) demonstrate their virtue, not their weaponry." Walking the king through the six points of his two-part argument, he first cites the "Hymns" (*song* 頌) and then urges the ruler to perfect his own virtue and cherish his people, in accordance with the instructions and institutions of former kings:

> As in the system of the previous kings, within the kingdom was the supply domain; outside the kingdom was the warning domain; on the outskirts of the warning domain was the subordinated domain; in the *Yi* and *Man* areas was the reinforcing domain; and in the *Rong* and *Di* areas was the wild domain. Those in the supply domain should have performed *Ji* Sacrifices; those in the warning domain, *Si* Sacrifices; those in the subordinated domain, *Xiang* Sacrifices; those in the reinforced domain paid the standard tributes; and those in the wild domain paid homage to the king. The *Ji* Sacrifices were daily; the *Si* Sacrifices monthly, and the *Xiang* Sacrifices seasonal. The standard tributes were paid yearly and the homage to the king was paid at his decease. The doctrine of the former kings says that: if there were (lords) who did not perform *Ji* Sacrifices, then (the previous kings) cultivated their minds; if there were (lords) who did not perform *Si* Sacrifices, they refined their own words; if there were (lords) who did not perform *Xiang* sacrifices, they refined the laws; if there were (lords) who did not pay the standard tributes, they refined the (system of) titles; and if there were (lords) who did not pay homage to the kings, they cultivated their own virtue. If these things were done one by one, yet there were still (lords) who did not send in their offerings, then (the former kings) refined the punishments. They then had to punish those who did not perform the *Ji* Sacrifices; to subjugate those who did not perform the *Si* Sacrifices; to chastise those who did not perform the *Xiang* Sacrifices; to reprimand those who did not pay the standard tributes; and to admonish those who did not pay homage to the kings. They then had rules for punishments and fines, weapons for launching assaults, supplies for punitive campaigns, commands to be used in stern reprimands, and rhetoric to be used in formal admonishments.
>
> 夫先王之制：邦內甸服，邦外侯服，侯、衛賓服，蠻、夷要服，戎、狄荒服；甸服者祭，侯服者祀，賓服者享，要服者貢，荒服者王；日祭、月祀、時享、歲貢、終王。先王之訓也：有不祭則修意，有不祀則修言，有不享則修文，有不貢則修名，有不王則修德，序成而有不至則修刑；於是

乎有刑不祭，伐不祀，征不享，讓不貢，告不王；於是乎有刑罰之辟，有攻伐之兵，有征討之備，有威讓之令，有文告之辭。[1]

As the Qing scholar Lin Yunming 林雲銘 (1628–97) notes: "[Duke Zhai's] argument is extremely well-ordered and well-cut, modeled as it is after ancient canons (*dian* 典), consultations (*mo* 謨), instructions (*xun* 訓), and announcements (*gao* 誥)."[2] The modern scholar Zhang Yiren (Chang Yi-ren 張以仁) comments that the layered and intricate structure of argument creates a euphonious whole reminiscent of court orchestra.[3] Duke Zhai's citation of the *Shijing*, along with his rehearsal of the ways of the former kings, showcases his comprehensive knowledge and literary cultivation while reflecting his deep historical consciousness. His reasoning is tight, but more important, his language has the resonance of "sounds of the ancestral hall" (Chang Yi-ren's phraseology), stately and sonorous, spoken at an unhurried pace and with a gentle diction.[4] The *Guoyu* is replete with ministerial remonstrations to either the Zhou Son of Heaven or other overlords, of which Duke Zhai's remonstrance is a prime example. Aside from recalling the former kings and citations from the *Shijing* or *Shujing* to create the proper basis for his argument, his speech exhibits his profound historical consciousness, broad cultivation, and above all, mildness of attitude, which serves to facilitate their relationship, ameliorating the conflict between the ruler and minister.

The instructive mode appears most often in remonstrances recorded in the *Guoyu* and *Zuozhuan* 左傳. Another good example, from the *Zuozhuan*, is Shi Que's 石碏 (n.d.) famous remonstrance with Duke Zhuang of Wei 衛莊公 (r. 757–735 BCE) for his undue fondness for Zhouxu 州吁, a son of his who was not the heir apparent.

---

1. Nienhauser, gen. ed., *The Grand Scribe's Records*, vol. 1, 68. This translation has been adapted from a similar passage in *The Grand Scribe's Records*, since the *Guoyu* has yet no formal English translation. Proper names have been converted into Pinyin phonetic spelling. The same applies for succeeding quotations. *Guoyu*, 7–11.

2. Lin Yunming, "Fanli" 凡例, in *Guwen xiyi*, 2.

3. See Zhang Yiren, "Cong *Guoyu* yu *Zuozhuan* benzhi shang de chayi shilun houren dui *Guoyu* de piping," 156–57.

4. See Zhang Suqing (Chang Su-ching), "*Guoyu* de 'yu,'" 3–8.

According to the hereditary system of lineage successions, the distinction between the first wife's sons and the secondary wives' sons ought to be enforced, yet Zhouxu is in this instance the favored successor. Shi Que therefore steps forward to remonstrate against this violation of the right of primogeniture. Beginning with Duke Zhuang's double roles as a ruler and father, Shi Que directs the duke's attention to his fatherly role first by suggesting that "if one loves a son, one teaches him the ways of duty" 愛子，教之以義方,[5] instructing him to apply his paternal feelings to moral considerations. In stirring up the father's protective feelings for his offspring, Shi Que acknowledges his affection for his son Zhouxu. Shi Que essentially argues that, if you cherish your son so, you ought to steer him away from "deviant paths" and stop "building steps to disaster."[6] By this reasoning, indulging one's son would bring about disaster, because, as Shi Que indicates:

> Pride, wastefulness, lewdness, and dissipation are origins of deviance. These four come when favor and reward are excessive. If you are going to establish Zhouxu as heir, then settle it now! If you are not ready to do this, then you are building steps to disaster. Few indeed are those who are indulged but do not become prideful; are prideful but able to step down; are able to step down but not be indignant; are indignant but able to keep within boundaries! Moreover, for the lowly to hinder the honored, for the young to insult the old, for the distant to come between kin, for the new to come between those with old ties, for the small to lord it over the great, for the lewd to destroy the dutiful, these are called the six violations. For rulers to be dutiful, for subjects to fulfill their tasks, for fathers to be kind, for sons to be filial, for older brothers to show love, and for younger brothers to be respectful, these are called the six compliances. To reject the compliances and follow the violations is the way to hasten disaster.

---

5. *Zuo*, Yin 3.6 (Yang, 31); Stephen Durrant, Waiyee Li, and David Schaberg, trans., *Zuozhuan*, Lord Yin, 3rd year. I sincerely thank these translators for allowing me to use their soon-to-be-published but still provisional translation of *Zuozhuan*. All subsequent translations of *Zuozhuan* are taken from their manuscript. Hereafter all references to the *Zuozhuan* will be marked, as in this note, by the ducal passage reference followed by the page number in Yang Bojun's translation.

6. *Zuo*, Yin 3.7 (Yang, 31–32).

> 驕、奢、淫、泆，所自邪也。四者之來，寵祿過也。將立州吁，乃定之矣；若猶未也，階之為禍。夫寵而不驕，驕而能降，降而不憾，憾而能眕者，鮮矣。且夫賤妨貴，少陵長，遠間親，新間舊，小加大，淫破義，所謂六逆也；君義，臣行，父慈，子孝，兄愛，弟敬，所謂六順也。去順效逆，所以速禍也。[7]

The "six violations" and "six compliances" are formulated with reference to Zhou ideas about proper social relations. Therefore, as Shi Que sees it, should someone of lower status such as Zhouxu become favored, and his given social role does not restrain him, he will rebel against, and cause disruptions to, the system. On this point, Shi Que stresses: "One who rules over men should devote himself to forestalling disaster; is it not then unacceptable that he should instead hasten it?" 君人者，將禍是務去，而速之，無乃不可乎？[8] As the head of state, if Duke Zhuang is made to realize that trouble is brewing, should he not work toward its deterrence? In this passage, from Shi Que's declaration regarding the origins of deviance to his claim that "[few] are indignant but able to keep within boundaries," the clauses are all four-characters long; at "six violations," they become three-characters long; when Shi Que begins to speak of the "six compliances" the clauses become two-characters long; but the opening and closing are composed in nonparallel sentences. The beauty of this passage lies partly in the alteration between phrases of odd- and even-numbered characters, and between nonparallel and parallel sentences, the patterning of which creates a poetic language embodying the 'asymmetrical' aesthetic.[9] As Shi Que teaches the ruler how he might fulfill his roles as ruler and father, the musicality of his speech is likewise reminiscent of the "sounds of the ancestral hall," orderly and evocative, while his language is mild and noncoercive.

While strong reasoning supports the remonstrance, the remonstrator still manages to adopt a mild attitude, usually because of the remonstrator's desire to avoid deepening a conflict. Even though "remonstrance" follows when the ruler and minister experience an initial conflict of opinion, the ruler retains final power to arbitrate

---

7. *Zuo*, Yin 3.7 (Yang, 31). Though this incident was recorded under the third year of Duke Yin in the *Zuozhuan* it had in fact taken place much earlier.

8. *Zuo*, Yin 3.7 (Yang, 33).

9. See Chen Yanhui, *Chunqiu ciling yanjiu*, 205–6.

government policy, settle succession disputes, and allocate power or favors among the ministers. Given the power dynamics between ruler and minister, the latter is still beholden to the former: regardless of how broad the minister's knowledge, how insightful his understanding, or how foolproof his reasoning, he can never usurp the ruler's decision-making powers. Consequently, insulting the ruler and rupturing the relationship would fail to help matters along; on the contrary, if the minister considered the whole picture, then the better strategy would be to minimize the threat or challenge to the ruler's authority through indirect and tentative means.

Two examples of such accommodative rhetoric are Shi Hui's 士會 (fl. 7th c. BCE) remonstrance with Duke Ling of Jin 晉靈公 (r. 620–607 BCE) and Zige's 子革 (fl. 6th c. BCE) remonstrance with King Ling of Chu 楚靈王 (r. 540–529 BCE). Having ascended the throne as a toddler, at this point of the narration, Duke Ling is still just a sixteen- or seventeen-year-old who indulges in juvenile pastimes and has little patience for anything else. In this episode Duke Ling has just executed a chef who served under-cooked bear paws, and when Zhao Dun 趙盾 (?–602 BCE; posthumously, Xuanzi 宣子) and Shi Hui learn of it, they immediately come forward to remonstrate. However, as the *Zuozhuan* narrates, "At that time the Jin prince was extravagant. Zhao Dun was in charge of policies. He repeatedly remonstrated with the ruler but was not heeded." 於是晉侯侈，趙宣子爲政，驟諫而不入。[10] Why, the text implies, would anyone expect Duke Ling to accept his ministers' remonstrances this time around? Both Zhao Dun and Shi Hui are already fairly pessimistic about the effects of further remonstrance, so having consulted each other, Shi Hui decides to give it a another attempt, and if no results are achieved, then Zhao Dun would give it a second try. Such desperation emerges from their sense of helplessness about the situation.

When confronted with a ruler whose selfish desires, drive for power, and ability to wield power are growing stronger by the day, Shi Hui treads cautiously, tempering his attitude and affecting a humble bearing. As he enters the inner court from the periphery, he halts his steps thrice, first at the palace gate, then the central

10. *Zuo*, Xuan 1.10 (Yang, 649).

courtyard, and only when he ascends the steps to the dais does Duke Ling look him in the eye. Preempting Shi Hui's speech, Duke Ling immediately says: "I know my errors. I will correct them." 吾知所過矣，將改之。[11] The scene here, in which Shi Hui advanced over "three stages . . . but only when he reached the eaves did the lord look at him" 三進，及溜而後視之 vividly depicts the subtle interactions between the ruler and minister.[12] The fact that Duke Ling preempts Shi Hui's planned comments suggests that he observed Shi Hui's presence early on, surmised what Shi Hui is about to say, but had no desire to hear any of it, wishing only that Shi Hui would be wise enough to bite his own tongue. Shi Hui, for his part, is fully aware of Duke Ling's impervious attitude, and thus decides to pay his respects all the more reverently when admonishing him. Responding to the duke's preemptive strike, he says:

> Who among men is without errors? Having erred and being capable of correction—there is no good greater than that. As it says in the *Odes*,
>
> There is none who does not have beginnings,
> Few are those who fulfill them as endings.[13]
>
> For if it is so, then those who can make good their errors are few. If my lord can persist to the end, then the altars of the domain will have a solid foundation. Surely it is not only your subjects who rely on that! As it also says in the *Odes*,
>
> The ritual vestment had holes—
> It was Zhongshan Fu who mended it.[14]
>
> This is about being able to make good one's errors. If my lord can do so, then the ritual vestment will not fall into disuse.

---

11. *Zuo*, Xuan 2.3 (Yang, 657).

12. *Zuo*, Xuan 2.3 (Yang, 656).

13. Mao, no. 255, "Dang" 蕩 18A.641.

14. Mao, no. 260, "Zhengmin" 蒸民 18.A.676. As Durrant, Li, and Schaberg note in their translation of *Zuozhuan*, "Zhongshan Fu was a minister who helped King Xuan revive the fortunes of Zhou. The vestment refers to embroidered robes of office for the king and the highest ministers. Here it is synecdoche for the king: holes refer to royal errors that Zhongshan Fu repairs by remonstrating with the king. [Shi] Hui is using the vestment to refer both to the dignity of Lord Ling's office and the stability of the Jin domain."

人誰無過，過而能改，善莫大焉。《詩》曰：「靡不有初，鮮克有終。」夫如是，則能補過者鮮矣。君能有終，則社稷之固也，豈惟群臣賴之。又曰：「袞職有闕，惟仲山甫補之」，能補過也。君能補過，袞不廢矣。[15]

Shi Hui emphasizes that, as no one is free of errors, the most important task is to remedy them—there is "no good greater" than this. In hoping that Duke Ling, who is becoming aware of his growing powers, could shape up as a good ruler, Shi Hui adds, "If my lord can persist to the end, then the altars of the domain will have a solid foundation," and if "my lord can [make good his errors], then the ritual vestment will not fall into disuse." Shi Hui's instructive remonstrance contains not one word of disparagement or denunciation; on the contrary, he insists upon appeasing and encouraging Duke Ling. But the result is that Duke Ling still "did not correct his errors" 猶不改. Since Shi Hui's efforts yield no result, Zhao Dun steps up to remonstrate several times, endangering his own life, as Duke Ling has long wanted to eliminate Zhao as the thorn in his side.[16] These life-or-death stakes illustrate that remonstrance in the instructive mode could still be a risky business.

In the next story, King Ling of Chu 楚靈王 (r. 540–529 BCE) is depicted as a ruler with an insatiable thirst for power who acts without regard for his ministers' plight. He sends troops to encircle the state of Xu 徐, but stations himself in the rear at Gan Xi 乾谿 among the reinforcement troops. While in the rear, he goes on a hunt, decked out in warm and opulent attire: leather cap, feathered coat, kingfisher-blue cape, leopard-skin boots. Returning from the expedition, he receives his deputy of the right, Zige 子革. Speaking of an ancient Chu king's service to King Kang of Zhou 周康王 (r. 1005/3–978 BCE), King Ling points out to Zige that, during that era, the vassal states Qi, Jin, Lu, and Wei all received their due rewards, while Chu did not. King Ling queries, "If we now send someone to Zhou to ask for a cauldron as our portion, will the king give it to us?" 今吾

---

15. *Zuo*, Xuan 2.3 (Yang, 657–58).

16. Duke Ling of Jin failed in his first attempt to assassinate Zhao Dun through a hitman, upon which the duke hid assassins at a banquet but failed again. While Zhao Dun fled to another state, Zhao Chuan murdered Duke Ling. Details are found in *Zuozhuan*, in the third year of Duke Xuan of Lu's reign.

使人於周，求鼎以爲分，王其與我乎？,[17] betraying his aspiration to become another King Zhuang (of Chu in earlier days) and take over power (the "cauldron") from the Zhou Son of Heaven.[18] King Ling pursues this quest for political dominance further, asking: What if I were to request land from the state of Zheng? To this Zige replies: If even the Zhou Son of Heaven is afraid of not complying with Chu's request for the cauldron, then how much less so would Zheng dare to refuse its land? King Ling then asserts that even though in the past other lords bowed to the state of Jin, given Chu's recent subjection of Chen, Cai, and the two Bugeng regions, certainly they would now be in awe of Chu. Zige ingratiatingly replies: Why of course they would be fearful of you, my king—why wouldn't they? At this moment, the deputy for artisans, Lu, requests the king's attention, whereupon the king departs momentarily, leaving a befuddled Xifu 析父, who has been listening on the sidelines, to question Zige: "You, sir, are the great hope of the domain of Chu. Now that you speak to the king like his own echo, what is the domain to do?" 吾子，楚國之望也。今與王言如響，國其若之何？[19] Zige responds: Just as one who sharpens his knives and swords await the right opportunity to strike, so "when the king emerges, my blade will cut him down." 王出，吾刃將斬矣。[20] Sure enough, when King Ling returns to discuss governance with him, Zige's rhetorical "sword" is unsheathed. As Yixiang 倚相, the scribe of the left, passes by, King Ling turns to heap praise on him, but Zige contradicts the king this time, arguing that Yixiang once professed ignorance of "Prayer Summons," a poem composed by Duke Moufu of Zhai 祭公謀父, when Zige tested his acquaintance with it. Zige's retort piques King Ling's curiosity, prompting him to ask if Zige can recite it.[21] Capitalizing on this moment, Zige replies:

---

17. In their translation of *Zuozhuan*, Durrant, Li, and Schaberg also note that "an earlier ruler of Chu, King Zhuang, had also had designs on Zhou cauldrons; see *Zuo*, Xuan 3.3. In this case, the king appears to want not the whole set of nine cauldrons, but only ritual status equal to that of the domains closest to the Zhou house."

18. *Zuo*, Zhao 12.11 (Yang, 1339).

19. *Zuo*, Zhao 12.11 (Yang, 1340).

20. Ibid.

21. *Zuo*, Zhao 12.11 (Yang, 1341).

I can. The poem says:	能。其《詩》曰：
Sonorous is the prayer summons,	祈招之愔愔，
Showing forth the sound of virtue.	式昭德音。
Think on our king's good order —	思我王度，
Like jade,	式如玉，
Like bronze.	式如金。
He makes the strength of the people his standard	形民之力，
And has no heart for drunken satiety.	而無醉飽之心。[22]

Zige appropriates the ideas in "Prayer Summons," imploring the king to devote himself to moral cultivation and the preservation of his people and resources, and to refrain from obsessing about military achievements. King Ling understands the lesson, but still proves unable to curb his ambitions, as he occupies Gan Xi indefinitely, with the result that ministers frustrated with the king seize the opportunity to rebel, leaving King Ling to commit suicide, overwhelmed by the pain of falling from the pinnacle of power.[23]

The *Zuozhuan* shows Duke Ling of Jin and King Ling of Chu both harboring deep political ambitions, a fact not lost on Shi Hui and Zige. Thus when they remonstrated, though their ethical positions may have been firm, their language is tactful, and though their stated aims are to edify and rectify their rulers, they try their best to avoid openly quashing their lords' ambitions, appeasing them first before seeking to change their minds. But however deft the ministers' maneuvers may be, their remonstrances fail to reverse their rulers' courses. For though the *Guoyu* and *Zuozhuan* also contain plentiful examples of successful remonstrances,[24] more often than not, we see rulers "not

---

22. *Zuo*, Zhao 12.11 (Yang, 1341).

23. In summer, the fourth month of the thirteenth year of Duke Zhao of Lu's reign, the Chu Prince Bi allied with the states of Chen and Cai to rebel against King Ling of Chu while the king was stationed at Gan Xi. The prince murdered the heir apparent Lu and Prince Pidi. Once King Chu realized that the situation had come to this, he hung himself.

24. Such successful examples of remonstrances are rare among transmitted documents. But in the battle at Bi between Jin and Chu (晉、楚邲之戰), the general of the central troops, Xun Linfu 荀林父, met with defeat, upon which he requested death as punishment. Duke Jing of Jin 晉景公 (r. 599–581 BCE) consented, but on account of Shi Wozhuo's 士渥濁 remonstrance, changed his mind, allowing Xun Linfu to resume his position.

listening" 弗聽 to and "not accepting" 弗從 their ministers' words. From the examples of Duke Moufu of Zhai, Shi Que, Shi Hui, and Zige above, we can see that the success or failure of the remonstrance often lies not in the remonstrator's rhetorical skill, but is determined by the ruler's own will and character. Since the ruler's and minister's roles are defined such that the ruler has the final say, as long as the ruler is aware of his superiority on this count, his will-to-power could be boundless, regardless of how culturally refined, rhetorically skilled, and well-intentioned his ministers may be.

As it is then, the ministers could do little but dutifully act within their traditional role as the ruler's enlightened teacher. As the "Remonstrance" chapter of the *Baihu tong* 白虎通 (*The Comprehensive Discussions in the White Tiger Hall*) explains:

> Why is it an obligation for a minister to remonstrate against his lord? So as to do his best and proffer his sincerity in service to the lord. As the *Analects* has it: "Can you love anyone without making him work hard? Can you do your best for anyone without educating him?"
>
> 臣所以有諫君之義何？盡忠納誠也。《論語》曰：「愛之能無勞乎？忠焉能無誨乎？」[25]

This passage likewise portrays ministers who remonstrate as occupying the role of a teacher uplifting his ruler. In *Zuozhuan*, Shi Kuang 師曠 provides the cosmological basis for treating the ruler as the receiver of instruction: the role of the ruler is ordained by a Heaven that "[gives] birth to the people and establishes rulers for them." 天生民而立之君。[26] The "ruler" is akin to Heaven, Earth, the spirits, and thunderbolts, yet he also shoulders the responsibility to sustain his people.[27] That should be the case, says Shi Kuang, because "Heaven" gave birth to the people, and established a "ruler" to tend to them: "Great indeed is Heaven's love for the people! Why would it let one person exert his will over the people and indulge his excesses while abandoning the nature of Heaven and Earth?" 天之愛民甚矣，豈其使

25. "Jian zheng" 諫諍, *Baihu tong shuzheng*, 226. Translated with reference to Tjan Tjoe Som, trans., *Po Hu T'ung* "Admonitions," 462.

26. *Zuo*, Xiang 14 (Yang, 1016).

27. Ibid.

一人肆於民上，以從其淫，而棄天地之性？[28] Though the ruler's power may be august, why would Heaven allow him to recklessly do as he pleases? As Shi Kuang further elaborates:

> There being rulers, Heaven establishes helpers for them to act as their teachers and guardians, not letting them exceed limits.[29] That is why the Son of Heaven has his lords, princes their ministers, ministers establish their collateral lineages, high officers have their secondary lines, officers their subordinate younger kinsmen or like-minded colleagues,[30] commoners, artisans, merchants, minions, lackeys, shepherds, and grooms all have their kin and close associates, so as to assist and support each other. When there is excellence, the helpers praise them; when there are wrongs, they rectify them; when there are troubles, they come to their aid; when there are errors, they change them.
>
> 有君而爲之貳，使師保之，勿使過度。是故天子有公，諸侯有卿，卿置側室，大夫有貳宗，士有朋友，庶人、工、商、皁、隸、牧、圉皆有親暱，以相輔佐也。善則賞之，過則匡之，患則救之，失則革之。[31]

From the Son of Heaven and below, those dukes, ministers, and grand masters who have fiefdoms all have officials to assist them, "to act as their teachers and guardians, not letting them exceed limits." For Shi Kuang, since the ruler is someone appointed by Heaven and, as such, is endowed with the powers to "reward excellence and punish excesses,"[32] it would behoove ministers to conceive themselves as the ruler's moral counselors whose job is to edify their rulers on the just exercise of his powers.

The Confrontational Mode

The same "Remonstrance" chapter of the *Baihu tong* also states: "The *shi* cannot remonstrate; owing to their lowly stature, they cannot interfere with politics, therefore, they cannot remonstrate." 士不得諫者，

---

28. *Zuo*, Xiang 14 (Yang, 1018).

29. Durrant, Li, and Schaberg, *Zuozhuan*: "The 'helpers' (*er* 貳) may also be translated as '(lesser) doubles.' In this vision of polity, the ruler is not unique and indispensable. His function is supported and duplicated by his officers and ministers, who also serve to keep him within proper bounds."

30. Ibid.: "Cf. Huan 2.8: *shi you li zi di* 士有隸子弟 'the officers have sons and younger brothers who are subordinate to them.'"

31. *Zuo*, Xiang 14 (Yang, 1016–17).

32. *Zuo*, Xiang 14 (Yang, 1016).

士賤，不得預政事，故不得諫也。[33] According to this understanding, the Son of Heaven, the feudal lords, ministers, grand masters, and *shi* 士 are aristocrats, but *shi* are generally ranked at the bottom, far from the center of power. Therefore, they neither "interfere with politics" nor, strictly speaking, have the responsibility or opportunity to remonstrate. As Shi Kuang states elsewhere as well, "[the *shi*] transmit opinions" and hence serve only to convey the voice of the people.[34]

However, in the Warring States period, members who rose from these lower ranks gradually constituted society's intelligentsia and political dissidents. Whether of aristocratic origins or not, they began to identify themselves as a distinct *shi* 士 class. Belonging to the educated stratum of society, they were rhetoricians who made a circuit of the various states, persuading rulers to sign onto the *shi*'s ideals, resolving rulers' difficulties and teaching them the art of governance from the various perspectives of the proliferating schools of thought. In this shifting social context, ruler-and-advisor power relations became such that advisors were not necessarily serving permanently and directly under a ruler's patronage; in fact, Mencius went so far as to proclaim that "when speaking to men of consequence, it is necessary to look on them with contempt" 說大人則藐之.[35] Although the advisors might draw upon past precedents, they subscribed to abstract notions of the "Way" (*dao* 道) or "righteousness" (*yi* 義) that apply to rulers and subjects alike, providing ethical checks and balances to the system. Confrontational remonstrators posing as dissenters emerged from this age of political division.

It may be a common misconception in our own time that, among pre-Qin thinkers, Confucians were particularly strident in advocating the subordination of ministers to the ruler's authority. But this point is quite open to debate. As one Han Confucian scholar Dong Zhongshu 董仲舒 (179–104 BCE) states, Confucius, who was anxious about the decline of the world, wrote the *Spring and Autumn Annals* to

---

33. Select translations of this and other primary texts are by Tan Yin Hoe, a former master's student in the Department of Chinese Literature at National Taiwan University.

34. *Zuo*, Xiang 14.6 (Yang, 1017).

35. See *Mengzi* 14.34; Lau, trans., *Mencius*, 201.

"humble the Son of Heaven, cause the feudal lords to repent, and take stock of the counselors" 貶天子，退諸侯，討大夫;[36] that is, he composed the work to criticize those in power. Other pre-Qin thinkers, such as Zisi (子思, 483–402 BCE), Mencius (Mengzi 孟子, ca. 380–300 BCE), and Xunzi (荀子, ca. 315–230 BCE), continued Confucius's critical legacy. Among the Chu bamboo slips in the Guodian cache 郭店楚簡, "Duke Mu of Lu Asks Zisi" 魯穆公問子思 contains this passage:

> Duke Mu of Lu asked Zisi, "How might one be fit to be called a loyal minister?" Zisi said, "One who consistently proclaims the iniquities of one's lord can be regarded as a loyal minister." The duke was unhappy. He bowed and sent Zisi away. When Chengsun Ge came to see the duke, the duke asked, "I once inquired Zisi about the qualities of a loyal minister. 'One who consistently proclaims the iniquities of one's lord can be regarded as a loyal minister,' was his answer. I am confused and could make no sense of it." Chengsun Ge replied, "Oh, excellent are his words! There had been ministers who sacrificed their lives for their lords. But I have yet to hear of a minister who consistently proclaims the iniquities of his lord. The ones who sacrificed their lives for their lords were after titles and emoluments. Those who proclaim the iniquities of their lords are renouncing their titles and emoluments. To renounce one's title and emolument for the sake of being righteous is such deed in which, other than Zisi, I have heard of none who is up to it."
>
> 魯穆公問於子思曰：「何如而可謂忠臣？」子思曰：「恆稱其君之惡者，可謂忠臣矣。」公不悅，揖而退之。成孫弋見，公曰：「向者吾問忠臣於子思，子思曰：『恆稱其君之惡者可謂忠臣矣。』寡人惑焉，而未之得也。」成孫弋曰：「噫！善哉，言乎！夫爲其君之故殺其身者，嘗有之矣。恆稱其君之惡者，未之有也。夫爲其君之故殺其身者，效祿爵者也；恆〔稱其君〕之惡〔者，遠〕祿爵者也，〔爲〕義而遠祿爵，非子思，吾惡聞之矣。」[37]

With the exception of this Guodian passage, many such dialogues between Zisi and Duke Mu of Lu among the transmitted texts have never attracted much attention. The loyal minister, according to Confucius's grandson, Zisi, is one who is unafraid of confronting his ruler, and in Chengsun Ge's view, those who choose righteousness

36. *SJ* 130.3297.

37. *Guodian chumu zhujian*, 141. Translation by Tan Yin Hoe.

over privileges would never think it worthy of themselves to live off of the ruler's power and privileges.

The above quoted passage compares well with one from *The Kong Family Masters*, in which Duke Mu of Lu 魯穆公 (r. 407–375 BCE) requests Zisi to recruit Gongyi Xiu 公儀休 (fl. 4th c. BCE) as his chief minister. Instead of simply complying, Zisi responds forcefully to what he perceives as the duke's design "to divide the state of Lu into three parts and let [Gongyi Xiu] have one" 參分魯國而與之一:

> If I deliver this message of yours, sir, then Gongyizi will have all the more reason not to comply. If you are eager to recruit the worthy and are ready to adopt their plans, then even if you were to offer a meal of plain vegetables and water, I, too, would like to be under your influence. Nevertheless, you are only trying to lure a superior man with a distinguished position and substantial salary, and you do not intend to make true use of him. If Gongyizi's intelligence were like that of a fish or a bird, then this plan of yours could be put into effect. But since this is not the case, then he will never in his life set foot in your court. Moreover, I am not a lackey and I am not obligated to hold a fishing rod for you and lower the hook in order to dislodge a gentleman who holds fast to his moral integrity.
>
> 如君之言，則公儀子愈所以不至也。君若飢渴待賢，納用其謀，雖蔬食水飲，伋亦願在下風。今徒以高官厚祿釣餌君子，無信用之意。公儀子之智若魚鳥，可也。不然，則彼將終身不躡乎君之庭矣。且臣不佞，又不任爲君操竿下釣，以傷守節之士也。[38]

Forthrightly refusing the Duke's request, Zisi berates Duke Mu for underestimating the acumen of worthy advisors. To treat high office and emolument as bait, and worthy *shi* as those who easily fall prey to such, impugns their dignity. Indeed, in his address Zisi himself displays the dignity of a *shi* who possesses "moral integrity." It is precisely his dignity and integrity that allows Zisi to be completely fearless in his comments to the monarch, to dare to speak so directly about his errors. The text *Kong Family Masters* may contain interpolations by later editors, but echoing across both the above excerpt and the Guodian passage "Duke Mu of Lu Asks Zisi" is the central idea that the upstanding minister would "renounce [his] title and emolument for the sake of being righteous." As part of his critique of the

38. Ariel, trans., *Kung-Tsung-Tzu*, 116; *Kongcongzi*, 49–50.

ruler, Zisi has not shied away from "proclaiming the iniquities of [his] lord." Without troubling himself to delicately cajole the ruler and having no regard for the duke's potential displeasure, Zisi delivers barbed admonitions. Mencius quotes a similar dialogue between Zisi and Duke Mu:

> Duke Mu frequently went to see [Zisi]. "How did kings of states with a thousand chariots in antiquity make friends with Gentlemen?" he asked. [Zisi] was displeased. "What the ancients talked about," said he, "was serving them, not making friends with them."
>
> 繆公亟見於子思，曰：「古千乘之國以友士，何如?」子思不悅，曰：「古之人有言曰：『事之云乎』，豈曰『友之云乎』?」[39]

As Zisi's supposed disciple, Mencius further elaborates on Zisi's message:

> The reason for [Zisi's] displeasure was surely this. "In point of position, you are the prince and I am your subject. How dare I be friends with you? In point of virtue, it is you who ought to serve me. How can you presume to be friends with me?"
>
> 子思之不悅也，豈不曰：「以位，則子，君也，我，臣也，何敢與君友也?以德，則子事我者也，奚可以與我友?」[40]

In terms of social and political stature, the ruler undoubtedly stands higher than the minister, the *shi* advisor; but in terms of moral stature, the *shi* often surpasses the ruler in his commitment to *de* 德 and *yi* 義. On account of his moral superiority, the *shi* exudes a kind of confidence admired by the ruler. If carrying out *de* and *yi* is the sole concern, then Zisi believes that it is the ruler who ought to "serve" the *shi*, thereby recalibrating the balance of power between the ruler and subject.[41]

It may have been the minister's obligation to remonstrate, as *Guoyu* and *Zuozhuan* remind their readers time and again, but in too

---

39. Mencius 5B, 7.4; Lau, trans., *Mencius*, 157.

40. Ibid.

41. In the "Intrigues of the State of Qi" in *Intrigues of the Warring States*, the remonstrances of Wang Dou 王斗 and Yan Chu 顏斶 (both fl. 4th c. BCE) with the king of Qi also play out the idea that the ruler's power derives from his given position, whereas the *shi* derives his from his commitment to the "way." As we can see, this understanding of their respective sources of personal capital was not limited to the Confucians but was a widely accepted belief.

many cases, rulers simply "refuse to listen" to or "refuse to follow" advice, insisting upon their own ways instead, so what good would "consistently proclaim[ing] his lord's iniquities" accomplish? Mencius and Xunzi both attempt to address this quandary. Should the ruler obstinately reject remonstrances, Mencius prescribes separate courses of action for what he distinguishes as "ministers of royal blood" as opposed to "those of families other than the royal house": the former could overthrow the ruler, while the latter should quietly depart. Mencius's audacious reply no doubt unsettled King Xuan of Qi 齊宣王 (r. 319–301 BCE). Xunzi refines the meaning of remonstrance by further subdividing it into four types of responses to a ruler's resistance to advice: "remonstrance" (*jian* 諫), "wrangling" (*zheng* 爭), "assistance" (*fu* 輔), and "opposition" (*fu* 拂).[42] He defines "remonstrance" as the choice whereby the minister would leave if his advice goes unheeded; "wrangling" as when the minister threatens suicide as either blackmail or pledge; "assistance" or "opposition" as when the minister acts on his own accord, resisting the ruler's command, usurping the ruler's prerogatives, and undermining his undertakings, such that the "behavior of the Lord of Pingyuan 平原君 in regard to Zhao may properly be called assistance" and the "conduct of the Lord of Xinling 信陵君 in regard to Wei may properly be called opposition."[43] The lords of Pingyuan (?–251 BCE) and Xinling (?–243 BCE) were both ministers of royal blood, or people whom Mencius and Xunzi would consider as having the privilege to employ more radical means to ensure the survival of the state. To these thinkers, this set of responses is a legitimate expression of the *shi*'s higher commitment to the impersonal ideal whereby the loyal minister "follows the way but not the ruler."

In the Warring States period, when Confucian and Mohist thought were equally influential, the Mohists may have been of the opinion that "[what] the superior takes to be right, all must take to be right. What the superior takes to be wrong, all must take to be wrong." 上之所是必皆是之，所非必皆非之。[44] But in the same breath, Mozi 墨子 (ca. 460–390 BCE) also avers, "If those above have faults, then

42. *Xunzi jijie*, 250.

43. Knoblock, trans., *Xunzi*, 199–200.

44. "Shang tong" 尙同, in *Mozi jiangu* 3.75; Johnston, trans., *The Mozi*, 93.

admonish and remonstrate with them." 上有過則規諫之。[45] The "Gong Meng" (公孟) chapter of *Mozi* says:

> Gongmeng Zi spoke to Master Mo Zi saying: "A gentleman folds his hands and waits. If he is questioned, then he speaks. If he is not questioned, then he desists. He is like a bell. If it is struck, then it sounds; if not struck, then it does not sound."
>
> Master Mo Zi said: "To this I say there are three conditions. You, Sir, know only of one, so you do not yet know what is being said. If a great officer behaves in a dissolute and cruel way in the state, to come forward to remonstrate is called not being humble. To remonstrate through those on either side is called privately criticizing. For the gentleman this is a perplexing matter. Now if the great officer who is governing is about to encounter some difficulty in the state, just like an arrow that flies from a bow, the gentleman must come forward to remonstrate, and be of benefit to the great officer. In this case, even if he is not struck, he must sound. Suppose a great officer undertakes some unusual enterprise that is not righteous. For example, suppose he acquires some ingenious device which can be employed in military matters and wishes to attack some unoffending state with it. If he has acquired it, he will certainly use it as a means of extending his territory and land, and illegally extorting goods and wealth. In going forth there is, however, unquestionably disgrace, and there is no benefit either to the one attacked or to the one attacking—that is, neither benefits. In such a case, although not struck, one should certainly sound."
>
> 公孟子謂子墨子曰:「君子共己以待,問焉則言,不問焉則止。譬若鍾然,扣則鳴,不扣則不鳴。」子墨子曰:「是言有三物焉,子乃今知其一(身) 〔耳」(也),又未知其所謂也。若大人行淫暴於國家,進而諫,則謂之不遜,因左右而獻諫,則謂之言議,此君子之所疑惑也。若大人爲政,將因於國家之難,譬若機之將發也然,君子之必以諫,然而大人之利,若此者,雖不扣必鳴者也。若大人舉不義之異行,雖得大巧之經,可行於軍旅之事,欲攻伐無罪之國,有之也,君得之,則必用之矣。以廣辟土地,著稅僞材,出必見辱,所攻者不利,而攻者亦不利,是兩不利也。若此者,雖不扣必鳴者也。」[46]

Qing commentators identify Gong Mengzi as one of Confucius's followers. If such is the case, then Mohist ideas may very well overlap with Confucian ideas concerning remonstrance, insofar as Mozi's

---

45. Ibid.

46. "Gongmeng" 公孟, in *Mozi jiangu* 12.449–50; Johnston, trans., *The Mozi*, 675.

metaphor of the gentleman as a bell essentially represents a passive, responsive stance. However, Mozi does identify two situations that would require the minister to "sound" though he has not been "struck": when the state meets with external threats, and when the ruler launches attacks on neighboring states to gain territory, unaware that no benefit can come from such action. At such a critical moment, the minister should not stand idle on the sidelines but should jump into the fray.

In the well-known story within the chapter "Gongshu" (公輸) where Mozi dissuades the state of Chu from attacking the state of Song, Mozi's active remonstrance applies principles that he lays out in "Condemning Offensive Warfare" (Feigong 非攻). As a skilled craftsman of the late Spring and Autumn period (722–468 BCE), Gongshu Pan 公輸盤 designed exquisitely made "cloud ladders" for the state of Chu, furnishing King Hui of Chu 楚惠王 (r. 488–432 BCE) with new means to attack the state of Song. In keeping with the positions he articulated in "Universal Love" 兼愛 and "Condemning Offensive Warfare," upon hearing word of Chu's imminent attack, Mozi immediately departs from the state of Qi, traveling with haste by day and night to Chu in the hopes of forestalling battle by remonstrating with the Chu king.[47] Mozi's remonstrances are presented in three stages. In the first, he chooses Gongshu Pan as his target, because Gongshu Pan is the inventor of the ladder. Mozi uses the following opening gambit: "In the northern region, there is one who has insulted me. I wish to make use of you to kill him" 北方有侮臣，願藉子殺之, causing Gongshu Pan to retort, "My righteousness is strong—I do not kill people." 吾義固不殺人。 Mozi later turns this very same retort against Gongshu Pan, underscoring Gongshu's self-contradiction: "To take as righteous not killing a few, yet to kill many cannot be called an understanding of analogy." 義不殺少而殺眾，不可謂知類。[48] Mozi additionally portrays Chu as a larger state that, as a land-grabber, would be unwisely and unjustly sacrificing its own people "[to] kill what there is not enough of in the struggle for what there is an excess of." 殺所不足，而爭所有餘。[49] If Gongshu

47. "Gongshu" 公輸, *Mozi jiangu* 50.483–89; trans. Johnston, *The Mozi*, 725–29.
48. *Mozi jiangu* 50.484; Johnston, trans., *The Mozi*, 725.
49. Ibid.

Pan agrees with Mozi on these counts but shrinks from remonstrating with the king of Chu, he "cannot be said to be loyal" 不可謂忠.[50] Pressing the point further, Mozi states that even if Gongshu Pan had made the good faith effort to remonstrate, were he unsuccessful, he "cannot be said to be strong" either 不可謂強.[51] Mozi's argument defeats Gongshu Pan completely, but Gongshu refuses to concede, foisting all responsibility for the decision to wage war on King Hui of Chu, since only the ruler can make such a decision. Thereupon, Mozi requests to see the king himself, embarking on a second round of persuasion.

Mozi uses concrete examples to illustrate larger ideas, employing a series of analogies to satirize Chu's attack on Song, which he says would be equivalent to a wealthy man stealing his neighbor's "broken-down carriage," "chaff and dregs," and "short jacket."[52] King Hui, for his part, does not disagree with Mozi's reasoning, but still clings to the pretext that since the ladders have already been built, the attack on Song should proceed. During the first and second rounds of remonstrance, Mozi deploys artful reasoning to win over Gongshu Pan and King Hui. However, seeing that verbal argumentation alone does not suffice, since both ruler and craftsman are eager to employ their technological superiority, Mozi makes his third move.

Mozi's third strategy consists in simulating combat with Gongshu Pan to compete with him on the level of technical skill ("Master Mo Zi took off his belt and made it a city wall. With little sticks he made weapons." 子墨子解帶爲城，以牒爲械。).[53] With clearly superior defensive strategies, Mozi corners and humiliates Gongshu Pan, resulting in Gongshu Pan's weighing whether to simply assassinate Mozi. But Mozi has not only already foreseen this result, but also made the proper preparations, for he says, "My disciple Qin Guli and three hundred such men have already prepared my machines of defence and are on the walls of Song awaiting the attack from Chu. Although you kill me, you will not be able to overcome [their defence]." 然臣之弟子禽滑釐等三百人，已持臣守圉之器，在宋城上而待楚寇矣。雖殺

50. Ibid.
51. Ibid.
52. *Mozi jiangu* 50.485; Johnston, trans., *The Mozi*, 727.
53. *Mozi jiangu* 50.486; Johnston, trans., *The Mozi*, 729.

臣，不能絕也。[54] At this point, the king of Chu cannot but quit his plan to invade Song. Gallantly, Mozi has not only "sounded" his counsel without being "struck," but has successfully convinced the king to desist, supplementing his remonstrance with a technical performance. The motivation behind Mozi's remonstrance lies not only in protecting Song or Chu, but in his broader wish to "promote what benefits the world and eliminate what harms it." 興天下之利，除天下之害。[55] Committed to this ideal, he opposes war that results in the killing of many, knowing that such wars are neither right nor beneficial to both sides—"either to the one attacked or to the one attacking." In accord with this belief, he undertakes to endure the hardship of travel, at the risk of execution, engaging in round after round of persuasion, thoroughly dismantling the idea of aggressive warfare, which harms the mutual benefit of the people of both states. In this particular case, Mozi's determination to speak on behalf of the people and to promote the ideal of "righteousness" ultimately forces the king of Chu to relinquish his notions pertaining to the power of the ruler and the state.

The Authoritarian Mode

Both Confucians and Mohists were wont to uphold the ways of ancient sage kings and invoke beliefs about circumscribing the ruler's absolute power. In contrast, the legalists, invested in buttressing the ruler's total authority, would not hesitate to ban private learning or discourage the participation of others in the formulation of statutes or policies. The authoritarian mode of rhetoric differs from the instructive mode in that legalists, arguing for the strengthening of central authority, would tend to favor new policies, boldly revamping old systems with little concern for historical precedents. Interestingly, this veneration of authority led to the organizing of formal debates (*yi* 議) in which ministers would present opposing arguments, but the ruler would retain the power of final arbitration. These debates on the floor of the court, held between ministers arguing contrary propositions, replaced the minister-to-ruler remonstrances. With this shift in argu-

---

54. *Mozi jiangu* 50.488; Johnston, trans., *The Mozi*, 729.
55. "Feiyue" 非樂, *Mozi jiangu* 32.251; Johnston, trans., *The Mozi*, 307.

mentative process, the ruler was rendered invisible and direct challenges to his authority were expertly deflected away.

Illustrating the difference between the legalist and previous two modes of rhetoric are two sets of argument debating the merits of abolishing or preserving the institution of enfeoffment (*fengjian* 封建), one between Shang Yang 商鞅 (?–338 BCE) and Gan Long 甘龍 at the time of Duke Xiao of Qin 秦孝公 (r. 361–338 BCE), and the other between Li Si 李斯 (?280–208 BCE) and Chunyu Yue 淳于越 during the reign of the first emperor of Qin (r. 246–210 BCE). According to the *Shiji*, in the first year of his reign Duke Xiao of Qin recruited talent to fill the ranks of his government, whereupon Shang Yang brought himself forward to present his argument in favor of scrapping the system of enfeoffment. Duke Xiao had already made up his mind to adopt Shang Yang's proposal, but hesitated on account of possible opposition from other ministers, so he resorted to the formality of handing the controversy over to a court debate (*tingyi* 廷議), which Shang Yang opened with these remarks:

> Indecision in one's actions will win no fame, indecision in one's enterprises will win no merit. Moreover, those whose actions are above the level of others are naturally abused by their age; those whose considerations are unique in their wisdom are sure to be despised by the common folk. The simple are blind to a task's successful conclusion, while the wise see it before it has begun. One cannot consider how to begin with the common people, one can only enjoy results with them. One who talks of the highest virtue will not be in accord with the vulgar, one who achieves great merit will not plan with the multitide. Thus, if it might strengthen a state, the sage will not follow its precedents; if it might benefit the people, he will not observe their social norms.
>
> 疑行無名，疑事無功。且夫有高人之行者，固見非於世；有獨知之慮者，必見敖於民。愚者闇於成事，知者見於未萌。民不可與慮始而可與樂成。論至德者不和於俗，成大功者不謀於眾。是以聖人苟可以彊國，不法其故；苟可以利民，不循其禮。[56]

Shang Yang portrays the ruler as a great leader possessing exclusive knowledge, whereas the people are benighted creatures. Since the ruler can consider himself everyone's superior, and thus beyond re-

56. *SJ* 68.2229; Nienhauser, gen. ed., *The Grand Scribe's Records*, vol. 7, 88–89.

proach, it is unnecessary to garner other people's support to attain "the highest virtue" or achieve "great merit" as long as he can "strengthen [the] state" and "benefit the people," even if it means ignoring the people's conservative tendencies in the name of innovation. Shang Yang places the ruler and his subjects into two camps, exalting and denigrating them respectively to the degree that those who oppose the policy change are scorned by Shang Yang as people who hold "plebeian" views. He defines their difference with his claims that "the wise make laws and the simple are bound by them" 智者作法，愚者制焉 and "the worthy change the social norms and the inferior are restrained by them." 賢者更禮，不肖者拘焉。[57] In Shang Yang's eyes, "vulgar" commoners, as well as scholars "obsessed with what they have learned" 溺於所聞, are fit only for complying with existing legislation, not for partaking in high-level discussions about policy changes. When another minister, Du Zhi 杜摯, voices opposition to the new policy, saying that "There is no error in following precedents" 法古吾過, Shang Yang rebuts him by saying that "[Tang] 湯 [of Yin] and Wu 武 [of Zhou] did not observe precedents yet became kings, while [Xia] 夏 and Yin 殷 did not alter social norms yet perished." 湯、武不循古而王，夏、殷不易禮而亡。[58] Contesting the traditionalist view, Shang Yang points out that the rulers of the Xia and Shang dynasties might have relied on time-honored institutions, but they still failed to escape their eventual demise. In contrast, the very rulers championed by the traditionalists, Tang and Wu, succeeded in founding the Shang and Zhou dynasties precisely because they were reformist figures. At this point in the debate, Shang Yang has transformed the sage rulers worshiped by traditionalists into symbolic figures for his own reformist discourse. Apparently convinced, Duke Xiao consequently pronounces his decision to abandon enfeoffments.

Upon closer examination, it is apparent that Shang Yang's speech rhetorically augments the ruler's authority, placing it in inverse proportion to the diminished power of his subjects: the premise that the

57. Nienhauser, *The Grand Scribe's Records*, vol. 7, 89.
58. Ibid.

ruler owns the absolute power to legislate changes legitimizes his dismissal of ideas that run contrary to his proposed changes. On the surface, Shang Yang and the likes of Gan Long or Du Zhi appear to openly and directly confront each other on the court floor, airing their respective views on whether or not to enact changes to the law. However, in reality, Shang Yang's position hews very close to the duke's from beginning to end, and as Shang Yang argues for the consolidation of the ruler's executive power, it surprises no one when the duke publicly sides with Shang Yang. In this round of formal court debate, Shang Yang is far from being a dissenter, or even much of a persuader. Indeed, it may fairly be said that he serves primarily as the duke's mouthpiece.

Another court debate illustrates similar dynamics between the ruler and ministers in disagreement over the same administrative issue regarding enfeoffments. In the *Shiji*'s account, during the thirty-fourth year of the First Emperor of Qin's 秦始皇 reign, many of his ministers are extolling the emperor's unification of the six states. The exception is Erudite Chunyu Yue 淳于越, who questions the systematic replacement of enfeoffments with commandaries and counties, insisting that one should appreciate the Shang and Zhou system of enfeoffment, which has worked for more than a thousand years and therefore merits emulation. The emperor asks his ministers to debate this issue on the floor of the court and commissions the Counselor-in-Chief Li Si to chair the debate. Li Si's presentation advances the view that since times, and institutional needs, have changed, if those advancing traditionalist notions continue to engage in policy discussions, chaos will ensue. He thus recommends the banning of outdated learning:

> Formerly the world was divided and in disorder, and none was able to unify it, therefore the feudal lords rose [to vie for hegemony] at the same time. In their words, they all talked about the ancient, thereby regarding the present [system] as harmful, and elaborated empty words to confuse reality. Each cherished what he had acquired from private learning to criticize what the sovereign has established. Now the emperor, having united and grasped the world, has discriminated between black and white and established a single authority. But they are partial to their learning and join together to criticize the laws and

teachings. Upon hearing an ordinance has been issued, each debates it according to his learning. In the court, they criticize it in their hearts; outside, they debate it on the streets. To discredit the ruler is a means to be famous, and to be inclined to opposition is a means of showing superiority. They lead their followers to fabricate slander. If things like this are not banned, then the ruler's power will be diminished above, and factions will form below. To ban them is appropriate.

古者天下散亂，莫之能一，是以諸侯并作，語皆道古以害今，飾虛言以亂實，人善其所私學，以非上之所建立。今皇帝并有天下，別黑白而定一尊。私學而相與非法教，人聞令下，則各以其學議之；入則心非，出則巷議，夸主以爲名，異取以爲高，率群下以造謗。如此弗禁，則主勢降乎上，黨與成乎下，禁之便。[59]

Li Si avers that all under Heaven should submit to one authority now that the First Emperor of Qin has unified the six states. He accuses officials and the people of stubbornly keeping to their custom of outspokenly criticizing government policies and statues, to no good purpose, for they do so only to heighten their own reputations, to aggrandize themselves, or to stoke oppositional public opinion. Since all such actions lead to the result that "the ruler's power will be diminished above," he suggests that the ruler has no choice but to suppress such customs. For Li Si, the particular question of whether to emulate the Shang and Zhou system of enfeoffment is not the crux of the issue at all; rather, he appears more broadly interested in squashing private learning and discussion, as is evident in his later recommendation to burn the books in a campaign to curtail critiques of imperial policies. As the emperor's advocate, Li Si seeks to have the emperor's edicts treated as law and thus allow "the ruler's power" to go unchallenged and unchecked. Pleased by this counsel, the First Emperor "approved" (*ke* 可) Li Si's recommendations. Evidently, Li Si chose not to continue the legacy of his teacher Xunzi to "follow the way but not the ruler" 從道不從君, preferring instead to contribute to Shang Yang's legalistic project of establishing the ruler's unassailable authority by subduing his subjects, restricting the space

59. *SJ* 6.254–55; Nienhauser, gen. ed., *The Grand Scribe's Records*, vol. 1, 147.

for open "debate," let alone any room for "remonstrance," "wrangling," "assistance," and "opposition."

Conclusion

In the pre-Qin era, ministers who remonstrated with their rulers could speak, as we have seen, in one or more of the three argumentative modes: the instructive, confrontational, or authoritarian mode. The first two modes call for respect for the past, a sense of historicity, and the emulation of former kings or the "Way," all of which foster and sustain a model of authority higher than the current ruler's. One of the differences between the instructive and confrontational approaches is that those remonstrating in the instructive mode would speak in circumspect ways, whereas those speaking in the confrontational mode would sound uncompromising when directing challenges to the ruler's authority. During the Warring States period, the dissemination of Confucian and Mohist thought spawned ideas that encouraged the adoption of the confrontational mode of rhetoric in the service of higher ideals. In contrast, the legalists, as represented by Shang Yang and Li Si, intimately involved as they were in court politics, gained the grace and favor of their rulers. These figures' speeches reflect an authoritarian mode of thinking and rhetoric as they worked to insulate the ruler's authority against objection or criticism. This last mode of rhetoric betrays the nature of raw power conferred upon the imperial ruler, as it reduces his subjects from the minister level and downward to a relative state of disempowerment. Perhaps due to the confrontational rhetorician's overt idealism, and the authoritarian rhetorician's excessively ingratiating support of the powers that be, the second and third modes of rhetoric gradually fell out of favor with remonstrators after the Han period (after 220 CE). So it is that the instructive rhetoric that gently steers the ruler to the right path eventually becomes the preponderant mode of remonstrance throughout most of China's imperial history.[60]

---

60. I would like to extend my sincere thanks to Pauli Wai, Ph.D. candidate in the Department of East Asian Languages and Cultures at the University of California at Berkeley, for translating this essay from the original Chinese.

CHAPTER 3

From Teachers to Subjects: Ministers Speaking to the Rulers, from Yan Ying 晏嬰 to Li Si 李斯

Yuri Pines, Hebrew University of Jerusalem

Two major studies inspired me to undertake the research that resulted in the present essay.[1] First was a section in Liu Zehua's 劉澤華 seminal work *Chinese Monarchism*, in which Liu Zehua analyzed the self-deprecating language employed by the leading Tang intellectuals Han Yu (韓愈, 768–824 CE) and Liu Zongyuan (柳宗元, 773–819 CE) in their correspondence with the throne. Through this analysis, Liu Zehua demonstrated the magnitude of the cultural and symbolical power of the emperor over his subjects—over even the most brilliant and audacious of them.[2] Second was a similarly inspiring "Playing at Critique" by David Schaberg, in which he noticed the proliferation of the genre of "indirect remonstrance" (*fengjian* 諷諫) from the second half of the Warring States (Zhanguo 戰國, 453–221 BCE)[3] period. Schaberg summarizes:

> The tellers of remonstrance tales registered a change in the status of court officials. Older tales of direct remonstrance had presumed near

---

1. This research was supported by the Israel Science Foundation (grant No. 511/11) and by the Michael William Lipson Chair in Chinese Studies. I am grateful for the participants in the workshop "Addressing the Autocrat" and to Garret Olberding for their comments on the draft of the essay.

2. See Liu Zehua, *Zhongguo de Wangquanzhuyi*, 263–79.

3. For Schaberg's earlier study of a "regular" remonstrance genre, see Schaberg, "Remonstrance in Eastern Zhou Historiography."

> parity between the ruler and the ministers who help to formulate his policies. Episodes of indirect remonstrance, on the other hand, took it as a given that the ruler might, with little fuss, put to death the men who presumed to criticize his action. While the first set of narratives reflects conceptions of hierarchy that prevailed before the middle Warring States period, the second reflects, probably in an exaggerated form, the concentration of power that took place thereafter.[4]

My study follows the lead of Liu Zehua and Schaberg by trying to analyze the changing status of members of the educated elite vis-à-vis the rulers from the late Spring and Autumn period (Chunqiu, 春秋, 770–453 BCE) through the Warring States and to the early imperial period, as reflected in their interaction with the rulers. By focusing on three leading figures from the preimperial period—Yan Ying (晏嬰, ca. 580–510 BCE), Mengzi (孟子, or Mencius, ca. 380–300 BCE), and Xunzi (荀子, ca. 315–230 BCE)—and briefly comparing them with the most important early imperial statesman, Li Si (李斯, d. 208 BCE), I shall demonstrate how the self-confident tone of a ruler's instructor and guide, a tone adopted by Yan Ying and to a certain degree by Mengzi, turned into the cautious tone of an advisor in the *Xunzi* and from there evolved into the subservient tone of a ruler's subject in Li Si's memorials. I hope to show that aside from reflecting differences in the source materials from which the speeches are taken, the changing mode of these putative conversations with the rulers may reflect the widening gap between the ruler and the minister, anticipating the situation of "elevated monarch and humble subject" depicted by Liu Zehua and Schaberg.

Yan Ying: Aristocrat Speaking

I begin my discussion with Yan Ying (Yanzi 晏子), one of the most colorful figures in the *Zuozhuan* 左傳, and one of the best-known personages from the Spring and Autumn period. Yan Ying belonged to a minor aristocratic lineage in the state of Qi 齊, the state which during his lifetime was engulfed in a life-or-death struggle among powerful aristocratic lineages amid overall weakening of the ruling house. Yan Ying became renowned for his wit, straightforwardness,

4. See Schaberg, "Playing at Critique," 196.

and ability to preserve the proper decorum during repeated outbursts of violent domestic struggles. Although politically speaking his career was not very impressive (he failed either to strengthen the state of Qi or to prevent the demise of its ruling house), his very ability to survive without compromising his moral integrity might have appealed to contemporaries and to later generations. Yan Ying's popularity is reflected in numerous anecdotes about him, which circulated broadly throughout the late Spring and Autumn and Warring States periods; some of these were incorporated already into the *Zuozhuan*, while many other circulated independently and eventually were collected in the *Yanzi chunqiu* 晏子春秋.[5] Here I focus exclusively on the *Zuozhuan* accounts, as they are definitely anterior to those of the *Yanzi chunqiu* and to other Warring States texts.[6]

During Yan Ying's lifetime the domestic crisis in Qi reached its peak. In a series of bloody coups, purges, inter- and intralineage conflicts between 546 and 532 BCE, one of the Qi rulers (Lord Zhuang [齊莊公, r. 553–548 BCE]) was assassinated, and four major ministerial lineages (Cui 崔, Qing 慶, Gao 高, and Luan 欒) were exterminated altogether, leaving the most powerful positions concentrated in the hands of Chen (陳 or Tian 田) and Bao 鮑 lineages. The Chens emerged as the great victors of these collisions: in 481 BCE (a few decades after Yan Ying's death), they succeeded to usurp power in the state of Qi and a century later, in 386 BCE, they had formally replaced the puppet ruling house of the "legitimate" Qi lords. Yan Ying appears in the *Zuozhuan* as both an active participant in these events and their astute commentator; in particular, a few of his important speeches deal with the future Chen ascendancy and rationalize it. We cannot know whether these speeches reflect original insights

5. For an example of what appears as an independently circulating anecdote, see the badly damaged *Jing Gong nüe* manuscript from the Shanghai Museum collection. See *Jing Gong nüe*, 157–91. For the composition of the *Yanzi chunqiu*, see, e.g., Zheng Liangshu, "Lun *Yanzi chunqiu* de pianxie ji chengshu guocheng."

6. As I have asserted elsewhere (*Foundations of Confucian Thought*), the *Zuozhuan* might have incorporated a variety of primary materials from the Spring and Autumn period states and reflects therefore the intellectual milieu of that age. This distinguishes it markedly from the *Yanzi chunqiu*, many of the anecdotes of which reflect the proud *shi* 士 spirit of the Warring States period, which is absent from the *Zuozhuan*.

of Yan Ying, or were edited or invented in the immediate aftermath of the 481 BCE Chen coup; yet as none of them refers to the Chen usurpation as final and irreversible they cannot date from much later than 481 BCE. For the current discussion, which focuses on Yan Ying's remonstrance speeches to his last master, Lord Jing of Qi (景公, r. 547–490 BCE), what really matters is not the authenticity of these speeches but that they are reflective of the intellectual atmosphere of the Spring and Autumn period; whoever composed or edited them might have done so in accordance with the norms of ruler-minister interaction of that age. As such, the Yan Ying remonstrance speeches provide us with a valuable glimpse at the late Spring and Autumn period intellectual atmosphere and the culture of addressing the ruler in particular.

Five of the most important remonstrance speeches by Yan Ying are collected in the end of the narratives of the twentieth and twenty-sixth years of Lord Zhao (i.e., 522 and 516 BCE respectively). Of these, two speeches deal (one directly and another indirectly) with the prospects of the Chen ascendancy; two others criticize the ruler for attempts to avert an illness or a potentially threatening omen through religious activities rather than through personal and political rectification; the fifth speech analyzes the nature of ruler-minister relations and warns the lord against relying on sycophants. These speeches have been translated and studied elsewhere; in what follows I shall analyze them exclusively from the point of view of ruler-minister relations.[7]

I shall begin with the lengthiest remonstrance, directed against Lord Jing's odd decision to punish two petty religious functionaries (a scribe and an invocator) for failing to solicit divine support for curing the lord's prolonged illness.[8] Yan Ying uses the pretext of this imprudent plan to criticize the lord's misdeeds. His speech is divided

---

7. For various translations and analyses of Yan Ying's speeches, see Pines, "The Search for Stability," 18–31; Schaberg, *A Patterned Past*; Waiyee Li, *The Readability of the Past in Early Chinese Historiography*.

8. This story appears in the *Jing Gong nüe* manuscript, cited above, and also in *Yanzi chunqiu yizhu*, "Nei pian jian shang" 內篇諫上 1.12, 27–30; "Wai pian shang" 外篇上 7.7, 327–28. Yet another of the Shanghai Museum manuscripts, *Bao Shuya yu Xi Peng zhi jian* 鮑叔牙與隰朋之諫, clearly borrows from Yan Ying's remonstrance, but attributes it to the courtiers of Lord Huan of Qi (齊桓公, r. 685–643 BCE).

into three sections. First, Yan Ying begins with an ostensibly innocent anecdote about Shi Hui (士會, fl. 630s–590s BCE), an eminent Jin 晉 statesman, whose uprightness and morality ensured his continuing political success. Yan Ying emphasizes that it was due to Shi's fine qualities that when his "invocators and scribes offered sacrifices, they presented the truth without dishonor," as a result of which Shi Hui was able to solicit divine and human support, allowing him sufficiently lengthy tenure "to aid five rulers [of Jin] in their role as hosts of the regional lords."[9] Shi Hui's political success and longevity are implicitly contrasted with the case of Lord Jing. Yet, as the lord pretends not to understand the hidden criticism, Yan Ying turns to a direct explanation about how a ruler should act to ensure the divine support:

> In the case of a ruler who has virtue, outside the palace and within it no one is lax about duties, superiors and inferiors have no complaints, when acting he does not transgress in any undertaking, and the invocators and scribes set forth the truth: there is nothing shameful. For this reason the spirits and deities consume the offerings and the state receives the blessings; the invocators and scribes have their part in these. The reason that he enjoys blessings and longevity is that [invocators and scribes] are employed by a trustworthy ruler, and in their words they have shown loyalty and trustworthiness to the spirits and deities.
>
> 若有德之君，外內不廢，上下無怨，動無違事，其祝、史薦信，無愧心矣。是以鬼神用饗，國受其福，祝、史與焉。其所以蕃祉老壽者，為信君使也，其言忠信於鬼神。[10]

Yan Ying first outlines the requirements of the ideal ruler, whom Lord Jing should emulate. The positive image of this virtuous sovereign who is able to ensure blessings and longevity for himself and for his subjects is contrasted with that of a bad ruler, with whom Lord Jing is implicitly associated:

> But it may happen that they encounter a profligate ruler, under whom there is irregularity and deviation outside of the palace and within it,

For the correct reconstruction of the *Bao Shuya* manuscript, see Lin Zhipeng, "Zhanguo zhushu *Bao Shuya yu Xi Peng zhi jian* yizhu."

9. See *Zuo*, Zhao 20 (Yang, 1415). In translating the *Zuozhuan* passages, I borrow heavily from the forthcoming translation by Durrant, Li, and Schaberg (University of Washington Press).

10. *Zuo*, Zhao 20 (Yang, 1416).

> under whom superiors and inferiors are resentful and jealous, whose every action is a transgression, who indulges his desires and satisfies his private wishes with lofty terraces and deep pools, with the striking of bells and girls' dancing. He cuts off the people's strength at its roots and purloins their stores to supply his own violations, taking no thought of future generations. Cruel and prodigal, unrestrained and guided by no standard, lacking any afterthought or prohibition, he gives no thought to the voice of critique and does not fear the spirits and deities. Though the deities grow angry and the people suffer, he does not repent in his heart. Should his invocators and scribes set forth the truth, this would amount to bringing an indictment against him. But should they cover up his failures and enumerate his better points, this would amount to falsehood. For advancing and withdrawing alike they have no words of justification, and so with empty words they curry favor. For this reason the spirits and deities do not consume the state's sacrifices, but bring calamity down upon it, and the invocators and scribes have their part in this. That the people die young, lose their wits, are orphaned, and suffer illnesses was caused by a cruel ruler, whose words are false and an insult to the spirits and deities.
>
> 其適遇淫君，外內頗邪，上下怨疾，動作辟違，從欲厭私，高臺深池，撞鐘舞女。斬刈民力，輸掠其聚，以成其違，不恤後人。暴虐淫從，肆行非度，無所還忌，不思謗讟，不憚鬼神。神怒民痛，無悛於心。其祝、史薦信，是言罪也；其蓋失數美，是矯誣也。進退無辭，則虛以求媚。是以鬼神不饗其國以禍之，祝、史與焉。所以夭昏孤疾者，爲暴君使也，其言僭嫚於鬼神。[11]

Yan Ying's invective is directed against a hypothetical bad ruler, but it is not too difficult to assert that its real target is Lord Jing, whose failure to obtain divine support is closely associated with his misdeeds. It is worth focusing on a few points in this speech. Yan Ying depicts the putative bad ruler as "cruel and prodigal, unrestrained and guided by no standard, lacking any afterthought or prohibition," the one who causes great suffering for his subjects, who "die young, lose their wits, are orphaned, and suffer illnesses." More ominously, Yan Ying depicts the ruler as a "cruel ruler" (*bao jun* 暴君), a designation that in certain contexts may justify the ruler's overthrow.[12]

---

11. *Zuo*, Zhao 20 (Yang, 1416–17).

12. In the *Mozi*, for instance, the term "cruel king" (暴王) is consistently used as a *terminus technicus* for the "last, evil" rulers of the Xia and the Shang dynasties. For

While Lord Jing is not directly referred to as a personification of this evil sovereign, he does not fail to understand the real target, asking: "If that is the case, then what is to be done?" 「然則若之何?」[13]

The lord's question indicates that he accepts Yan Ying's criticism. He tries neither to protest, nor to say that his rule is still much better than that of the "cruel ruler." Rather, he acts as a model object of remonstrance should do: demonstrate a willingness to mend his ways rather than punish the offending minister. Yan Ying does not lack practical advice:

> [Yan Ying] replied, "Nothing can be done. The timber on the mountainsides is watched over by foresters. The rushes in the marshes are watched over by boatmen. The firewood and kindling in the lowlands are watched over by wardens. The salt and mussels in the sea are watched over by coast guards. Men from dependent and outlying territories enter his government; duty-stations just outside the capital exact heavy duties for their private gains; hereditary nobles forcefully buy commodities. Rules are promulgated without principles, taxes are levied without limits, palaces and homes increase by the day, and there is no departure from excess and merry-making. Concubines who enjoy favor within the palace seize property wantonly in the marketplace. Personnel who enjoy favor outside the palace usurp command for themselves in the outlying territories. When private desires are fostered and pursued but are not satisfied, incriminations follow. The people suffer and fret, and man and woman alike curse you. If an invocator's prayer brings benefits, then curses also bring harm. From Liao and She to the east, from Gu and You to the west, many are the men who live there. How could even an excellent invocator overcome the curses of so many millions? If you wish to execute the invocator and the scribe, then you may do so only after you have cultivated your virtue."
>
> Pleased, the lord had the responsible officers ease government policies, tear down the duty-stations, eliminate the controls on resources, reduce taxes, and forgive tax debts.
>
> 對曰:「不可爲也。山林之木,衡鹿守之;澤之萑蒲,舟鮫守之;藪之薪蒸,虞候守之;海之鹽、蜃,祈望守之。縣鄙之人, 入從其政;偪介之關,暴征其私;承嗣大夫, 強易其賄。布常無藝,徵斂無度;宮室日更,淫樂

a general discussion about the right to overthrow an evil sovereign, see Pines, "To Rebel Is Justified?"

13. *Zuo*, Zhao 20 (Yang, 1417).

不違。內寵之妾，肆奪於市；外寵之臣，僭令於鄙。私欲養求，不給則應。民人苦病，夫婦皆詛。祝有益也，詛亦有損。聊、攝以東，姑、尤以西，其爲人也多矣。雖其善祝，豈能勝億兆人之詛？君若欲誅於祝、史，修德而後可。」

公說，使有司寬政，毀關，去禁，薄斂，已責。[14]

Yan Ying's enumeration of the lord's misdeeds focuses on the economic burden that his wanton and corrupt administration puts on the populace rather than on the lord's personal misconduct; as such, this last part of the remonstrance appears somewhat milder than the previous one. However, the mildness is undermined by the assertion that "the people suffer and fret, and man and woman alike curse you." This succinct picture of universal dissatisfaction with Lord Jing's reign implies that the populace is wishing the lord's swift demise and that his illness hence is a kind of divine retribution for his inadequate rule. Once again, Yan Ying dangerously approaches the line of questioning the very legitimacy of the sovereign's rule. Nonetheless, the harshness of his verdict on Lord Jing is not presented as exceptionally audacious or subversive; rather, the narrator tells us of Lord Jing's humble acceptance of Yan Ying's proposals, which might have indeed improved the lord's fortunes: he reigned for another thirty-two years after the recorded remonstrance; and although his line died out soon after his death, individually speaking he surely benefited from heeding his advisor's remonstrance.

The question of the impending demise of the ruling house of Qi is another pertinent feature in Yan Ying's conversations with Lord Jing. In a short anecdote, recorded under the year 522 BCE, Yan Ying warns the lord of inevitability of decline of the ruling dynasties by reminding him that the territory of Qi was previously occupied by several polities, each of which came to its end.[15] Although this historical digression does not overtly trespass the norms of political propriety, its message appears to be offensive or at least inauspicious. We are not told of the lord's reaction; but apparently he got the message, as is evident from the next anecdote, placed six years later:

---

14. *Zuo*, Zhao 20 (Yang, 1417–18).
15. *Zuo*, Zhao 20 (Yang, 1418–19).

> Lord [Jing] of Qi was sitting with Yanzi in his private chambers. With a sigh, the lord said, "How lovely these chambers are! Who will it be who possesses these?"
>
> Yanzi said, "May I presume to ask what you mean?"
>
> The lord said, "I take it to be a matter of virtue."
>
> [Yanzi] replied, "As you have put the matter, it will be the Chen lineage. Although the Chens lack any great virtue, they are generous to the people. By measure of *dou* 豆, *qu* 區, *fu* 釜, and *zhong* 鍾, they collect for the lord's sake sparingly and give to the people generously. Because you tax generously and the Chens give generously, the people have gone over to them. The *Odes* say: "Although I have no virtue to share with you, we shall sing and dance." The people sing and dance in response to the benefits of the Chen lineage. If future generations are even slightly remiss, and the Chen lineage does not perish, then the state will be theirs."
>
> 齊侯與晏子坐于路寢。公嘆曰：「美哉室！其誰有此乎！」晏子曰：「敢問何謂也？」公曰：「吾以為在德。」對曰：「如君之言，其陳氏乎！陳氏雖無大德，而有施於民。豆、區、釜、鍾之數，其取之公也薄，其施之民也厚。公厚斂焉，陳氏厚施焉，民歸之矣。《詩》曰：『雖無德與女，式歌且舞。』陳氏之施，民歌舞之矣。後世若少惰，陳氏而不亡，則國其國也已。」[16]

The new exchange between the lord and Yan Ying (which is also the last appearance of Yan Ying in the *Zuozhuan*) begins where the previous anecdote ended: it is the turn of Lord Jing now to raise the issue of the possibility of his dynasty's fall due to his insufficient virtue. Yan Ying eagerly endorses this topic to attack the lord's oppressive economic policy and to hail the lenient "populist" measures of the Chen lineage, whose heads manipulated their private weights and measures to the benefit of the populace, giving up part of their income to acquire political support.[17] While Yan Ying is careful to

---

16. *Zuo*, Zhao 26 (Yang, 1480).

17. Yan Ying explains the Chen policy in a conversation with a conservative Jin minister, Shuxiang 叔向: the Chen employed two sets of measures: their private measures and smaller ones, authorized by the ruling house. When lending grain they used their private set, while when collecting it they used the official set; thus they lost income, but gained the population's support. Yan Ying summarized then, back in 539: "[The people] love [the Chens] as their parents and turn to them as flowing water. Even if they did not intend to attain the people, can they avoid this?" (*Zuo*, Zhao 3 [Yang, 1236]).

avoid the overall endorsement of the Chens, and even provides the lord, in the later part of the speech, with the means of preventing the Chen ascendancy (through full implementation of the norms of ritual hierarchy, which would ensure that "family's favors do not exceed those of the state . . . and the nobles dare not seize lord's profits"),[18] his conclusion is still highly unfavorable of Lord Jing. Indeed, even though "the Chens lack any great virtue" their small virtue evidently exceeds that of Lord Jing.

Yan Ying skillfully plays between two major meanings of the term *de* (德, virtue): a sacred charismatic substance that qualifies a person and a lineage to rule the land, and a more concrete "kindness" or "grace."[19] The Chens may lack *de* in its former (and more important) meaning, but their kindness to the people is nonetheless indicative of their possession of a certain "virtue." The direct implication of this assertion is that Lord Jing lacks even this minor *de*, which, again, turns him unfit to rule the country. This verdict is moderated in the second part of the discussion where ritual propriety is proposed as the only means to sustain current sociopolitical hierarchy and prevent the Chen ascendancy, but the implications remain harsh. Although Yan Ying is clearly absolved of the suspicion of being the Chens' accomplice, he still transgresses the norms of ruler-minister relations by explicitly doubting the sovereign's fitness to maintain his—and his progeny's—power.

Yan Ying's rhetorical skill softens his harsh message, but the bottom line is nonetheless clear: in both quoted dialogues he depicts Lord Jing as unfit to rule his country, as lacking sufficient virtue, as hated by the populace and as leading the ruling house to its doom. What is remarkable, though, is not his outspokenness itself, but the humility with which the lord accepts it: twice he faces the criticism with a humble "so what can be done about this?" The anecdotes suggest that this was a normal or even a normative reaction: a brave remonstrator was not supposed to be punished. What are the reasons behind this remarkable leniency? Surely, Yan Ying's impeccable record

---

18. *Zuo*, Zhao 26 (Yang, 1480).

19. For the early meaning of the term *de* see Kominami, "Tenmei to toku"; for the later developments of this term, see, e.g., Onozawa, "Toku ron"; Martynov, "Kategoriia *de*"; Pines, *Foundations of Confucian Thought*, 125–32.

of loyalty to the ruling house might have precluded interpretation of his statements as outright treason or subversion, but I believe that this is only a partial explanation.[20] The *Zuozhuan* records dozens of instances of remonstrance, which was not always heeded but which only very rarely and exceptionally brought about persecution of a remonstrating official. Even in extreme cases, when a remonstrating official broke the rules of decorum and publicly humiliated or even threatened the ruler, punishment was far from inevitable.[21] Acceptance of the legitimacy of criticism from below was a norm, not a manifestation of particular tolerance and the ruler's broadmindedness.

The reasons for this toleration are not difficult to find. The world of the *Zuozhuan* was the world of hereditary aristocrats, whose military, economic, and administrative power at times equaled or even surpassed that of their nominal superiors, the regional lords; and the latter had little choice but to swallow the haughtiness of their underlings. Punishing a powerful minister was a dangerous gamble, as the ministerial response could have disastrous consequences for the lord. It was safer to display acquiescent attitude toward ministerial criticism or even to their overt insubordination; only exceptionally powerful monarchs, such as King Ling of Chu (楚靈王, r. 540–529 BCE), could occasionally cow the dissenters into submission. In a world where a ruler frequently was either a *primus inter pares* or just a hapless

20. Yan Ying braved Cui Zhu 崔杼 and his accomplices in 548 when he violated Cui Zhu's prohibition to mourn the slain Lord Zhuang of Qi (齊莊公, r. 553–548 BCE); in 532 BCE he again displayed remarkable devotion to the lord, protecting him during the violent outburst of domestic turmoil (*Zuo*, Xiang 25 [Yang, 1098]; Zhao 10 [Yang, 1316]).

21. For instance Yu Quan (鬻拳, d. 675 BCE) of Chu threatened King Wen (楚文王, r. 689–675 BCE) with weapons and prevented the king from entering the royal capital to encourage the ruler to conquer more lands; he was not punished, but committed suicide after King Wen's death, to die along with the monarch. Xian Zhen (先軫, d. 627 BCE) of Jin spat on the ground in front of his lord to protest the latter's decision to release the Qin 秦 captives; he was not punished, but rushed to death in a battle to punish himself. Qing Zheng (慶鄭, d. 645 BCE) of Jin, frustrated by Lord Hui's (晉惠公, r. 650–637 BCE) rejection of Qing's advice, taught the ruler a harsh lesson by causing the Jin military defeat and Lord Hui's imprisonment by the Qin army; and he is the only one to be executed for his break of norms; this does not prevent the *Zuozhuan* from treating him as a loyal minister, however. See more in Pines, *Foundations*, 146–53.

figurehead, it was much safer to behave in the way of Lord Jing of Qi rather than, for example, in the way of Lord Ling of Jin (晉靈公, r. 620–607 BCE), who tried to eliminate his outspoken critic, prime minister Zhao Dun 趙盾, but instead was murdered by Zhao's henchmen.

It is worth noting here that there is a certain exceptionality in Yan Ying's lengthy admonitions to Lord Jing; namely, there are relatively few examples of admonishing of the ruler in the later part of the *Zuozhuan*. While in the early part of the book the absolute majority of remonstrating speeches are directed at regional lords, by the sixth century most of the addressees are powerful ministers or foreign dignitaries. Some of the most eloquent speakers of the *Zuozhuan*, such as Zichan 子產 of Zheng 鄭, are never cited as talking to their lord at all. Nothing better indicates the decline of the ruler's power: the nominal lords were so meaningless as not to merit even a minister's admonition.[22] This sign of the declining authority of the rulers provides us with another clue for Lord Jing's complacency. A weak sovereign, who had been enthroned in place of his slain brother by a powerful potentate and who barely survived several rounds of domestic turmoil, Lord Jing was not in a position to punish his outspoken aide. That Yan Ying bothered at all to criticize Lord Jing's errors might have perpetuated the illusion of the lord's power and might have even made the lord glad. His descendants, after all, would no longer merit admonitions, but will be simply ruthlessly replaced by their rebellious underlings. In retrospect, being accused "only" of unfitness might have been a blessing in disguise for the lord.

Mengzi: A Proud Shi

The two centuries that separate Mengzi (Mencius) from Yan Ying witnessed tremendous changes in China's sociopolitical landscape. Loose polities of the aristocratic age were replaced by new, tightly organized "ruler-centered" Warring States, the lords of which enjoyed immeasurably more power than their Spring and Autumn period

22. It is worth remembering that remonstrance, while allowing critical stance toward the ruler, is based on the supposition of the ruler's absolute superiority over his subjects: it is up to him to heed admonitions or reject them. See more in Zhang Fentian, *Zhongguo diwang guannian*, 520–38.

predecessors. The very stratum of proud hereditary power holders who turned the ruler into *primus inter pares* had all but disappeared, being largely submerged within a new and much broader elite, the *shi* 士, the members of which did not enjoy hereditary positions and were much weaker politically, economically, and militarily than the Spring and Autumn period aristocrats.[23] All this should have made ministers of the Warring States period more deferential toward their lords. And yet, many of Mengzi's dialogues with regional lords echo Yan Ying's audacity, and at times even surpass it.

Mengzi's attitude toward the rulers appears at a first glimpse as somewhat puzzling, even conflicted. Few texts of the Warring States period can rival the *Mengzi*'s harsh criticism of contemporary sovereigns, who are intermittently referred to as "criminals," "devourers of human flesh," and "those who have the proclivity to kill humans";[24] and Mengzi is likewise renowned for manifold demarches against his employers, the regional lords. And yet throughout most of his life, Mengzi relentlessly sought engagement with those very sovereigns whom he repeatedly criticized; so that his career appears as an almost endless chain of appointments and resignations.[25] Mengzi's contemporaries and disciples were at times puzzled by his simultaneous attraction to and aversion toward the rulers, causing Mengzi to explain the reason for his odd behavior:

> Mengzi said: "It is not enough to criticize others; it is not enough to blame the government. Only the Great Man is able to rectify the wrongs in the ruler's heart. When the ruler is benevolent—everybody is benevolent; when the ruler is righteous—everybody is righteous; when the ruler is correct—everybody is correct. Just rectify the ruler and the state will be stabilized."
>
> 孟子曰：「人不足與適（過）也，政不足與間也，惟大人爲能格君心之非。君仁莫不仁，君義莫不義，君正莫不正，一正君而國定矣。」[26]

23. See detailed discussions in Lewis, "Warring States," and Pines, *Envisioning Eternal Empire*.

24. See respectively, *Mengzi yizhu*, "Gaozi xia" 告子下 12.7: 287; "Li Lou shang" 離婁上 7.14: 175; "Liang Hui Wang shang" 梁惠王上 1.6: 12–13.

25. For a brief outline of Mengzi's career, see Yang Bojun's "Introduction" (導言) in *Mengzi yizhu*, 1–15.

26. *Mengzi yizhu*, "Li Lou shang" 7.20: 180; cf. "Li Lou xia" 離婁下 8.5: 187.

This unwavering belief in the importance of "rectification of the ruler" may explain the nearly religious zeal with which Mengzi addressed the sovereigns and also his audacity when speaking to them. Of course, we cannot know to what extent multiple dialogues with the rulers scattered throughout the *Mengzi* reflect real encounters, or whether they were heavily polished or outright invented by Mengzi's disciples, who compiled the eponymous book; yet like in the case of Yan Ying, we can assert that the authors of the *Mengzi* could not have deviated considerably from what was believed to be an acceptable form of ruler-minister conversation of their age. As such, Mengzi's repeated assaults against the rulers' perceived immorality and unfitness may be suggestive of the court atmosphere of the middle Warring States period.

The *Mengzi* opens with a series of five anecdotes that narrate the thinker's encounter with King Hui of Wei (魏惠王, r. 369–318 BCE). Yoav Ariel has suggested (in a still unpublished talk, which I freely paraphrase) that these five anecdotes can be read as a sequence of psychoanalysis sessions, during which Mengzi effectively strips the king of his self-confidence and reduces him from a position of a patron to that of a humble disciple.[27] Indeed, one can discern a certain escalation in Mengzi's criticism of the king. Already at their first encounter Mengzi confounds the ruler for inappropriately speaking of "benefit" instead of "benevolence and righteousness." In the second anecdote, he denies the king the right to enjoy the pleasures of the royal garden, insofar as the populace cannot share the king's joy. The third anecdote turns to political questions: the king is puzzled why his subjects do not appreciate his concern for their economic well-being. Mengzi explains that the king's efforts, even if laudable, still fall short of proper concern for the people, and that his policy in fact is as exploitive as that of other rulers of the age.[28] The gradually escalating criticism peaks in the fourth anecdote.

---

27. Ariel's talk was at the Hebrew University of Jerusalem in 2003. For a different and no less engaging analysis of these passages, see Nylan, "Mencius on Pleasure."

28. For these three exchanges, see *Mengzi yizhu*, "Liang Hui Wang shang" 1.1–1.3: 1–5.

King Hui of Liang [Wei] said, "I am willing to accept your teachings." Mengzi replied: "Is there any difference between killing a man with a staff and killing him with a dagger?"

"There is no difference."

"Is there any difference between killing him with a dagger and killing him with [bad] government?"

"There is no difference."

"There is fat meat in your kitchen and there are well-fed horses in your stables, yet the people look hungry and in the countryside men drop dead from starvation. This is to lead the animals to devour men. Even the devouring of animals by animals is hated by the people. If the government of the 'father and mother of the people' cannot avoid leading animals to devour men, wherein is he father and mother to the people? Confucius said, 'The inventor of human-shaped burial figurines deserves not to have any progeny'—because he uses [figurines] that resemble human beings. So what should be done to the one who causes the people to starve to death?"

梁惠王曰:「寡人愿安承教。」孟子對曰:「殺人以梃與刃,有以異乎?」曰:「無以異也。」「以刃與政,有以異乎?」曰:「無以異也。」曰:「庖有肥肉,廄有肥馬,民有饑色,野有餓莩,此率獸而食人也。獸相食,且人惡之;爲民父母,行政不免於率獸而食人,惡在其爲民父母也?仲尼曰:『始作俑者,其無後乎!』爲其象人而用之也。如之何其使斯民飢而死也?」[29]

Mengzi leaves no doubt: despite his self-proclaimed care for the people, King Hui does not differ from the worst tyrants of old. His malpractices cause the people to die prematurely, and as such the king deserves no lenience: at the very least he should have no progeny, that is, his dynasty should end. Interestingly, the compilers of the *Mengzi* framed this harsh statement within an anecdote that begins with the king's humble request to teach him. The contrast between the king's humility and Mengzi's harshness serves here to reinforce the pride shown by an intellectual who acts as the superior's teacher—a topic to which we shall return below.

The motif of the ruler's fitness for his office permeates the *Mengzi* and is duly present in his conversations with another of Mengzi's major employers, King Xuan of Qi (齊宣王, r. 319–301 BCE). Thrice

---

29. *Mengzi yizhu*, "Liang Hui Wang shang" 1.4: 8–9.

the issue is raised in discussions between the two, and these instances deserve a focused treatment.

> King Xuan of Qi asked about high ministers [*qing* 卿]. Mengzi said: "Which high ministers are you asking about?"
>
> The king said: "Are there differences between high ministers?"
>
> "Yes. There are high ministers who are related to the lord, and those of other clans."
>
> "What about high ministers who are related to the lord?"
>
> "If the ruler made a serious transgression, they should remonstrate with him, but if he does not heed repeated remonstrations, they should replace him."
>
> The king flushed with anger.
>
> "The king should not treat my answer as odd. Since you asked me, I dared not give you anything but the proper answer."
>
> The king's color stabilized and he asked about high ministers from other clans. "If the prince made a serious transgression, they should remonstrate with him, but if he does not heed repeated remonstrations, they should leave him."
>
> 齊宣王問卿。孟子曰：「王何卿之問也？」王曰：「卿不同乎？」曰：「不同，有貴戚之卿，有異姓之卿。」王曰：「請問貴戚之卿。」曰：「君有大過則諫，反覆之而不聽，則易位。」王勃然變乎色。曰：「王勿異也。王問臣，臣不敢不以正對。」王色定，然後請問異姓之卿。曰：「君有過則諫，反覆之而不聽，則去。」[30]

Mengzi raises here two important points. The last one, namely the right of the minister to leave the king, will be addressed below; here we shall focus on the right of the minister to "replace" (literally, "change places with"—*yi wei* 易位) the king. While the right to replace the sovereign is confined to his kin, so that the dynasty would survive, it is remarkable that the conditions for the coup are quite quotidian: the ruler's failure to heed remonstrance. It is not surprising then that the king flushes with anger: should Mengzi's views proliferate, not a single sovereign will ever be safe on his throne. This exchange recurs, in an even harsher form elsewhere:

> King Xuan of Qi asked: "Did it happen that Tang expelled Jie, while King Wu attacked Zhou[xin]?"[31]

---

30. *Mengzi yizhu*, "Wan Zhang xia" 10.9: 251–52.

31. Jie 桀 is the "last, evil" king of the Xia dynasty; Zhouxin 紂辛 (d. ca. 1046 BCE) is the "last, evil" king of the Shang.

> Mengzi replied: "This is reported in the *Traditions*."
>
> [The king] said: "Is it permissible that a minister murders his ruler?" Mengzi said: "One who commits crimes against benevolence is called 'criminal'; one who commits crimes against righteousness is called 'a cruel one.' A cruel and criminal person is called 'an ordinary fellow.' I heard that an ordinary fellow Zhou[xin] was punished, but did not hear of murdering a ruler."
>
> 齊宣王問曰:「湯放桀,武王伐紂,有諸?」孟子對曰:「於傳有之。」曰:「臣弒其君,可乎?」曰:「賊仁者,謂之賊;賊義者,謂之殘。殘賊之人,謂之一夫。聞誅一夫紂矣,未聞弒君也。」[32]

The topic of "righteous rebellion" was part and parcel of the political discourse of the Warring States period, but nowhere is the support for the right to rebel stated as unequivocally as in the *Mengzi*.[33] In marked distinction from most other thinkers who approved of rebellion only under truly exceptional circumstances, such as those associated with the paradigmatic overthrows of Jie and Zhouxin, Mengzi refers to routine violations of the norms of benevolence and righteousness as sufficient justification to rebel and execute the culprit. Any reader of Mengzi's philippics against contemporary rulers will not fail to notice that these rulers do not differ considerably in his eyes from Jie and Zhouxin. What practical conclusion then can come from this analysis? Should contemporary rulers face replacement and execution just like the past tyrants? And if so, who will decide upon such an execution? Most remarkably, Mengzi fails to mention Heaven (which elsewhere in the *Mengzi* is attributed with important political tasks)[34] as a major factor behind the demise of Jie and Zhouxin. Does this mean that rebellion is a normative action against an immoral sovereign? Mengzi does not raise this dangerous question in a conversation with the king, but certain clues in the text apparently strengthen this conclusion.[35]

To moderate Mengzi's affront we should recall that King Xuan of Qi had a problematic background (he belonged to the same Chen

---

32. *Mengzi yizhu*, "Liang Hui Wang xia" 梁惠王下 2.8: 42.

33. For details, see Pines, "To Rebel Is Justified?"

34. For the role of Heaven in the *Mengzi*, see, for instance, *Mengzi yizhu*, "Wan Zhang shang" 9.5–9.6: 219–22.

35. See further discussion in Pines, "To Rebel Is Justified?" 15–16.

lineage, the ascendancy of which worried Yan Ying, and his ancestors deposed the line of legitimate lords of Qi), so he might have even be secretly glad for Mengzi's legitimation for the dynastic replacement. Needless to say, this conjecture cannot be verified; and even if it is correct, then the third exchange between the king and the ruler leaves no doubt with regard to Mengzi's audacity:

> Mengzi said to King Xuan of Qi: "Suppose your subject has entrusted his wife and children to a friend, and traveled to Chu. When he returned, he discovered that his friend let his wife and children to suffer cold and hunger. What should be done about it?"
>
> "Cast [the friend] away."
>
> "When the Master of the *shi* is unable to rule the *shi* properly, what should be done about it?"
>
> "Remove him."
>
> "If there is no proper rule within the domain, what should be done about it?"
>
> The king turned to his attendants and changed the subject.
>
> 孟子謂齊宣王曰：「王之臣有托其妻子於其友而之楚游者，比其反也，則凍餒其妻子，則如之何？」王曰：「棄之。」曰：「士師不能治士，則如之何？」王曰：「已之。」曰：「四境之內不治，則如之何？」王顧左右而言他。[36]

Mengzi's message is unequivocal: the malfunctioning king should be removed like any petty official. The implications are clear, and the king once again understands the harshness of Mengzi's message, but dares not punishing his aide; the only way to express his dissatisfaction is dropping the matter. Much like King Hui of Wei, King Xuan of Qi appears astonishingly accommodating toward his aggressive advisor. While the king does not hide his occasional dissatisfaction with Mengzi's remonstrance, especially whenever Mengzi touches upon the most sensitive issue of the legitimacy of the lord's reign, he never punishes his counselor, nor accuses him of subversion. Flushing of anger or turning to other attendants is his strongest reaction. Even firing a troublesome aide does not appear to be an option: whenever we know of the reasons for Mengzi's disengagements from various courts, these are invariably related to the thinker's dissatisfaction

36. *Mengzi yizhu*, "Liang Hui Wang xia," 2.6: 40.

with insufficiently polite treatment by the rulers rather than his being dismissed by appalled employers.

What are the reasons for this surprising complacency of the rulers of the Warring States with Mengzi's strong criticism, which at times approximates overt subversion? After all, unlike an aristocrat of the Spring and Autumn period, Mengzi (and other contemporary thinkers) was economically and politically dependent on the ruler's will, and could not retaliate against the lord if the latter decided to punish him. A possible answer, as I have extensively discussed elsewhere, was a peculiar situation of an interstate "market of talent" of the Warring States.[37] During that period, members of the educated elite were moving freely across the Zhou 周 world in search of better appointment. In the situation of acute competition between rival courts, insofar as the demand for gifted statesmen exceeded the supply, *shi* intellectuals were in an excellent bargaining position. Rulers dared not offend them, tolerating harsh criticisms of Mengzi and his like, since should a disgruntled *shi* leave an inhospitable court, this could cause a severe brain drain, benefiting the lord's rivals. A following dialogue from the *Mengzi* may exemplify the ruler's plight:

> Mengzi declared to King Xuan of Qi: "If a ruler treats his subjects as his hands and feet, they will treat him as their belly and heart. If he treats them as his horses and hounds, they will treat him as a mere fellow. If he treats them as mud and weeds, they will treat him as a mortal enemy."
>
> The king said: "Ritual requires of a minister to wear mourning for his ruler. How in these circumstances will it be possible to wear mourning?"
>
> [Mengzi] said: "The ruler should follow [the minister's] remonstrance, heed his advice, and benefit the people below. If [the minister] has a reason to leave the country, the ruler should send someone to conduct him beyond the border, and somebody to prepare the way ahead. Only if after three years abroad [the minister] did not return, the ruler might take over his fields and dwellings. This is called 'the three courtesies.' If the ruler behaves so, then it is the minister's duty to wear mourning for him. Today the remonstrance is not followed, advice is not heeded, the people below see no benefits. When a minister has the reason to leave, the ruler has him arrested and put in

37. See Pines, "Friends or Foes"; *Envisioning Eternal Empire*, 163–80.

> chains, makes things difficult for him in the state he is going to, and confiscates his fields and dwellings the day he leaves. This is what is meant by 'mortal enemy.' What mourning is there for a mortal enemy?"
>
> 孟子告齊宣王曰:「君之視臣如手足,則臣視君如腹心;君之視臣如犬馬,則臣視君如國人;君之視臣如土芥,則臣視君如寇讎。」王曰:「禮,爲舊君有服。何如斯可爲服矣?」曰:「諫行言聽,膏澤下於民;有故而去,則使人導之出疆,又先於其所往;去三年不反,然後收其田舍。此之謂三有禮焉。如此則爲之服矣。今也爲臣,諫則不行,言則不聽,膏澤不下於民;有故而去,則君搏執之,又極之於其所往;去之日,遂收其田舍。此之謂寇讎。寇讎何服之有?」[38]

This exchange does not merely illustrate again Mengzi's audacity when addressing the ruler, but it is also revealing with regard to the connection between ministerial boldness and employment flexibility. Mengzi clearly implies that a minister has no fixed obligations toward a ruler: their relations are based on a *quid pro quo*, and the ruler cannot expect a better attitude than the one he displays toward his aide. Moreover, the minister, in Mengzi's eyes, has an inalienable right to leave the ruler and go to another state; with a remarkable nerve, Mengzi even demands that the ruler respect the right of the minister to leave the court for a rival state and yet still preserve his emoluments!

We do not know whether or not King Xuan of Qi accepted Mengzi's arguments, but if he and other rulers, as the authors of the *Mengzi* want us to believe, repeatedly tolerated Mengzi's affronts, this may have been precisely because they feared that a harsh reaction would cause Mengzi (and other advisors and ministers) to shift allegiance to a rival court. Actually, Mengzi's audacity was not exceptional in the Warring States period; rather, like Yan Ying, he was simply the most eloquent representative of the self-confident *shi* of his age. Manifold texts and anecdotes from the Warring States period reflect the almost overbearing pride of the members of the *shi* stratum. Some texts tell of haughty *shi* like Yan Chu 顏斶, who humiliated King Xuan of Qi just in order to convince him of the superiority of the *shi* over the sovereigns; other texts postulate that a *shi* may leave the ruler whenever he is dissatisfied with the ruler's treatment;

38. *Mengzi yizhu*, "Li Lou xia," 8.3: 186.

others abound with effusive panegyrics to the proud *shi*: "The Five Thearchs could not obtain them as friends, the Three Kings could not obtain them as teachers; only when they cast aside their Thearchs' and kings' airs could they approach and be able to attain them." 五帝弗得而友，三王弗得而師，去其帝王之色，則近可得之矣。[39] Thus, while the *shi* were economically dependent on the throne and anxious to find a proper employer or patron, insofar as interstate market of talent continued functioning, they remained in an advantageous position, and were able to maintain a haughty stance. And yet, the pride of the *shi* had its price. Even if the rulers refrained from retaliating against their hypercritical aides, many of them were visibly irritated by the haughtiness of Mengzi and his like, whose posture as the ruler's superiors undermined the very foundations of the ruler-minister relations.[40] In this situation, a novel, more moderate approach had to come into existence—the one that would allow the *shi* to retain their pride while preserving political hierarchy intact. This approach is exemplified best in the writings of the relentless critic of Mengzi, Xunzi.

Xunzi: A Cautious Voice

Xunzi is one of the most sophisticated political thinkers in China's history, the one who contributed decisively toward the formation of China's imperial political culture. His manifold similarities and differences with other "Confucian" thinkers, such as Mengzi, have been discussed extensively elsewhere and shall not be addressed here anew; suffice it to say that Xunzi is commonly considered as belonging to what is often deemed as a more "authoritarian" or, more precisely, ruler-oriented current within what is broadly defined as "Confucian" thought.[41] This assessment is correct insofar as it reflects Xunzi's commitment to strengthening the ruler's authority;

---

39. *Lüshi chunqiu jiaoshi*, "Xia xian" 下賢 15.3: 879. For earlier examples, see *Zhanguo ce zhushi*, "Qi ce 齊策 4," 11.5: 395–96; *Guodian Chumu zhujian*, "Yu cong" 語叢 3, slips 1–5. See more in Pines, *Envisioning Eternal Empire*, 115–84.

40. Pines, *Envisioning Eternal Empire*, 136–84.

41. For systematic accounts of Xunzi's thought, see Goldin, *Rituals of the Way*; Sato, *The Confucian Quest for Order*; I have addressed many aspects of Xunzi's thought in the *Envisioning Eternal Empire*.

but it should not obliterate his unequivocally critical stance with regard to many of the contemporary rulers. Thus, Xunzi warns them:

> Hence when some ministers murder their rulers, when inferiors kill their superiors, when [the people] are timid about defending the walls, turn back on their obligations, and are not ready to die in [the rulers'] service—it is for no other reason than the ruler had chosen this [that is, being assassinated or abandoned] himself.
>
> 是以臣或弒其君，下或殺其上，粥其城，倍其節，而不死其事者，無它故焉，人主自取之。[42]

The harshness of this pronouncement cannot be ignored. A ruler who behaves improperly loses his right to rule; he bears the sole responsibility for his future dethronement and "while he was enfeoffed as a regional lord and is named 'a ruler,' he does not differ from a mere fellow and a robber" 如此者，雖封侯稱君，其與夫盜無以異。[43] These sayings directly resemble those of Mengzi and suffice to undermine plain identification of Xunzi with the ruler. However, while critical toward contemporary sovereigns, Xunzi radically differs from Mengzi with regard to the proper mode of ruler-minister interactions.

The *Xunzi* is built as a series of shorter and longer essays, and unlike *Mengzi*, it is almost devoid of dialogues. In particular, the book narrates only very few encounters between Xunzi and contemporaneous rulers: although we know that Xunzi's career was longer and generally more successful than that of either Confucius or Mengzi, he (and/or his disciples and followers) opted not to preserve most of the records of his conversations with power holders. Only a single such dialogue with the sovereign is preserved in the text—Xunzi's encounter with the most powerful ruler of his age, King Zhao of Qin (秦昭王, r. 306–250 BCE). Since it is highly likely that this single dialogue was included with a deliberate purpose to highlight a proper tone that, in the eyes of Xunzi and his followers, one should adopt when speaking to a ruler, it deserves a closer focus.

---

42. *Xunzi jijie*, "Fu guo" 富國 6.10: 182–83.
43. *Xunzi jijie*, "Zheng ming" 正名 16.22: 431.

King Zhao asked Master Sun Qing [Xunzi]:[44] "Are Ru ["Confucians"] useless to the state?"

Master Sun Qing said: "The Ru take the former kings as their model, they exalt ritual and propriety, scrupulously observe the position of sons and subjects, and esteem their superiors. When they are employed, they are positioned at the court and act appropriately; when they are not employed, they retreat, organize the hundred clans, and behave sincerely: surely they will behave compliantly in the inferior position. Even if impoverished, freezing, and starving, they will not follow evil ways to satisfy their avarice; even when having not enough land to place an awl they are clear at upholding the great propriety of the altars of soil and grain; when they shout but nobody responds, they still comprehend penetratingly the guidelines of accumulating myriad things and nourishing the hundred clans. When positioned above, they are of the qualities of kings and dukes; when positioned below, they are the ministers of the altars of soil and grain, the treasure of the ruler. Even when obscure in an impoverished lane in a leaking house, nobody will fail to esteem them—it is because the Way of esteem[45] truly rests [with them]. . . . When in court, the Ru beautify the government; when in an inferior position they beautify the customs. This is how the Ru behave when they are positioned below."

秦昭王問孫卿子曰:「儒無益於人之國?」孫卿子曰:「儒者法先王,隆禮義,謹乎臣子而致貴其上者也。人主用之,則勢在本朝而宜;不用,則退編百姓而慤,必爲順下矣。雖窮困凍餧,必不以邪道爲貪;無置錐之地,而明於持社稷之大義;嗚呼而莫之能應,然而通乎財萬物、養百姓之經紀。勢在人上則王公之材也,在人下則社稷之臣、國君之寶也。雖隱於窮閻漏屋,人莫不貴,(之)[貴]道誠存也。儒者在本朝則美政,在下位則美俗,儒之爲人下如是矣。」[46]

This exchange differs markedly from what we saw in the Mengzi. The ruler's attitude is not that of a humble student; nor is he interested in impressing his guest; rather, he asks Xunzi dismissively whether or not the Ru, on whose behalf Xunzi is speaking, are useless to his state. In response, the thinker extols the Ru's usefulness,

---

44. Xunzi (Xun Qing 荀卿) is rendered here Sun Qing because the book's compiler, Liu Xiang (劉向, ca. 79–8 BCE) avoided the tabooed character Xun 詢, the name of Emperor Xuan of the Han (漢宣帝, r. 73–49 BCE). See Wang Xianqian's gloss in *Xunzi jijie* 117.

45. Following Wang Xianqian, I emend 之 to 貴 (*Xunzi jijie* 118).

46. *Xunzi jijie*, "Ru xiao" 儒效, 4.8: 117–120.

strongly emphasizing their ability to contribute to the state's well-being and to proper social *mores* even when in an inferior position or lacking an official appointment. Significantly, Xunzi emphasizes from the very beginning that the Ru "scrupulously observe the position of sons and subjects and esteem their superiors" and that they "behave compliantly in the inferior position." It seems that Xunzi was anxious to distinguish the true Ru of his kind from troublemakers of Mengzi's ilk. With this emphasis on compliance, the entire exchange is marked by Xunzi's defensiveness and accommodating spirit. This changes only slightly in the second half of the dialogue:

> The king said: "If so, how do they behave when positioned above?"
>
> Sun Qing said: "When above, they are broad and great: their will and intentions are stabilized within, ritual norms are maintained at the court, laws, and measures are ordered among the officials; loyalty, trustworthiness, and the love for benefits is formed among the inferiors. They will never do anything inappropriate or kill an innocent person to attain All under Heaven. The dutifulness of these lords is trusted by the people, penetrates the four seas, and then All under Heaven replies to it joyously: why is it? This is because their esteemed name is clear, and All under Heaven is properly governed. Hence, those who are close are chanting and are pleased with them; the distant exert themselves to approach them; all [within] the four seas are like a single family, and wherever they reach everybody is submissive: this is called being the Master of the people. The poem says: 'From the west, from the east, / from the south, from the north, / there is none who is not submissive.' It is told about this. Thus, such are they when positioned below, such are they as positioned above—how can you say that they are useless for the state?"
>
> King Zhao said: "Good!"
>
> 王曰:「然則其爲人上何如?」孫卿曰:「其爲人上也廣大矣;志意定乎內,禮節脩乎朝,法則度量正乎官,忠信愛利形乎下,行一不義、殺一無罪而得天下,不爲也。此君主義信乎人矣,通於四海,則天下應之如讙。是何也?則貴名白而天下治也。故近者歌謳而樂之,遠者竭蹶而趨之,四海之內若一家,通達之屬莫不從服,夫是之謂人師。 詩曰:「自西自東,自南自北,無思不服。」此之謂也。夫其爲人下也如彼,其爲人上也如此,何謂其無益於人之國也?」昭王曰:「善。」[47]

47. *Xunzi jijie*, "Ru xiao" 4.8: 120–21. The quoted poem is "Wen Wang you sheng" 文王有聲 from the *Shijing* (Mao no. 244).

The second part of the exchange may contain seeds of criticism of the king: Xunzi's flattering depiction of the moral and political superiority of a Ru when the latter is placed in a position of a ruler may hint at a king's inadequacy: after all, King Zhao was surely neither the person who would shun morally inappropriate acts when facing the possibility to attain "All under Heaven," nor was he a kind of the leader to entice universal voluntary submission. Yet if Xunzi indeed targeted the king, he succeeded in making the criticism as inoffensive as possible. In marked distinction from Mengzi or Yan Ying he did not raise the tiniest issue related to King Zhao personally, and remained on a highly theoretical level of discussion. Therefore, the king's reaction was just to say "good" rather than to ask, "How can I attain this blessed state of affairs?" as such an exchange would probably end in the *Zuozhuan* or the *Mengzi*.

Why did Xunzi and/or his followers decide to preserve this exchange with King Zhao despite the thinker's humble and defensive stance vis-à-vis the ruler? I think that the inclusion aims at demonstrating what Xunzi believed to be a proper mode of the ruler-minister interactions. Xunzi was not a flatterer, and he recognized the importance of remonstrance, but he might have felt that Mengzi and his like were alienating rulers rather than encouraging them to improve their ways; it is not impossible that King Zhao's provocative question "Are the Ru useless to the state?" was placed as an indirect reference to the "vulgar Ru" (*su Ru* 俗儒) of Mengzi's type. Xunzi explained elsewhere how the minister should interact with the ruler:

> In serving a sage ruler, be attentive and compliant without remonstrance and arguments. In serving an average ruler, remonstrate and argue without flattery and servility. In serving a violent ruler, you should mend his deficiencies without ostensibly opposing him. When encountering a calamitous age, living in poverty in a violent state and having nowhere to escape, you should praise [the ruler's] fine character, hail his goodness, avoid [exposing] his badness, conceal his mistakes; speak of his advantages and do not mention his shortcomings—turning this into your habit. The *Poems* say: "When the state has the Great Decree, do not tell it to others, just preserve your body." It speaks just about this.
>
> 事聖君者，有聽從無諫爭；事中君者，有諫爭無諂諛；事暴君者，有補削無撟拂。迫脅於亂時，窮居於暴國，而無所避之，則崇其美，揚其

> 善，違其惡，隱其敗，言其所長，不稱其所短，以爲成俗。《詩》曰：「國有大命，不可以告人，妨其躬身。」此之謂也。[48]

There are four possible ways to interact with a ruler, and remonstrance is only one of them, although perhaps the most common, since it is prescribed for the "average ruler." Importantly, though, of the proposed ways of action Xunzi omits the one that was the most natural for most of his contemporary office holders, namely, leaving for another state. By speaking of conditions in which "there is nowhere to escape," Xunzi apparently envisions a future unified empire that effectively monopolizes the market of talent, putting an end to free boundary crossing by members of the elite. In this soon-to-be-established new world order a critical minister will lack the ability to leave and will no longer be able to defy the sovereign with Mengzi's haughtiness. This insight of Xunzi became a reality soon after his death, when the great-grandson of King Zhao, King Zheng 政 of Qin unified "All-under-Heaven," establishing a new, imperial polity that was to last for 2,132 years.

Epilogue: Li Si—From Teacher to Servant

The imperial unification can be considered the second major change in the ruler-minister relations in China history after the decline of hereditary aristocracy. When King Zheng of Qin—now the First Emperor/August Thearch of China (秦始皇帝, r. 246–221 BCE as king, to 210 BCE as emperor)—proudly proclaimed, "Wherever human traces reach, / There is none who does not declare himself [the Thearch's] subject" 人跡所至，無不臣者,[49] he did not exaggerate much. The interstate market of talent had ended and a firm monopoly on employment of the intellectuals had become established throughout the "civilized" world. In these new conditions, Xunzi's assessment of the proper forms of ruler-minister interactions proved to be prescient.

The new mode of ruler-minister relations transpires through the interaction between Qin ministers and the First Emperor, as is

48. *Xunzi jijie*, "Chen Dao" 臣道 9.13: 251–52. The quoted poem is not a part of the current *Shijing*. Cf. Xunzi's recommendations for dealing with different types of rulers in "Zhongni" 仲尼 3.7: 109–10.

49. *SJ* 6.245; Kern, *Stele Inscriptions of Ch'in Shih-huang*, 32–33.

reflected in the "Basic Annals of the First Emperor" in the *Shiji* 史記. Discussion continues about the reliability of this chapter of the *Shiji*, but I believe that insofar as Sima Qian incorporated, at least in part, original Qin court materials, then, possible manipulations aside, his account represents reliably the Qin court atmosphere.[50]

Let us look briefly at one of the most famous memorials presented by Li Si and his colleagues to the First Emperor at the very beginning of the imperial rule. The topic was the adoption of a new title by the King of Qin in the aftermath of the successful unification of All under Heaven. The memorialists—the chancellor Wang Wan 王綰, the imperial secretary Feng Jie 馮劫, and the commandant of justice Li Si—proposed:

> In antiquity, the lands of the Five Thearchs were one thousand *li* squared, beyond which was the regional lords' domain and the aliens' domain. Regional lords sometimes came to the court and sometimes did not, and the Son of Heaven was unable to regulate this. Now, your Majesty has raised a righteous army, punishing the savage criminals, has pacified and stabilized All under Heaven, turning the territory between the seas into commanderies and counties; and laws and ordinances have a single source. From antiquity it has never been so; the Five Thearchs could not reach this!
>
> 昔者五帝地方千里，其外侯服夷。服諸侯或朝或否，天子不能制。今陛下興義兵，誅殘賊，平定天下，海內爲郡縣，法令由一統，自上古以來未嘗有，五帝所不及。[51]

The beginning is flattering enough, which is expected, not only because of the officials' understandable desire to win the king's favor, but also because of the undeniable magnitude of the king's achievements. After all, it was King Zheng who realized the dreams of preimperial thinkers, Mengzi and Xunzi included, to put an end to endless war and turmoil of the Warring States period. Now, the officials turn to their practical recommendation:

> *We, your subjects* have respectfully consulted with the court erudites who tell us that in antiquity there was the Heavenly August, Earthly

50. For doubts toward the reliability of Sima Qian's account, see van Ess, "Emperor Wu"; for attempts to discern reliable information from this account, see, e.g., Kern, *Stele Inscriptions of Ch'in Shih-huang*.

51. *SJ* 6.236; modifying Watson, *Records of the Grand Historian*, 43.

> August, and Greatly August, of which the Greatly August was the most esteemed. Therefore, *on pain of death your subjects propose upwards* the following titles: the king shall become "the Greatly August"; his commands—"edicts"; his orders—"decrees"; the Son of Heaven shall refer to himself by the pronoun *zhen* 朕.
>
> 臣等謹與博士議曰:『古有天皇,有地皇,有泰皇,泰皇最貴。』臣等昧死上尊號,王爲『泰皇』。命爲『制』,令爲『詔』,天子自稱曰『朕』。[52]

Let us put aside for a moment the content of the proposal and focus on its form: twice the ministers refer to themselves as "we, your subjects" (*chen deng* 臣等); and then they precede their concrete recommendations by the formula "speaking on pain of death" (*mei si* 昧死). The self-reference "your subject" (*chen* 臣) is not new, of course: it appears, albeit infrequently, in texts from the Spring and Autumn and the Warring States periods. Yet the term "speaking on pain of death" is apparently novel.[53] This formula, which implies that the proponents may somehow be responsible for a transgression that warrants the death penalty, is pronounced neither in a daring remonstrance nor in a speech that is supposed somehow to enrage the ruler, but in a relaxed situation of a flattering proposal aimed at answering the king's aspirations. That the assembled ministers use these words reflects nothing but a new court atmosphere: henceforth, addressing the ruler meant taking into consideration the possibility that he would be somehow enraged and put his advisor(s) to death.

The compound *mei si* recurs in Li Si's presentations to the throne, including his most (in)famous speech in which he recommended imposing a ban on "private learning."[54] It appears that the most powerful Qin courtier applied it from the first moment of the imperial unification. Accordingly, Cai Yong (蔡邕, 135–192 CE) assessed that the *mei si* formula came into existence from the time of Qin unifica-

---

52. *SJ* 6.236. Italics mine.

53. I have found only one instance of this term in preimperial texts: in a memorial supposedly submitted to the king of Qin either by Zhang Yi (*Zhanguo ce zhushi,* "Qin ce 1," 3.5: 88–91) or by Han Feizi (*Han Feizi jijie*, "Chu xian Qin" 初見秦 1.1: 12). In that memorial, braving death is not a formula but a very real suggestion, followed by the proposal to execute the memorialist if his plan of action fails. Evidently, *mei si* did not exist as a fixed formula of speech in the Warring States period.

54. See *SJ* 6.254, 267.

tion, and eventually it became common in the imperial court exchanges.[55] Its proliferation during the Qin dynasty had been recently confirmed by a discovery at the site of Liye 里耶 of what appears to be an extract from the Qin court communication, which contains the *mei si* formula.[56] The application of this formula is indicative of a deep change in a minister's standing vis-à-vis the sovereign.

It would be an oversimplification to contrast Mengzi and Li Si as representatives of change in ruler-minister relations from the middle Warring States period to the time of Qin unification. Not only does this comparison ignore individual differences (Li Si was not a courageous remonstrator but a skillful courtier), but it also does not take into consideration difference in our sources: Li Si's memorials and speeches come, in all likelihood, directly from the Qin court documents and are not embellished by the thinker's followers as may be the case with Mengzi, Xunzi, and, less likely, Yan Ying. Moreover, ending the discussion with Li Si's *mei si* formula may obscure the fact that it was Mengzi, not Li Si, who remained a model intellectual for the majority of the imperial literati.

This said, the difference between Li Si and his predecessors is not just a matter of my selective approach. The transformation of Li Si from a traveling persuader into the imperial chancellor is indicative of the broader transformation of the members of the educated elite into a much more dependent stratum than was the case before the unification. In the Spring and Autumn period, the educated elite was almost equivalent to the ministerial stratum, the members of which, due to a peculiar situation of the rulers' weakness, could treat the lords as *primus inter pares*. In the Warring States period, the elite became much broader, comprising both active and aspiring officials, and its members lost their power vis-à-vis the throne. Yet insofar as the interstate market of talent continued to function, the appointment flexibility of the *shi* allowed them a relatively independent stance of any specific ruler, encouraging haughty admonitions of Mengzi and his like. Now, in the newly unified world, members of the educated elite could focus their aspirations only on a single court,

---

55. For Cai Yong's views, see Giele, *Imperial Decision-Making and Communication in Early China*, 92–94.

56. See Chen Wei, *Liye Qin jiandu jiaoshi*, 376, slip 8-1668.

ruled by the most powerful universal monarch. With the power of an emperor dwarfing that of any ruler of pre-Qin world, it was no longer possible to defy him in the harsh way characteristic of Yan Ying and Mengzi.

The self-deprecating tone adopted by Li Si and his fellow ministers dominated the ruler-minister interaction during the imperial era; and the figure of a semi-independent advisor to the throne, of Mengzi's kind, disappeared. The emperors were protected by the *lèse majesté* laws, which could turn any critical comment into the criminally punishable "great irreverence" (*da bu jing* 大不敬); and as they gradually assumed the posture of sages (*sheng* 聖), they were less inclined to behave as the thinkers' disciples.[57] While it was expected of the emperor to behave modestly and to recognize the superior ideological expertise of his aides (see the example of Emperor Wu [漢武帝, r. 140–87 BCE] in Sarah A. Queen's essay in this volume), it was up to the emperor to decide when to dispense with the accommodating spirit and punish his critics—not just for direct remonstrance but even for the "crime of [criticizing the government] in the stomach" (*fu fei zui* 腹非罪).[58] Hence, although ostensibly "direct words" were welcome, and the office of remonstrating officials was established, in practice overt criticism could be suicidal, as many courtiers of Emperor Wu came to learn very well.

Yet having become the ruler's servitors rather than his teachers, the imperial literati were not necessarily cowed into senseless subservience. Amid flatterers and sycophants there always was a substantial conscientious minority that followed Xunzi's imperative "Follow the Way and not the ruler."[59] Some, like Dong Zhongshu (董仲舒, ca. 195–115 BCE) in Queen's essay, preferred a subtle remonstrance, hidden behind the veneer of ritualized speech that emphasized the minister's humility and the emperor's exaltedness; others, like Dong's

57. For the complexity of the concept of imperial sagacity in the early empire, see, e.g., Xing, "Qin Han huangdi yu 'shengren,'" 50–83.

58. See *HS* 24B.1168 for the execution of the minister of agriculture under Emperor Wu, Yan Yi 顏異, for this crime. See more on the atmosphere of terror against outspoken officials under Emperor Wu in Wu, *Written at Imperial Command*, 13–15.

59. See *Xunzi jijie*, "Chen Dao," 9.13: 250, and the discussion in Pines, "Friends of Foes."

contemporary, Sima Xiangru (司馬相如, 179–118 BCE) opted for even subtler "indirect remonstrance"; yet none of these men became the emperor's obedient tool. And while throughout the imperial era the criticism of the monarch had normally to be expressed in a much more self-deprecating language than before, there was also a distinct minority of diehard critics, who dared to directly assault the throne, willing at times to sacrifice their careers and even their lives for the sake of preserving their moral integrity—much in the way of Mengzi, but usually with much harsher consequences.[60]

Yet putting aside both sycophants and radical critics, I can summarize that in the final account, it seems, that Xunzi—as in many other cases—properly grasped the essential norms of a future imperial interaction between a ruler and his aide. A prudent minister would continue to "follow the Way," but he would express his reservations in an accommodating language without either offending or alienating the ruler. The model of Xunzi's cautious admonition to King Zhao appears thus as a more viable form of communicating with the sovereign than the fierce and offensive criticism practiced by Yan Ying and Mengzi. It seems then that Xunzi poses a reasonable compromise between Yan Ying's and Mengzi's audacity and Li Si's subservience.

---

60. For "indirect remonstrance" see Schaberg, "Playing at Critique"; for Sima Xiangru's case, see Wu, *Written at Imperial Command*, 16–21; for the complexity of expressing one's dissatisfaction in the imperial court, see e.g., Declercq, *Writing against the State*; cf. Liu Zehua's analysis in *Zhongguo de Wangquanzhuyi*, 263–79. For the diehard critics of the throne, see Pines, *The Everlasting Empire*, 97–100.

CHAPTER 4

Riddles, Concealment, and Rhetoric in Early China

Wai-yee Li, Harvard University

Xunzi (ca. 340–245 BCE) sums up succinctly the predicament of the subject whose only tool in persuading the ruler is his rhetoric: "For such is the difficulty of persuasion: there can be no easy, straightforward way to get the most exalted to meet the lowest, or to have the vision of ultimate governance imposed on the greatest disorder. One who encompasses far-ranging references is blamed for fabrication; one who stays close to mundane affairs is blamed for insipidity." 凡說之難，以至高遇至卑，以至治接至亂，未可直至也。遠舉則病繆，近世則病傭。[1] The skillful persuader must therefore command range without appearing far-fetched, adhere to practicality while rising above the pedestrian. He has to, in other words, master the art of transformation: "He changes and moves with the times, rears up and bows low with his generation, slows down the urgent and adds to the diminished. Gamely instrumental, he is to himself like a dam is to water or a straightening instrument is to wood. To call this condition bending or concealed would be apt. He does not, however, suffer rupture or harm." 與時遷徙，與世偃仰，緩急嬴絀，府然若渠匽檃栝之於己，曲得所謂焉，然而不折傷。[2] The ideal persuader fashions

1. *Xunzi jianshi*, chap. 5, 53. All translations in this chapter are my own.

2. *Xunzi jianshi*, 53. I follow Yang Shuda 楊樹達 and read *fu* 府 as *fu* 俯, "the manner of fitting to things" 就物之貌. Liang Qixiong, the compiler of the 1936 edition of *Xunzi jianshi*, claims that *qu* 曲 in *Xunzi* means "all-encompassing" (*zhoupian* 周徧),

himself according to changing times and circumstances, improving situations through apposite ameliorations. This calls for extreme self-discipline: he restrains and molds himself just as the dam holds water and the straightening instrument shapes wood. Lest this suggests mere expediency, Xunzi posits pliancy and concealment that nevertheless forestall harm and perhaps, by extension, damaging compromises.

According to Xunzi, "the art of persuasion" (*tanshuo zhi shu* 談說之術) should be "approached with proud dignity, treated with proper sincerity, upheld with unyielding strength, expressed through analogies and references, illuminated through distinctions, brought forth through joy and harmony." 矜莊以莅之，端誠以處之，堅彊以持之，譬稱以喻之，分別以明之，欣驩芬薌以送之。[3] Such associations with reverence, integrity, and clarity are possible because the persuader's eloquence and transformations are rooted in fundamental moral concerns. Here "clever words" (*qiaoyan* 巧言) are not by definition suspect (differing in this from the *Analects*):[4] while "the petty man's eloquence" (*xiaoren zhi bian* 小人之辯) is pernicious, "the noble man's eloquence" (*shi junzi zhi bian* 士君子之辯) and "the sage's eloquence" (*shengren zhi bian* 聖人之辯) serve moral goals. Of the latter two figures it is the noble man who functions as the true exemplar. The sage's eloquence "has no prior calculation, no planning in advance. Once manifested, it is apposite, forming the right words in proper categories. Staying put or moving, it has endless power to respond to changes." 不先慮，不早謀，發之而當，成文而類，居錯遷徙，應變不窮。It transcends method and is therefore inimitable. By contrast, the noble man's eloquence "has prior calculation, and is planned in advance. Every passing word is worth listening to. Finely crafted, his words yet bring concrete results. Broad in sympathy, he yet sides with what is correct." 先慮之，早謀之，斯須之言而足聽，文而致實，博而黨正。[5]

---

as distinct from the usual usage of the word. I have opted for its more common associations with "bending" and "concealed" (as in *yinqu* 隱曲). Kubo Ai 久保愛 thinks "no rupture or harm" refers to the addressee, but more likely it pertains to the speaker.

3. *Xunzi jianshi*, 54.

4. See *Analects* 1.3: "Those sporting clever words and an ingratiating appearance—rarely do they realize the virtue of humaneness!" 巧言佞色，鮮矣仁。

5. *Xunzi jianshi*, 54–56.

If Xunzi's ideal persuader still abides by normative methods and standards despite keen awareness of transformations as the means of ultimate control, his counterpart in *Han Feizi* is dogged by a heightened awareness of the political dangers threatening the persuader to eschew normative criteria in favor of psychological manipulation. In "Difficulties of Speaking" ("Nan yan" 難言), Han Feizi 韓非子 (d. 233 BCE) elaborates the litany of pitfalls awaiting the subject addressing his ruler, who may well regard grand eloquence as mere flourish without substance, reverence and probity as ineptness and tactlessness, copious references and broad analogies as insubstantial impracticality, restraint and simplicity as offensive bluntness, probing concern and empathy as immodest interference, unyielding expansiveness and profundity as useless exaggeration, concern with immediate circumstances as short-sighted pettiness, prudent avoidance of offense as cowardly pandering, detachment from the mundane world as delusion, ready wit and literary adornment as scribal trade, rejection of erudition in favor of practicality as vulgarity, and knowledge of the classics and antiquity as mere pedantry.[6] Han Feizi goes on to enumerate paragons of wisdom, loyalty, and eloquence who met with rejection, calumny, or persecution when they tried to urge their ideas upon those in power.

In "Difficulties of Persuasion" ("Shui nan" 說難), Han Feizi probes the psychological explanations for such dangers. More than knowledge, courage, and rhetorical prowess, successful persuasion depends on reading the mind of the ruler and fashioning eloquence to match his stated and hidden goals. Even while astuteness and psychological penetration are indispensable, however, such qualities must remain hidden, for persuasion is a cat-and-mouse game that depends on the persuader's hiding the very qualities responsible for his success. The ruler's power and mystique are rooted in secrecy, and the persuader must not on any account threaten it. Again and again Han Feizi elaborates this theme:

> For affairs succeed because of secrecy; and words that leak out cause failure. The persuader may not personally leak them, but if his words

---

6. My paraphrase of the beginning passage in "Nan yan," *Han Feizi shiping*, chap. 3, 1.236.

> allude to the hidden affairs, then he is in danger. The ruler claims an overt motivation to act, but has other intentions. If the persuader knows not only the overt motivation but also the hidden intention, then he is in danger. If in planning an important affair that matches the ruler's wish, some clever person not privy to it yet figures it out and leaks it, then the ruler will certainly blame it on the persuader, who will be in danger. When the relationship with the ruler has yet to deepen, but the persuader's words show comprehensive knowledge about the ruler, then if his persuasion is followed and brings achievements, he will invite jealousy, and if his persuasion is not followed and leads to failure, he will invite suspicion: he will be in danger.
>
> 夫事以密成，語以泄敗；未必其身泄之也，而語及所匿之事，如此者身危。彼顯有所出事，而乃以成他故，說者不徒知所出而已矣，又知其所以爲，如此者身危。規異事而當，智者揣之外而得之，事泄於外，必以爲己也，如此者身危。周澤未渥也，而語極知，說行而有功，則見忌，說不行而有敗，則見疑，如此者身危。[7]

Han Feizi goes on to enumerate more ways whereby the persuader is imperiled, reworking some of the formulations that appear in "Difficulties of Speaking." In some cases, the underlying agonistic momentum of the cited passage persists: for example, the persuader is cautioned against urging lofty moral principles when a ruler is obviously at fault (lest he be accused of highlighting his error). Likewise, he must not reveal that he knows the ruler is claiming (undue) merit.

The obverse side of such perils is success through the skilful manipulation of the ruler's desires, hopes, and fears. "What persuasion should focus on is knowing how to highlight what the person being persuaded takes pride in and to extinguish what he is ashamed of." 凡說之務，在知飾所說之所矜，而滅其所恥也。The recurrent word in "Difficulties of Persuasion" is *si* 私, the secret, private, personal preferences that the persuader rationalizes and upholds as public good and moral principles. Compromises and self-abnegation (*ziwu* 自汙) are the means to gain the ruler's trust, so that the persuader's views "will be heeded, carried on, and thus rouse his generation" 聽用而振世. In other words, the persuader hides his true concerns but will in the end be able to openly avow his views once he prevails. He will "then give full rein to his knowledge and eloquence" 然後極騁智辯焉. Having

7. *Han Feizi shiping*, 1.442–43.

built a relationship of "closeness and trust" 親近不疑, he can "push his words to their limit" 得盡之辭, "strategize unfathomably without inviting suspicion, bring up contention without being blamed. He will openly dissect gain and damage to achieve merit, directly point out right and wrong to rectify the ruler's person. In this way the two sides regard each other: this is the fruition of successful persuasion" 深計而不疑，引爭而不罪，則明割利害以致其功，直指是非以飾〔飭〕其身，以此相待，此說之成也.[8] The interplay of submission and mastery is summed up in the final image of the chapter: "For the dragon is a beast, it can be treated gently and intimately and ridden. But under its throat is a foot-long scale that grows backward, and anyone who touches [it] will certainly be killed. A ruler also has a scale that grows backward. So long as the persuader does not touch it, he will be close to success." 夫龍之爲蟲也，可柔狎而騎也，然其喉下有逆鱗徑尺，若人有嬰之者，則必殺人。人主亦有逆鱗，說者能無嬰人主之逆鱗，則幾矣。

The chapter "Expedient Persuasion" ("Shun shui" 順說) in *Lüshi chunqiu* (3rd c. BCE) also elaborates the theme of the persuader's transformations. A skilful persuader "relies on another's strength and makes it his own strength, relies on another's coming and comes along, relies on another's going and goes forth. He does not set forth form and images, but follows another's rise and growth, like echo is to words. He goes along another's high points and nadir, taking it as his point of reference." 因人之力以自爲力，因其來而與來，因其往而與往，不設形象，與生與長，而言之與響，與盛與衰，以之所歸。[9] "Another" refers to the ruler. The persuader's apparent pliancy and dependence notwithstanding, the examples that follow demonstrate moral instruction via seduction and empathy. King Kang of Song 宋康王 declares interest in "valor and strength," not "humaneness and righteousness," but the persuader Hui Ang 惠盎 is able to lure him into grudging admiration (if not acceptance) of the sages Kongzi 孔子 and Mozi 墨子 by appealing to his interest and vanity through metaphorical extensions of valor and strength. By the same token, the Qi persuader Tian Zan 田贊 is able to use his own shabby clothes

8. *Han Feizi shiping*, 1.448.
9. *Lüshi chunqiu jiaoshi*, 905.

to draw a Chu king's attention to the misery of his people caught in incessant warfare. In some ways, "Expedient Persuasion" rehearses the same argument as "Difficulties of Persuasion," although psychological tension and potential competition between the ruler and the persuader are much more evident in the latter.

Riddles and the Persuader's Dilemma

It is in the context of these Warring States discussions of persuasion and rhetoric that we can fully appreciate the appeal of anecdotes about riddles. Recurrent references to transformations, concealment, and inscrutability in such contexts summon association with riddles.[10] A riddle is a paradoxical combination of opacity and clarity, commanding sudden transformations of one into the other. It deals with hidden meanings and hidden agency, leaving room for the psychological tug-of-war between the ruler and the persuader, as well as the latter's fantasies of stealthy control and mastery. As a form of entertainment, it provides pleasure, but its solution often encodes moral instruction. Anecdotes about riddles answer anxieties about the persuader's dilemma: how to establish authority through subjugation, offer instruction via seduction, and promise revelation by way of concealment.

One of the most famous riddle anecdotes, with variants appearing in *Han Feizi*, *Lüshi chunqiu*, and chapters 40 and 126 in Sima Qian's (ca. 145 BCE–ca. 87 BCE) *Shiji* (Records of the historian), features a king (King Wei of Qi 齊威王 in chapter 126 of *Shiji*, King Zhuang of Chu 楚莊王 in all other accounts) who has neglected his duties for three years. The remonstrating character, variously identified as a minister, a courtier, or a jester, presents a riddle about an inert and silent bird. Thus *Han Feizi*:

> King Zhuang of Chu took charge of government for three years and neither issued any commands nor made any policies. The supervisor of the military on the right was in attendance and offered the king this riddle: "A bird stops at the mound of the south. For three years it did not spread its wings, fly, or cry out. Taciturn, it made no sound.

10. Cf. Plaks, "Riddle and Enigma in Chinese Civilization"; Harbsmeier, *Language and Logic.*

> What is its name?" The king said, "For three years it did not spread its wings, so as to let feathers and plume grow; it neither flew nor cried, so as to observe the people's standards. Although it did not fly, when it flies it will certainly soar to the heavens; although it did not cry out, when it cries it will certainly command everybody's attention. You, sir, should desist. I, the inadequate one, already understand this."
>
> 楚莊王莅政三年，無令發，無政爲也。右司馬御座，而與王隱曰：「有鳥止南方之阜，三年不翅，不飛不鳴，嘿然無聲，此爲何名?」王曰：「三年不翅，將以長羽翼；不飛不鳴，將以觀民則。雖無飛，飛必沖天；雖無鳴，鳴必驚人。子釋之，不穀知之矣。」[11]

The story concludes with a litany of King Zhuang's achievements and is capped with a quotation from *Laozi*, as is consonant with its chapter title, "Illustrating the Meanings of *Laozi*" ("Yu Lao" 喻老). The emphasis here on King Zhuang's agency and his timely, inevitable transformation diminishes the role of the persuader. "It was because King Zhuang did not perform paltry goodness that he had a great name; it was because he did not manifest his success early on that he could accomplish great things. That is why it says in *Laozi*, 'The great vessel takes long to make, the great note spares sound.'" 莊王不爲小善，故有大名，不蚤見示，故有大功。故曰：「大器晚成，大音希聲。」 Like the ideal ruler in *Laozi* and *Han Feizi*, King Zhuang is inscrutable, and his hidden agency reveals itself only when confronted with the minister's "hidden meanings" or "hidden words," the literal translation of the term for riddle in Chinese (*yin* 隱、讔).

In *Lüshi chunqiu*, a version of this anecdote appears in the chapter "Weighing Words" ("Zhongyan" 重言). King Zhuang is no longer the embodiment of the Daoist ideal of latent worth and hidden power; rather, he is the misguided ruler who does not heed remonstrance but loves riddles 不聽而好讔. Remonstrance is built on normative words, whereas riddles play with meanings and are potentially frivolous. King Zhuang's aversion and inclination thus bespeak a deeper malaise—he rejects earnest counsel but prefers the game of words, whose remonstrative potential is occluded. Cheng Lord Gu 成公賈, the person offering remonstrance in this version of the anecdote, has to disavow all intentions of remonstrance and to profess its

11. *Han Feizi shiping*, 2.715–16.

antithesis, entertainment with riddles: "I do not dare remonstrate. I beg to offer you, my king, a riddle." 臣非敢諫也，願與君王讔也。The riddle about the inert and silent bird, substantially the same as in *Han Feizi*, here plays a more clearly transformative role, and the riddle thus redeems itself by being turned into the instrument of remonstrance. To "weigh words" (or regard words as weighty), as announced by the chapter title, is to be careful, deliberate, and sparing with words. The cryptic nature of riddles qualifies it as "weighty": it realizes its moral purpose by forcing the listener to examine his past, present, and future as he seeks the answer. The passage concludes by quoting lines from the *Classic of Odes* to sum up King Zhuang: "Why do you take so long? / There must be a reason. / Why do you linger? / There must be something to give." 何其久也，必有以也。何其處也，必有與也。[12]

The chapter begins with an anecdote about the Shang king Gaozong 高宗who does not speak for three years after ascending the throne. Gaozang is silent out of vigilance: "For I, the lone person, have to rectify the four directions. I am fearful only that my words do not match the proper categories of excellence. That was why I did not speak." 以余一人正四方，余唯恐言之不類也，茲故不言。 It concludes with an anecdote about Lord Huan of Qi 齊桓公 and Guan Zhong 管仲, whose secret plans to invade Ju come to light because Lord Huan's carriage driver has uncanny powers of discernment. King Zhuang's initial silence thus bears superficial resemblance to Gaozong's vigilance over words (*shenyan* 慎言), and it may also be justified by the ruler's supposed need for secrecy and inscrutability. The genius of Cheng Lord Gu's riddle is to make King Zhuang's transformation appear so seamless. Deviance becomes potential greatness because "weighty words" operative in the construction and decoding of the riddle allow for maximum room of maneuver, inasmuch that the ruler's lapse can be reclaimed as ultimate control.

The errors of the ruler become more extreme and the corrective function of the riddle correspondingly more pronounced in *Shiji*. In *juan* 40, "The Hereditary Family of Chu" ("Chu shijia" 楚世家), King

---

12. Mao, no. 37, "Mao qiu" 旄丘, in *Shi ji zhuan*, 27. The received text has the sequence reversed: 何其處也，必有與也。何其久也，必有以也。*Lüshi chunqiu jiaoshi*, 1156.

Zhuang neglects government and wallows in sensual pleasures, giving the order that "anyone who dares to remonstrate will be put to death with no hope of reprieve!" 有敢諫者死無赦。[13] He is embracing beautiful women and seated among bells and drums when the Chu minister Wu Ju 伍舉 presents his riddle (*jinyin* 進隱) about the bird that neither takes flight nor cries out for three years. The king's reply here is much shorter than in the analogous passages in *Han Feizi* and *Lüshi chunqiu*, pertaining not to the past but only to the future. In other words, the promise of great and successful endeavor is not rooted in any attempt to explain past failure. Despite his promise, however, the king's excesses become even more reprehensible after a few months, and another minister, Su Cong 蘇從, braves the threat of death to remonstrate: "To suffer death in order to enlighten the ruler is my very wish." 殺身以明君，臣之願也。 Only then does King Zhuang change his ways, entrust policies to Wu Ju and Su Cong, and rise to become overlord. In this account, forthright remonstrance is shown to be more effective than the psychological manipulation of the riddle.

In "The Biographies of Jesters" ("Huaiji liezhuan" 滑稽列傳), Sima Qian gives a slightly different version of the anecdote. The substance of the exchanges remains more or less the same, but the characters involved are here King Wei of Qi and the jester Chunyu Kun 淳于髡. He was a son-in-law who took the place of a son in his wife's family (*zhuixu* 贅壻), which probably indicated humble origins.[14] Of short stature and sporting a name (Kun) that means "the punishment of having one's head shaved," "he mastered the game of words and the art of disputation, and was never humiliated when he was sent on diplomatic missions to the lords." 滑稽多辯，數使諸侯，未嘗屈辱。 King Wei's indulgence in sensual pleasures and neglect of government bring the realm to the brink of ruin. His excesses are mentioned in conjunction with his "fondness for riddles" (*xiyin* 喜隱), which leaves Chunyu Kun room to maneuver meanings and "persuade through a riddle" 說之以隱. The persuader's "class change"

---

13. *SJ* 40.1700.

14. The word *zhui* 贅, which means "superfluous" or "burdensome," implies that the son-in-law taken into the wife's (usually heirless) family is extraneous to her lineage. Only men of humble background would concede to such an arrangement.

is emblematic of how a dire situation calls for a more drastic reversal of roles. The entertainer or jester (*you* 優) can "speak without fear of incurring blame" 言無尤[15] because his words are supposed to entertain rather than have a practical function, thus making room for remonstrance when there is none. Chunyu Kun's riddle of the silent and inert bird calls forth the same response from the king as in the analogous passage in King Zhuang's story cited above, with the difference that King Wei's transformation into a determined and successful ruler is immediate and complete.

The Ming scholar, poet, and playwright Yang Shen 楊慎 (1488–1559 CE) comments on King Wei's "fondness for riddles": "One who is fond of riddles prides himself on clarity and keen intelligence. That is why the persuader can enter [his mind] and quickly convince him. Otherwise this method would not suffice as a fitting match." 喜隱者，自恃其明與智也，故其入也，速于遊說，不然者不足稱也。[16] Taking my cue from Yang Shen, I submit that "fondness for riddles" is presented as a redeeming trait that opens the way to self-correction. One may argue with equal justification that King Wei's predilection is but one aspect of a more general fascination with excesses. In other words, manipulating deviance furnishes the instrument for rectification.

In these versions of the great bird riddle, the ruler's image ranges from potential greatness biding its time to pleasure-loving deviance fascinated with excess, and the persuader's role varies from minister to jester, implying methods of earnest counsel or apparent entertainment. These differences define the boundaries of the relationship between the ruler and the persuader and also address some of the anxieties surrounding persuasion. As noted above, both the ruler and the persuader rely on concealment and transformation. The persuader must read the ruler's mind but also hide his perspicacity, or else he risks threatening the ruler. The ruler has to follow good counsel but must confirm (or at least present) his change of heart as rooted in his own reasoning and agency. The riddle gives the persuader maximum cover by allowing him to both dramatize and hide

---

15. "I am an entertainer, I can speak without incurring blame." 我優也，言無郵（尤）。See *Guoyu jijie*, Jin yu 晉語 2.1, 276.

16. Yang Shen's comment is cited in Ling Zhilong 凌稚隆, *Shiji pinglin* 126.2768.

his powers and by upholding the ideal of the unfathomable ruler capable of unpredictable transformations.

Riddles and Seduction

In structure Chunyu Kun's riddle is similar to other ploys in the jester's repertoire: mime, enigmatic gestures, gross exaggeration, and unlikely analogies, which share the underlying principle of instruction through seduction. In all these cases, told with gusto and admiration in Sima Qian's "Biographies of Jesters," the jester gains the ruler's attention by an apparently incomprehensible or outrageous proposition, and achieves the goal of remonstrance through decoding (either by himself or by his listener). An example we may consider is Chunyu Kun's reply to King Wei's question as to how much he could drink before succumbing to inebriation: "Your subject can become drunk with a dipper, or with a picul." 臣飲一斗亦醉，一石亦醉。He proceeds to enumerate five scenarios whose different demands determine the gradation of his capacity for drinking.

> King Wei said, "If you, sir, get drunk after drinking one dipper of wine, how can you drink a whole picul? May I ask what you have to say about this?" Kun said, "If wine is bestowed on me in your presence, with officers of the law on the side and the official of censure behind, then I will bow low and drink in trepidation, and I will be drunk already with less than a dipper. . . . As for the gatherings of districts and villages, when men and women mingle and the wine circulated can be made to stay, when we can invite each other to play arrow tossing and the six gambling games, when holding hands incur no blame and staring or flirting is not forbidden, when in front are fallen earrings and behind are hairpins let go, I enjoy myself and can drink up to eight dippers and be only twenty or thirty percent drunk. As the sun sets and drinking is more than half done, what remains of the feast is gathered and brought close, men and women are at the same table, shoes get mixed up, cups and dishes are in disarray, candles are snuffed in the hall, and the host asks me to stay while sending off the guests. The lapels of silken garments are untied, and I can faintly smell the fragrance of the ladies. At this moment, I am the happiest, and can drink a picul. Hence it is said: drinking pushed to extremes brings disorder, and pleasure pushed to extremes brings grief. All things are like this—which is to say nothing can be pushed to extremes, for doing so brings decline." Thus did he offer indirect

criticism. The Qi king said, "Excellent." He then stopped nightlong drinking, and made Chunyu Kun the hosting official receiving the lords. When nobles related to the ruling house held feasts with wine, Kun was often by their side.

威王曰:「先生飲一斗而醉,惡能飲一石哉。其說可得聞乎。」髡曰:「賜酒大王之前,執法在傍,御史在後,髡恐懼俯伏而飲,不過一斗徑醉矣。。。若乃州閭之會,男女雜坐,行酒稽留,六博投壺,相引爲曹,握手無罰,目眙不禁,前有墮珥,後有遺簪,髡竊樂此,飲可八斗而醉二參。日暮酒闌,合尊促坐,男女同席,履舄交錯,杯盤狼藉,堂上燭滅,主人留髡而送客。羅襦襟解,微聞薌澤,當此之時,髡心最歡,能飲一石。故曰:酒極則亂,樂極則悲,萬事盡然,言不可極,極之而衰。」以諷諫焉。齊王曰:「善。」乃罷長夜之飲。以髡爲諸侯主客。宗室置酒,髡嘗在側。[17]

How does Chunyu Kun earn the right to regulate other people's drinking? He gives a compelling account of how disorder ensues when there is excessive drinking, but the disorder itself, so lovingly described, seems more like the celebration of pleasure than its castigation. No wonder the Song poet and scholar-official Su Shi 蘇軾 (1037–1101) comments: "This is almost encouragement. What remonstrance is there?" 幾於勸矣,而何諷之有?[18]

This method of apparently agreeing with a ruler's perverse inclination, describing it with relish and exaggerating it to such an extent that its absurdity is revealed, also obtains in other instances of remonstrance by jesters in Sima Qian's chapter. King Zhuang of Chu had a beloved horse, which he fed with delicacies and clothed in fine silks. When it died, he wanted to bury it in a coffin with rituals proper for high officers, and he also issued the command that anybody who remonstrated about the horse would incur the death penalty. Entertainer Meng's 優孟 response is to wail and lament that the horse deserves to be buried like a ruler, that is, like the king himself. He then goes on to enumerate the pomp and rituals for burying a ruler and recommends their use for the dead horse. His point is that King Zhuang mistreats his subjects and holds them in lower esteem than his horse, and the only way to make him realize this confusion of standards is to put the king and the horse on the same level. The

17. *SJ* 126.3199.
18. Ling, *Shiji pinglin* 126.2769.

difference between this anecdote and Chunyu Kun's excursus on drinking is that the punch line here is more direct and unfolds more logically. After describing how the dead horse should receive sacrifices from a settlement of ten thousand households, Meng adds: "When the other rulers hear of this, they will all know that you, great king, demean people and value horses." 諸侯聞之，皆知大王賤人而貴馬也。[19] Although Meng claims to comply with the king, the critical intent is unmistakable, and the prospect of being branded a bad ruler by his peers makes the king desist.

With analogous ploys, the midget entertainer Zhan 優旃 corrects two Qin kings' attempts at self-aggrandizement by inflating their desires with the language of exaggerated compliance. When the First Emperor of Qin wanted to expand the imperial park, Zhan said, "Excellent. Release many birds and beasts in there. When the raiders come from the east, it will suffice to just let the deer and antelope charge at them." 善。多縱禽獸于其中，寇從東方來，令麋鹿觸之，足矣。[20] The Qin ruler gave up his plan. After the Second Emperor acceded to the throne, he wanted to paint the city walls. Zhan said, "Excellent. Even if your majesty had not said anything about it, I was about to request it. Although the people may fret about the cost of painting the walls, it will be so great! The painted walls will be so smooth that the raiders who come will not able to climb up. We will want to go about it right away. It will be easy enough to paint the walls, but setting up the cover for drying them will be difficult." 善。主上雖無言，臣固將請之。漆城雖於百姓愁費，然佳哉。漆城蕩蕩，寇來不能上，即欲就之，易爲漆耳。顧難爲蔭室。[21] The Second Emperor laughed and gave up his plan because of Zhan's intervention.

Despite comparable logic, Chunyu Kun's speech about drinking is actually quite different from the remonstrance of Zhan or Meng. With the latter, the irony and absurd exaggeration unmistakably exposes the fatuousness of the ruler's desire, while the spectacle of inebriated abandon in Kun's speech is ambiguous enough to inspire either excitement or disquiet, depending on the audience's disposition. More generally, this ambiguity underlies the role of pleasure in

---

19. *SJ* 126.3200.
20. *SJ* 126.3202–3.
21. *SJ* 126.3203.

persuasion. The balance or tension between pleasure and political intervention remains a persistent issue in the discussion of court rhetoric in early China. Pleasure may be derived from the allure of the subject matter, the beauty, cadence, and symmetry of crafted words, or the manner of performance.

Riddles are linked to the idea of pleasure in two ways—as a verbal game that brings pleasure, and as the operative principle of revelation through concealment that has secret affinities with the paradoxical fusion of excess and regulation in indirect remonstrance. It is noteworthy that the riddles in chapter 26 of *Xunzi* should come to be identified as early examples of *fu* 賦 (variously translated as poetic exposition, rhyme prose, or rhapsody). A mixture of verse and prose, these pieces begin by posing a riddle, giving as clues the moral-philosophical meaning of the concept in question, and then elaborate a series of metaphors before providing the solutions. While the title of the chapter ("*Fu*") in the received text might have been added later, the dialogic, argumentative structure of its pieces, as well as their moments of equivocation and uncertainty, announce affinities with what comes to be known as *fu* in the Chinese literary tradition.[22] The stabilization of meaning in the process of answering riddles is implicitly compared to the imposition of order on political chaos: "The times are out of joint; please allow me to set forth transforming, transformative verses." 天下不治，請陳佹詩。[23]

Riddles and indirect remonstrance are thus intertwined in late Warring States and early Han writings. The link between riddles and *fu* also suggests that the jester has much in common with the court poet, and by extension with the subjects whose relationship with the emperor is an unpredictable mix of intimacy, influence, and vulnerability, as Sima Qian notes in his letter to Ren An: "Those who master fine words, records, astrology, and the calendar are indeed the ones his majesty toys with and treats like entertainers. They are the ones slighted by the common run of society." 文史星曆，近乎卜祝之

22. The answers to the riddles are rites, knowledge, clouds, silkworms, and needles; see *Xunzi jianshi*, 357–63. On these riddles in *Xunzi*, see Knechtges, "Riddles as Poetry."

23. *Xunzi jianshi*, 361. Yang Shuda glosses *gui* 佹 as *gui* 恑, meaning *bian* 變 (according to *Shuowen* 說文), cited in *Xunzi jianshi*, 361.

間，固主上之戲弄，倡優畜之，流俗之所輕也。[24] The court poet Mei Gao 枚皋 (b. 153 BCE) also reportedly said that "to compose *fu* is to curry favor through wit, and to be regarded as an entertainer. I regret being in the same category as entertainers." 爲賦乃俳，見視如倡，自悔類倡也。[25] What the jester and the court poet share is the unstable balance between celebrating pleasure and offering admonition, between the seduction of hidden meanings and the clarity of the revealed message.

The fact that Han (and later) writings often refer to the distinction between "mere entertainers" and their more morally high-minded and politically more effective counterparts means that political intervention remains a constant goal for some practitioners of wit, eloquence, and concealed meanings.[26] Sometimes the same person encompasses poles of performance and political intervention. Dongfang Shuo 東方朔 (154 BCE-93 BCE), who used riddles to demonstrate his superiority over a rival wit at court and amuse the emperor, also remonstrated with Emperor Wu 漢武帝 (r. 141 BCE-87 BCE) against the expansion of imperial hunting grounds and urged him to curb the wealth and power of Dong Yan 董偃, the lover of an imperial princess. Although favored and rewarded by Emperor Wu, Dongfang Shuo, "whose words, amounting to tens of thousands, focus on the discourse of Shang Yang and Han Fei, with far-ranging references that are also marked by extravagant wit, was ultimately not appointed [to important positions]." 其言專商鞅、韓非之語也，指意放蕩，頗類詼諧，辭數萬言，終不見用。[27]

Dongfang Shuo expresses his political aspiration as nostalgia for preunification China, when warring domains left the itinerant persuader much greater room to maneuver: "That was then, and this is now. How can they be the same!" 彼一時也，此一時也。夫可同哉！[28] This excursus on how a more rigid hierarchy of ruler and subject

---

24. *HS* 62.2731–32.

25. *SJ* 51.2367.

26. Martin Kern emphasizes "performance, display, and pleasure" and discounts "political intervention" in his study of Western Han *fu*; see his "Western Han Aesthetics and the Genesis of the *Fu*," 436–37.

27. *HS* 65.2864.

28. *HS* 65.2864.

diminishes the political efficacy of rhetoric, subsequently anthologized in Xiao Tong's 蕭統 (501–31 CE) *Wenxuan* 文選 as "Response to the Guest's Challenge" (Da ke nan 答客難), is almost an indirect apology for recourse to the entertainer's tricks.[29] Another disquisition, "Sir Nonexistent" (Feiyou xiansheng 非有先生), presents the official Sir Nonexistent, who has been silent for three years and finally explains why persuasion is no easy feat 談何容易 and delineates the ideal of forthright remonstrance upon the urging of the king of Wu.[30] The king follows his advice and achieves good governance. The speaker's name, however, announces this exchange as fictitious wish fulfillment. In his concluding remarks, Ban Gu 班固 (32–92 CE) defends Dongfang Shuo against charges of shallowness and immorality: "The reason why Shuo's dubious reputation exceeds the facts is because he was expansive, excessive, and multifaceted, unclassifiable as to any particular conduct: in his witty responses he was like an entertainer, in his inexhaustible knowledge he seemed to be wise, in his direct remonstrance he seemed upright, in his dubious virtue he seemed hidden." 然朔名過實者，以其詼達多端，不名一行，應諧似優，不窮似智，正諫似直，穢德似隱。[31] In being intractable and hidden, Dongfang Shuo also gives new meanings to reclusion: "As for people like me, we can be said to be escaping the world by being in court, whereas the ancients escaped the world in the midst of wild mountains." 如朔者，所謂避世於朝廷間者也。古之人，乃避世於深山之中。[32] He admonished his sons to "rely on being hidden to take pleasure in the world, and challenge the times without meeting danger." 依隱玩世，詭時不逢。[33] As noted above, the persuader's transformations and unknowability are crucial for his protection and

29. Chu Shaosun 褚少孫 (1st c. BCE) adds the section on Dongfang Shuo in "The Biographies of Jesters" in *SJ* 126.3205–8. In this chapter, it is the academicians (*boshi* 博士) who pose the challenge to Dongfang Shuo. In the much fuller account of his life in *Hanshu,* 65.2841–76, the interlocutor is simply identified as "the guest" (*ke* 客). Dongfang Shuo's response in *Hanshu* is longer than its counterpart in *Shiji*. The *Wenxuan* account follows *Hanshu*; see Xiao Tong, *Zhaoming wenxuan*, 45.627–28.

30. *HS* 65.2868–72.

31. *HS* 65.2783–84.

32. *SJ* 126.3205.

33. *HS* 65.2874.

effectiveness. In Dongfang Shuo's case, however, such attributes suffice only to protect him and facilitate "direct remonstrance that made him seem upright" 正諫似直. Such remonstrance bespeaks the desire for political intervention, which nevertheless remains out of reach.

If "direct remonstrance" is but one of Dongfang Shuo's many facets and is in that sense one manifestation of his hidden core, then his contemporary, the court poet Sima Xiangru 司馬相如 (179–127 BCE), embodies the paradox of hidden intention in indirect remonstrance. Dongfang Shuo masters both verbal entertainment and direct remonstrance but keeps them separate (except when he promotes political ideals with fictional devices), whereas Sima Xiangru professes a continuum between entertainment and remonstrance. Like Dongfang Shuo, Sima Xiangru is said to be adept at manipulating his image and enhancing his reputation. Perhaps more than Dongfang Shuo, Sima Xiangru's life and writings are marked by seduction, role playing, performance, and unpredictable transformations.[34]

According to *Shiji* and *Hanshu*, Sima Xiangru honed his craft in rhetoric and composition with "itinerant persuaders" (*youshui zhi shi* 遊說之士) in the court of Prince Xiao of Liang 梁孝王 (d. 144 BCE). After the prince died, Sima Xiangru returned to his native Shu, where he gained fame when his old friend Wang Ji 王吉, the administrator of Linqiong 臨邛, spread his fame by making a show of demonstrative deference so that Xiangru had a chance to show his superiority with studied indifference. His reputation enhanced, Sima Xiangru was invited to the residence of Zhuo Wangsun 卓王孫, a rich man in Linqiong, where he played the *qin* to seduce Zhuo Wenjun 卓文君, Zhuo's widowed daughter. Their romance ended in elopement, and their union finally gained Zhuo Wangsun's financial

34. "The Biography of Sima Xiangru" is almost identical in *Shiji* and *Hanshu*. The reference to Yang Xiong 揚雄 (53 BCE-18 CE) in the Grand Historian's comment indicates interpolation, and some have averred that the comment in *Shiji* is taken from *Hanshu*. See the comments of Zhou Mi 周密 and Yu Youding 余有丁 in Ling, *Shiji pinglin*, 117.2639. Others have argued that the entire *Shiji* account of Sima Xiangru is taken from *Hanshu*; see Zhu Dongrun, *Shiji Kaosuo*, 268; Yang Ximei, *Xian Qin wenhua shi lunji*, 542–46; Kern, "The 'Biography of Sima Xiangru' and the Question of *Fu* in Sima Qian's *Shiji*," 303–16.

support when Wenjun and Xiangru shamed him into submission by becoming vendors in a wine shop. It is hard to ascertain the historical veracity of these fanciful stories, but there is a compelling continuity between the biography and the writings: we find the same motifs of seduction, masking, false appearance, and manipulation of image and reputation.

In Sima Xiangru's *fu*, remonstrance is made possible through, but is also at the same time blunted by, the device of fictional bracketing. The inclusion of a critical dimension paradoxically legitimizes excesses. This is nowhere more evident than in "*Fu* on Shanglin" 上林賦, with which Sima Xiangru first gained imperial favor. The historian introduces it by alluding to the contradictions of indirect remonstrance:

> Xiangru uses Master Unreal (meaning unreal words) to speak on behalf of Chu; Sir Nonexistent (meaning such events do not exist) to give the Qi counterargument; Lord Not-Thus (meaning there is no such person) to illuminate the principles of the Son of Heaven. He thus borrows the phrases of these three characters to praise the parks of the Son of Heaven and of the lords. The last section [of the *fu*] reverts to restraint and thereby offers remonstrance. He presented the composition to the Son of Heaven, who was greatly pleased.
>
> 相如以「子虛」，序言也，爲楚稱；「烏有先生」者，烏有此事也，爲齊難；「無是公」者，無是人也，明天子之義。故空藉此三人爲辭，以推天子諸侯之苑囿。其卒章歸之於節儉，因以風諫。奏之天子，天子大說。[35]

The glosses of the obviously allegorical names emphasize self-conscious fictional bracketing, which playfully qualifies both the description of excesses and the final remonstrance. The bracketing device apparently produces little critical distance, however. The emperor's great pleasure is more likely the result of sensual gratification than of moral edification.

The "*Fu* on Shanglin" unfolds as a rhetorical contest. Master Unreal, a Chu envoy in Qi, tells Sir Nonexistent and Lord Not-Thus how he responded with an elaborate account of the splendor of the Chu park Yunmeng when the Qi king tried to impress him with his teams of horses and chariots. The Chu king enjoys extravagant plea-

35. *SJ* 117.3002; *HS* 57A.2533.

sures "in the calmness of nonaction; dispassionately, with self-restraint" 泊乎無爲，澹乎自持,[36] thereby demonstrating his superiority to the Qi ruler who is totally immersed in the pursuit of amusement and gratification. Sir Nonexistent criticizes Master Unreal for "speaking extravagantly about licentious pleasures and glorifying profligacy" 奢言淫樂而顯侈靡: "If such things exist and you speak of them, you are magnifying your ruler's faults; if they do not exist and you speak of them, you are harming your own good faith." 有而言之，是章君之惡，無而言之，是害足下之信。 He claims that Qi exceeds Chu in every way and that the Qi king only desists from replying to Master Unreal because "in his position as lord, he did not dare to speak of the pleasures of games." 然在諸侯之位，不敢言游戲之樂。[37] Lord Not-Thus chides both Master Unreal and Sir Nonexistent for defying the limits and obligations proper to subsidiary domains, and proceeds to show how Qi and Chu parks are negligible compared to the emperor's Shanglin Park. Even as the Qi king retains inward detachment, the emperor comes to a sudden realization of his duties at the height of pleasure—as with Yunmeng this is represented through music and the seductive dance of beautiful, semidivine maidens. The emperor now understands the pleasures of hunting allegorically, as he

Roams in the Enclosure of the Six Arts,	游乎六藝之囿
Races his steeds in the Paths of Humaneness and Duty,	騖乎仁義之塗
Feasts his eyes on the Forest of the *Spring and Autumn Annals*.	覽觀春秋之林
. . . He adorns himself in the Garden of *Rites*,	。。。修容乎禮園
Speeds through the Field of *Documents*,	翺翔乎書圃
Tells of the Way of the *Changes*.	述易道
He lets go of strange beasts,	放怪獸
Ascends the Bright Hall,	登明堂
Sits in the Pure Temple,	坐清廟
And Gives his subjects free rein	恣羣臣
To submit judgments of policies.	奏得失
Within the four seas,	四海之內
None fails to receive the hunt's bounty.	靡不受獲[38]

36. *SJ* 117.3014; *HS* 57A.2544.
37. *SJ* 117.3015; *HS* 57A.2545.
38. *SJ* 117.3041; *HS* 57A.2573.

Good government ensues, and hunting is thus turned to good account. In the end, Master Unreal and Sir Nonexistent bow to the superior vision and judgment of Lord Not-Thus.

The agonistic momentum behind "*Fu* on Shanglin" suggests that the moral arguments against excess voiced by all three characters are just part of a rhetorical competition. By the same token, the Chu king's supposed detachment and the emperor's sudden conversion support claims of superiority. Despite the apparent disparagement of excess, the possibility of transcending pleasure either through indifference or enlightenment paradoxically condones pleasure. After all, it is through the sensuous delights of Shanglin that the emperor arrives at an allegorical understanding of hunting in terms of moral and spiritual self-cultivation. The word *zi* 恣 (to give free rein to), usually used in connection with unrestrained desires, here applies to unfettered expression for ministers and officials, who can now judge the pros and cons of policies with impunity. In this "fantasy of transference," the ruler's unrestraint is transformed, through successful indirect remonstrance, into the removal of constraint for the minister to make room for unimpeded direct remonstrance.

"Shanglin" pleased Emperor Wu, who rewarded Sima Xiangru with the post of palace officer (*lang* 郎). There is, however, no mention of the emperor heeding the supposed admonition against wastefulness, and Sima Qian sums up the accounts of Yunmeng and Shanglin as "extravagant, excessive, and surpassing facts. Moreover, this is not what proper principles should uphold. That is why one should pare it down and take the essentials, and return it to the right way for consideration." 侈靡過其實。且非義理所尙，故刪取其要，歸正道而論之。[39] Traditional dichotomies of encouragement (*quan* 勸) or remonstrance (*feng* 諷) and entertainment or edification in the evaluation of compositions such as "Shanglin" implicitly question their political efficacy. More recent attempts to transcend such polarities with ideas of fictionality or performance do not reinstate political intervention.[40]

39. *SJ* 117.3043; *HS* 57A.2575.

40. See Wai-yee Li, *Enchantment and Disenchantment*, 1–46; Kern, "Western Han Aesthetics and the Genesis of the *Fu*."

Do the elaborate description and the sense of indirectness and deliberate paradox that characterize Sima Xiangru's *fu* persist in his more overtly political arguments? For an example we can turn to his writings on Emperor Wu's expansionist policies in the Southwest, which follows right after "*Fu* on Shanglin" in the chapter.[41] His proclamation (*xi* 檄) to the inhabitants of Ba and Shu is meant to placate them in the wake of the unpopular policies of the imperial envoy Tang Meng 唐蒙. In addition to his levy of soldiers and laborers, Tang had used military law to punish those who transported grains without permission.[42] Sima Xiangru blames Tang Meng for causing anxiety and disquiet among the people of Ba and Shu, but also chides the latter for evading their duties and for misunderstanding the peaceful intentions of the emperor. Acknowledging the envoy's error briefly is a way to demand loyalty from the people of Ba and Shu in greater length: "Thus is his majesty troubled by his envoy, and such is the way he mourns the disloyalty of his benighted subjects." 陛下患使者有司之若彼，悼不肖愚民之如此。[43]

Sima Xiangru also paints a picture of universal harmony and order, wherein imperial missions only function to parcel out rewards: "For those who did not submit had been cut down, while those who did good had not yet been rewarded. That was why we sent the overseer of officers to host them as guests, recruiting five hundred men from Ba and Shu, respectively, to carry gifts of coins and cloth to defend the envoy should unforeseen circumstances arise. There will be no incidents of armed conflict or fear of war." 夫不順者已誅，而爲善者未賞，故遣中郎將往賓之，發巴蜀士民各五百人，以奉幣帛，衛使者不然，靡有兵甲之事，戰鬬之患。[44] This stands in stark contrast to the historian's account of the baleful consequences of the mission. As Tang Meng, relying on the momentum of having reached Yelang,

41. Sima Xiangru's involvement with Emperor Wu's southwestern policy may explain the placement of his chapter right after the account of the "southwestern barbarians" in *Shiji*.

42. The people transporting grain without permission (*shan* 擅) were probably seeking to profit from the expedition. This is subsequently anthologized in *Wenxuan* under the title "Proclamation to the Elders of Ba and Shu" 喻巴蜀檄 (Xiao Tong, *Zhaoming wenxuan*, 613–14).

43. *SJ* 117.3046; *HS* 57B.2580.

44. *SJ* 117.3044; *HS* 57B.2577–78.

continued to "open the way to the southwestern barbarians," "he recruited laborers from Ba, Shu, and Hanguang, rousing men numbering tens of thousands. After two years of building, the road was not yet completed, and most of the soldiers and laborers died. The cost came to millions. Many among the people of Shu and the ministers in court questioned the mission's viability." 因通西南夷道，發巴、蜀、廣漢卒，作者數萬人。治道二歲，道不成，士卒多物故，費以巨萬計。蜀民及漢用事者，多言其不便。[45] Elsewhere in the *Shiji*, Sima Qian is unstinting in his criticism of Emperor Wu's expansionist policies, including these expeditions to the southwest.[46]

Despite these setbacks, Sima Xiangru supported southwestern expansion, citing Qin precedent and urging the establishment of "provinces and prefectures" (*junxian* 郡縣) in the wake of initial forays. By the time he was appointed envoy to Shu, the chorus of discontent was getting ever louder. "Xiangru wished to remonstrate, but he did not dare to do so because he had originally supported the policy. He thus wrote a piece, using the elders of Shu as his mouthpiece, and offering counterarguments in his own voice, in order to subtly criticize the emperor and also to spell out his mission's goals, so that the people can understand the emperor's intention." 相如欲諫，業已建之，不敢，乃著書，籍（藉）以蜀父老爲辭，而己詰難之，以風天子，且因宣其使指，令百姓知天子之意。 The notion that literature can facilitate communication between the ruler and his subjects came to be idealized as an indispensable component of good governance.[47] In fact, however, the two stated objectives of this piece, realized in two sections of a dialogic structure, are not compatible. The elders of Shu criticize southwestern expansion as wasteful and destructive—"cutting off the common people to bring the Yi and Di barbarians closer, decimating what the state relies on to serve a useless cause" 割齊民以附夷狄，弊所恃而事無用—and, citing precedents, urge the court to seek instead peaceful coexistence (*bing* 並). If this were

45. *SJ* 117.3046; *HS* 57B.2581.

46. See *SJ* 30, "Treatise of Balance and Standard" 平準書, 1421; *SJ* 116, "Account of the Southwestern Barbarians" 西南夷列傳, 2995.

47. See, for example, the "Great Preface" to *Shijing*: "Those above use the Airs to morally transform those below, and those below use the Airs to indirectly criticize those above." 上以風化下，下以諷刺上。

meant to be Sima Xiangru's remonstrance, then it is rendered innocuous by Sima Xiangru's lengthy reply that contains a substantial defense of the emperor's position. The reply is also rhetorically more complex and subtle. It takes issue with the elders' plea for the southwestern barbarians' difference, which justifies noninterference: "Following this logic, Shu would not have changed its costumes and the mores of Ba would not have been transformed." 必若所云，則是蜀不變服而巴不化俗也。 In other words, while the elders see Ba and Shu as part of Han, a cultural-political entity whose coherence is undermined by expansion, Sima Xiangru turns to their peripheral status and argues that their very identity as part of Han is a consequence of such expansion. He then lauds the "extraordinary men" (*feichang zhi ren* 非常之人) and their "extraordinary achievements" (*feichang zhi gong* 非常之功) in history, implicitly comparing Emperor Wu to such culture heroes as the sage-king Yu, the controller of floods. This preposterous comparison is further integrated into a panegyric of Han greatness, a seductive vision of inevitable expansion. A great ruler cannot be tied down to conventions and traditions, for his goal is not merely to "please his generation" 當世取說: "He must therefore uphold discourses and broaden opinions, open up new endeavors to lay down foundations and become the model for ten thousand generations hence. That is why he gallops and flies high in the realm of all-encompassing inclusiveness, and assiduously strives to be third to heaven and second to earth." 必將崇論閎議，創業垂統，爲萬世規。故馳騖乎兼容并包，而勤思乎參天貳地。[48] Here the elevation of "discourses" and "opinions" is prelude to the emperor's grand ambitions of lofty ideals and territorial expansion, and the envoy's affirmation of his own rhetoric becomes inseparable from his political argument. The rhetoric of laudatory *fu*, whereby the ambition of being all-encompassing is both verbal and political, takes over.

Sima Xiangru's piece concludes with the elders of Ba and Shu being convinced by his own speech as envoy. It was likely presented to Emperor Wu, but we are not told about his reactions and his southwestern policy did not change. Silence thus follows his explicit

---

48. *SJ* 117.3051; *HS* 57B.2585.

political intervention, in contrast to his other works for which Sima Qian describes the contexts of presentation and the emperor's responses. Sima Xiangru's forthright remonstrance against hunting seems to have been the only criticism that met with the emperor's comprehension and approval. Some later readers consider the *fu* lamenting the second Qin emperor a warning intended for Emperor Wu, although the neo-Confucian thinker Zhu Xi 朱熹 (1130–1200 CE), for one, faults the criticism (if indeed intended) for being too hesitant and muted. The fact that no response from Emperor Wu is recorded suggests that if remonstrance is intended, it misses the target. Others consider his "*Fu* on the Great Man" ("Daren fu" 大人賦) as ironic deflation of Emperor Wu's quest for immortality, adducing as evidence its pathetic image of the Queen Mother of the West 西王母 and the ambiguous final apotheosis of the Great Man's journey as he surveys a limitless void.[49] However, the final void, like the emperor's sudden conversion in "Shanglin," may be regarded as the one necessary step beyond ultimate power and glory, a crowning complement of totality rather than its ironic negation. Sima Xiangru's stated intention is to invoke a world more splendid than "Shanglin," and the emperor was indeed "greatly delighted, as if floating away on clouds and wandering between heaven and earth" 天子大說，飄飄有淩雲之氣，似游天地之間意。[50] From beyond the grave Sima Xiangru urges the performance of sacrifices to heaven and earth in "Writing on Feng and Shan Sacrifices" ("Feng shan wen" 封禪文), combining flattery with injunctions of moral vigilance.[51] Emperor Wu duly performs those sacrifices some years later, with scant regard for the supposed burden of moral perfection.

---

49. See, for example, Xu Fuguan, "Xi Han wenxue lun lue," 350–84. On the ambivalent vindication of immortality in "Fu on the Great Man," see Wai-yee Li, "On Becoming a Fish: Paradoxes of Immortality and Enlightenment in Chinese Literature," 29–59.

50. *SJ* 117.3063; *HS* 57B.2600: 天子大說，飄飄有陵雲氣游天地之間意。

51. The Qing scholar Zhang Yuzhao 張裕釗 (1823–94) reads "Writing on Feng and Shan Sacrifices" as "indirect remonstrance" 譎諷 with a "hidden and paradoxical" 隱詭 message, cited in Qian Zhongshu, *Guan Zhui bian*, 1.368. Xu Fuguan also argues in "Xi Han wenxue lunlue" that the enumeration of moral qualities necessary for the *feng* and *shan* sacrifices implicitly warns Emperor Wu that his virtue is inadequate for such an undertaking.

In his final comments, Sima Qian invokes hidden and manifest meanings, direct and indirect references, in the classics: "The *Spring and Autumn* probes the manifest to reach the hidden, the *Changes* is based in the hidden and moves toward the manifest. The *Greater Odes* speak of kings, lords, and great men, yet their virtue extends to the common people. The *Lesser Odes* criticize the mistakes and faults of the lesser officials, yet its flow reaches to those above. Although externally the words are different, in combining virtues they are the same. Although Xiangru has many unsubstantiated words and extravagant arguments, his main concern is to point the way to restraint and frugality. How is this different from the indirect criticism offered by the *Odes*?" 春秋推見至隱，易本隱之以顯，大雅言王公大人而得逮黎庶，小雅譏小己之得失，其流及上。所以言雖外殊，其合德一也。相如雖多虛辭濫說，然其要歸引之節儉，此與詩之諷諫何異。[52] Despite the final approbation, Sima Qian shows in the chapter how eloquence, erudition, and expansive imagination often fail as political intervention. Critical communications to the throne often have to be indirect in order to be countenanced at all; in the process the message is often lost. Compared with the itinerant persuader of the preceding era, the new figure of the court poet is more glamorous yet more subservient; he can only bury his remonstrative intention under an ever grander and more paradoxical rhetoric.[53] This remains the case even when the intention of political intervention is unmistakable, as in Sima Xiangru's writings about Ba and Shu.

Riddles, Ugly Women, and Hidden Agency

If indirect remonstrance often entails seduction or pandering, how do persuaders reclaim the authority to urge their message? The question of how to manipulate the resources of indirectness while at the same time preserving autonomy or even asserting power over the ruler might have bred the fantasy of the riddle maker who, by rousing the audience's curiosity and expectation, drives home the lesson. As noted above, a riddle is a kind of verbal pleasure; it is seduction by enigmatic concealment. But it is also a challenge: as distinct from

---

52. *SJ* 117.3073; *HS* 57B.2609.
53. Cf. Pines's essay in this volume and his *Envisioning Eternal Empire*, 115–84.

other forms of hidden meanings, it calls for a solution and puts the speaker immediately in a position of authority. Authority augmented by the dramatic revelation of hidden meaning also marks the difference with anecdotes that leave the decoding to the listener and thereby restores that listener's agency and powers of self-transformation (as in the great bird riddle discussed above).

For example, we may consider the story of Zhongli Chun 鐘離春 from *Lienü zhuan* 列女傳 (tenth entry in the chapter "Rhetorical Prowess" ["Biantong" 辯通]) and *Xinxu* 新序 ("Miscellany" ["Zashi" 雜事] 2.20), both attributed to Liu Xiang 劉向 (ca. 77–ca. 6 BCE). Zhongli Chun, an extremely ugly woman from Wuyan in Qi, sought marriage but found no match. Rejected and wandering, she offers herself at age forty as consort to the Qi king. She claims to admire the king's "beautiful righteousness" and to excel at riddles.

> King Xuan said, "Riddles are certainly what I desire. Give it a try." Before she finished speaking, she was all of a sudden not seen. Greatly taken aback, he immediately unearthed *The Book of Riddles* and read it. He withdrew and pondered this but could not fathom the meaning at all.
>
> The next day, he summoned her again and asked her, and she did not respond with riddles. But then she lifted her eyes and clenched her teeth, raised her hands and slapped her knees, saying, "Danger! Danger!" She went on like this four times.
>
> King Xuan said, "I wish to heed your command."
>
> Zhongli Chun replied, "Now you, great king, as ruler of the domain, face the danger of an aggressive Qin to the west, and the enmity of a dominant Chu to the south. From without you have the threat posed by these two domains, while within you have gathered deviant ministers. The multitudes do not support you. At forty years of age, you have not established a grown son as heir. You concern yourself not with many worthy men, but with your many consorts. You uphold what strikes your fancy and ignore what you need to rely on. The day will come when the great one succumbs, and the domain will be in chaos. This is the first danger. The Jian Terrace has five levels and is decked out in yellow gold and white jade, precious stones and elaborate woodwork, gems and jewels, while the people are worn out in the extreme. This is the second danger. Worthy men hide in mountain forests, sycophants lord it over others by your side. Deviant and deceitful ones are established at your very court, while those who remonstrate with you cannot gain admittance. This is the third

danger. Mired in indulgence in drinking through dusk and dawn, you abandon yourself to the reckless mirth of female musicians, jesters, and entertainers. In external affairs you have not attended to ritual propriety for other rulers, in internal affairs you have not taken on the government of the domain. This is the fourth danger. That is why I said, 'Danger! Danger!'"

King Xuan then heaved a sigh and said, "Sharp indeed are the words of Lady Wuyan. Only now do I get to listen to them!"

He then took down the Jian Terrace, disbanded the female musicians, sent the sycophants away, removed the elaborate decorations, chose armor and horses, and filled the treasury and arsenal. The lord's gates opened in four directions, inviting those with forthright words to come forward, and extending reach to the worthy among the lowly and obscure. He divined and chose an auspicious day for establishing the heir. He promoted his kindly mother, and bowed to honor Lady Wuyan as queen. That the domain of Qi was able to enjoy great peace was due to the effort of the ugly woman.

The noble man said, "Zhongli Chun was upright and had effective words."

宣王曰:「隱,固寡人之所願也,試一行之。」言未卒,忽然不見。宣王大驚,立發《隱書》而讀之,退而推之,又未能得。明日,又更召而問之,不以隱對,但揚目銜齒,舉手拊膝,曰:「殆哉!殆哉!」如此者四。宣王曰:「願遂聞命。」鍾離春對曰:「今大王之君國也,西有衛秦之患,南有強楚之讎,外有二國之難,內聚奸臣,眾人不附。春秋四十,壯男不立,不務眾子,而務眾婦,尊所好,忽所恃。一旦山陵崩弛,社稷不定,此一殆也。漸臺五重,黃金白玉,琅玕籠疏,翡翠珠璣,幕絡連綿,萬民罷極,此二殆也。賢者匿于山林,諂諛強于左右,邪僞立于本朝,諫者不得通入,此三殆也。飲酒沈湎,以夜繼晝,女樂俳優,縱橫大笑,外不修諸侯之禮,內不秉國家之治,此四殆也。故曰:『殆哉!殆哉』」于是宣王喟然而嘆曰:「痛哉!無鹽君之言,吾乃今一聞。」于是拆漸臺,罷女樂,退諂諛,去雕琢,選兵馬,實府庫,四辟公門,招進直言,延及側陋。卜擇吉日,立太子,進慈母,拜無鹽君爲后。而齊國大安者,醜女之力也。君子謂鍾離春正而有辭。[54]

Zhongli Chun is one of three ugly women in the chapter on "Rhetorical Prowess" in *Lienü zhuan*.[55] Fine rhetoric is sometimes linked

---

54. He and Zhu, eds., Gu Lienü zhuan *yu xian Qin liang Han dianji chongjian ziliao huibian* (hereafter *Lienü zhuan*), 143–44.

55. The other two are "the Qi woman with a goiter" 齊宿瘤女 and "the expelled orphan girl of Qi" 齊孤逐女.

to pleasing appearance: both are regarded as potentially deceptive.[56] Ugliness divests the persuader (and his or her rhetoric) of suspicions of seduction.[57] In Zhongli Chun's case, the absence of sexual attraction confirms the validity of her advice: despite her eventual position as King Xuan's queen, private emotions and public concerns will not be entangled.

On another level, ugliness speaks to the discrepancy between surface and meaning, appearance and reality: such distinctions are especially important in appointing advisors and ministers who might otherwise have seemed unlikely choices. Thus Warring States and Han texts refer often to worthy men in humble circumstances elevated by discerning rulers—examples include Yi Yin 伊尹, a cook who draws the attention of Tang, founder of Shang; Fu Yue 傅說, a conscript builder raised to high office by the Shang king Wuding 武丁; Lü Wang 呂望 (Taigong Wang 太公望), said to be a fisherman or butcher until in his old age he meets the future King Wu of Zhou 周武王; and Baili Xi 百里奚, subject of the vanquished domain, Yu, bought for five sheepskins by Lord Mu of Qin 秦穆公, who then relies on him to achieve the status of overlord. Indeed, Zhongli Chun's story comes after other stories of hidden worth and the dynamic of ruler-minister relationship in "Miscellany" in *Xinxu*, indicating common concerns.

Zhongli Chun attracts the king's attention with riddles. As noted above, the word for riddles, *yin*, also means "to conceal" or "to vanish."

---

56. In "Master Dengtu Enamored of Beauty" (Dengtu zi haose fu 登徒子好色賦), attributed to the nebulous Song Yu 宋玉 (ca. 3rd c. BCE?), the poet is accused of being a seducer, "pleasing and elegant in his deportment, and mouthing many clever, subtle words" 體貌閑雅，口多微辭, in Xiao Tong, *Zhaoming wenxuan*, 253. Yang Xiong famously compares excessive rhetoric to an overly adorned woman: "Or put it this way: a woman has beauty; does writing have beauty also? The answer is yes. The worst thing for a woman is to have her inner beauty beclouded by cosmetics; the worst thing for a piece of writing is to have its rules and standards confounded by excessive rhetoric." 或曰：「女有色，書亦有色乎？」曰：「有。女惡華丹之亂窈窕也，書惡淫辭之淈法度也。」. See Yang Xiong, "Wuzi" 吾子, in *Fayan yishu*, 57.

57. There is also a more general suspicion of beauty in *Lienü zhuan*. Beauty is consistently mentioned only in the seventh chapter on *femme fatales* (*Lienü zhuan*, 157–92). Virtuous women downplay their beauty for fear of beguiling the ruler (e.g., Queen Xuan Jiang of Zhou 周宣姜后, *Lienü zhuan*, 45).

In the received text of both *Lienü zhuan* and *Xinxu*, Zhongli Chun's riddles end in a vanishing act. Commentators aver textual corruption (based presumably on a misunderstanding of *yin* as "the vanishing act" when Zhongli Chun declares that she excels at *yin*) or try to rationalize the line "she was all of a sudden not seen" by restoring the "unseen" to the realm of rhetoric and meanings. Thus the late Qing woman scholar Xiao Daoguan 蕭道管 (1850–1907 CE): "'All of a sudden not seen' are words that the ancients use to describe how the principles of something cannot be fathomed. This is basically not about concealing one's form." 忽然不見，在古人乃事理難明之辭，本非隱形之謂也。 Another commentator, Chen Hanzhang 陳漢章, ties concealment to intention: "All of a sudden she hides her meaning about the failing domain and withdrew, that is why the text says she is 'not seen.'" 忽然隱其亡國之意而退，故云不見。[58]

Yet on another level there is continuity between the riddle and the vanishing act. Both test the boundaries of reason, both dramatize the need to rise above appearance, and both legitimize and heighten the otherwise questionable authority of the speaker or performer through remonstrance. We are not told the content of Zhongli Chun's riddles, we know only that they have the effect of rousing King Xuan from his stupor and sending him to search for answers in *The Book of Riddles*. When Zhongli Chun presents herself at court again, she refrains from riddles but enigmatically conveys anger or distress through expression and gestures that culminate in dramatic declarations of "danger." Her final remonstrance is straightforward; its effectiveness depends on the preceding stages of concealment and dramatization.

The psychological process of persuasion is marked more emphatically in the *Xinxu* version of the story. King Xuan has been listening to Zheng-Wei music (often decried as licentious) and is moved as much by the affective power of Zhongli Chun's performance as by the intellectual content of her arguments. His reaction to her remonstrance is likewise marked in dramatic, emotive terms: "Then King Xuan, subdued, made not one sound. His spirit, having entered the

58. The comments by Xiao Daoguan and Chen Hanzhang are both cited in Huang Qingquan, ed., *Xin yi Lienü zhuan*, 322.

Yellow Springs, all of a sudden reared up." 於是，宦工掩然無聲，意入黃泉，忽然而昂。[59]

Riddles allow an otherwise unlikely candidate to engage the ruler's attention. This also obtains in the story about Zhuang Zhi 莊姪, virgin of Chu, who also appears in the chapter "Rhetoric Prowess" in *Lienü zhuan*. The twelve-year-old Zhuang Zhi, troubled by the errors of King Qingxiang of Chu 楚頃襄王 (extravagance, unregulated travels, negligence regarding the succession, and rejection of remonstrance) and the mounting crisis facing Chu with Qu Yuan 屈原 in exile and Qin harboring aggressive designs, waylays the king against the explicit injunction of her mother not to do so. Catching the king's attention with banners by the road, she further addresses the king with riddles:

> "The great fish has lost its water. There is a dragon but it has no tail. The walls are about to collapse inward, but the king does not see it." The king said, "I do not understand this." Zhi replied, "The great fish has lost its water: this refers to how you, my king, have left the domain and are five hundred *li* away. With pleasures ahead of you, you do not think about the disasters that will come up later. There is a dragon but it has no tail: you are already forty years old but have no heir apparent. The domain has no strong support and will certainly be in great danger. The walls are about to collapse inward, but you do not see it: disasters and chaos are brewing, but you are not changing your ways."
>
> 「大魚失水，有龍無尾，墻欲內崩而王不視。」王曰：「不知也。」姪對曰：「大魚失水者，王離國五百里也，樂之於前，不思禍之起于後也；有龍無尾者，年既四十，無太子也，國無弼輔，必且殆也；墻欲內崩而王不視者，禍亂且成而王不改也。」[60]

The king's continued incomprehension (repeated three times) allows Zhuang Zhi to further elaborate the meanings of the riddles, the king's mistakes, and the dangers facing Qi. Finally convinced, the king returns with Zhuang Zhi to the Chu capital, just in time to quell a rebellion. He then honors her as chief consort. The noble man comments: "Although Zhuang Zhi goes against ritual propriety, she finally guards what is correct." 君子謂莊姪雖違于禮而終守以正。 A

59. The account from *Xinxu* is included in *Lienü zhuan*, 144–45.
60. *Lienü zhuan*, 149–50.

woman who remonstrates with the king and ends up becoming his consort always risk being deemed immodest and opportunistic. In this case, boldness is compounded by Zhuang Zhi's defiance of her mother.

Zhongli Chun and Zhuang Zhi use riddles to make their points, but they eschew the verbal resources associated with the riddle, such as equivocation, exaggeration, indirectness, and irony. Perhaps women are too easily suspected of seduction to be shown resorting to rhetorical performance that exaggerates the appeal of sensual pleasure. A female Chunyu Kun wallowing in the pleasures of immoderate drinking (only to urge restraint) or a female Sima Xiangru celebrating hunting in the imperial park (only to present its allegorical application to learning) would be hard to imagine.

The stories about women persuaders often dwell not on the vagaries of hidden meanings but on their hidden agency. A case in point is the orphan girl of Qi 齊孤逐女, also included in the chapter on "Rhetorical Prowess" in *Lienü zhuan*.[61] Expelled from her village because of her extreme ugliness, and having passed the time for marriage, she seeks an audience with King Xiang 齊襄王, who regards her misfortunes as a sign of extraordinary destiny and speaks to her for three days. On the first day, she asks the king about "the pillar of the domain" 國之柱 and explains how it refers to the prime minister. On the second day, he asks her opinion of his prime minister, whom she judges equal to the task if he has the proper helpers and associates.

> On the third day, the king said, "Can my prime minister be changed?" The expelled girl replied, "He is of middling talent. Someone like that cannot yet be found. If there is one who exceeds him, why can't it be done? But now there isn't anyone yet. I have heard that when an enlightened king uses people, he extends his reach. That is why Chu used Yu Qiuzi and obtained Shusun Ao; Yan used Guo Wei, and obtained Yue Yi. If you, great king, can spur him, then this one can be used."
>
> 其三日，王曰：「吾相其可易乎？」逐女對曰：「中才也，求之未可得也。如有過之者，何爲不可也？今則未有。妾聞明王之用人也，推一而用之，故楚用虞丘子，而得叔孫敖；燕用郭隗，而得樂毅。大王誠能厲之，則此可用矣。」

61. *Lienü zhuan*, 147–48.

To the king's question of how he should use his prime minister, the expelled girl elaborates on how things will inevitably have their "corresponding manifestations," so much so that by honoring the prime minister, he will attract other worthy helpers. The king follows the girl's advice and gives her to the prime minister as wife.

Zhongli Chun and Zhuang Zhi disappear into the harems of their respective rulers. The expelled girl from Qi resolves doubts about the prime minister's ability by shoring it up from within enclosed domestic space. The woman becomes the hidden agent who augments the judgment of ruler or minister but is herself not seen. This probably answers (or reflects) anxieties about the possibly pernicious role of women in public life and the potential conflict or competition between consort and minister. However, ultimately these stories about women persuaders are probably less about the historical reality of women in early China than about the dangers and possibilities of political persuasion. Their method may imply discontent with or suspicion of indirect remonstrance, yet they retain the aura of enigma (sometimes through the riddle, sometimes just by virtue of their mysterious charisma) to establish their authority to present direct arguments. Their hidden agency may also speak broadly to the fantasies and anxieties of persuaders: their *modus operandi* limited by the increasing power of the ruler, these stories imagine escape from the rigid hierarchy of ruler and subject by gaining the ruler's absolute trust, their authority becoming incontrovertible as their power and influence are enhanced by being invisible and indefinable.

The politics and aesthetics of the persuader's craft in early China are thus intertwined. Both the ruler and his subject can regard transformations and inscrutability as the source of power. Effective political persuasion often has to hide the wherewithal of its success, even as the ruler, swayed by his subject, may have to present acceptance of the persuader's views as his own inexplicable self-transformation. As noted above, various versions of anecdotes about riddles illustrate interpretations of the psychological tug-of-war between the ruler and the persuader. The riddle also shares enough common ground with other devices of indirect remonstrance for us to consider its affinity with the principle of instruction through seduction, a tactic shared by the remonstrating minister, the jester, and the court poet. All these associations are potentially troubling, and the anecdotes about ugly and unlikely women persuaders answer the anxieties about indirect remonstrance and uphold its promise of security and efficacy: they enact scenarios whereby the speaker retains the aura of enigma (sometimes through riddles) while keeping at bay any suspicion of seduction, and they conclude with affirmations of her silent integration into the inner circle of political influence, exercising control with stealth, while she remains ultimately intractable.

CHAPTER 5

How Did Ministers Err?

Garret P. S. Olberding, University of Oklahoma

The Power of the Historian

Much has been made of the singular commitment of premodern Chinese historians to moral didacticism, and to their use of historical tales or anecdotes to recommend a particular moral (or immoral) vision, particularly in relation to state governance. In his study of *Zuozhuan* 左傳, Henri Maspéro succinctly notes that "where we look for facts, nothing but facts, [a Chinese literatus] looks for a rule of life, a moral."[1] This priority on the moral is reinforced by the early Chinese commentaries to the *Spring and Autumn Annals* (*Chunqiu* 春秋). For many premodern Chinese commentators, all events in *Chunqiu* were treatable as signs or symbolic indicators addressing a religiomoral concern. Also common among premodern historians was the assertion that the *Annals* were composed or compiled by Confucius (孔子, 551–479 BCE), the "uncrowned king," who, as the title suggests, arrogated the official prerogative of the monarch to pronounce judgment on events. In classical China, the monarch was the head of both the religious and political community. Any final judgment or prognosis about the meaning of events, whether religious or political, required his imprimatur. Thus, in the religious sphere, only the ruler could authorize the interpretation of oracular

1. Maspéro, "La composition et la date du Tso tchouan," 207.

signs;[2] in the political sphere, it was also only the ruler who could authorize a historical record.[3] Those "scribes" (史), or "historians," who defied the ruler's wishes were liable to receive the death penalty for "treasonously" offering critique where none was requested. An oft cited tale from *Zuozhuan*, Cui Zhu's assassination of Lord Zhuang of Qi 齊莊公 (r. 553–548 CE), exemplifies the scribe's idealized function:

> The grand scribe wrote, "Cui Zhu assassinated his ruler." Cui Zhu put him to death. The scribe's younger brothers succeeded him and wrote the same thing, and so two more persons were killed. Another younger brother again wrote it, whereupon Cui Zhu desisted. The scribe of the south, having heard that the grand scribes had all died, clutched the bamboo strips and set out. When he heard that the record had already been made, he turned back.
>
> 大史書曰：「崔杼弒其君。」崔子殺之。其弟嗣書，而死者二人。其弟又書，乃舍之。南史氏聞大史盡死，執簡以往。聞既書矣，乃還。[4]

---

2. As David Keightley states, "The diviners might formulate the charges and preside over the divinatory rituals, but with few exceptions, only the king . . . had the ability to read the cracks. . . . His monopoly of the crucial interpretive act may plausibly be explained in terms of his kin relationship to the ancestors." See Keightley, "The Shang," 247.

3. 「世衰道微，邪說暴行有作，臣弒其君者有之，子弒其父者有之。孔子懼，作《春秋》。《春秋》、天子之事也；是故孔子曰：『知我者其惟《春秋》乎！罪我者其惟《春秋》乎！」In D. C. Lau's translation: "When the world declined and the Way fell into obscurity, heresies and violence again arose. There were instances of regicides and parricides. Confucius was apprehensive and composed the *Spring and Autumn Annals*. Strictly speaking, this is the Emperor's prerogative. That is why Confucius said, 'Those who understand me will do so through the *Spring and Autumn Annals*; those who condemn me will also do so because of the *Spring and Autumn Annals*.'" See Lau, trans., *Mencius*, 114. This ritualized sanctification of the power of the royal family overrode any claims to historical accuracy. For instance, Western Zhou records, such as the bronze inscriptions, did not "accommodate well the complexity and diversity of historical detail. . . . Reducing historical knowledge to a normative and ideal account, they create a memory sanctified by its performance in ancestral sacrifices and other rituals, a linguistically constructed parallel reality that with its own authority overrules the 'factual' one." The preeminence of ritual concerns over factual accuracy seemed to have been preserved in later eras. See Kern, "Poetry and Religion," 61–62.

4. *Zuo*, Xiang 25 (Yang, 1099). Translation is taken from Durrant, Li, and Schaberg, trans., *Zuozhuan*.

Though this tale is generally mentioned to reinforce an ideal model of the historian's mandate, it also reveals the implicit norm: scribes, in their writings, were not to contradict the ruler's judgments on affairs.

As the compiler of *Chunqiu*, Confucius ostensibly violated this norm. Assuming the king's prerogative, he, in essence, "ruled" through the text, subversively dispensing reward and punishment through his subtly encoded annalistic notations on late Zhou events. In the absence of a "true" king, Confucius, appointed by high Heaven, created a " 'true history' as a way of restoring the realm to the rites and the Right."[5] The attribution of the authorship or editing of *Chunqiu* to Confucius is now given little credibility, but the story achieves a phenomenally transformative effect: by ascribing to the "sage-king" Confucius the monarchical prerogative of passing judgment, early Chinese historians thus authorized themselves to do so. Through this, they asserted the separation of executive power from juridical power, the power of physical coercion ascribed to the executive from the normative authorization of power ascribed to scholars, the power to distinguish what is from what should be. In claiming the judge's mantle, scribes were asserting an independence that would forever frustrate the executive's desire to maintain hegemony over his own legacy. It is this standard that informs the enormous prestige conferred by the Chinese literati on those who have the courage to speak truth to power, to "directly remonstrate" (*zhijian* 直諫).[6]

Facts and Historical Logic

Maspéro's judgment that the Chinese histories do not emphasize, and thus devalue, factual accuracy is a very common one. Some scholars, such as Paul Goldin, have offered an even bolder thesis, that not only did early Chinese intellectuals *not* concern themselves with carefully representing the details of events, they went so far as to actively *distort* such details. For Goldin, Chinese scholars were representing events accurately in accordance with available evidence; in-

---

5. Nylan, *The Five "Confucian" Classics*, 265.

6. On the topic of "remonstrance," see, for instance, Schaberg, "Remonstrance in Eastern Zhou Historiography." In more modern terms, the right to "directly remonstrate" would probably be put in terms of "free speech."

deed, he is not sure that many of the major intellectual figures of early China, including such "rationalists" as Xunzi 荀子 (ca. 315–230 BCE), even "had a concept of evidence."[7] Referring to Xunzi's representation of the past, Goldin avers, "there is not much support for the inference that [he] would have taken care not to 'distort' history in order to buttress his ethical theories."[8] In sum, according to Goldin, "our notion of illegitimately 'distorting' the past would have been quite alien to the early Chinese intellectual world."[9] It is incorrect to suppose that Chinese historians "would have looked down on deliberate distortions of history."[10]

Evidence, for Goldin, "necessarily involves a concept of fact"; experience, by contrast, need not involve such. Early Chinese thinkers and writers, including the historians, "valued statements about the past that embodied what should have been true, regardless of whether they embodied what was true. History was expected to be edifying, not necessarily factual."[11] Goldin offers intriguing cases (such as the *Shi Qiang Pan* 史牆盤) in which the facts were garbled by those who must have known what had happened and wonders how this could have been possible. His conclusion, like Maspéro's, is that factual truth was often sacrificed on the altar of a grander moral truth.

Goldin and Maspéro rightly acknowledge the general carelessness or lack of interest among historians regarding the *precise* representation of the facts, and are certainly correct that many premodern Chinese historical documents are not reliable in every particular they represent. However, it remains unclear that historians were utterly unconcerned with preserving the general outline of the facts, or, to put it in Goldin's even bolder formulation, that they would simply not appreciate the importance of accuracy and the problems involved in willfully distorting the facts, that they would have had no sense about the ideal of avoiding the commission of factual errors. Though early Chinese historians, such as Sima Qian (司馬遷, 145–?86 BCE),

7. Goldin, "Appeals to History in Early Chinese Philosophy and Rhetoric," 80.
8. Ibid.
9. Ibid.
10. Ibid.
11. Ibid., 81.

seem not to have developed a robust commitment to factual accuracy, this is not due, I argue, solely to personal or cultural blindness to the salience of facts or the importance of accuracy. I hypothesize that it is also due to basic limitations on debate and discourse within a monarchic environment.[12] It was not that early Chinese historians had no concern with preserving facts but that in the uncertain monarchic climate, all knowledge was politicized and thus ultimately unreliable.[13] Because of this, I suspect, it was difficult for a historian to be certain whether his sources contained a factual error. Furthermore, for a government official much more worrisome than a simple factual error was risking the charge of slander, of an intentional, politically motivated distortion. In the intrinsically politically charged monarchic climate, a climate of intrigue and manipulation, the factual reliability of one's sources was, in all likelihood, extremely difficult to assess, or achieve.

The thesis I wish to forward in this essay is that not only were the facts not relied upon in court discussions; they were not consistently relied upon for just this reason, that is, the unreliability of most information in the distorting climate of intrigue and slander that is intrinsic to the monarchic circumstance. My ultimate aim in this study is to achieve a better understanding of how the use of "facts" in court discussions might have affected the outcome of state action and thus ultimately the course of the historical narrative. My analysis will largely focus on sample debates, addresses, and quoted remarks in the early Han histories as they speak to the value of facts. In particular, my analysis will attempt an answer to the following questions: (1) Did

---

12. Any number of studies in other areas of history reinforce my basic suspicion about the possibility of truth in unstable political climates. See, for instance, Walton, *Policing Public Opinion in the French Revolution*.

13. There of course may be notable exceptions to this general claim, such as Sima Guang 司馬光 (1019–86 CE). But even Sima Guang's standards for acceptable materials would be deemed relatively loose by our reckoning. He appeared to have had only two main criteria for distinguishing acceptable (true) from unacceptable (false) materials: positive evidence, "chiefly in the form of contradictions with known facts such as the calendar, and . . . inherent probability." Even in Sima Guang's case, it is not clear to what extent the facts were unexposed to political alteration. See Pulleyblank, "Chinese Historical Criticism," 157.

the emperor (or any other executive audience) reveal a discernable interest in receiving factually accurate information? (2) What did the employment of positive terms relating to "information" or the "substance of an affair," such as *shishi* 事實, or corresponding negative terms relating to error and mistake, such as *wu* 誤, *cuo* 錯, *e* 訛, or *yao yan* 妖言, suggest about the criteria by which information presented to the court was evaluated? (3) If not by a criterion of factual reliability, by what critical standard were ministerial discussions and remarks evaluated? Did such a critical standard share any resonance with factual accuracy?

Given its laconic annalistic form, any judgmental message discerned in *Chunqiu* needed to be decoded. It is thanks to the commentaries later associated with *Chunqiu*, particularly *Zuozhuan*, that we begin to have a tradition of historical narration in which anecdotal accounts flesh out the events merely indicated in *Chunqiu*. These anecdotes are romanticized, clearly, but they both align with known astronomical events and with other early records (such as the *Bamboo Annals*) to such an extent that we can rely on their general factual accuracy. Their romantic aspects appear not in the outline of events they record, but in the dramatization of these events, specifically in the included speeches and other narrative embellishments.

As David Schaberg has persuasively argued, while the speeches are clearly embellished, they are nonetheless central to the conception of the historical narrative, to its narrative logic, not only insofar as the story narratively progresses but also insofar as the story is represented as making any sense. Schaberg remarks that, in *Zuozhuan*, "narrative imports the events of the world into the text and in the process naturalizes assumptions of all sorts. But it is speech that makes assumptions patent."[14] In previous interpretations of the agenda of the documents or speeches recorded in the early commentaries and histories, the emphasis has been on norms and symbolic gestures through which the documents or speeches indicated their underlying moral lesson. My concern is to offer a renewed perspective into the basic construction of historical narrative, to ask to in what way the facts were acknowledged within cited debates and

14. Schaberg, *A Patterned Past*, 22.

addresses and, more specifically, in what ways error was perceived. To what extent was error related to the misuse of evidence, of the facts?

The Emperor's Desire for Accurate Information

Though the precise configurations of the emperor's power were neither as certain nor as far-reaching as those of modern totalitarian rulers, his executive authority was nevertheless sufficient to sustain the apparent general consensus that comments should be addressed *as if* he were the ultimate arbiter of state affairs. Thus he appears in the addresses and in many portrayals of court interaction as if he were the possessor of centralized, autocratic authority.[15] Access to the emperor was restricted and, as Liao Boyuan 廖伯源 has noted, news about the state of affairs in the empire was subject to official filtering. Officials were cognizant of the need to supervise, and, if necessary, censor the information the emperor received. If the emperor wished to obtain unfiltered reports from the various regions of the empire, he was often forced to depend on local officials and clerks to act as his eyes and ears.[16] Naturally, such information was never perfectly secure, and thus was not absolutely reliable. There was always the danger of the information being corrupted or altered before the emperor received it.[17] And yet Former Han emperors are repeatedly described in the histories of the Former Han (206 BCE–9 CE) as being interested in reliable information about the actual state of the empire

15. Yet, as Michael Loewe remarks, the Han dynasty "witnessed a number of occasions when the personal powers of the emperor were reduced to a point of disappearance, in favour of the control of government by other parties." See Loewe, "The Authority of the Emperors of Ch'in and Han," 82.

16. Liao, *Shizhe guanzhi yanbian*, 105

17. One measure to prevent the alteration of documents sent to the court was to mark at the end of the document the total number of graphs, to ensure that nothing was either excised or added. Such is a common feature in the provincial statistics from the end of the Former Han dynasty recorded in the administrative documents found at Yinwan 尹灣, Jiangsu province. See Enno Giele's article: Ji Annuo, "Yinwan xinchutu xingzheng wenshu de xingzhi yu Handai difang xingzheng," 21–45. See also Giele, *Imperial Decision-Making and Communication in Early China*, 138. Of course, such measures could not prevent absolutely the outright forgery of a new set of documents; thus, the continued concern on the emperor's part that the information received was false or distorted.

and the prosecution of governmental affairs. They frequently sent emissaries to "travel to the various commanderies and kingdoms" (*xing junguo* 行郡國), to "conduct a general review" (*xingshi* 行視), or "to travel to the various parts of All-Under-Heaven [to observe general trends]" (*xunxing tianxia* 巡行天下). The reviews had two principal aims. One was to root out corruption: to determine if the people were being ill-treated or if they were unable to make a living or if the local officials were taking bribes or were overly punitive. A second was to determine whether there were extraordinary situations or projects to which the emperor needed to devote particular attention. No matter what the concern, one could reasonably suppose the emperor hoped for the delivery of relevant, generally accurate information to make an informed, appropriate decision. The less accurate the information, the less effective his executive responses.

The recent discovery of administrative records at sites such as Juyan 居延, Yinwan 尹灣, Zhangjiashan 張家山, and Zoumalou 走馬樓 afford a much deeper insight into Han administrative practice, but few archaeological finds as yet show us what information might have arrived at court. By contrast, in the historical records, we are afforded numerous detailed representations of the processes by which the business of state was conducted, and, more specifically, the manner in which discursive exchanges between the monarch and his subjects unfolded. If the *Yili* 儀禮 is any indication, there were manifold prescriptions detailing how a subject was to present himself at court, whether related to the manner of dress or the direction in which he was permitted to look.[18] During these interviews, monarchs were clearly concerned with handling state affairs efficiently and quickly. They wanted to know, presumably as succinctly as possible, just what was at issue and what bore on it. Monarchs repeatedly complain about being "wearied" by eloquent men; ministers, correspondingly, were quite aware of the dangers of wasting the monarch's time. A Warring States persuader-diplomat, Fan Sui 范睢 (?–255 BCE), phrases his hesitance even to address his monarch in this way: "Now since my neck can't stand up to a chopping block and ax

18. For instance, never were subjects supposed to look directly into the monarch's face. See *SJ* 87.2558; Watson, trans., *Records of the Grand Historian: Qin Dynasty*, 198.

and my waist can't fend off a battle-ax or war-ax, how would I dare to offer dubious matters before Your Majesty?" 今臣之胸不足以當椹質，而要不足以待斧鉞，豈敢以疑事嘗試於王哉！[19] Here, Fan Sui worries openly that his remarks will exhaust his monarch's patience. Just as significantly, he asserts that the affairs are troubling, "dubious," matters on which a decision cannot easily be made, whether because of their complexity, or because the information on which any decision had to depend was unreliable, incomplete, or simply suspicious. The term, *yishi* 疑事, translatable as "dubious matters," or, better yet, "troubling matters," although not seen very frequently in the early Han histories, almost uniformly refers to those matters that result in indecision and insecurity.[20] "Troubling" matters were those that were difficult to sort out and monarchs were loath to have to resolve them. Zhao Gao 趙高 (?–207 BCE), for instance, in his plot to take control of governmental affairs, advises the Second Emperor of Qin 秦二世 (r. 209–207 BCE) not to handle matters himself and risk looking foolish but to entrust the administration to his ministers. Zhao Gao asserts that the emperor's removing himself from daily affairs will make officials reluctant to bring forward "troubling matters." While it is not entirely clear why Zhao Gao believes the emperor's withdrawal will suppress the number of ministers requesting an audience, I argue that it almost certainly reveals a concern on those ministers' part of imposing on the emperor.[21]

---

19. Nienhauser, gen. ed., *The Grade Scribe's Records*, vol. 7, 235. For another translation of this, see Watson, trans., *Records of the Grand Historian: Qin Dynasty*, 134.

20. Two of the eight appearances of the term in the *Shiji* and the *Hanshu* are used within what seems to have been a familiar maxim: "You will attain nothing if you are (continuously) in doubt about how to handle a matter. You will win no reputation if you are (continuously) in doubt about how to act" 疑事無功，疑行無名. See *SJ* 43.1807 and 68.2229. For another compelling instance, see *SJ* 122.3139. But there are several substantiating references from other sources. See, for instance, *Liji*, "Quli" *shang*: "Do not positively affirm what you have doubts about; and (when you have no doubts), do not let what you say appear (simply) as your own view" 疑事毋質，直而勿有. *Liji zheng yi*, vol. 1, 9; Legge, trans., *Li Chi*, vol. 1, 62. See also Wei Shou, comp., *Weishu* 魏書 82.1798.

21. 「今坐朝廷，譴舉有不當者，則見短於大臣，非所以示神明於天下也。且陛下深拱禁中，與臣及侍中習法者待事，事來有以揆之。如此則大臣不敢奏疑事，天下稱聖主矣。」See *SJ* 87.2558. I contend that my and Nienhauser's translation of *yi* 疑 as "troubling" or "dubious," with the nuance of suspiciousness or questionability, is

While at court, the emperor's principal task was to listen to various reports and addresses, and decide how to respond. Zhao Gao, in the same passage mentioned above, explains how, with a competent leader such as the Second Emperor's father, none of the officials would dare present false or misleading reports, for fear of punishment:

> Zhao Gao persuaded the Second Emperor, saying:
>
> The First Emperor personally administered All-Under-Heaven for a long time. The many ministers did not dare to act falsely or forward slanderous statements. Now, Your Majesty is rich in the number of years left to You and has just recently ascended to his position. For what reason would You convene with high ministers in court to decide matters? If the matters were to be mistakenly handled, this would expose to the many ministers Your shortcomings. The Son of Heaven refers to himself as *zhen* (which symbolizes his superior status). One definitely should not hear His voice.
>
> 趙高說二世曰:「先帝臨制天下久,故群臣不敢爲非,進邪說。今陛下富於春秋,初即位,柰何與公卿廷決事?事即有誤,示群臣短也. 天子稱朕,固不聞聲。」[22]

Though Zhao Gao's most salient concern is with the emperor's committing an error, the root of the error lies with the emperor being misled by false actions (*wei fei* 爲非) or malicious statements (*xie shuo* 邪說). It thus appears that the essence of the emperor's error is grounded in his misperception of the matter at hand, and it is unclear whether the emperor could ever have had access to the unbiased, unfiltered materials necessary to correct any error. Here the term that can be translated as "mistake" or "mistakenly" is *wu* 誤. Its appearance in this instance does not explain what is meant by a "mistake," nor does its appearance at any other point in the *Shiji*. Indeed, upon examination, any number of terms plausibly translated as "mistake," "error," or "falsehoods" either do not appear in the *Shiji* or *Hanshu* at all (as in the

---

more accurate than the more general "problematic" or "difficult," as Watson proposes in some of his translations. See Watson, trans., *Records of the Grand Historian: Han Dynasty II*, 387. Doubt, in early China, was very intimately connected with the suspiciousness of the claim, of the unreliability of the source and the general culture of suspicion. See, for instance, *HS* 53.2419.

22. See *SJ* 6.271.

case of *huang* 謊),[23] or appear in contexts that suggest excesses in conduct or judgment, not inaccuracies in sources or materials. One might suspect that scarcity of references to inaccurate information indicates a general lack of interest in considering facts when discussing state business in the early Chinese court, that facts were either not deemed of much use or were not important for the historical representations of state affairs. This suspicion, however, is challenged by much in the records.

In many of the multifarious addresses submitted to the emperor, particulars relating to concrete circumstances, whether they were of the quantifiable sort or not, were judged of utmost relevance and were regularly cited in discussions of state affairs. More to the point, in those instances where his questions or responses elaborate upon the submitted addresses, the monarch's responses reveal his interest in the particulars relating to concrete circumstances.[24] His responses also acknowledge the import of concrete particulars and his judgment of their applicability to the matter at hand. However, the type of response that would definitively confirm the emperor's interest

23. The term is hardly used in much of early Chinese literature. It is used in none of the "Confucian" classics, though it does appear in *Lüshi chunqiu* 16.3: 「瞑士未嘗照，故未嘗見，瞑者目無由接也。無由接而言見，謊。」

24. Though the following instance is not a monarchical response to a debate or address, it very clearly reveals Emperor Yuan's interest in knowing exactly what is going on: "In the first year of the *yung-kuang* era (43 BCE), frost fell in the spring, the summer was cold, and the sun shone gray and lusterless. The emperor once more issued an order berating the chancellor and imperial secretary on a number of counts, saying, 'Palace attendants returning from the east tell me that the people are in such desperate straits that father and son turn their backs on one another. Are the officials under your jurisdiction hiding the truth and failing to report it to you? Or are those who come from the east exaggerating the true state of affairs? Why should there be such discrepancies? I want to know the truth! It is too soon to predict what kind of harvest we will have this year, but if there should be floods or droughts, the damage will be far from slight. You, the high officials, are supposed to be able to take steps to prevent future disasters and to remedy those which have already occurred, are you not? I want each of you to give a sincere reply, without fear of saying anything that will offend me!" 「永光元年，春霜夏寒，日青亡光，上復以詔條責曰：「郎有從東方來者，言民父子相棄。丞相、御史案事之吏匿不言邪？將從東方來者加增之也？何以錯繆至是？欲知其實。方今年歲未可預知也，即有水旱，其憂不細。公卿有可以防其未然，救其已然者不？各以誠對，毋有所諱。」 See *HS* 71.3044–45; Watson, trans., *Courtier and Commoner in Ancient China*, 169.

not only in concrete particulars in general but also in their *accuracy* is notably absent. We nowhere find an announcement by the monarch that information presented to him is actually just demonstrably *wrong,* succeeded by his forwarding other concrete particulars that justify his contradiction of the erroneous materials. Nowhere in early Chinese historical documents (at least none I have read) does a monarch assert that such and such description of a concrete matter is directly contradicted by reliable information.[25] The closest approximation we have to an outright contradiction is the monarch's calling into question the relevance of the proffered information. For instance, in Zhao Chongguo's celebrated address to Emperor Xuan, the young emperor, exasperated by Zhao Chongguo's refusal to aggressively attack the Qiang, overtly confronts him. At one point in their exchange, after Zhao Chongguo had again insisted on pursuing a war of attrition by encroaching on Qiang lands using military colonies, Emperor Xuan insinuates that Zhao Chongguo's detailed plan will never lead to the defeat of the Qiang:

> His Highness responded:
>
> "The August Thearch questions the General of the Rear Zhao Chongguo about his remarks about his wish to disband the cavalry, leaving ten thousand people in the agricultural fields. Even if we act according to the General's plans, when will the Qiang vermin submit to punishment [i.e., military defeat]? When will the army achieve decisive action? After you consider carefully the expediency of your plan, present another address."
>
> 上報曰：「皇帝問後將軍，言欲罷騎兵萬人留田，即如將軍之計，虜當何時伏誅，兵當何時得決？孰計其便，復奏。」[26]

---

25. It is significant to note that in the various exchanges between ministers, such as are captured in *Zhanguoce* 戰國策, the early Han histories, or the *Debates on Salt and Iron* (*Yantielun* 鹽鐵論), the ministers, even among themselves, never appear to contradict, directly or indirectly, the assorted concrete particulars. For an extended examination of this, see Olberding, *Dubious Facts,* chaps. 6 and 8.

26. Olberding, *Dubious Facts,* 140. The late Edward Dreyer offers the following version of the passage: "The Emperor has heard that the General of the Rear says he wants to disband his cavalry and retain [only] 10,000 men to till the fields. What sort of general would plan this? When will the enemy be exterminated? When will our troops gain a decision? If you can figure out why this plan is to our advantage, memorialize again!" See Dreyer, "Zhao Chongguo," 696.

Emperor Xuan is plainly not convinced by Zhao's proposals, in spite of the extraordinary level of detail and Zhao's meticulous exposition about how his plan will work. The emperor either does not believe military colonies will be at all effective or believes they must be used in tandem with more aggressive measures.

There are, in sum, clear indications in the exchanges between monarch and ministers that securing the accuracy of relevant concrete particulars is among the monarch's interests in his deliberative process. He confesses this interest in his queries to ministers. The ministers acknowledge it in their presentations and sometimes the emperor even seeks to secure it rather directly. In no way do we see monarchs ignorant of the essential function of accurate concrete particulars and their need of such to develop effective policy.

Perception of "Reality"

With these select exchanges between monarchs and their ministers we can begin to prove general interest in accurate representation, but more broad-ranging signs of interest in the accurate representation of concrete reality are also found in the use of various terms pertaining to the perception of a state of affairs. Positive expressions include *ran* 然 "it is so," *shi* 是 "corresponds to this state of affairs," and *shishi* 事實 "the substance (or reality) of affairs," often translated simply as the "facts."[27] There are also, of course, negative expressions that imply a contradiction of an actual state of affairs, such as *fei* 非 "to contradict,"

27. Vogelsang argues that Ying Shao's 應劭 (fl. 2nd c. CE) comment regarding Ban Gu's appraising Sima Qian's *Records* as a *shilu* 實錄 is the reason for subsequent assertions that Sima Qian was an "objective" historian. Ying Shao defines the *shilu* as that which records *shishi* 事實, which are, in Vogelsang's translation, the "facts of the matter." In a footnote, Vogelsang insists that translating the term *shishi* as "facts of the matter" is well supported by its appearances in the *Hanshu*, citing *HS* 25B.1251 and 30.1715. The term appears a total of eight times in the *Hanshu* and twice in the *Records*. Though it is clear that it has something to do with truth, as opposed to erroneous, empty, or sycophantic speech, it is not at all clear in its appearances whether it really can be translated as "facts" or "facts of the matter." Indeed, in a very illuminating passage, Zuo Qiuming is said to have "given form" in *Zuozhuan* to the *shishi* noted in *Chunqiu*. See *HS* 30.1715 and Vogelsang, "Some Notions of Historical Judgment in China and the West," 152, n. 41. Various other scholars agree that *shishi* should be translated as "facts of the matter." See also Kern, "Poetry and Religion," 53–54.

as well as terms that seem to imply the use of incorrect or mistaken information (and not simply an incorrect or mistaken viewpoint): terms such as *wu* 誤, of course, but also *bu shi* 不實 ("not in accord with the substance [of the affair]"), *bu dang* 不當 ("not fitting"), and *yao yan* 妖言 ("deceptive statements").

As already mentioned, in most instances there is little that precisely defines just what the source of an error was. A typical example of an unexplained attribution of error is the above quoted excerpt from Zhao Gao's conversation with the Second Emperor of Qin, Huhai 胡亥.[28] In his speech, the term translated as "error" is *wu* 誤, and the error involved how a matter or affair (*shi* 事) could be handled.[29] Other instances of the use of *wu* reveal nuances of deception or being misled, instances such as King Hui of Yan's 燕惠王 (r. 278–272 BCE): "I, King Hui of Yan, was new in my position and those around me [at court] led me into error" 寡人新即位,左右誤寡人.[30] Fortunately, a few exchanges in the *Records of the Grand Historian* reveal more about the kinds of errors that led to distortions of perception and judgment. In the following exchange between the king of Zhao 趙, Zhang Ao 張敖 (r. 202–198 BCE), and his supporters, Zhang Ao castigates them for their "erroneous" characterization, and thus their perception, of Gaozu, the first emperor of Han (r. 206–195 BCE):

> In the seventh year of Han, Gaozu on his way from Pingcheng passed through Zhao. The king of Zhao, Zhang Ao, morning and evening bared his shoulders, donned sleeve guards and apron, and personally offered food to the emperor, behaving with extreme deference in his ritual conduct, acting in accord with the rites for a son-in-law. Gaozu sat with his legs sprawled and cursed Zhang Ao, showing extreme disrespect toward him. Guan Gao, the chancellor of Zhao, Zhao Wu and others, men over sixty years of age who had long ago been Zhang Er's retainers and who always gave vent to their tempers, were furi-

28. Quoted in the previous section of this essay.

29. Indeed, I find the employment of *wu* to be more revelatory in any notion of evidentiary error than many other terms commonly used to denote error, such as *guo* 過 or *guoshi* 過失, which are more accurately translated as "excess"; *cuo* 錯, which should be translated as "confused" or "confusion"; or *miu* 謬, which denotes an error in judgment, not in perception or fact.

30. *SJ* 80.2430.

> ous, saying, "Our king is a weak king!" They then argued with the king of Zhao, saying, "When the outstanding men of All-Under-Heaven rose up together [against Qin], it was those who were capable who were first established as rulers. Now the King serves Gaozu with extreme deference and yet Gaozu has no manners. We beg to kill him for the King!" Zhang Ao bit his finger so hard that he drew blood, saying, "You all speak erroneously! When my father lost his state, he depended on Gaozu to reclaim it. Gaozu's virtue flows to the sons and grandsons of my father. Even the smallest hair on my body is owed to Gaozu's power. I wish you all do not again open your mouths about this." Guan Gao, Zhao Wu, and the other ten or so men all responded saying, "Then we all have spoken incorrectly. Our king is an exemplary man who will not betray Gaozu's virtuous conduct."
>
> 漢七年，高祖從平城過趙，趙王朝夕袒韝蔽，自上食，禮甚卑，有子壻禮。高祖箕踞詈，甚慢易之。趙相貫高、趙午等年六十餘，故張耳客也。生平爲氣，乃怒曰：「吾王孱王也！」說王曰：「夫天下豪桀並起，能者先立。今王事高祖甚恭，而高祖無禮，請爲王殺之！」張敖齧其指出血，曰：「君何言之誤！且先人亡國，賴高祖得復國，德流子孫，秋豪皆高祖力也。願君無復出口。」貫高、趙午等十餘人皆相謂曰：「乃吾等非也。吾王長者，不倍德。」[31]

By contradicting their perceptions, Zhang Ao wishes to dissuade his men from murdering Gaozu. His men have spoken "erroneously" (*yan zhi wu* 言之誤), their judgment about Gaozu "incorrectly" ignoring the protection Gaozu offered Zhang Ao's father in the past, an arrangement that may not be completely accurate, but that Zhang Ao offers as established fact and that none dare to contradict. Because of Gaozu's past favor, Zhang Ao insists that he has a duty to be deferential, in spite of Gaozu's poor behavior.

Such appraisals of character and of what characters deserve are a common area of erroneous perception. Though these errors often involved judgments about action, they significantly center on the perceptions that inform judgment. Two additional instances further substantiate this: first, the dispute about the ranking of Xiao He 蕭何 (?–193 BCE) over Cao San 曹參 (?–190 BCE)[32] and, second, the dispute

---

31. *SJ* 89.2583. For alternate translations, see Watson, trans., *Records of the Grand Historian: Han Dynasty*, vol. 1, 142, and Nienhauser, gen. ed., *The Grand Scribe's Records: The Memoirs of Han China,* Vol. 8, 20.

32. See *SJ* 53.2016.

about whether Han Xin 韓信 (?–196 BCE) should trust Gaozu.[33] In both instances, two objectors, Gentleman E 鄂君 (E Qiu 鄂秋, ?–193 BCE) and Kuai Tong 蒯通 (fl. 3rd–2nd c. BCE), make cases in which they explicitly assert that others have been mistaken in their perceptions. But as with the above instance, the insistent identification of error does not contradict what has been perceived. Returning to the example discussed above, Zhang Ao does not contest that Gaozu has been rude or disrespectful; rather the source of his men's error about Gaozu's character is their lack of cognizance of or emphasis on Gaozu's early support of Zhang's father. In the case of the ranking of Xiao He over Cao San, Gentleman E avers that the many courtiers who advocated ranking Cao San over Xiao He had overlooked or undervalued Xiao He's numerous contributions. Regarding whether Han Xin should trust Gaozu, Kuai Tong insists that Han Xin is wrong (*wu* 誤) to put any faith in his relationship with Gaozu, saying that even the most secure relationships are prone to betrayal when political interests are involved. In all three of these instances, the basis of the error is less inaccuracy in perception than lacking (*que* 缺) the proper information. Indeed, their error is akin to the error of a document that "lacks" complete information: a document is "lacking" and thus flawed or mistaken.

Notably, in the above-cited instances in which people's perceptions are deemed erroneous, as lacking in some respect, there is tacit sympathy between the speaker and his audience. Zhang Ao shares his men's irritation with Gaozu; Gentleman E 鄂, in contrast to other courtiers, shares the emperor's stated preference for Xiao He over Cao San. Thus "error" in both circumstances—and, I would suggest, in most circumstances—is not an objectively incontestable error. It is instead an error of emphasis or of ignorance, a deficiency that allows the original perception of the interlocutor to remain basically unaltered. The loose boundaries of the sources of error—that it commonly appears to be treated as stemming from the manner in which information is communicated or received rather than any objective discrepancy between what is perceived and what is the case—

33. See *SJ* 92.2624–25.

permits an expanded boundary on what could have been treated as reliable and useful.

Rumor and Natural Signs as Information

If error is not commonly characterized as a stark error in perception, the issue is less perception than what is deemed most salient in its representation.[34] Such a hypothesis would seem to be supported by various applications of not only *wu* 誤 to discussions of court affairs but also other terms such as *e* 訛, generally translatable as "rumor." In the Han histories, at first glance, the term appears to denote a kind of false representation. In the following example, a young girl comes to the capital to report that a great flood was approaching the capital, terrifying the government clerks. The emperor blames this reputedly "false rumor" on the mistreatment of the common people by the local government officials:

> In the fall, there was a great flood in the capital area, the Area Within the Pass. In the seventh month, a young girl from Tishang named Chen Chigong heard that a great flood was coming and ran into the Hengcheng Gate, and without proper documentation entered a side gate into the Weiyang Palace gardener's office [and announced the news]. The clerks and commoners climbed the city walls in fright. In the ninth month, the emperor issued an edict: "Recently, certain commanderies and kingdoms suffered flooding, which led to the drowning of many people, as many as several thousand. Members of the court without basis spread the rumor that a great flood was coming. The clerks and the commoners were frightened and fled to climb the city walls. This occurred probably because the cruel, violent, and harshly punitive [local] clerks have not yet desisted [in their acts of cruelty] and a multitude of commoners have unfairly been deprived of their livelihoods. I hereby dispatch Grand Master of Remonstrance Lin, among others, to make a tour of All-Under-Heaven."
>
> 秋，關內大水。七月，虒上小女陳持弓聞大水至，走入橫城門，闌入尚方掖門，至未央宮鉤盾中。吏民驚上城。九月，詔曰：「乃者郡國被水災，

34. This distinction would certainly be in keeping with the ancient practice of intentionally misrepresenting embarrassing past events. See Kern, "Poetry and Religion," 57–58 and 60.

> 流殺人民，多至千數。京師無故訛言大水至，吏民驚恐，奔走乘城。殆苛暴深刻之吏未息，元元冤失職者眾。遣諫大夫林等循行天下。」[35]

Though it does not appear very often in the Han historical records, the employment of *e* 訛 is significant in several respects. It almost invariably describes the reaction of the common people to extraordinary natural phenomena, such as an eclipse, an earthquake, or, as in the example above, a flood, reactions that were communicated using folk songs and rhymed chants, the common vehicles of rumor. The promulgation of such rumors is often mentioned in conjunction with attempts to divine with lots, commonly phrased as, "The commoners spread rumors and cast lots" 民訛言行籌.[36] These rumors—accusatory words or chants—were perceived by members of the court, and by the emperor himself, to indicate the state of the common people. Thus though they are denigrated by officials as false representations of events, they nevertheless are important sources of information for the court, for they reveal the underlying discomfiture or unease among the populace, a sign that the governance of the empire is flawed, corrupt, or somehow inadequate.

While peasants could theoretically communicate their grievances through the presentation of an official petition at court,[37] in practice,

---

35. See *HS* 10.306–7. See also *HS* 97.3979, 75.3181, 82.3370 for references to the same story.

36. See *HS* 85.3476, 85.3479, 86.3496, 72.3091, 45.2184.

37. Enno Giele notes that, starting in 68 BCE, submissions could be presented directly to the emperor, with the introduction of *fengshi*, or memorials of "sealed matters," submissions that were not screened by the secretariat. "The Biography of Huo Guang" in the *Hanshu* "reveals that direct submissions were not merely a prerogative of the high-ranking officials, but were principally also an option for common people." Yet even these direct submissions "were not really directly communicated from subject to emperor, but had to make use of the eunuch institution of palace secretaries (or perhaps also palace receptionists)," and thus were also subject to tampering. Once instituted under Emperor Xuan 宣帝 (r. 73–49 BCE), Giele notes, the practice of these direct submissions continued through the Han and into later eras. Though direct submissions were not in the majority of submissions, they were an important source of information about the empire, for as Giele, referring to Liao Boyuan's research, mentions, "they served the emperor in multiple ways by providing a source of more, speedier and better information and by forcing the officials to disclose their attitudes and thereby to keep them under control." See Giele, *Imperial Decision-Making and Communication in Early China*, 69–71.

most presumably did not, either because of the difficulty of verifying its transmission to the proper authorities (venal local authorities could interfere) or because the personal risks were too great. Instead, most of the information gathered from the populace appears to have been gathered informally or through the emperor's own emissaries. Indeed, there are a host of references in early Chinese literature to the need for the monarch to listen to the grievances of the common people. Martin Kern notes that, starting with *Zuozhuan*, anonymous folk songs "frequently announce major calamities like the untimely death of a ruler, a major military defeat, or even the fall of a state. Such prophecies are couched in simple rhymes and gain much of their authority from the ideal of innocent and undistorted truth embodied in the minds and voices of the common people or, quite often, children."[38] Clearly, the major purpose of these folk songs or chants was the communication of bad news. Early employments of *e* 訛 in the *Shijing* emphasize the critical nature of folk songs, as illustrated in this passage:

> Layers of frost in the first month,
> My heart suffers with worry.
> [Accusatory] chants among the common people
> Are already very prevalent.
>
> 正月繁霜，我心憂傷. 民之訛言，亦孔之將。[39]

---

38. Kern, "Poetry and Religion," 67.

39. "Zhengyue" 正月, Mao, no. 191. See Li, ed., *Maoshi zhengyi*, vol. 2, 706–7. In Zheng Xuan's 鄭玄 (127–200 CE) commentary, he notes that the "first month" is meant to refer to the fourth month of summer; thus the poet's concern about the unnatural weather. Zheng Xuan also defines *e* 訛 as "falsehoods" (*wei* 僞), interpreting the phrase as indicating that moral turpitude is so prevalent that people are using falsehoods to trick each other, leading the king to apply extremely harsh punishments, an unnatural state of affairs that has produced the the natural world itself to act unnaturally. Thus, Zheng Xuan concludes, the narrator speaks of the falsehoods of the common people as being especially flagrant. (人以僞言相陷，人使王行酷暴之刑，致此災異，故言亦甚大也。) In this instance, I believe Zheng Xuan's interpretation might be incorrect. In many of the appearances of *jiang* 將 in the *Odes*, its meaning relates to dissemination, offering, presentation—moving about. For instance, in the ode "Full," the female narrator speaks of her wish to leave with a handsome man, saying, "I regret that I did not go with him" 悔予不將兮. ("Feng" 丰, Mao, no. 88; *Maoshi zhengyi*, vol. 1, 309). In "Zhengyue", I argue, the narrator is actually speaking to the prevalence of the commoners' remarks, not their falseness. If my argument is correct, clearly, by Zheng Xuan's time, peasant chants were perceived by

Although these rumors, or accusatory chants, came to be treated, perhaps intentionally, by the authorities as false representations of the actual state of affairs, they were not therefore to be dismissed out of hand. Faced with the pervasive corruption of official channels, the monarch was obliged to marshal every possible resource. Indeed, monarchs were repeatedly adjured by their (presumably well-meaning) advisers to pay close attention to what the common people were saying, or risk social unrest.[40] As Liu Tao 劉陶 (?–185 CE) advocated in the Latter Han (25–220 CE) to Emperor Huan 桓 (Liu Zhi 劉志, r. 147–167 CE),

> Listen to the folk tunes of the commoners; inquire after that about which the old man on the road worries; scrutinize the patterned brilliance of the sun, moon, and stars; observe the convolutions and curves of the mountains and rivers. Then will you immediately understand the mind of All-Under-Heaven, the great affairs of the states and households, and there will be no confusion born of oversight and omission.
>
> 聽民庶之謠吟，問路叟之所憂，瞰三光之文耀，視山河之分流。天下之心，國家大事，粲然皆見，無有遺惑者矣。[41]

---

officials in a very negative light, and often dismissed as falsehoods, a possible indication of the concern about the upheaval that might be brought about were commoners given a voice.

40. For instance, in the *Record of Rites* (*Liji* 禮記), the "Master" remarks: "If the monarch weighs carefully the words of the common people, then His subjects will [feel as if they are receiving] Heaven's bestowed favors. If the monarch does not weigh carefully the words of the common people, then they will oppose Him. If His subjects do not [feel as if they are receiving] Heaven's bestowed favors, then disorder will ensue. Therefore if the Gentleman supervises the common people in a trustworthy and humble manner, the common people's reciprocity will be impressive. The *Odes* say, 'In ages past the common people have said that [to understand how to govern], one need inquire with the wood-cutter.'" (子云：上酌民言，則下天上施；上不酌民言，則犯也；下不天上施，則亂也。故君子信讓以蒞百姓，則民之報禮重。詩云：先民有言，詢於芻蕘。) See *Li ji zheng yi*, vol. 2, 1406–7.

41. *HHS* 57.1846. In footnote 6, there is a fascinating reference to a passage from the *Liezi* that might offer further support for my claims here: "Liezi said, "Previously Yao managed All-Under-Heaven for fifty years and did not know if the empire was managed properly or was in disorder. Yao thus traveled in disguise about the thoroughfares. [On one] a young boy chanted, 'If [You, the emperor] pacify our common people, there will be no limit to the reaches of Your [bounty]. [The commoners] do not comprehend, do not understand [governance], [they just] fol-

Since they apparently arose from the general populace, these folk chants avoided the corruptions that frequently plagued official information. Indeed, the repeated attention given to rumor in the early histories, I argue, highlights the general problem of informational reliability, whether official or unofficial, and the serious, entrenched problem of active misinformation, of intrigue and deception. It is highly significant that doubts or questions are rarely raised in early Han court discussions relating to the reliability of the information received from the commoners. Since all channels were somewhat unreliable, it appears that unattributed and unverified information, even rumor, was to be taken seriously, at least until there was some reason to reject it.

The catholic examination of various sources of information, both social and natural, is exactly what Li Xun 李尋, a member of the staffs of Chancellor Zhai Fangjin 翟方進 (?–7 BCE) and Marshal of State Wang Gen 王根 (?–2 BCE), advocates in his address to Wang Gen.[42] A student of natural signs, Li Xun was concerned about the inauspicious signs for the Han imperial house. He counsels extreme care in the choice of assistants, for "when worries and responsibilities are extremely heavy, the crux is obtaining the [right] people" 憂責甚重，要在得人.[43] He then elaborates:

> Success or failure is a consequence of whom you hire. You must take the utmost care with this. In the past, Duke Mu of Qin took pleasure in silver-tongued orations and employed incautious bravos. He personally

---

low the emperor's rules.'" (列子曰：「昔堯理天下五十年，不知天下理亂。堯乃微服遊於康衢。兒童謠曰：『立我蒸人，莫非爾極，不識不知，順帝之則。』」) The passage is somewhat different and more expansive in the received *Liezi*:「堯治天下五十年，不知天下治歟，不治歟？不知億兆之願戴己歟？不願戴己歟？顧問左右，左右不知。問外朝，外朝不知。問在野，在野不知。堯乃微服游於康衢，聞兒童謠曰：『立我蒸民，莫匪爾極。不識不知，順帝之則。』堯喜問曰：『誰教爾爲此言？』童兒曰：『我聞之大夫。』問大夫。大夫曰：『古詩也。』」 See "Zhongni" in *Liezi jishi*, 143–44.

42. In his address, Li Xun urges Wang to make "broad inquiries" (*bo wen* 博問), emphasizing not only the quality but the number of people Wang formerly employed who could have offered divergent perspectives: "The scholar-officials are the great treasures of the nation and lie at the root of its accomplishment and reputation. You, General, had within your gates nine feudal lords and twenty [men of] the Red-Wheeled Chariot. Since the Han Dynasty arose, your ministers have been well-treated and very numerous . . . until now."「夫士者，國家之大寶，功名之本也。將軍一門九侯，二十朱輪，漢興以來，臣子貴盛，未嘗至此。」See *HS* 75.3180.

43. *HS* 75.3179.

> experienced great disgrace and his state was almost lost. He regretted his excesses and blamed himself. He thought about the yellow-haired [Jian Shu 蹇叔, who had advised him not to wage the disastrous attack on Zheng].[44] He took into his employ Bailixi, who eventually became the earl of the Western Reaches. His virtue was in keeping with the Way of the Kings. The misfortune and fortune of these two being like this—how could one not take heed [of their experiences]?
>
> 得人之效，成敗之機，不可不勉也。昔秦穆公說諓諓之言，任仡仡之勇，身受大辱，社稷幾亡。悔過自責，思惟黃髮，任用百里奚，卒伯西域，德列王道。二者禍福如此，可不慎哉！[45]

Duke Mu of Qin was heedlessly uncritical of the various advice he received from people such as Qizi 杞子, Fengsun 逢孫, and Yangsun 楊孫 and therefore met with disaster in his attack against Zheng 鄭. With this example, Li Xun expands on his argument that not just the number but the *quality* of one's advisors, and thus the information and advice one receives from them, is crucial to the survival of the state and the preservation of one's reputation: "I pray you have worthy friends and stalwart assistants. These subjects can protect your life, extend your family line, and bring peace to the nation." 唯有賢友彊輔，庶幾可以保身命，全子孫，安國家。[46]

For Li Xun, the signs of the natural world should be treated as sources of information that are as reliable as that received from one's officials. He avers that these signs must be thoroughly scrutinized in order to know better what administrative measures to take and for advance warnings about future opportunities or disasters.[47] For instance, were one to foment a rebellious insurrection—which he is almost certainly insinuating that Wang Gen should not do—"if calamitous defeat will be the result, signs and omens will reveal this beforehand" 咎敗將至，徵兆爲之先見.[48] All available signs of future changes of

---

44. Duke Mu of Qin 秦穆公 (r. 659–621 BCE) was advised by the "yellow-haired" Jian Shu 蹇叔 not to wage an attack on the state of Zheng. His troops, led by Meng Mingshi 孟明視, Xi Qishu 西乞逑, and Bai Yibing 白乙丙 fell prey to a ruse and were routed by Jin troops led by Duke Xiang 襄 of Jin.

45. *HS* 75.3179; *HSBZ* 75.22b.

46. *HS* 75.3180.

47. 「《書》曰『曆象日月星辰』，此言仰視天文，俯查地理，觀日月消息，候星辰行伍，揆山川變動，參人民繇俗，以制法度，考禍福。」 *HS* 75.3180.

48. *HS* 75.3180.

fortune must be surveyed: one must regard the heavenly patterns, investigate the principles of the earth, observe the waxing and waning of the sun and moon, study the movements of the stars, look into the alterations in the mountains and rivers, and pay close attention to developments in the songs and customs of the people (人民繇俗). Yet since these signs are "dark" and "hidden," they require expert readers of the natural patterns to discover them. In spite of their need to be interpreted, he asserts their truth is nonpartisan, for there is an undisputable relation between the patterns of the natural and those of the social world. Since government is necessarily affected by the changes in the natural world, one must attempt to follow these changes. The signs revealing these changes are the means by which one can know in what ways government must be adjusted. Just as iron arises out of the conjoining of iron ore with the coal fires in the extraction process, so government arises out of the conjoining of the natural forces of yin and yang. In each process, the effect is "trustworthy," believable.[49]

Reliability and Information

Li Xun's phrasing his assessment on the "correctness" of the influence of natural processes on the political world in terms of "trustworthiness" (*ke xin* 可信) is indicative of the tendency to evaluate the worth of information or arguments in these terms.[50] The "trustworthiness" of the information was judged not only in relation to its purveyor but also in relation to the quality of the information itself. Wu Zixu 伍子胥 (?–485 BCE), for instance, remonstrated against the King of Wu 吳 for employing the plan formulated by an official, Great Steward Bo Pi 伯嚭 (?–473 BCE), who had been repeatedly bribed by King Goujian of Yue 越王句踐 (r. 496–465 BCE), saying that the king of Wu "trusted," or better, "believed," "the airy phrases and deceptive falsehoods" forwarded by Bo Pi on Yue's behalf.[51] In

49. *HS* 75.3182.

50. As Kai Vogelsang notes, "*Kaoxin* 考信 is the word used by Sima Qian, not *kaoshi* 考實. Indeed, *xin*, 'trustworthiness, realibility,' seems to have been the most prominent epithet for historiography in Han times." Vogelsang, "Some Notions of Historical Judgment in China and the West," 155.

51. 伍子胥諫曰:「夫越,腹心之病,今信其浮辭詐僞而貪齊。」 *SJ* 66.2179. Because the trust expressed in these arguments is clearly not simply a personal trust, I

the evaluation of arguments, all information and all analyses were judged for "believability," for "reliability," whether because their specific origins or purveyors were unreliable, or because, more broadly, no source was absolutely reliable. Because concern regarding the "believability" or "trustworthiness" of a source is so pervasive in court addresses and debates, because this concern seems not to be particularly directed at any one type of source or individual, it would appear that the problem is a holistic one, a concern about the unbelievability, the untrustworthiness of almost *any* source. And if all sources were potentially untrustworthy, then the primary concern in deciding to rely on them would not, at least initially, be the accuracy but rather the *plausibility* of a source's representation of a general state of affairs. In such a circumstance, it is not surprising that natural signs, such as the phases of the moon or sun, were accepted as indicators of underlying regular processes and of the correct course of action. Indeed, they might very reasonably have been deemed by some to be more believable than reports received through the usual political channels. Compared with these reports, the impersonal symbols of the natural world might have appeared well-nigh objective, as close to the undistorted factual truth as one could get.

Whatever the case, the problem of error was thus reduced to the reliability of one's informant, of whether he, and thus his information, could be trusted or believed. Those who could not be believed were deemed "slanderers." "Believing slanderous remarks" (*xin chan* 信讒) is repeatedly raised as a concern in the Han histories.[52] Executives were highly susceptible to the influence of false or misleading reports or remarks. Having no basis to judge, they could be utterly deceived merely by the repeated assertion of a false statement, as King Anli of Wei 魏安釐王 (r. 276–243 BCE) was by the false insinu-

argue that, in instances relating to the quality of the information or arguments received, a more precise translation should actually be "belief." Indeed, I might suggest that *xin* 信 would regularly be better translated as "belief" or "believe" to accommodate this application, whether as in "believing in" someone or "believing" a statement. For other instances of *xin* being used in terms of a "belief" in a statement, see *SJ* 79.2425 and *SJ* 83.2473.

52. See, for instance, *HS* 35.1907, *HS* 49.2296, *HS* 76.3235, and *HS* 95.3851.

ations repeatedly forwarded by spies from Qin.[53] Most terms for "lying"—*chan* 讒, *chan* 諂, *yu* 諛, *hui* 毀, *huo* 惑, *feibang* 誹謗—are more properly translated as "slander," "flattery," or "distortion," not as the outright contradiction of a verifiable report. Lying at court, as with other forms of erroneous speech acts, was not defined by a discrete utterance involving the clear negation of specific information or the substitution of a false piece of information for a correct one. Lying was the act of misdirecting and confusing the audience's perceptions, and thus, their judgments. If my reading is correct, if the monarch did not have ready access to reliable materials, he would have few means by which to rectify any confusion or misdirection and thus was extremely vulnerable to being manipulated. But should then the monarch strive to verify the information he receives? Wouldn't he then be less prone to manipulation? Actually, as the *Hanfeizi* insightfully recommends, it would be better if he didn't bother; his aim should only be to determine the agenda of his addressors. Knowing that they will attempt to structure their remarks based on his reactions, he can assess their motives by analyzing their attempts at manipulation. It is only natural, the *Hanfeizi* asserts, to assume that the monarch's addressors will attempt to play upon and take advantage of his moods. In a calmer hour, the self-conscious monarch, through careful analysis of their responses to his reactions, can "obtain the signs of their vilification and aggrandizement, of their public and private [faces]" 以得毀譽公私之徵.[54]

Surrounded by self-interested persuaders aiming to manipulate him toward their favored course of action, monarchs would naturally have been distrustful, even paranoid, about the advice they received. Monarchs would regularly voice their concern regarding corruption at court and the threat of manipulation by nefarious advisors. Concomitantly, certain monarchs also repeatedly expressed a desire for forthright, honest advice, advice that was untainted by

---

53. See *SJ* 77.2384, where Sima Qian states that the king of Wei, having repeatedly heard slanderous remarks, "could not not believe them" 不能不信.

54. The entire sentence reads:「明主之道，已喜則求其所納，已怒則察其所搆，論於已變之後，以得毀譽公私之徵。」 See "Bajing" 八經, in *Han Feizi xinjiaozhu*, 1075.

personal agendas. Not surprisingly, in this climate of unrelenting suspicion, even straightforward, forthright advisors were vulnerable to charges of slander and manipulation. Emblematic of this problem, ministers themselves sometimes sardonically refer to honest critics as "slanderers" (*feibang de ren* 誹謗的人), as in Jia Shan's 賈山 address to Emperor Wen of Han (漢文帝, r. 179–157 BCE) about the First Emperor of Qin. Jia Shan's argument is that when the empire is weak, as in the final years of the Qin dynasty, there is no commitment to its strengthening, and thus to offering direct, critical advice. Why did the Second Emperor not know of the problems of the empire? Because there were none who dared report honestly what was going on. And why was that? Because government officials, and the emperor in particular, gave little concern to the problems of the empire, to taking care of those who needed help. Instead of having their advice considered seriously, those who attempted to speak honestly to the court were either "retired" or murdered:

> Why did the First Emperor of Qin live among ruins and not himself know about [the empire's decline]? Because among All-Under-Heaven, there were none who dared make a report [about the poor state of the empire]. For what reason were there none who dared to make a report? There was no righteous commitment to take care of the elderly, there were no ministers willing to assist, there were no *shi* who would come forward to remonstrate.[55] The emperor unrestrainedly executed punishments, forcing those who "slandered" into retirement, killing those *shi* who directly remonstrated. For this reason, the ministers speak flatteringly to curry favor and ingratiate themselves. When they assess the emperor's virtue, he is more worthy than Yao and Shun; when they evaluate his accomplishments, then he is more worthy than Tang or Wu. All-Under-Heaven has already crumbled and none report it. The *Book of Odes* states, "It is not that words are inadequate. Why would you refrain out of fear or worry? If he listens, then respond. If he slanders you, then retire."[56] This is the point. It also states, "Marvelous are the many *shi* with whom King

---

55. All of these negative developments were obviously being blamed on the emperor's style of governance.

56. See Mao, no. 257, "Sang rou," in *Maoshi zhengyi*, vol. 3, 1187. My translation borrows from Waley, trans., *The Book of Songs*, 268. The last two phrases are not in the received text.

> Wen brought tranquility to the empire."[57] All-Under-Heaven by no means had lost its *shi*. So why did the ode about King Wen only mention those who brought tranquility? When King Wen gave preference to benevolence, then benevolence flourished. When he acquired *shi* and treated them respectfully, then the *shi* were employed. He employed them with an eye to the rites and propriety.
>
> 秦皇帝居滅絕之中而不自知者何也？天下莫敢告也。其所以莫敢告者何也？亡養老之義，亡輔弼之臣，亡進諫之士，縱恣行誅，退誹謗之人，殺直諫之士，是以道諛媮合苟容，比其德則賢於堯舜，課其功則賢於湯武，天下已潰而莫之告也。詩曰：「匪言不能，胡此畏忌，聽言則對，譖言則退。」此之謂也。又曰：「濟濟多士，文王以寧。」天下未嘗亡士也，然而文王獨言以寧者何也？文王好仁則仁興，得士而敬之則士用，用之有禮義。[58]

Jia Shan's ironic application of "slanderer" to those who offer forthright, genuine advice is indicative of the trend to label "false" speech, whether truly false or only politically unacceptable, as slanderous. To forward an honest appraisal of a state of affairs that could contradict what the monarch wished to hear was often highly dangerous, and self-conscious emperors knew that.[59] For the monarch and thus the court in general, "liars" are not simply those who intentionally contradict true reports; they are those who contradict the political aims and preferences of the court.[60] As Emperor Wen himself forthrightly acknowledges, when a leader who wishes to be honestly apprised of the conditions of the empire holds aims and preferences that encourage such, then the criticisms of his advisors will be more effective. Emperor Wen admits that if he is not virtuous and perceptive, the benefit of intelligent ministers will be for naught: "Were I not yet

57. See Mao, no. 235, "Wen Wang," in *Maoshi zhengyi*, vol. 3, 961.

58. See *HS* 51.2333.

59. Emperor Wen, at one point, vows he will not punish those who are extremely direct with him: "There are many who are able to speak forthrightly and remonstrate extensively. In the future, they can use such criticisms to correct me without [fear of] being arrested." 「能直言極諫者，各有人數，將以匡朕之不逮。」 See *HS* 49.2290.

60. Of course, our consciousness of a broad, and sometime ironic, charge of slander, even by the historians themselves, must force us to reconsider its veracity. In other words, we cannot assume that the statements behind the charges of slander were false; nor can we assume they were true. As with the monarch, we must look to the possible motives behind its assertion or denial.

virtuous or perceptive, [even if] I were enlightened, I would not be able to bring [problems] to light, and [even if] I were knowledgeable, I would not be able to govern [properly]." 朕既不德，又不敏，明弗能燭，而智不能治。[61] With an open-minded, sensitive monarch, "truth" perhaps would more closely correlate with the facts and "slander" with falsehood. But whether or not this is the case, "slander" is consistently the operative term by which false, distorted speech is described. Indeed, it is not so much falsehood as distortion and confusion that are specifically at issue.

Because of this association between slander and political aim within the operations of the government, Chinese literati repeatedly engaged with the problem of distortion and confusion. Although they could not guarantee the monarch's own interest in discovering the actual state of affairs, they were well aware that many in the court wished, through eloquent artifice, to contribute to its obscuration. In the early Chinese texts, direct, "truthful" speech is almost always represented as being antithetical to eloquent and thereby misleading speech. In *Laozi* 81 this is stated explicitly: "Trustworthy words are not beautiful, beautiful words are not trustworthy." 信言不美，美言不信。 Eloquent speakers are incessantly denigrated, as when Sima Jizhu 司馬季主 states that "rhetoricians" were obligated to use extended displays of verbal trickery to catch their rulers' attention.[62] The danger of manipulative remarks was extreme, for they could corrode even the strongest bonds of affection and loyalty. The Former Han official Du Qin 杜欽 speaks specifically to this problem in his remarks to Emperor Cheng's (漢成帝, r. 32–7 BCE) maternal uncle, Wang Feng 王鳳 (?–22 BCE), about slanderous statements promulgated by King Wu of Zhou's (r. 1045–1043 BCE) older brothers, Guanshu Xian 管叔鮮 and Cai Shudu 蔡叔度, about the Duke of Zhou. These slanderous statements, Du Qin cautioned, could have influenced King Cheng of Zhou, were it not for King Cheng's own resolute sense of the Duke of Zhou's overwhelming virtue. Du Qin then adds a more contemporary example: before the Warring States persuader-diplomat Fan Sui 范睢 spoke with the king of Qin, the

61. See *HS* 49.2290.
62. See Kern, "Poetry and Religion," 54.

king and the marquis of Rang 穰侯 had been inseparable. In the monarchic environment, no relationship, no commitment, whether to a person or to a view of the world, even to those views grounded in fact, was invulnerable to manipulation and distortion.[63]

Misinformation and Ministerial Error

In the discussion above, I have highlighted the apparent consensus that all sources required circumspect treatment. Yet the veracity or accuracy of documents submitted to the central court is almost never explicitly discussed in the historical texts. There is never in the received Former Han histories (or, it appears, even in the pre-Han historical documents) any extended discussion of whether the information in a report or missive—either from an official, an office, or a region—is false, forged, or distorted. The most we have are bare, unsupported assertions that a claim or document is false, such as in the following exchange, when Emperor Zhao 昭 of Han (r. 86–74 BCE) insists to Huo Guang 霍光 (?–68 BCE) that a document composed at the behest of the king of Yan 燕 charging Huo Guang with wishing to arrogate power is false:

> "The General may put his cap back on. I know this document is a swindle. The General has committed no offence." Huo Guang said, "How does Your Majesty know this?" The emperor said, "The General went to Guangming to conduct a review of the gentlemen [and the Feathered Forest Corps] and it has not even been ten days since the transfer and promotion of colonels [to your command]. How did the king of Yan become cognizant of [both of these events]? Furthermore, even if the General were acting falsely, you would not need these colonels [to carry out any plot]."
>
> 上曰:「將軍冠. 朕知是書詐也。將軍亡罪。」光曰:「陛下何以知之?」上曰:「將軍之廣明,都郎屬耳。調校尉以來未能十日,燕王何以得知之?且將軍爲非,不須校尉。」[64]

---

63. See *HS* 60.2676. Of course, an additional subtext is that, like Wang Feng, both of these (as with the third figure with which Du Qin makes an analogy, Tian Fen 田蚡), were open to the charge of attempting to claim too much power.

64. See *HS* 68.2936. The address was submitted on behalf of the king of Yan, Liu Dan 劉旦 (r. 117–80 BCE), Emperor Zhao's half-brother, who resented Huo Guang's influence.

Though the basis of the emperor's assertion is a personal faith, however genuine, in Huo Guang, this instance reveals that the possible "falsity" or, better, "deceptiveness" of the document was recognized, that, just as with oral address, written documents could not simply be taken at face value.

In the classical corpus, extended discussions of how a monarch should evaluate the presentations made by his officials, discussions that occupy significant portions of the *Hanfeizi*, appear to be meant to apply to all data received by the monarch. In these discussions, concern with the veracity of received documentation is identical with the concern with veracity in general. In the following excerpt, the *Hanfeizi* offers an illuminating passage about how the monarch should dispose himself toward what he receives:

> If you do not critically attend to what you hear then you will have no means by which to interrogate your inferiors. If their speech is not evaluated with regard to its applications then you'll be faced with duplicitous persuasions. With regard to speech, people frequently believe what is said. When the concrete particulars are not apposite, if a few people assert them, then you doubt them; if many people assert them, then you take it to be the case; if a multitude of people asserts them, your conviction will not be shaken.
>
> 聽不參則無以責下，言不督乎用則邪說當上。言之為物也以多信。不然之物，十人云疑，百人然乎，千人不可解也。[65]

Even though in the *Hanfeizi* there is the recognition that a speech that attends to relevant concrete particulars (*wu* 物) is one that deserves the most secure assent, the *Hanfeizi* discusses it only perfunctorily, which suggests that this type of speech was relatively rare. For the rest of the essay, attention is directed at what was probably a much more common occurrence, namely, when the asserted relevant concrete particulars were not reliable or were not the central piece of the forwarded argument. Because there are so many ways to confuse and distract the monarch, to play to his sympathies, or even to blame him for a policy failure, the *Hanfeizi* urges repeatedly that the monarch force his advisors to assert a strong position on a focused question and not equivocate. Yet the monarch must not defer his judg-

65. "Bajing," *Han Feizi xinjiaozhu*, 1074.

ment while awaiting further information or intensive scrutiny of the proposals: "If the ruler of men does not vent his anger [at extended, ornate, complicated arguments] but waits to see if they accord with investigation, his power will be accorded to his inferiors." 人主不饜忿而待合參，其勢資下也。 Instead, the monarch must attend to the applied consequences and constructive uses of forwarded policy proposals: "The wise ruler listens to speeches, assesses their applied consequences, and evalutes their constructive uses. From his evaluations of their constructive uses, rewards and punishments arise." 有道之主，聽言，督其用，課其功，功課而賞罰生焉。

Consequently, the penultimate task of the monarch, as really with any executive, is to be cognizant of the prejudicial selection of information, of the personal interests that his advisors may have in the success or failure of a policy, and to extricate that interest from the mass of information and argument provided. Given that the monarch must decide swiftly how to respond, he cannot himself spend the requisite time evaluating the veracity of the facts themselves, and ministers were certainly aware of this. If the success or failure of a proposal was not dependent on the correctness of its information but rather the applied consequences or the constructive use of such a proposal, it is not surprising that proposals often lacked such concrete information or were not careful about its accuracy. Accordingly, the standard by which ministers are to be evaluated is not the factual correctness of their proposals but their ability to carry out their duties, to speak carefully about the problems at hand and follow through successfully with what they propose. Whether or not the information they use to formulate their argument is correct is actually irrelevant. This is not to say that their proposals do not need to be buttressed by relevant and accurate information—indeed, the *Hanfeizi* states explicitly that they do[66]—but it is not the duty of the executive to verify this, nor is it politically wise for him to do so. If the majority of that with which the monarch is presented does not contradict what a minister proposes and the proposal itself appears to be worthy on its own merits, then the monarch has sufficient basis to consider it seriously, regardless of what figures are used.

---

66. 「言必有報，說必責用也。」 *Han Feizi xinjiaozhu*, 1075.

This standard, of course, falls well short of what we might ourselves believe rigorous investigation and complex government should demand. But it is one that is frequently applied, in both the ancient and modern world, to political spheres in which time is of the essence and information is often not terribly trustworthy. The greatest error that the monarch can commit in his own deliberations is to let his personal feelings about the matter get in the way (or even to be divulged), for it benefits only those who wish to manipulate him.

In conclusion, I offer a provisional answer to the question inspiring my analysis: How could a minister err in the early Chinese court? First, he could err by not thoroughly knowing his duties and those matters pertaining to his duties. Second, he could err on the side of vagueness that would encourage indecision, of asserting something with too many qualifications or equivocations to serve as effective advice or recommendation. Third, most egregiously and most dangerously, the minister could attempt to use his knowledge of the emperor's predilections to manipulate him for personal or professional advantage. This would be not only a personal error (for which he could be severely punished) but also a professional error, for his policies, no matter how good or reasonable, might not be accepted and his word would be less valued.

Consequences

If the explanations I propose for deemphasizing factual evidence and the general irrelevance of factual errors to success or failure at court are correct, then the common identification of objective truth with some kind of "moral" or consequential truth in early Chinese documents is even more comprehensible, for the truth most in play is not a matter of accuracy but of plausible relevance to how the empire should be governed. These explanations also bear on our appraisal of the early Chinese historiographical project itself. We can perhaps see somewhat more clearly why it might have been uncommon or even impossible for a "purely" objective standard to be used in the appraisal of an early work of historiography; for instance, in Ban Gu's judgment of Sima Qian's history as a "veritable record."[67] When facts

67. 「不虛美，不隱惡，故謂之實錄。」 See *HS* 62.2738.

cannot be the determining feature of a politically charged environment, it would be difficult for them to be, when one is drawing upon the same documents, the determining feature of the historical representation of that environment. It is perhaps partly because of the politically charged atmosphere that Confucius, in a *Gongyang zhuan* passage,[68] could both acknowledge a factually inaccurate remark in *Chunqiu* and nevertheless insist that *Chunqiu* is called a trustworthy history (*xinshi* 信史).[69] The factual inaccuracies may serve to indicate an intentionally placed *aporia*, forcing the reader to look between the lines for the truthful, "reliable" insinuations. All of this is not to deny that there seems to be something of, in Kai Vogelsang's phrase, "a disregard for the distinction between historical record and historical judgment, that blends fact and fiction and focuses on history as a literary artefact."[70] What I have hoped to achieve with this study is to pose an alternative to the unflattering portrayal of the early Chinese as being unable to recognize a fact when they saw one, or to have any idea of evidence. They clearly did, I maintain, and not only that, they would have used it, if it would have helped. But in the poisonous early Chinese political environment, facts not only did not matter, they *could not* matter as much as one ideally would have hoped.[71]

---

68. 子曰:"我乃知之矣。"在側者曰:"子苟知之,何以不革?"曰:"如爾所不知何?《春秋》之信史也。" *Chunqiu gongyangzhuan zhushu*, vol. 8, 493–94.

69. See Vogelsang, "Some Notions of Historical Judgment in China and the West," 156. I take issue with Vogelsang's assertion that *Chunqiu* is a "reliable" or "trustworthy" history "because it gives a wrong account" and his succeeding assertion that "quite obviously, *xin* does not mean 'truth.'" *Xin* clearly cannot be absolutely identified with factually accurate truth but it does correlate with a measure of truth, of what Vogelsang might call the "heart of the matter."

70. Ibid., 143.

71. I would like to thank the members of the workshop "Addressing the Autocrat," held at the University of Oklahoma in 2009, for their remarks, especially Yuri Pines and Michael Nylan.

CHAPTER 6

The Rhetoric of Dong Zhongshu's Imperial Communications

Sarah A. Queen, Connecticut College

Dong Zhongshu's career spanned several decades during the reigns of Emperors Jing and Wu. He held official posts both at the central court and in outlying areas of the empire providing many opportunities to communicate with the power holders of his day. This essay will discuss three such official exchanges. In the first example, Dong addresses Emperor Wu as an academician recently recommended to the court to participate in an imperial inquiry. In the second example, Dong exchanges words with the king of Jiangdu as his recently appointed administrator. In the third example, Dong speaks to Emperor Wu as a retired official through Zhang Tang, the chamberlain of law enforcement, who is sent by the emperor as an emissary to question him on the Suburban Sacrifice. Each provides an example of the different ways that a monarch could be addressed: (1) directly (the memorials); (2) indirectly through a king (the exchange with King Yi); and (3) indirectly through an emissary (the exchange with Zhang Tang). Moreover each dates from a different moment in Dong's career, addresses different policy issues, and in each Dong holds a different official rank. Thus collectively they cover a long span of time during Dong Zhongshu's career and can speak to any consistent use of conventions and whether or not he maintained a consistent approach to the monarch throughout his career.

Scenario 1: The Academician Dong Zhongshu and the Young Emperor Wu

The first official exchange to be discussed is preserved in Ban Gu's biography of Dong Zhongshu in Ban Gu, *Hanshu* 56. Ban Gu's introductory comments indicate that this communication between Emperor Wu and Dong Zhongshu was the result of an imperial inquiry (對策) held early in Emperor Wu's reign:[1] "After assuming the throne, he [called for] the recommendation of scholars who were 'worthy, excellent, and learned'[2] numbering several hundred. Dong Zhongshu was among those recommended as 'worthy and excellent' who responded to the imperial inquiry."[3] The rhetoric of Liu Che's introductory remarks initiating the inquiry provide a palpable sense of how the young emperor wished to portray himself to both the scholars presently gathered to respond to his inquiries and those who would later read his edict:

> The imperial edict states: We have secured and inherited [this position of] utmost reverence and refined virtue, and [wish] to transmit its legacy without flaw, so that it operates everywhere. Yet the responsibility is great and the undertaking weighty. Thus day and night [We] take no time to rest, thinking constantly of the governance of the myriad affairs, ever fearful that [We] have fallen short. Therefore [We] have searched widely and deeply for the "eminent and brave"[4] from the four quarters [of the empire], and [ordered] the feudal lords and dukes of the commanderies and kingdoms to recommend scholars who are "worthy and excellent," who cultivate their integrity, and who are widely versed [in the classical literature], because [We] desire to hear the essentials of the great Way and the ultimate truths of its

---

1. For the dating of these documents see Queen, *From Chronicle to Canon*, appendix 2.

2. See Hucker, *A Dictionary of Official Titles in Imperial China*, 242.

3. *HS* 56.2495.

4. *Huainanzi* 20.23 explains: "Those whose knowledge surpassed ten thousand men were called 'talented'; those whose knowledge surpassed a thousand men were called 'eminent'; those whose knowledge surpassed a hundred men were called 'brave.'" All citations of the text are to Lau et al., eds., *A Concordance to the Huainanzi*, in the form chapter/page/lines. Hereafter cited as *HNZ*. For an English translation, see Major et al., trans. and eds., *The Huainanzi*, 833.

> highest principles. Now you, gentlemen, have been honored to stand at the head of those recommended. We deeply admire this [achievement]. You gentleman, refine your thoughts and stretch your minds, for We have condescended to listen to and question you.
>
> 制曰:朕獲承至尊休德,傳之亡窮,而施之罔極,任大而守重,是以夙夜不皇康寧,永惟萬事之統,猶懼有闕。故廣延四方之豪儁,郡國諸侯公選賢良修絜博習之士,欲聞大道之要,至論之極。今子大夫褎然爲舉首,朕甚嘉之。子大夫其精心致思,朕垂聽而問焉。[5]

Throughout his introductory remarks, and those that follow in the second and third edict of this imperial inquiry, the emperor employs a number of formulaic conventions and specialized vocabulary reserved for his use alone, that assert his supremacy over the scholars he addresses. For example, we find the ubiquitous self referential "royal We" (*zhen* 朕),[6] and the set phrase "Verily, We have heard" (*gai wen* 蓋聞) or simply "Verily" (*gai* 蓋), expressions employed by the emperor when referring to historical precedents or citing traditional sayings. In addition, the emperor insists that he will, for example, "condescend to listen" (*chui ting* 垂聽) or "condescend to inquire of [*chui wen* 垂問] his scholars." Emperor Wu's introduction also employs a distinct vocabulary of highly emotional terms. Thus, for example, the emperor expresses either his deep admiration for (*zhen shen jia zhi* 朕甚嘉之) or deep remorse toward (*zhen shen dao zhi* 朕甚悼之) a given subject.

Beyond these rhetorical conventions that implicitly assert the preeminence of the emperor and subordinate status of his scholars, the content of the edict suggests a relationship of utter dependency in which the emperor occupies an inferior status relative to his officials. The effusive language of Liu Che's introductory remarks portray the young emperor as living in a perpetual state of fear and anxiety that he is insufficiently equipped to deal with the responsibilities that face him. Though he has "inherited [this position of] utmost reverence and refined virtue," if he is to successfully transmit the legacy of his forebears, he must seek the help of his best scholars and rely upon

---

5. *HS* 56.2495.

6. According to Sima Qian, after the First Emperor of Qin united the empire in 221 BCE he approved of his officials' suggestion to adopt this term of address. See *SJ* 6.236 and Watson, trans., *Records of the Grand Historian: Qin Dynasty*, 42–43.

them to share the burden of leadership. The ruler simply cannot go it alone, and thus he urges those gathered for this imperial inquiry to share their "finest sentiments and deepest thoughts." As we will see throughout the examples discussed below, while the formulaic conventions of imperial communication assert the superior political status of the emperor, the hierarchy posited in these formal conventions stands in constant tension with the hierarchy of moral knowledge, which posits the officials versed in the classical literature as the masters of the Way and the emperor as their first and foremost disciple.

Historical Precedents and Policy Concerns

Having drawn in his audience—present and future—with this emotionally charged preamble, Emperor Wu next clarifies the historical precedent—the flourishing and decline of the Way of the Five Thearchs and Three Kings—meant to frame the five specific questions he will pose. Emperor Wu searchingly inquires: "Is the Mandate ordained by Heaven irrevocable?" Reflecting on the long centuries of futile efforts to restore the Way, Emperor Wu wonders whether his efforts will end in similar failure or whether he can stem the tide of decline. If he is the legitimate heir to the Way of the Five Thearchs and Three Kings, what auspicious signs confirm his contemporary reception of the Three Dynasties' mandate? Why would disasters and anomalies continue to appear? How does Heaven's Mandate manifest itself at the level of the individual? What specific policies should the emperor support to restore the Way so that the human community will flourish? Lastly, what policies should he initiate to attract the assistance of the numinous world of Heaven and the spirits?

The emperor concludes his edict with a number of requests:

> You, gentlemen, understand the achievements of the Former Sages, and are well versed in the alternations of customary change and the proper sequence of their cycles. The days you have been discussing and deliberating these lofty and proper principles have been long. Communicate your insights to Us. Explain every detail as a separate item. Do not crowd your points together. Select each item in accordance with a clear technique. Carefully consider your reply. If you know of any instance of impropriety, dishonesty, disloyalty, laxity, or negligence, write a letter, do not leak the information, and submit it to Us personally. Do not dread the repercussions. You, gentlemen,

> speak your mind. Do not conceal anything. We will personally examine [your responses].
>
> 子大夫明先聖之業，習俗化之變，終始之序，講聞高誼之日久矣，其明以諭朕。科別其條，勿猥勿并，取之於術，慎其所出。乃其不正不直，不忠不極，枉于執事，書之不泄，興于朕躬，毋悼後害。子大夫其盡心，靡有所隱，朕將親覽焉。[7]

In closing, Emperor Wu urges the participating scholars to speak the truth: to share their insights thoughtfully and in every detail. Moreover, should they know of any miscreant activities among the officials they are encouraged to submit a secret letter directly to the emperor so that the precious information communicated inside will not be made public. The extent to which the ruler is ultimately dependent upon his officials for reliable information is clear. As we will see below, though following the emperor's questions religiously, Dong's responses go far beyond his agenda to challenge him at every turn.

The First Response to Emperor Wu

Dong's response exhibits several characteristics that illuminate important aspects of communication between emperor and scholar in the Western Han generally, and between Emperor Wu and Dong Zhongshu more particularly. A given communication between the emperor and his officials necessarily followed the rhetorical conventions of imperial exchange but the content that participants of a dialogue wished to communicate was shaped by a number of more complicated factors: the sociopolitical realities of the moment, the personality, age, and experience of a given emperor and respondent, and the personal agendas each brought to the communication. As will become apparent in the examples below, Dong introduces his responses to the emperor with a number of typical self-abasing rhetorical conventions meant to demonstrate his lowly status compared to the lofty status of the emperor. Chief among them was the ubiquitous term "Your Highness" or "Your Majesty" (*bixia* 陛下); the Chinese term literally means "below the steps of the throne" but was likely a contraction of a longer self-abasing term that must have meant something like "You whom this utterly unworthy servant addresses from

7. *HS* 56.2498.

beneath the steps of Your Throne." In answering the emperor's queries, Dong also consistently employs one of two set phrases: either "Your servant has respectfully examined" (*chen jin an* 臣謹案) or "Your servant has heard" (*chen wen* 臣聞). Moreover, he repeatedly describes himself as "lowly and vile" or simply too "ignorant" to provide an adequate response.

The structure of Dong's responses also appears to have been constrained by certain conventions of composition operative in this form of imperial exchange. For example, Dong responds to each topic raised by the emperor following the exact order of the queries in the imperial edict. Furthermore, each response reiterates the precise language of the question raised in the imperial edict, typically at the end of an individual answer but sometimes at its beginning. Within the confines of this rhetorical frame meant to mirror linguistically the political hierarchy operative between emperor and scholar, however, the message Dong sends to the emperor is anything but humble. The content of Dong's response, in fact, reveals a good deal of hubris. As we will see, though the rhetorical conventions employed throughout by emperor and scholar uphold the superiority and supremacy of the emperor in contrast to the inferiority and humility of his scholar, the content of Dong's communications inverts and subverts this rhetorical hierarchy from beginning to end.

From Dawn to Dusk Unceasing Mirroring the emperor's introductory remarks, Dong begins his response with equally flattering platitudes as well as the requisite self-effacing conventions: "Your Highness has spoken in virtuous tones and sent down this enlightened announcement inquiring into Heaven's mandate and into the disposition and nature. These are all beyond the reach of your ignorant servant." 陛下發德音，下明詔，求天命與情性，皆非愚臣之所能及也。[8] With these formulaic conventions of imperial exchange out of the way, Dong is now free to address the substance of the emperor's first question. In contrast to the opening claim that he is too ignorant to craft a worthy response, Dong displays his erudition through his mastery of the canonical literature. Drawing upon the authority of

---

8. *HS* 56.2498.

the *Spring and Autumn Annals*, complemented by flourishes from the *Book of Odes* and *Book of Documents*, and capping his argument with a quotation from Confucius, Dong challenges the emperor on two important accounts. If the emperor is to understand how the Mandate of Heaven operates, he must first understand the mutuality that exists between Heaven and humankind and Heaven's desire to support the ruler as long as the ruler makes the appropriate effort to practice the Way. More specifically, Dong explains what values and policies exemplify the Way and how it is that the Way has not, as the emperor posits, completely disappeared as a consequence of centuries of declining rule: the educational and transformational power of ritual and music has ensured and will ensure the continued existence of the Way. Ultimately, however, whether or not the Way will prevail under any particular ruler rests with the policies pursued. The ruler must hire the right men and follow the correct path of rulership if he hopes to retain the Mandate. Thus, contrary to the emperor's claim that the Mandate is irrevocable, all depends on the actions of the emperor who will set the course of his dynasty on either a path of order and prosperity or one of chaos and decline. As Dong concludes: "If he exerts himself to practice the Way, then his virtue will increase daily and he will be in possession of great achievements. These efforts will enable him to quickly achieve results. The *Odes* declare: 'From dawn to dusk unceasing.' The *Documents* declare: 'Make the effort. Make the effort.' Both refer to exerting oneself."

彊勉行道，則德日起而大有功：此皆可使還至而立有效者也。《詩》曰「夙夜匪解」，《書》云「茂哉茂哉！」皆彊勉之謂也。[9] Implicit in Dong's argument is a thinly veiled remonstrance: the emperor must make greater efforts to practice goodness.

Virtue Never Stands Alone Dong continues to explain his theory of the mutuality of Heaven and humankind in the second leg of his response, addressing the emperor's questions concerning auspicious and inauspicious omens. Here again, availing himself of the past to discuss the present, Dong suggests that omens are earned not fated: when the ruler accrues enough goodness and amasses enough virtue,

---

9. *HS* 56.2498–99.

Heaven will reward him with auspicious signs. Conversely, when he abandons moral instruction and relies instead upon coercive measures, he will engender an imbalance in the cosmic *qi* and inexplicable evils will arise. Again the implicit remonstrance: if the emperor hopes to set his empire in order, he must exert himself to institute moral instruction and ease up on punitive measures.

Like Clay on a Potter's Wheel Next Dong turns to the emperor's question on the Mandate (命) as it relates to the nature (性) and disposition (情) of human beings and responds with some of his most powerful imagery. Moral instruction is potentially efficacious because human beings are ultimately malleable. But human beings are not uniform, Dong explains, because their inner attributes are ultimately shaped and brought to completion by external influences: "Thus for the ruler to transform the ruled and for the ruled to submit to the ruler resembles clay upon a potter's wheel: only a potter can shape it. It resembles metal in a mould: only a metalsmith can cast it." 夫上之化下，下之從上，猶泥之在鈞，唯甄者之所為；猶金之在鎔，唯冶者之所鑄。[10] As rulers and circumstances differ, human development tends in different directions. Good rulers who practice virtue engender humane subjects and enjoy long life; bad rulers who practice evil engender degenerate subjects who die prematurely. But even good rulers may live in challenging times that make the task of moral transformation ever more difficult.

The King's Rectification Proceeds from Heaven In his role as potter and metalsmith, where then does the emperor turn for his template to shape and mould the malleable nature and disposition of human beings? Dong finds his answer in the prescribed structure of the *Spring and Autumn*. He explains:

> Your servant has respectfully examined [*chen jin an*] the text of the *Spring and Autumn* in search of the starting point of the Kingly Way and has found it in the term *zheng* (the first). [In the first entry for each reign period in the *Spring and Autumn*] the term *zheng* (the first) follows the term *wang* (king), and the term *wang* (king) follows the

---

10. *HS* 56.2501.

term *chun* (spring).[11] The spring is established by Heaven; the first [month] is established by the king. The intention of the *Spring and Autumn* is to say that the ruler receives what Heaven establishes and he utilizes it to rectify his activities. This is what I mean when I say that *zheng* (the first) is the starting point of the Kingly Way.

臣謹案春秋之文，求王道之端，得之於正。正次王，王次春。春者，天之所爲也；正者，王之所爲也。其意曰，上承天之所爲，而下以正其所爲，正王道之端云爾。[12]

Thus as the potter and metalsmith to the unshaped clay and unformed metal of human nature, the ruler is the chief but not the final or sole arbiter of human moral development. He must take his cues from Heaven and pattern his rectification of the human community on Heaven's yin and yang, giving priority to moral instruction over punitive measures. When the opposite conditions abide, as Dong implicitly argues is the case under Emperor Wu's reign, government is synonymous with tyranny:

To govern through a reliance on coercive punishment does not conform to Heaven. Thus none among the Former Kings dared do so. Is not the present dismissal of officials who promote the moral instruction of the Former Kings and the sole reliance on officials who uphold the rule of law to bring order to the people, a case of relying upon coercive punishments? Confucius said: "To impose the death penalty upon those you have not educated is called tyranny."[13] When tyrannical government is applied to the lower reaches of society it is exceedingly difficult to fulfill the desire to spread moral instruction throughout the world within the Four Seas!

爲政而任刑，不順於天，故先王莫之肯爲也。今廢先王德教之官，而獨任執法之吏治民，毋乃任刑之意與！孔子曰：「不教而誅謂之虐。」虐政用於下，而欲德教之被四海，故難成也。[14]

Moral Transformation Proceeds from the Greatness of the Origin Despite his criticisms of the emperor, Dong maintains, in his closing remarks below, it remains possible for Emperor Wu to rectify his rule if he is will-

11. The first entry for each lord reads: "Spring. The royal first month" 春王正月.
12. *HS* 56.2501–2.
13. *Analects* 20.2.
14. *HS* 56.2502.

ing to take the *Spring and Autumn* as his blueprint for reform. Once again, turning to the formulaic structure of the *Spring and Autumn* to build his argument, Dong articulates a vision of rectification that begins with the emperor to proceed to the farthest reaches of the world:

> Your servant has respectfully examined [*chen jin an*] the reason why the *Spring and Autumn* refers to "the first [year of each lord's reign]" (*zheng*) as "the originating [year]." The first is that from which all things begin. The Origin is that which the Great Appendix calls "great." To refer to the first as the originating [year] is to recognize the importance of the beginning and to desire to rectify the root [of all things.] The *Spring and Autumn* explores deeply into the root [of things] and so it reverts back to begin from the noble. Therefore the one who would rule others rectifies his mind to rectify the court; rectifies the court to rectify the numerous officials; rectifies the numerous officials to rectify the myriad people; rectifies the myriad people to rectify the Four Quarters of the world. If the Four Quarters of the world are rectified, then no one, near or far, will dare to fail to be one with his rectitude, and there will be no noxious *qi* to defile those among them. For this reason, yin and yang will be harmonious, and wind and rain will arrive in their appropriate seasons; all living things will be in harmony and the multitudes will prosper; the Five Grains will reach fruition and the subsidiary crops will flourish. All within Heaven and Earth will be showered by these blessings and all within the Four Seas will hear of the ruler's flourishing virtue and flock to him to become his subjects. Of all possible blessings and every conceivable auspicious omen that may be summoned, none will fail to arrive, and the Kingly Way will be fulfilled.
>
> 臣謹案春秋謂一元之意，一者萬物之所從始也，元者辭之所謂大也。謂一爲元者，視大始而欲正本也。春秋深探其本，而反自貴者始。故爲人君者，正心以正朝廷，正朝廷以正百官，正百官以正萬民，正萬民以正四方。四方正，遠近莫敢不壹於正，而亡有邪氣奸其間者。是以陰陽調而風雨時，群生和而萬民殖，五穀孰而草木茂，天地之間被潤澤而大豐美，四海之內聞盛德而皆徠臣，諸福之物，可致之祥，莫不畢至，而王道終矣。[15]

In contrast to the tragic figure of Confucius, who possessed the ability to summon auspicious signs from the gods but could never do so because he lacked the requisite political station to fulfill his messianic vision of reform, Emperor Wu is eminently equipped to make Confucius's

15. *HS* 56.2502–3.

vision a reality. He need only apply himself to the task of reforming the institutions of moral instruction throughout the empire. In short, Dong concludes, the time is long overdue for the emperor to enact reform: "The ancients had a saying: 'Looking down into the pond and coveting the fish does not compare to withdrawing and weaving a net.' Now looking down at the government and desiring to govern for more than seventy years does not compare to withdrawing and instituting reform. Having instituted reform, it will be possible to govern well. If the state is well governed, disasters will diminish day by day and blessings will increase." 古人有言曰:「臨淵羨魚,不如(蛛)〔退〕而結網。」 今臨政而願治七十餘歲矣,不如退而更化;更化則可善治,善治則災害日去,福祿日來。[16]

EMPEROR WU APPRAISES DONG'S FIRST RESPONSE AND ISSUES A SECOND EDICT

Given that each and every one of Dong's responses challenged Emperor Wu to recognize his shortcomings or criticized the state of affairs under his reign, it is not surprising that the emperor, upon examining Dong's response, voiced his disapproval. Ban Gu reports: The Son of Heaven examined Dong Zhongshu's reply, but took exception to it, and so issued another imperial instruction.[17] The beginning of this edict, however, does not exhibit the flowery language and rhetorical conventions present in the first. Perhaps as a follow-up to the first edict, the emperor was able to dispense with the formulaic conventions that typically marked the beginning of his official communications. Whatever the case, in the second edict, the emperor continues to probe the Way of the thearchs and kings but raises new and more detailed questions. This second edict consists of four questions, the first three of which ask the respondents to explain the different policies adopted by the various thearchs and kings of the past. Why, for example, could Shun sit idle doing nothing at all while King Wen toiled frenetically to bring order to the world? Why were the Zhou rulers so extravagant compared to the frugality of Shun?

---

16. *HS* 56.2505.

17. *HS* 56.2506. For the general meaning of the term *ce*, see Giele, *Imperial Decision-Making and Communication in Early China*, 268–84.

What explains the differing reliance upon mutilating punishments among the Later Kings? Finally, the emperor expresses concern that, despite his many efforts to encourage agriculture, employ the worthy, and comfort the orphaned and infirm, anomalies and disasters continue to appear, and he reads as cosmic verification that "the common people have yet to find relief" and the honest and corrupt within his bureaucracy remain unidentified.[18]

Having raised all his questions the emperor proceeds to the following closing comments and instructions, where he voices his frustration at the recondite references and obscure responses his ministers have provided thus far:

> Thus, who among the scholars that [We] have so carefully selected, will speak the truth? Presently, among you one hundred or so gentlemen who await this imperial announcement, some have said that the challenges of the present age have yet to be relieved. You have explicated the different policies of remote antiquity but when applying them to the present circumstances you have [claimed that they are] difficult to implement. Is it not the case that you have been so fettered by the constraints of literary form that you have been unable to avail yourself of your talents? Or is it that you have recommended conflicting methods [to be adopted] or informed me with differing advice? Each of you should consider well your response and write it down in clearly defined sections (篇).[19] Do not conceal your opinions from the responsible officials. Illuminate both your specific points and broader overviews. Cut and polish your investigations in order to fulfill Our wish.
>
> 故詳延特起之士，庶幾乎！今子大夫待詔百有餘人，或道世務而未濟，稽諸上古之不同，考之于今而難行， 毋乃牽於文繫而不得騁與？ 將所繇異術，所聞殊方與？各悉對，著于篇，毋諱有司。明其指略，切砵究之，以稱朕意。[20]

The Second Response to Emperor Wu

Like the emperor's second edict, Dong's second response is also free of the excessive platitudes that opened the first round of exchange.

18. See *HS* 56.2506–7.

19. For the possible meanings of *pian* in this context, see Giele, *Imperial Decision-Making and Communication in Early China*, 193.

20. *HS* 56.2507.

Instead, Dong proceeds directly to address the emperor's four questions. In response to Emperor Wu's pointed questions that demand Dong to take notice of the distinctions in his broad-brush moralizing representations of the thearchs and kings, Dong confirms the different leadership styles of Shun and King Wen. He explains their divergence in terms of two critical factors: the legacy of rulership they inherited from the preceding dynasty and the relations they built with their officials. Shun was able to sit idly because his predecessor Yao, in essence, had labored endlessly to perfect his governance by seeking out and employing virtuous officials to assist him. King Wen, on the other hand, was preceded by Zhou, a ruler who was infamous for treating his officials brutally and tyrannically: worthy officials under Zhou, such as Bo Yi and Tai Gong, had no choice but to retreat to a life of eremitism. Unable to secure the proper assistance from worthy officials, Zhou's dynasty quickly unraveled. Thus, upon assuming the throne, King Wen, in contrast to Shun, inherited a legacy of chaotic rule and was required by the exigencies of the circumstances to work overtime to restore order. He did so by procuring the worthy talents of such officials as Hong Yao, Tai Dian, and San Yisheng, who, upon discovering King Wen's desire to restore the proper relationship between ruler and minster, gravitated to his court. Thus each ruler inherits a potentially different geopolitical arrangement and therefore must adopt different policies to restore the one thread that binds them all together: the eternal and unchanging Way. Chief among them, Dong argues, is an ideal of ruler-minister relations whose negation, history has demonstrated, assuredly entails the demise of the ruler and his dynasty altogether.

After responding in the briefest and most perfunctory manner to the emperor's second and third questions, which speak to contemporary fiscal and juridical policies that challenge Dong to acknowledge the limitations of his unified moral picture, Dong then turns to the heart of his position in the last and longest portion of his response. He argues that the later kings of the Three Dynasties, in contrast to the earlier thearchs, followed different policies because it was necessary to rectify the faults they inherited from their predecessors. Likewise in the present, Emperor Wu must adopt policies that will rectify the faults of his Han predecessors. Chief among them is the sorry state of official recruitment, which, Dong insists, is surely the source of the anomalies that plague Emperor Wu's reign:

> Presently the governors of the commanderies and prefects of the provinces are the teachers and leaders of the common people. They are the ones who have been commanded to propagate transformation [among the common people]. Thus if the teachers and leaders are not worthy, then the virtue of the ruler will not be proclaimed and his benevolent and saturating [moral influence] will not flow forth. Now the subofficial functionaries[21] are lacking in education and instruction in the lower echelons of government. Some fail to accept and employ the laws of their ruler and superiors. [Instead] they tyrannize the common people and proffer deals with the treacherous so that the poor and destitute, and orphaned and infirm suffer injustice and hardship and consequently lose their livelihoods. Surely such actions are hardly a declaration of Your Highness's intent! This is why yin and yang are out of step and noxious *qi* fills and chokes the heavens so that the numerous forms of life rarely reach maturity and the common people have yet to find relief. In all cases, it is the lack of enlightenment among the chiefs and subofficial functionaries that brought this about.
>
> 今之郡守、縣令，民之師帥，所使承流而宣化也；故師帥不賢，則主德不宣，恩澤不流。今吏既亡教訓於下，或不承用主上之法，暴虐百姓，與姦爲市，貧窮孤弱，冤苦失職，甚不稱陛下之意。是以陰陽錯繆，氛氣充塞，羣生寡遂，黎民未濟，皆長吏不明，使至於此也。[22]

The solution, Dong proposes, is thoroughgoing reform:

> The chiefs and subofficial functionaries mainly derive from the ranks of the gentleman of the interior[23] and the inner gentlemen,[24] who are in turn selected through recommendation from the sons and younger brothers of two-thousand-bushel subofficial functionaries. Just because they are wealthy does not necessarily mean that they are worthy. Moreover in antiquity those who were deemed meritorious were ranked in accordance with the degree to which officials fulfilled the

21. See Hucker, *A Dictionary of Official Titles in Imperial China*, 301.
22. *HS* 56.2512.
23. See Hucker, *A Dictionary of Official Titles in Imperial* China, 301.
24. See ibid., 191.

responsibilities of their assigned posts and not in accordance with the length of time they served. Thus those officials who possessed limited capabilities remained in minor posts even if they served for a long time, while those who exhibited worthy capabilities, even if they had not served for long, were not precluded from possibly being promoted to a high post. This is why officials employed all their strength and fully developed their knowledge, exerting themselves to the utmost to master their tasks and thereby accrue merit. Nowadays the circumstances are not so. Officials earn various honors due to their seniority; the longer their tenure in office, the higher their post. This is why the honest and the corrupt are mixed together and the worthy and degenerate are confused, and their true abilities are not yet ascertained. Your servant, in his ignorance, is of the opinion that Your Highness should direct the enfeoffed lords, the governors of commanderies and two-thousand-bushel officials, each to select the most worthy men among their functionaries and annually supply two men to serve as guards of the lodgings and observe the abilities of the great ministers. Those who recommend worthy men should be rewarded; those who recommend unworthy men should be punished. In this manner, the imperial marquises and two-thousand-bushel officials will devote their minds to seeking out worthies and it will be possible to secure the scholars of the empire and employ them in office. If everywhere in the empire worthy men are ascertained, then the prosperity of the Three Kings will be readily achieved and the reputation of Yao and Shun will be attained. Do not consider the longevity of an official's tenure to be meritorious but rather give priority to substantiating and testing an official's worthiness and ability. Assess their capabilities and appoint them to office; appraise their virtue and determine their rank and then the honest and the corrupt will follow distinct paths and the worthy and foolish will occupy different posts.

夫長吏多出於郎中、中郎，吏二千石子弟選郎吏，又以富訾，未必賢也。 且古所謂功者，以任官稱職爲差，非（所）謂積日絫久也。故小材雖絫日，不離於小官；賢材雖未久，不害爲輔佐。 是以有司竭力盡知，務治其業而以赴功。今則不然。（累）〔絫〕日以取貴，積久以致官，是以廉恥貿亂，賢不肖渾殽，未得其真。臣愚以爲使諸列侯、郡守、二千石各擇其吏民之賢者，歲貢各二人以給宿衞，且以觀大臣之能；所貢賢者有賞，所貢不肖者有罰。夫如是，諸侯、吏二千石皆盡心於求賢，天下之士可得而官使也。徧得天下之賢人，則三王之盛易爲，而堯舜之名可及也。毋以日月爲功，實試賢能爲上，量材而授官，錄德而定位，則廉恥殊路，賢不肖異處矣。[25]

25. *HS* 56.2512–13.

This acerbic and cutting response analyzing the Liu family's hiring policies leaves no doubt the lengths to which Dong would go to express his disapproval of policies emanating from the emperor.

Self-Deprecating Conclusions Having ended his second response with a biting account of the problems in the current official recruitment system and proposals for their reform, Dong concludes with a number of self-abnegating references to seemingly soften the blow of his critique:

> Your Highness has been most generous in overlooking your servant's crimes. [Your Highness] has sent down an imperial command not to be fettered or constrained by the demands of literary form, enabling [your servant] to cut and polish [his] investigations of these matters. Your servant's daring not to fully develop [his response] is due to his ignorance.
>
> 陛下加惠，寬臣之罪，令勿牽制於文，使得切磋究之，臣敢不盡愚。[26]

These last ritually obliged comments restore the proper hierarchal relationship between ruler and minister that the preceding critique has challenged through and through. Perhaps this is the very point of these formulaic self-effacing conventions: coming at the beginning and end of an official document and, as we will see below, just before particularly disapproving comments, they demarcate a linguistic safe zone wherein vital input, often critical in nature, may be expressed. Insofar as that information necessarily abrogates or suspends the proper status of superior emperor to inferior minister, it must be ritually marked off from the rest of the text and thereby contained and neutralized.

Emperor Wu's Third Edict

At the conclusion of Dong's second response Ban Gu notes that "subsequently the Son of Heaven again issued an imperial edict." As his opening remarks in the third edict make clear, the emperor is clearly unhappy and disgruntled with the responses he has received:

> The edict states: Verily, [We] have heard, "Those who excel at speaking of Heaven invariably find verification in humankind; those who

26. *HS* 56.2513.

excel at speaking of the past, invariably find proof in the present." Thus We have condescended to question you concerning the [mutual] responsiveness between Heaven and humankind. [We] have shown admiration for Yao and Shun and expressed remorse for Jie and Zhou with regard to the gradually diminishing and extinguishing, and gradually brightening and shining Way, with the purest of intentions to enact reform. Now, you gentlemen understand how yin and yang create and transform, and you are well versed in the Way of the Former Kings, yet your literary compositions have yet to reach the ultimate. Could it be that you are confused concerning which endeavors are most appropriate to the present age? Or does the fact that the threads of your arguments do not connect, the central skein [of your formulations] does not compass the subject, indicate that you feel We will not understand? That we will listen as if dazed? Now, [some claim] that the teachings of the Three Kings differed in their origins and each had its failings. [Yet] others say that to endure without changing is the Way. How strange this opinion is! Now, you gentlemen have already expounded upon the highest principles of the Great Way and the starting point of order and chaos. You have elaborated on these issues in great detail. Who will return to these issues once more? Does not the *Odes* declare: "Alas! You Noblemen! Do not anticipate that your repose endure forever. . . . The spirits are listening to you and will bring you radiant happiness!" We will personally examine [your responses]. You gentleman, do your utmost to clarify the issues raised.

制曰：蓋聞「善言天者 必有徵於人，善言古者必有驗於今」。故朕垂問乎天人之應，上嘉唐虞，下悼桀紂，寖微寖滅寖明寖昌之道，虛心以改。今子大夫明於陰陽所以造化，習於先聖之道業，然而文采未極，豈惑虖當世之務哉？條貫靡竟，統紀未終，意朕之不明與？聽若眩與？夫三王之教所祖不同，而皆有失，或謂久而不易者道也，意豈異哉？今子大夫既已著大道之極，陳治亂之端矣，其悉之究之，孰之復之。詩不云虖？「嗟爾君子，毋常安息，神之聽之，介爾景福。」 朕將親覽焉，子大夫其茂明之。[27]

The Third Response

In recognition of the emperor's frustrations, Dong's third introduction is weighted more heavily with self-abasing conventions and laudatory speech directed toward the emperor. He begins with an apt

27. *HS* 56.2513–14.

quote from the *Analects*, implicitly depicting the emperor as a sage and praising him for his persistence in seeing his questions through to the end. He then proceeds to describe himself as an ignorant, lowly, and vile servant of the emperor, whose performance has been less than adequate:

> Your servant has heard that the *Analects* states: "It is perhaps the sage alone who, having started something, will always see it through to the end." Presently Your Highness has sent down favor and bestowed kindness by retaining and heeding his servant who has inherited the learning [of the sages] and once again promulgating this enlightened edict, to parse his ideas so as to fully investigate the virtue of the sages. This is not something Your ignorant servant, with his limited capabilities, is equipped to do. Previously in the response submitted to the Throne, the thread [of the arguments] did not connect, the central skein [of the formulations] did not compass the subject, the language was not clear and the principles not distinguished. This is all due to the faults of Your servant who is vile and lowly.
>
> 臣聞論語曰:「有始有卒者,其唯聖人虖!」今陛下幸加惠,留聽於承學之臣,復下明冊,以切其意,而究盡聖德,非愚臣之所能具也。前所上對,條貫靡竟,統紀未終,辭不別白,指不分明,此臣淺陋之罪也。[28]

Following this self-flagellating preamble, however, the tone of the memorial once again changes dramatically as Dong's responses, drawing upon the authority of the *Spring and Autumn* and the sage Confucius, exhibit a pride and confidence that demonstrates the utter insincerity of his preamble. This pride is perhaps clearest in the third leg of Dong's response where his criticisms of the emperor are most fully expressed. For his part, Emperor Wu is frustrated that his various official interlocutors have yet to serve up the requisite historical precedents to legitimize the institutional innovations he hopes to establish, such as the iron and salt monopolies. Though the emperor repeatedly appeals to the models of the Later Kings to legitimate the innovative economic policies he hopes to pursue, Dong refuses to acquiesce:

> The Way has endured for ten thousand generations without flaw. If flaws should arise, this means that the Way has been lost. The Way of the Former Kings necessarily possessed aspects that were biased and

28. *HS* 56.2514–15.

> undeveloped because the governments [they inherited] were in certain respects unenlightened and ineffective. They implemented biases in order to repair such flaws and nothing more.
>
> 道者萬世亡弊，弊者道之失也。先王之道必有偏而不起之處，故政有眊而不行，舉其偏者以補其弊而已矣。[29]

Moreover, the present emperor's circumstances are analogous to the Former Kings of the Three Dynasties, not their predecessors the great thearchs of remote antiquity, Yao, Shun, and Yu, whose reigns were flawless: "The great source of the Way emanates from Heaven. Heaven does not change; the Way also does not change. Thus when Yu succeeded Shun and Shun succeeded Yao, these three sages received and safeguarded the same Way. There were no policies to repair flaws and so there is no discussion of what they diminished and what they augmented." 道之大原出於天，天不變，道亦不變，是以禹繼舜，舜繼堯，三聖相受而守一道，亡救弊之政也，故不言其所損益也。[30] Dong here admonishes the emperor not to think of the Way as alterable and thus that he can compromise in his own political policies. Nonetheless, there are flaws to repair. What then, according to Dong, were the flaws that Emperor Wu needed to repair? Before unloading his next diatribe against Emperor Wu, Dong seemingly shields himself with the following prefatory wall of obsequious and self-demeaning verbiage:

> Your Highness, being in possession of enlightened virtue and the outstanding Way, is saddened by the dissipating customs of our age and remorseful that the Kingly Way does not shine forth. Thus Your Highness has recommended scholars who are worthy and excellent and straightforward and upright[31] to discuss and deliberate and to be tested and questioned, desiring to restore the excellent virtues of humaneness and righteousness, to clarify the laws and institutions of the thearchs and kings, and establish the Way of Great Peace. Your servant being stupid and degenerate, merely transmits what he has heard and recites what he has studied, speaking the words of his teachers, and in doing so, is scarcely able to avoid error. To discuss the

29. *HS* 56.2518.

30. *HS* 56.2518–19.

31. For this recommendation, see Hucker, *A Dictionary of Official Titles in Imperial China*, 242.

successes and failures of governmental policies and investigate what the empire is at stake to lose or gain, are the duty of the bulwarks and assistants of the grand ministers, and the responsibility of the Three Dukes and Nine Ministers. They are not issues Your servant Zhongshu is capable of addressing. Nonetheless, Your servant humbly submits the following perversity.

陛下有明德嘉道，愍世俗之靡薄，悼王道之不昭，故舉賢良方正之士，論（誼）〔議〕考問，　將欲興仁誼之休德，明帝王之法制，建太平之道也。臣愚不肖，述所聞，誦所學，道師之言，厪能勿失耳。若乃論政事之得失，察天下之息秏，此大臣輔佐之職，三公九卿之任，非臣仲舒所能及也。然而臣竊有怪者。[32]

The Rhetoric of the Virtuous Minister Gongyi Xiu Dong begins his "perversity" by appealing to a heavenly principle and ancient precedent, a strategy characteristic of policy statements articulated throughout his exchange with Emperor Wu:

Now Heaven has that which it gives in proportion. [Thus] those who are given upper teeth are not given horns; those to whom wings are attached are given [only] two feet. Likewise, those who have been endowed with great things may not appropriate small things as well. In antiquity those who were given salaries did not eat by means of their own physical labor, nor did they participate in the branch occupations. This is also a case of being endowed with great things, not appropriating small things, and thereby identifying with Heaven's will. Now, if Heaven could hardly provide sufficiently for those who, having received great things, also sought to appropriate small things, how much less can man!

夫天亦有所分予，予之齒者去其角，傅其翼者兩其足，是所受大者不得取小也。古之所予祿者，不食於力，不動於末，是亦受大者不得取小，與天同意者也。夫已受大，又取小，天不能足，而況人乎！[33]

The failure of the emperor to follow this principle of Heaven as the ancients did is the root source of suffering among the common people:

This is why the people wail bitterly about their insufficiencies. How can the people tolerate those who are favored with positions

32. *HS* 56.2519.
33. *HS* 56.2520.

of eminence, having warm houses and enjoying substantial salaries, availing themselves of the resources of their wealth and position to compete for profit with them? They increase the numbers of their servants; multiply the numbers of their livestock; enlarge the sizes of their land and estates; augment the products of their professions, and amass their supplies of grain. They exert their utmost on these endeavors and nothing else, oppressing the common people so that as the days and months pass by, the common people are gradually reduced to utter destitution.

> 此民之所以囂囂苦不足也。身寵而載高位，家溫而食厚祿，因乘富貴之資力，以與民爭利於下，民安能如之哉！是故眾其奴婢，多其牛羊，廣其田宅，博其產業，畜其積委，務此而亡已，以迫蹴民，民日削月朘，寖以大窮。[34]

Having reduced the lower echelons of society to destitution, rampant crime is unavoidable:

> If the wealthy are extravagant and wasteful, the poor will become destitute and grieved. If the poor become destitute and grieved and the emperor does not relieve them, then the people will find no joy in living. If the people find no joy in living, they will do nothing to avoid death; how is it possible that they will avoid committing crimes? This is why depravity cannot be overcome, even if punishments are increased.
>
> 富者奢侈羡溢，貧者窮急愁苦；窮急愁苦而上不救，則民不樂生；民不樂生，尚不避死，安能避罪！此刑罰之所以蕃而姦邪不可勝者也。[35]

What then is to be done? Dong proposes the following solution:

> Therefore the households that receive an official salary should live off their official salaries and nothing more. They should not compete for resources with the common people. Only then will benefits be distributed equally and the people will be able to provide sufficiently for their households. Such policies esteem the principles of Heaven and also the Way of Remote Antiquity and they are what the Son of Heaven should emulate in devising his institutions, and what officials ought to follow and implement. Thus when the prime minister of Lu, Master Gongyi,[36] returned home and saw his wife weaving silk, he grew angry and banished her. When he went home to dine and

34. *HS* 56.2520–21.

35. *HS* 56.2521.

36. Gongyi Xiu 公儀休, prime minister under Duke Mu of Lu (r. 407–376 BCE), enjoyed a reputation for frugality and incorruptibility.

[saw his servants] pickling vegetables, he grew vexed and rooted up the vegetables, exclaiming: "I already live off of an official salary. How could I deprive the farmers and weavers of their profit?"[37] The worthy and noble men of antiquity who took up various official positions, all were like this. Thus their subordinates all admired their conduct and followed their teachings while the common people were transformed by their incorruptibility and were no longer scornful. But coming to the decline of the Zhou dynasty, in contrast, the chief ministers were lax to practice righteousness yet frantic to pursue profit. Though utterly lacking retiring and deferential habits, they were full of lawsuits to vie for land. Thus the poets despised them and satirized them saying: "How lofty is the Southern Mountain! How massive its boulders! How awesome are you, Master Yin! The people all admire you."[38] If you[39] are fond of righteousness, the people will turn to humaneness and custom will become good. If you are fond of profit, the people will grow fond of depravity and customs will become corrupt. From this perspective it is clear that the Son of Heaven and his chief ministers are those whom the common people watch and emulate, and those whom the inhabitants of distant regions from all sides look to for guidance. Surely it is not possible for one to whom people both near and far look for their example to occupy the position of the worthy yet conduct himself as a mere commoner! If the August Emperor seeks after wealth and profit, ever fearful that he will not have enough, he will possess the intent of a commoner. If the August Emperor seeks after humaneness and righteousness, ever fearful that he will not be able to transform the people, he will possess the intent of a nobleman. The *Changes* states: "Carrying his burdens on his back, he avails himself of a carriage and thereby invites robbers to attack him." To avail oneself of a carriage reflects the station of the noble man; to carry a burden's on one's back reflects the station of the small man. This means that one who occupies the station of the nobleman yet follows the pursuit of the common man will inevitably be overtaken by disaster. If one wishes to occupy the position of a nobleman and engage in conduct appropriate

---

37. For other Han versions of this popular narrative, see *HNZ* 12.113.22–26 and *Shiji* 119. 3101–2. For English translations see Major et al., *The Huainanzi*, 463–64, and Watson, trans., *Records of the Grand Historian: Han Dynasty*, vol. 2, 375–76.

38. Mao, no. 191

39. Note the use of the more formal second person pronoun *er* 爾 as compared to *ru* 汝.

> to that station, then one can never forsake the example of Gongyi Xiu when he was a minister in Lu.
>
> 故受祿之家，食祿而已，不與民爭業，然後利可均布，而民可家足。此上天之理，而亦太古之道，天子之所宜法以爲制，大夫之所當循以爲行也。故公儀子相魯，　之其家見織帛，怒而出其妻，食於舍而茹葵，慍而拔其葵，曰：「吾已食祿，又奪園夫紅女利虖！」古之賢人君子在列位者皆如是，是故下高其行而從其教，民化其廉而不貪鄙。及至周室之衰，其卿大夫緩於誼而急於利，亡推讓之風而有爭田之訟。故詩人疾而刺之，曰：「節彼南山，惟石巖巖，赫赫師尹，民具爾瞻。」爾好誼，則民鄉仁而俗善；爾好利，則民好邪而俗敗。由是觀之，天子大夫者，下民之所視效，遠方之所四面而內望也。近者視而放之，遠者望而效之，豈可以居賢人之位而爲庶人行哉！夫皇皇求財利常恐乏匱者，庶人之意也；皇皇求仁義常恐不能化民者，大夫之意也。《易》曰：「負且乘，致寇至。」乘車者君子之位也，負擔者小人之事也，此言居君子之位而爲庶人之行者，其患禍必至也。若居君子之位，當君子之行，則舍公儀休之相魯，亡可爲者矣。[40]

Dong crafts his polemic to build an argument as to why the government should not take an active role in the economy. The imagery is deliberately extreme: Gongyi Xiu is shown becoming furious with his wife and household servants for doing what would ordinarily be the norm: weaving silk and growing fresh vegetables for household consumption. Because he was a government official, according to Dong, Gongyi Xiu felt it was obligatory for him to spend his government salary on these basics rather than producing them for himself as *any other household would do*. This is argument by hyperbole: Gongyi Xiu was unwilling to "compete" with the people in even such an innocuous way, how much less should the Han government do so by establishing an enterprise like the salt monopoly?

None of the extant passages from verifiably Warring States sources, such as the *Hanfeizi*, cast the image of Gongyi Xiu in quite this light: his refraining from luxuries like fish in Warring States texts is not a matter of refusing to compete with the people, but of remaining personally incorruptible in the face of the temptations of power. This reading of Gongyi Xiu continued well into the Han, as testified, for example, by its appearance in the *Huainanzi* and *Shiji*.[41]

---

40. *HS* 56.2521.

41. See *HNZ* 12.113.22–26, and Major et al., *The Huainanzi*, 463–64; *SJ* 119.3101–2 and Watson, trans., *Records of the Grand Historian: Han Dynasty*, Vol. II, 375–76.

Dong Zhongshu, however, has embroidered and updated the iconographic Gongyi Xiu to suit his own rhetorical purposes in the debates that were current in the Han.

Scenario 2: The Administrator Dong Zhongshu and the King of Jiangdu

Chunqiu fanlu 32 and *Hanshu* 56 each preserve a recension of the exchange between the king of Jiangdu and the administrator Dong Zhongshu. The *Chunqiu fanlu* version is replete with the formulaic speech of an official communication, suggesting that it preserves or mimics an official exchange that occurred in historical time. This official report of the exchange must have then been sent up to the central court to be stored in the imperial archives, making it available to Ban Gu, who years later selected it to craft his biography of Dong Zhongshu. Thus in thinking about the characteristics of early imperial court discourse the reader must be mindful that the rhetoric of imperial communication preserved in the official documents comes to us filtered through a second screen of rhetoric, that of the historian. As will be demonstrated below, Ban Gu has staged and framed these documents to yield a particular reading.

The *Chunqiu fanlu* recension of the exchange between Dong Zhongshu and Liu Fei, the king of Jiangdu, begins in the following succinct manner: "A royal command to the administrator stated."[42] The *Hanshu* account, however, sets a more elaborate scene for reading the exchange both implicitly and explicitly. First, by positioning the exchange between the newly promoted administrator of Jiangdu and the local king immediately after Dong's communications with Emperor Wu, Ban Gu creates a stunning contrast between Emperor Wu and his brother Liu Fei: their personalities, the manners in which they deport themselves, the rulers they cite as historical precedent, the policies they wish to promote, and finally their relationships to their officials as expressed in the language of exchange could not be more different. Moreover, the manner and content of Dong

42. *Chunqiu fanlu zhuzi suoyin* 32.41.3. All citations of the text are to D.C. Lau et al., eds., *A Concordance to the Chunqiu fanlu*, in the form chapter/page/lines. Hereafter cited as *CQFL*.

Zhongshu's response to the emperor can now be compared to that of his brother and local king, Liu Fei who, according to Ban Gu, was a ruler with pointedly different proclivities, yet one whose uncouth ways Dong had already begun to reform:

> When his [i.e., Dong Zhongshu's] responses drew to a conclusion, the Son of Heaven appointed Dong Zhongshu to be the administrator to Jiangdu to serve King Yi. King Yi was the elder brother of the emperor. He was unrefined and haughty, and was fond of bravado. Zhongshu employed propriety and rightness to correct and rectify [the king]. [Consequently] the king respected [Dong] and took him seriously. After some time had passed the king inquired of Zhongshu stating . . .
>
> 對既畢，天子以仲舒爲江都相，事易王。易王，帝兄，素驕，好勇。仲舒以禮誼匡正，王敬重焉。久之，王問仲舒曰:[43]

As Ban Gu's comments indicate, when the imperial inquiry drew to a conclusion, Emperor Wu appointed Dong Zhongshu to the post of administrator to the kingdom of Jiangdu. Apparently Dong Zhongshu's responses were simply too forthright and critical for the young emperor to withstand. The emperor effectively neutralized the outspoken scholar with an assignment far from the central court. Sending Dong to Jiangdu not only removed him from the central court; it also established Dong as an effective muzzle for Liu Fei and monitor for an area that recently had experienced a rebellion.

At the time, the kingdom of Jiangdu was under the jurisdiction of Emperor Wu's elder brother Liu Fei, who reigned as King Yi. King Yi was well known for his martial inclinations, having established a reputation for his military acumen during the Revolt of the Seven Kingdoms, when he quelled the rebellion in Wu on behalf of the imperial court. Sima Qian and Ban Gu also insist that he was arrogant and extravagant.[44] A ruler with such character traits was hardly a good match for the uncompromising and frank Dong Zhongshu. The two men could not have had more different personalities and agendas. Yet, Ban Gu's comments suggest that Dong was able to in-

43. *HS* 56.2523.

44. See *SJ* 59.2096 and Watson, trans., *Records of the Grand Historian: Han Dynasty, Vol. I*, 391.

fluence the king and ultimately "rectify and correct" him, as a teacher does his disciple.

Dong served King Yi at a time when both central and local officials were increasingly concerned with the mounting challenges posed by the Xiongnu. In 133 BCE, Emperor Wu issued an imperial edict asking his ministers whether the time was ripe to attack the Xiongnu, and receiving the support of his highest officials, proceeded to sanction what turned out to be an abortive attack on the Xiongnu led by General Wang Hui.[45] Perhaps it was General Wang Hui's abysmal failure that prompted King Yi to step forward to propose leading the next military incursion against the Xiongnu. Whatever the particular motivations, for his part, King Yi was clearly contemplating a military solution to the ongoing Xiongnu crisis. The *Shiji* reports: "In the fifth year of the *yuanguang* era (130 BCE), when the Xiongnu were invading and plundering Han territory in great numbers, [Liu] Fei submitted a letter [to Emperor Wu] requesting permission to attack the Xiongnu, but the Throne did not grant permission." 元光五年，匈奴大入漢爲賊，非上書願擊匈奴，上不許。[46] The official exchange between King Yi and Dong Zhongshu also testifies to the king's desire to employ a military solution to resolve the Xiongnu crisis. As will be demonstrated below, it is best understood as a veiled discussion of the mounting Xiongnu crisis: the humiliations suffered by Goujian at Kuaiji when surrounded and defeated by the army of Fuchai, king of Wu, serves as a powerful substitute for the recent embarrassments Emperor Wu had suffered at the hands of the Shanyu leader of the Xiongnu. This is the most likely context for the discussion recorded below.

The King of Jiangdu's Question

How then does each address his respective audience? Does the language of their communication ultimately affirm or negate Ban Gu's representations of King Yi? And what does it betray of the respective participants' views on the ideals of the ruler-minister relations? King Yi initiates the dialogue as follows:

---

45. For the details of the imperial instruction *zhao* 詔 requesting the attack and the opinion *yi* 議 sanctioning military action, see *HS* 6.162.

46. *SJ* 59.2096.

> The king of Yue together with the five great officers—[Fan] Li, [Wen] Zhong, [Shi] Yong, Gao, and Che Cheng made a plan to attack [the state of] Wu. After they destroyed Wu, they [considered themselves] avenged for the humiliation they suffered at Kuaiji. Ultimately [the king of Yue] became a Hegemon. Fan Li left the state; Wen Zhong died there. I, the Orphaned One, consider that these two great officers both were worthy men. Confucius said: "There were three humane men [during] the Yin [dynasty]." Now considering the worthiness of the king of Yue and the capabilities of Fan Li and Wen Zhong, I, the Orphaned One, submit that there were also three humane men in Yue. What is your opinion? As Duke Huan [of Qi] deferred his questions to Guan Zhong, so do I, the Orphaned One defer mine to you.
>
> 大夫蠡，大夫種，大夫庸，大夫睪，大夫車成，越王與此五大夫謀伐吳，遂滅之。雪會稽之恥，卒爲霸主。范蠡去之，種死之。寡人以此二大夫者爲皆賢。孔子曰：「殷有三仁。」今以越王之賢，與蠡，種之能，此三人者，寡人亦以爲越有三仁。其於君何如？桓公決疑管仲，寡人決疑於君。[47]

What is most interesting about the exchange between King Yi and Dong Zhongshu is the extent to which the language utilized by the emperor's brother differs from that employed by the emperor in the previous exchange. Gone are the elaborate formulaic conventions that ensure the proper ritual space between superior and inferior. The king observes the ritual protocols of courtly communication in a most limited fashion: he employs the term *guaren* 寡人, a stylized regal form of self-address employed by Warring States monarchs in classical texts. Meaning "the orphaned one" or "the lonely one," it refers to the fact that the king only becomes king on the loss of his father. Further research is required to determine whether this was customary usage among the Han feudal kings or a deliberate archaism on the part of Liu Fei to reinforce his rhetorical appeal to the model of Duke Huan. Whatever the case, it is clear that the language generally employed by Liu Fei was far more informal and lacking in ritual protocol compared to the official exchanges between Emperor Wu and Dong Zhongshu described above. Could they have served as linguistic confirmation of Ban Gu's claims concerning Liu Fei's "un-

---

47. *CQFL* 32.41.31–42.3. See also *HS* 56.2523.

refined" manners? Moreover, what of King Yi's portrayals of the ruler-minister relationship? Situated within several layers of the text, we find them at the surface level of the document, in the discursive exchange itself and the extent to which that speech follows the formulaic conventions of official exchange; in the brief analogy King Yi draws between his relationship to Dong Zhongshu and that of Duke Huan and Guan Zhong; and in King Yi's reading of the well-known narrative of Goujian, king of Yue and his "humane ministers." At all three levels, King Yi confirms his self-styled identity as a latter-day hegemon aspiring to the likes of his predecessors beginning with Duke Huan of Qi and ending with King Goujian of Yue.[48] Like these rulers, King Yi readily dismisses the efficacy of ritual for that of the sword and strives to redefine humaneness in terms of notions of justified warfare. The only way to avenge the humiliation Emperor Wu has suffered in the face of ongoing attacks initiated by the Xiongnu is to do as Goujian has done, follow his minister's advice and attack when the time is right.[49]

Dong's Response to King Yi

In contrast to King Yi's lack of etiquette, the beginning of Dong's response is chock-full of self-effacing rhetoric; the respondent engages in a number of ritual acts both physical and linguistic to confirm his subordinate and lowly status in comparison to that of the ruler he addresses: "Dong Zhongshu prostrated himself and bowed twice. His response stated: 'Zhongshu's knowledge is petty and his learning superficial. They do not suffice to decide these questions. Nonetheless, when a king has a question for his servant, his servant cannot dare but do his utmost to respond, for [such are the rules of] propriety.'" 仲舒伏地再拜，對曰：仲舒知褊而學淺，不足以決之。雖

48. It may be that part of Liu Fei's agenda was an actual revival of the office of "hegemon" for the Han era. Just as the hegemons had held their positions under the auspices of the Zhou "Son of Heaven," Liu Fei may have wished his position of preeminence among the Han feudal kings to be formalized by this title. As "hegemon" he would then effectively be subruler and military commander-in-chief under his brother, the emperor.

49. For an outstanding new study of more recent political readings of Goujian, see Cohen, *Speaking to History*.

然，丰有問於臣，臣不敢不悉以對，禮也。[50] Having served up the requisite language to reconfirm his inferior status to that of the king and his inferior standing as a scholar, yet bound by the demands of official protocol, Dong, posing an analogy between himself and Liuxia Hui, reluctantly responds:

> Your servant Zhongshu has heard that in earlier times the Lord of Lu asked Liuxia Hui: "I wish to attack Qi. What do you think?" Liuxia Hui responded: "You cannot." Liuxia Hui returned home with a worried expression and said: "I have heard that when [the ruler] is going to attack another state, he does not question those who are humane. Why were these questions directed at me?" Having only been asked, Liuxia Hui was ashamed, how much more [would he have been ashamed] if he had plotted [like Fan Li and Wen Zhong with Goujian] to treacherously attack Wu? The inappropriateness of such a scheme is clear. Looking at the question from this perspective, [the kingdom of] Yue fundamentally lacked even one humane man, much less having three. A humane man is one who corrects his Way but does not calculate what benefits that will bring him, who adheres to principles without hurrying after success. The righteousness of the *Spring and Autumn* honors trustworthiness and censures deceit. To deceive others to achieve victory, even if successful, is not something a noble man would do. This is why even a five-foot-tall [i.e., young] boy who follows the teachings of Confucius is ashamed to mention the Five Hegemons because they placed treachery and force before humaneness and righteousness. They simply engaged in treachery and nothing else. Therefore they are not worthy of being mentioned within the gate of the great noble man [Confucius]. Compared to other lords of the land, the Five Hegemons were worthy; compared with the worthiness of the sages what worthiness did they possess? It is like comparing coarse stone to polished jade. Your servant Dong Zhongshu [again] prostrates himself and salutes twice, [in gratitude] for being heard.
>
> 臣仲舒聞：昔者，魯君問於柳下惠曰：「我欲攻齊，何如？」 柳下惠對曰：「不可。」退而有憂色，曰：「吾聞之也，謀伐國者，不問於仁人也。此何為至於我？」 但見問而尚羞之，而況乃與為詐以伐吳乎！其不宜明矣。以此觀之，越本無一仁，而安得三仁！ 仁人者，正其道不謀其利，修其理不急其功。是以仲尼之門，五尺之童子，言羞稱五伯。為其詐以成功，苟為而已也。故不足稱於大君子之門。五伯者， 比於他諸侯

50. *CQFL* 32.42.3–4.

爲賢者。比於聖賢，何賢之有？譬猶碔砆比於美玉也。臣仲舒伏地再拜以聞。[51]

Though King Yi likens his relationship with Dong Zhongshu to that of Goujian and his ministers Fan Li and Wen Zhong on the one hand, and Duke Huan of Qi and Guan Zhong on the other, Dong Zhongshu, in contrast, looks to the duke of Lu and Liuxia Hui. Dong's reading of Liuxia Hui not only follows that of the *Analects* and *Mencius*, but quite self-consciously and deliberately draws upon it.[52] According to the *Mencius*, Liuxia Hui was a sage who "was not ashamed of a prince with a tarnished reputation."[53] The entire exchange is best read as a form of rather thinly veiled, coded communication between King Yi and Dong in which Dong remonstrates with the king. King Yi "queries" Dong on particular historical models to sound him out on his present dispositions: "If I have the ambition to be a Goujian or a Duke Huan, would you be my Fan Li or Guan Zhong?" Dong responds with an emphatic no. The model Dong responds with unequivocally rejects one ideal of ruler-minister relations for a decidedly different one: "You've got it wrong: you are no Duke Huan and I am no Guan Zhong. You are, in fact, the unworthy duke of Lu and I am Liuxia Hui. I only tolerate serving a tainted ruler like yourself out of a sense of duty to save you from your own worst inclinations." Liuxia Hui's shame for the duke of Lu mirrors Dong Zhongshu's own shame for King Yi, who has proposed not only pursuing military action but pursuing self-aggrandizing military action that could be seen as a challenging arrogation of power, a challenge that follows the very troubling uprising by Liu Pi, of 154 BCE. This in turn explains the excessive ritual courtesies Dong loads into his concluding remarks: he has to find some way of softening the insult he is delivering to Yi by way of giving him some face.

Where then does the response ultimately leave Dong Zhongshu? Though the *Chunqiu fanlu* recension of the official exchange concludes with Dong's remarks and does not indicate whether King Yi

---

51. *CQFL* 32.41.31–.42.12. See also Giele, *Imperial Decision-Making and Communication in Early China*, 97–100.

52. See *Analects* 18.8.

53. See *Mencius* 2A.9 and 5B.1.

accepted or rejected Dong's position, Ban Gu's account supplied a resolution: "The King responded: Excellent!" 王曰:「善。」[54] Not only does Ban Gu provide the reader with King Yi's response, but the inclusion of this response supports Ban Gu's likely mythic claim that Dong was able to reform the recalcitrant king. Thus the official document, in the hands of the court historian, becomes both *is* and *ought*—both the present and posthumous testimony of the truth of Ban Gu's claims concerning not only the character of this particular official and the nature of his relationship to imperial power but also the way that relationship ideally ought to be. This the historian bequeaths to readers of later ages as the ultimate historical judgment.

Scenario 3: The Retired Dong Zhongshu Responds to Emperor Wu via an Emissary

The third document, preserved in *Chunqiu fanlu* 71 under the title "An Official Response on the Suburban Sacrifice" 郊事對, affords another view of the highly ritualized formalities and intricacies of early imperial court discourse. As the chapter title and the content of the communication suggest, it is also an official response (*dui* 對) addressed to Emperor Wu. It differs, however, in several important respects from the document discussed at the outset of this essay, as can be seen from the following opening lines of Zhang Tang's letter: "The chamberlain for law enforcement, your servant [Zhang] Tang, risking death for daring to report [to your Majesty] states: Your servant [Zhang] Tang has received an imperial decree to question the former administrator of Jiaoxi, [Dong] Zhongshu, regarding the Suburban Sacrifice." 廷尉臣湯昧死言曰:臣湯承制,以郊事問故膠西相仲舒。[55] Dong Zhongshu is not summoned to the central court as an expectant academician hoping to secure an official appointment but rather answers Emperor Wu's questions through an emissary from his home as a retired official, who reports his answers to the emperor with an official letter. This reading is further supported by the conventions of imperial exchange found throughout the docu-

54. *HS* 56.2524.
55. *CQFL* 71.70.22.

ment. For example, in the opening line, Zhang Tang employs the phrase "risking death for daring to report [to Your Majesty] (*mei si yan* 眛死言)." As Enno Giele has noted, the phrase "risking death (*meisi* 眛死)" was actually an abbreviation of "risk committing a crime that merits capital punishment" (*mei fan si zui* 眛犯死罪), a convention employed by Qin officials when submitting letters to the throne which Han officials continued to employ.[56]

Ban Gu's "Biography of Dong Zhongshu" provides the background to situate the official exchange under consideration here. Dong's biography notes that after a brief tenure as administrator to Liu Duan, King Yu of Jiaoxi, another elder brother of Emperor Wu, who was no less reprehensible than Liu Fei, King Yi of Jiangdu,[57] Dong retired to his home in fear for his life: "Zhongshu feared that if he remained long [in this post] he would be implicated in a crime and so retired on the grounds of illness." 仲舒恐久獲辠，病免。[58] In this last portion of the biography, Ban Gu describes Dong's postretirement communications with the imperial court as follows: "When Zhongshu was retired, if the central court held an important deliberation, [the emperor would] send emissaries, including even the chamberlain for law enforcement Zhang Tang himself, to travel to his home and question him. His responses all possessed clear standards." 仲舒在家，朝廷如有大議，使使者及廷尉張湯就其家而問之，其對皆有明法。[59] Presumably, then, Emperor Wu sent Zhang Tang, in his capacity as chamberlain for law enforcement, to solicit Dong Zhongshu's opinions at home after he retired from active office around 123 BCE.[60] The year 123 was a momentous one for the Suburban Sacrifice: Emperor Wu resumed performing this rite after a hiatus of more than a decade. As the emperor looked to resume the rite, it would have made sense to seek Dong's advice on the many details

---

56. See Giele, *Imperial Decision-Making and Communication in Early China*, 92.

57. See *SJ* 59.2097, Watson, *Records of the Grand Historian: Han Dynasty*, 393, and *HS* 56.2525.

58. *HS* 56.2525.

59. *HS* 56.2525.

60. Zhang Tang was active in the above-named post from 126 to 121 BCE but Dong Zhongshu did not retire before 123 so the document must date no earlier than 123 and no later than 121. See Queen, *From Chronicle to Canon*, 31–36.

of a ritual he knew intimately and had written about extensively.[61] Chapter 71 of the *Chunqiu fanlu* is likely the official report of such an exchange in which Zhang Tang reports to the emperor the questions directed to Dong and his respective responses.

As mentioned above, in the first line of the official document Zhang Tang employs the phrase "risking death for daring to report [to Your Majesty]" (*mei si yan* 昧死言). Aside from this chilling expression of the emperor's power over the lives of his subjects, Zhang Tang's comments are relatively free of linguistic gestures of humility. The questions and responses that constitute the body of the letter follow a straightforward, concise, and consistent formula. Zhang Tang typically reports his questions with the formulaic "Your servant Tang asked Zhongshu" 臣湯問仲舒 or "Your servant Tang respectfully asked Zhongshu" 臣湯謹問仲舒."[62] As the letter emanated from an official who occupied the high station of chamberlain for law enforcement, perhaps he did not need to pepper his report to the emperor with the kind of self-abasing language officials of lower status like Dong were required to employ when addressing the emperor. Moreover, an official letter submitted to the throne likely did not require the same level of ritual pomp and circumstance as an imperial inquiry.

For his part, Dong's responses to Zhang Tang, though a messenger of the emperor, were relatively unadorned. Most answers are consistently reported with the set phrase "Your servant Zhongshu responded by stating" 臣仲舒對曰.[63] There are, however, two important exceptions. When proffering his opinions Dong twice adopts the rhetoric of feigned "stupidity" and introduces his position with the set phrase "Your servant, in his stupidity, is of the opinion that . . ." 臣愚以爲. Why in these two instances does Dong avail himself of this false modesty? In his study of imperial communication, Giele proposes that this convention was frequently employed in responses to questions or general calls for opinions by the emperor when disputing

61. See *SJ* 28.1384, *HS* 25A.1216, *HS* 6.162, 6.174, 6.175, 6.183, 6.185, 6.193, 6.195, and *HFHD*, II, 57, 60, 74, 76, 89, 93, 113, 248, 313, 325, and 329. See also Loewe, *Crisis and Conflict in Han China*, 167–68.

62. See the numerous examples throughout *CQFL* 71.70.2–71.71.10.

63. See the numerous examples throughout *CQFL* 71.70.22–71.71.10.

the pro and cons of an orthodox position or the status quo.[64] This is precisely the case here. However, some background is required to understand how pointedly Dong is challenging the emperor in these seemingly banal details concerning the appropriate colors of various sacrificial victims.

In keeping with his other writings on the rite, Dong emphasized the primacy of the Suburban Sacrifice to Heaven as the emperor's most important rite of veneration. Indeed, the emperor's obligations to perform the Suburban Sacrifice trump all other ritual obligations: "It is well known that among the rituals of the Son of Heaven in ancient times, none was more important than the Suburban [Sacrifice]. The Suburban [Sacrifice] was always offered in the first month on the first *xin* day. In order to precede the sacrifices to the numerous spirits it was placed at the very beginning [of the sacrificial schedule]." 所聞古者天子之禮，莫重於郊。郊常以正月上辛者，所以先百神而最居前。[65] It was even more paramount, as ancient precedent demonstrated, than the emperor's filial obligations to his deceased father: "In accordance with the rites, during the three-year mourning period, one did not sacrifice to the ancestors but one did not dare to abandon the Suburban [Sacrifice]. The Suburban [Altar] was more important than the ancestral temple [just as] Heaven is more venerable than humankind." 禮，三年喪，不祭其先，而不敢廢郊。郊重於宗廟，天尊於人也。[66] Though performed only a few times by the Han emperors that preceded Emperor Wu, and only intermittently by Emperor Wu himself, the established practice was that the Suburban Sacrifice was reserved for the emperor alone. Breaking with this orthodox position, in the first example, Dong defends as legitimate the Lu performance of the rite as performed by the duke of Zhou. The duke of Zhou's virtuous service to King Cheng, as the young ruler's regent, earned him the prerogative to perform a rite normally reserved for the Son of Heaven alone. Thus the young king sanctioned the duke's performance but because of the unusual circumstances of the supplicant, made sure that the color of the sacrificial victim the duke employed differed from that used by the Son of Heaven:

---

64. See Giele, *Imperial Decision-Making and Communication in Early China*, 193.
65. *CQFL* 71.70.23.
66. *CQFL* 71.70./23–24.

> King Wu had died and King Cheng had been established [as Son of Heaven], but he was still a child. The duke of Zhou inherited the undertaking of Kings Wen and Wu, and brought to completion the merit of these two sagely kings. His virtue extended to all that lay between Heaven and Earth and his generosity filled all within the four seas. Thus King Cheng recognized his virtue and ability and revered and respected him. The *Odes* declare: "No virtuous deed is without recompense."[67] Thus when King Cheng ordered the sacrificial offering, the duke of Zhou used a white-colored bull. With respect to his superior, he was not allowed to use the same color sacrificial victim as that used by the Son of Heaven; with respect to his subordinates, [the color of the sacrificial victim] differed from that of the lords of the land. Your servant Zhongshu, in his stupidity, is of the opinion that this was an act of propriety to repay the duke of Zhou's virtue.
>
> 武王崩，成王立而在襁褓之中，周公繼文武之業，成二聖之功，德漸天地，澤被四海，故成王賢而貴之。《詩》云：'無德不報。'故成王使祭周公以白牡，上不得與天子同色，下有異於諸侯。臣仲舒愚以爲報德之禮。[68]

In the second example in which Dong employs the convention of polite "stupidity," he challenges imperial authority once again, but this time with regard to an innovation the emperor desires to introduce with respect to the ancestral sacrifices: the proposition being considered is whether or not a domesticated duck (*mu* 鶩) may be substituted for a wild one (*fu* 鳧). Dong responds:

> A domesticated duck is not a wild duck; a wild duck is not a domesticated duck. Your servant has heard that when Confucius entered the ancestral temple of the Son of Heaven he made inquiries concerning each thing he encountered. This was the epitome of vigilance. Your Highness personally performs the sacrifices. [Prior to performing the sacrifice, Your Highness] fasts and purifies himself, cleansing body and mind. In offering sacrifices at the ancestral temple he is extremely reverent. Why then substitute a domesticated duck for a wild duck? Neither the name nor the reality of the thing would match. Using a domesticated duck to sacrifice at the ancestral temple would be quite a mismatch! Your servant Zhongshu, in his stupidity, considers that such a substitution is not permissible.

---

67. Mao, no. 256.
68. *CQFL* 71.70.29–71.2.

> 鶩非鳧，鳧非鶩也。臣聞孔子入太廟，每事問，慎之至也。陛下祭躬親，齊戒沐浴，以承宗廟，甚敬謹，奈何以鳧當鶩，鶩當鳧？名實不相應，以承太廟，不亦不稱乎？臣仲舒愚以爲不可。[69]

Ultimately, Dong's responses express what would amount to a desire to reform the Suburban Sacrifice along the lines of Zhou practices. Judging from the accounts of Emperor Wu's performance of this sacrifice in the years that followed, Dong lost out to rivals' proposals.[70] Dong's unorthodox and dissenting positions on the Suburban Sacrifice suggest that he was swimming against the tide. Perhaps that is why, beyond the demands of protocol, he concluded his responses with the following hyperbole:

> Your servant is but a decrepit hound or broken-down horse, having been granted permission [to rest his] weary bones and to live out his days in this humble lane. Still Your Highness has graciously sent one of the Nine Ministers to question your servant on an important matter of the court. Your servant is stupid and vulgar. [His abilities] do not suffice to receive this enlightened imperial announcement (*ming zhao*) and submit a significant response. Your servant Zhongshu risks death to inform [Your Majesty].
>
> 臣犬馬齒衰，賜骸骨，伏陋。陛下乃辛使九卿問臣以朝廷之事。臣愚陋，曾不足以承明詔，奉大對。臣仲舒昧死以聞。[71]

Conclusion

Throughout the official documents explored in this essay we find a pervasive tension between the formalistic language of imperial exchange that elevates the position of the ruler and humbles that of his ministers and the content of the exchanges themselves that confirms the ruler's inferiority vis-à-vis the superior erudition of his ministers. Though the administrative hierarchy of the empire is mirrored in the conventions of imperial exchange, beneath the veneer of such ritual protocols, this hierarchy is subverted time and again by the specific arguments of the officials and even that of the emperor himself when young and more vulnerable. Whether as interpreter of the eternal

---

69. *CQFL* 71.71.7–8.
70. *SJ* 28.1387, 1389, 1393–96.
71. *CQFL* 71.71.8–10.

and unchanging principles of the Way or as expert in the minutiae of ritual sacrifice and the raison d'être for each and every detail, Han officials like Dong Zhongshu not only saw themselves as teachers of the student emperors they served, but were in certain respects *de facto* teachers. For as long as they possessed the ritual expertise and moral knowledge to guide and legitimate the emperor and his empire, the emperor was necessarily inferior and dependent with respect to their mastery of the traditions of the past which were to guide present policy decisions. Even though Dong portrays himself as a broken-down nag utterly dependent on the emperor's grace to survive, through the ritual expertise of scholars like Dong Zhongshu the emperor sought to authenticate the dynasty that sustained his power.

In sum, scholars at the Han court like Dong Zhongshu drew readily upon the formulaic language developed during the Warring States and Qin to confirm that the ruler was hierarchically miles above his ministers and advisors. Though Han officials addressed the emperor with this more formal and hierarchical vocabulary of empire, the content of their arguments continued to draw inspiration from Warring States ideals and precedents that conceived of the minister-ruler relation as analogous to that of teacher and disciple. Thus, their use of self-abasing language, created a rhetorical "safe zone" that enabled them to speak authoritatively and candidly to the ruler, disagree with, and even upbraid him, to provide the critical information upon which the emperor depended to perpetuate his reign. Within the linguistic empire of self-deprecating conventions, the educated elite held tenaciously to such pre-Qin ministerial ideals as the duke of Zhou and Gongyi Xiu embodied, calling them forth to challenge the assumptions of the very linguistic edifice they were now required to uphold.[72]

---

72. I am indebted to Professor Olberding for inviting me to participate in the conference "Addressing the Autocrat," which inspired the research for this essay, and to the National Endowment for the Humanities, whose grant supported a sabbatical to further my work on Dong Zhongshu. I would also like to thank Paul Cohen, John Major, and Andrew Meyer for sharing their invaluable insights and comments on earlier drafts of the essay.

CHAPTER 7

Kinship and Kingship in Han China: The 120 CE Case against Liu Chang, King of Lecheng

Griet Vankeerberghen, McGill University

Most of this essay is devoted to an analysis of a legal case brought in 120 CE against Liu Chang 劉萇, the king of Lecheng 樂成, by two officials of the central government. The two documents relating to the case that are preserved in the received historical sources focus on the struggles over imperial succession that marked Empress Dowager Deng's 鄧太后 (81–121 CE) years in power and the years following her death in 121 CE. As tempting as it might be to analyze the case solely in terms of political struggles at the central court in the first quarter of the second century CE and to see Liu Chang merely as a helpless pawn in the hands of emperors and empresses jockeying for power, Liu Chang's case should be examined as a significant part of the history of the institution of kingship during the Han dynasty.

That institutional history is usually given short shrift, eclipsed as it is by the dramatic events of the first half-century of the Western Han. The Han founder, Liu Bang 劉邦 or Gaozu 高祖 (r. 206–195 BCE), had installed his comrades-in-arms as kings over large swaths of territories, only then to dethrone them, one by one, replacing them with kings who were members of the Liu clan (either his own brothers or sons).[1] These Liu kings and their descendants, as well as

---

1. With the exception of the royal line at Changsha 長沙, where non-Liu kings ruled until 157 BCE, this process of replacement was more or less complete by 195 BCE.

the kings installed by subsequent emperors, had extensive powers over the large territories that they ruled. The kings soon became the targets of officials at the central court who sought to limit both the territories assigned to each king and the degree of control they exercised over those territories. The conflict between kings and officials came to a head in the Seven Kingdoms Rebellion of 154 BCE. Suppression of that rebellion by the Chang'an court gave the emperor's officials a free hand in dealing with the kings.[2]

According to the standard narrative, by 154, the kings no longer played a major role on the historical scene. For the remainder of the Han dynasty, with their political and economic significance shriveled, the kings endured as mere shells of their former selves: having become princes rather than kings, they were useful only as a pool of reserve candidates in case the emperor produced no regular heir; with both the governance and the economic exploitation of their territories wholly in the hands of the central administration, they carried only nominal authority over their territories; they were compensated for this loss of real power not only by receiving large living allowances commensurate with the size of their kingdoms, but also by participation in the frequent exchanges of luxury and ritual items between their courts and the central court at Chang'an.

While the broad outline of this historical sketch is correct, it fails to capture the fact that the institution of kingship held meaning even after its political and economic functions had fallen victim to the forces of centralization.[3] This raises intriguing questions: Why was the institution of kingship not abolished *tout court*? Why were the kings allowed to continue to claim territories to the east, north, and south of the imperial capital, from which they and their descendants could be evicted only after being found guilty of crimes? Why do the histories dedicate specialized chapters to the kings' lives? From those histories it is clear that legal cases against the kings were treated differently from cases against other subjects of the emperor: the emperor was required to review them and almost routinely commuted the

---

2. Emmerich, "Die Rebellion der Sieben Könige, 154 v. Chr.," 397–497.

3. Here I take my lead from Huizinga, who made a similar point about the late medieval European nobility; see Huizinga, *The Autumn of the Middle Ages*, chap. 3.

sentences of the kings to lesser charges. Why was this? What symbolic capital did these kings possess?

The historian Ban Gu 班固 (32–92 CE), in his *Hanshu* 漢書, points to 138 BCE as a defining moment in the history of kingship. No important military event or grand state action marked that historical moment. The turning point, it seems, was the simple delivery of a powerful and effective speech by Liu Sheng 劉勝, the king of Zhongshan 中山 (r. 154–112 BCE), during a banquet at the imperial court that established, in Ban Gu's view, the parameters that would define the future relationship between the emperor, his officials, and the kings. By invoking kinship, the one trump card the kings still held, Liu Sheng's speech not only restored dignity to the battered egos of the Han kings, but also, as Ban Gu suggests, ensured the viability of the institution for a long period to come.[4]

This essay will pause to examine briefly Ban Gu's *mise-en-scène* of Liu Sheng's speech and Ban Gu's understanding of the consequences of that speech. The reason for this digression is that I am interested in discovering the extent to which the parameters that, according to Ban Gu, defined and supported the institution of kingship in the years after 138 BCE remained valid some 250 years later when Liu Chang, the king of Lecheng, was charged by officials with impiety. I believe that they did remain valid, albeit in slightly altered form; that they are crucial to understanding why Liu Chang's case evolved as it did; and that these parameters engendered the specific instances of rhetoric that have been preserved to this day.

An Effective Remonstration from 138 BCE *and a New* Modus Operandi

Ban Gu tells us that, in 138 BCE, during a banquet at the imperial court, Liu Sheng, the king of Zhongshan, burst into tears during

4. *HS* 53.2422–26. That *Shiji* does not mention that Liu Sheng's speech is likely significant. The speech might, indeed, be seen as a fictionalization of Ban Gu's interpretation of the history of the kings. For evidence that doubts on the authenticity of the speech were raised earlier, see *HSBZ* 53.10a, 1121, where Shen Qinhan 沈欽韓 (1775–1831) uses a *fu* attributed to Liu Sheng in *Xijing zaji* to show that the king was accomplished in literary composition, against anonymous commentators who posited that his speech was an invention by later literati. See *Xijing zaji* 6.1, 254.

a musical performance. To channel his overflowing emotions, the king extemporized a beautiful, subtly phrased remonstration for the edification of his host, Emperor Wu 武 (r. 141–87 BCE), and the several other kings who happened to be paying a court visit at the time.[5] In his speech, Liu Sheng evokes the pain and humiliation inflicted upon the kings by the massive but unjust campaign that officials of the central government had organized against them in the wake of the Seven Kingdoms Rebellion. The underlying message of his speech was to insist that the officials relent. He argued that the ties of kinship between the emperor and the kings are impossible to dissolve.

The speech stands out for its explicit invocation of kinship. On the one hand, it paints the officials as men who "drove the imperial clan from power, and dissolved ties of flesh and blood" 使夫宗室擯卻，骨肉冰釋;[6] on the other, it claims that the kings' status as members of the imperial clan makes them invulnerable to any efforts of the officials to exterminate them. Kinship alone ultimately ensures the survival of both their persons and the institution. As a passage at the height of the speech puts it,

> As it is said: that one cannot drown a mouse under the altar, or fumigate a rat from the ceremonial room is because of the place where they have settled. Even though I am insignificant, I, nonetheless, am His Majesty's close relative. Even though my position is humble, I still head a vassal state in the East, and, in kinship terms, He [i.e., the emperor] still calls me "older brother."
>
> 臣聞社鼷不灌，屋鼠不熏。何則？所託者然也。臣雖薄也，得蒙肺附；位雖卑也，得爲東藩，屬又稱兄。[7]

An earlier passage from the speech makes clear that the kings' survival is not merely a sentimental issue but, rather, a matter crucial to

5. Since it had become customary for each reigning emperor to entrust his sons or brothers with a hereditary fief, at any given point, the reigning kings could include both close and more distant relatives of the emperor, from his own siblings and sons, to cousins several times removed. At the 138 BCE banquet, the company included two brothers of the emperor (Liu Sheng and Liu Fa 發, king of Changsha) and two of his cousins (Liu Ming 明, king of Jichuan 濟川, and Liu Deng 登, king of Dai 代).

6. *HS* 53.2425.

7. *HS* 53.2424.

the well-being of the greater political order. By implicitly comparing the kings with moral paragons such as King Wen (r. 1099–1050 BCE) and Confucius, two men known for having fought back the forces of evil when faced with a desperate situation, Liu Sheng suggests that the kings, precisely because their relation of kinship with the emperor cannot be dissolved, have a crucial role to play within the existing system of checks and balances. If the officials as a group were ever to connive and pursue their own interests rather than the common good, the kings could be called upon to warn the emperor and help him to restore moral order.

> If a crowd blows against it, the mountain moves; a swarm of mosquitoes creates a sound like thunder; a cooperating group of men can take on a tiger; ten men can break a hammer. Hence, that King Wen was imprisoned in Youli or that Confucius was in distress between Chen and Cai was because those in favor set the tone, and, there being too many of them, they caused harm.
>
> 夫眾煦漂山，聚蟁成吒，朋黨執虎，十夫橈椎。是以文王拘於牖里，孔子阨於陳、蔡。此乃烝庶之成風，增積之生害也。[8]

In other words, Liu Sheng alerts the emperor to the fact that the officials have partisan interests and, as a group, pose potential harm to the emperor's own interests; the kings, bound to the emperor by ties of kinship, can be counted on to come to the emperor's aid in such situations. This need not imply that actual governing responsibilities must be assigned to the kings: it would be sufficient for them to exist as a dormant group that could be activated for the emperor's defense whenever circumstances demanded.

As I noted earlier, Ban Gu believed that Liu Sheng's speech was effective in stopping the officials' assault on the kings. Ban Gu related how the officials' war on the kings in the period after 154 BCE was fought mostly by legal means rather than in policy debates at court. Officials "presented numerous memorials to the throne detailing the kings' faults" (*shu zou bao qi guo'e* 數奏暴其過惡), and often unjustly targeted individual kings: "The officials would blow apart the hairs upon a fur to find faults; through beatings they would

8. *HS* 53.2423.

get the kings' officials to testify against their lords." 有司吹毛求疵，笞服其臣，使證其君。[9]

Liu Sheng's speech, in Ban Gu's view, did not stop officials from using legal means to attack the kings, but confined it to relatively strict boundaries. Not only should the officials' powers of prosecution be more clearly circumscribed; there was a strong expectation that the emperor, as head of the imperial clan, would reach out to the kings with measures of kindness whenever legal cases were brought against them. The speech, as Ban Gu sees it, also awarded the kings a more sharply defined place in the ritual system, providing a sort of guarantee for the continued existence of the institution of kingship. Here is how Ban Gu put it: "After [the speech], the emperor treated the kings with greater courtesy. He reduced the number of pretexts officials could use to present memorials against them. [Cases that did get forwarded] he treated with the kindness due a close relative." 於是上乃厚諸侯之禮，省有司所奏諸侯事，加親親之恩焉。[10]

Liu Sheng's speech seems to have prompted a new *modus operandi* for the emperor, his officials, and the kings. While the kings may have been forced to abandon their claims on real power, they received ritual prestige; while officials could continue to bring legal cases against the kings, they had to tread more carefully, knowing that the emperor would intervene and only accept sanctions appropriate to the elevated kinship status of the kings. The emperor could continue to avail himself of both groups: the officials as an active, administrative force; the kings as a dormant group that could be drawn upon when needed.

It is no coincidence that Liu Sheng was the one to deliver this epoch-making speech. Liu Sheng, as we know from exchanges that are reported between him and his brother, Liu Pengzu 彭祖, the king of Zhao 趙 (r. 152–92 BCE), was one of the few kings able to reconcile himself with the idea that his kingship would bring him great ritual and economic privileges, but no real powers.[11] He is, therefore,

---

9. *HS* 53.2422.

10. *HS* 53.2425.

11. Liu Sheng posited that, "My brother's ways as king are to take control so that he can rule instead of his officials, whereas a king should daily listen to music, and

a prime example of the new kind of king born in the wake of the post-154 campaign: given to conspicuous consumption, but without an overtly political role. Fittingly, the extent of the material and ritual privileges to which Liu Sheng was entitled by virtue of being king was revealed by the discovery, in the late 1970s, of the rock-cut tombs of both himself and his queen in the hills at Mancheng 滿城 (current Hebei 河北 province). Among the rare finds not to have been disturbed by robbers, these well-stocked, multichambered abodes for the afterlife allow us not only to reconstruct the economies of exchange that existed between the courts at Zhongshan and Chang'an 長安, but also to imagine how the king and the queen—herself a member of the powerful Dou family—would have passed their days in the Zhongshan palace, amid their numerous children and grandchildren, priding themselves on the fact that the privilege of their birth had not only provided them with wealth and title, but also with extensive territories that they could inscribe, via tombs and shrines, with their branch of the imperial family.[12]

The Kings in Imperial Communications

When one reads through the various collective biographies of the kings contained in the *Hanshu* or the *Hou Hanshu* 後漢書, it seems as if the new *modus operandi* between the emperor, the kings, and the officials, captured by Liu Sheng's speech, indeed held for the next few centuries, until the end of the Eastern Han. On a regular basis reigning emperors would confer kingships on his sons, and many of these kings were successful in maintaining their lines over multiple generations. The kingdoms were now much smaller than they had been at the beginning of the Western Han dynasty, roughly coinciding with the size of a prefecture, and were administered in the same way

allow himself to be enticed by beautiful sounds and women." 兄爲王，專代吏治事·王者當日聽音樂，御聲色. Liu Pengzu countered that "the king of Zhongshan indulges in extravagances, and fails to assist the emperor in guiding the people. How can he be called a vassal king!" 中山王但奢淫，不佐天子拊循百姓，何以稱爲藩臣! Liu Sheng, reportedly, sired more than 120 children. *HS* 53.2425–26. Unlike Liu Sheng's speech, the exchange between the two brothers is found in *Shiji*. See *SJ* 59.2099.

12. Zheng Shaozong, *Mancheng Hanmu*.

as prefectures, by centrally appointed officials. From Emperor Xuan's 宣帝 (r. 74–48 BCE) reign onward, kings with the closest kinship relationship with the reigning emperor were often retained at the capital before being sent to live at their own courts. Officials assigned to supervise the kings continued the well-established practice of attacking the kings via legal charges presented as memorials to the throne.[13] The emperor, expected to review all cases brought against the kings, routinely invoked the language of kinship to impose alternatives to punishments that, in the case of ordinary offenders, would have attached to their crimes.

Few texts are preserved that document regular events in the lives of the kings, even though we know that the superintendent of the imperial clan (*zongzheng* 宗正) must have entered their births, deaths, marriages, and appointments into his register, which he kept at the central court. However, a good number of examples of the communications that flew back and forth during legal cases against the kings are preserved in the histories: memorials of officials, advice proffered to the emperor, imperial edicts, letters in which the kings sought to establish their innocence or apologize for their faults, and so on. These communications form an important subset of the imperial communication at large, set apart from other such subsets by their frequent recourse to the rhetoric of kinship.[14]

Reserving a more comprehensive treatment of the rhetorical exchanges involving the Han kings for another publication, I will, in this essay, confine my analysis to just one case dating to the Eastern Han: that of Liu Chang 萇, the king of Lecheng 樂成, who was charged with impiety in 120 or 121 CE. Analysis of this case will allow

13. I am using the term "legal" loosely here; some cases concern matters that might seem domestic, and some cases were brought to the central court's attention by courtiers or even close relatives of the accused. Once a case arrived at the central court, several government offices would have been involved, including that of the superintendent of trials (*tingwei* 廷尉) and that of the superintendent of the imperial clan (*zongzheng* 宗正), as well as various agencies charged with imperial communication, including the Secretariat (*shangshu* 尚書). Cases brought against kings were handled differently from ordinary legal cases, as the emperor always had to review them, and as kings were not usually subjected to the regular set of punishments.

14. For an outstanding monograph on the topic of imperial communication, see Giele, *Imperial Decision-Making and Communication in Early China*.

us to observe how the new *modus operandi* described by Ban Gu worked in concrete, historical cases. While the broad outlines of Ban Gu's analysis can be left to stand, a concrete case such as Liu Chang's is likely to reveal how the established patterns that characterized the relations and exchanges between the emperor, the king, and his officials varied according to particular historical circumstances and conflicting political objectives.

I will first present the details of Liu Chang's life to the extent that we are able to reconstruct them given the limitations of our sources, and only then turn to an analysis of the two rhetorical exchanges that are preserved regarding his case. To analyze the rhetorical exchanges, I will draw on the terminology developed by David Schaberg regarding the organizational features of speeches in the *Zuozhuan* 左傳: the statement of one or more *principles* ("utterances that admit of no debate," e.g., citations, general truths, historical precedents), the *application* of those principles to the facts of the case at hand, and a *judgment* (the conclusion to be reached from the statement of facts).[15] This terminology, I believe, is both concrete and flexible enough to be applied to persuasions from the early imperial period; it also helps us recognize the speeches as coherently organized wholes. As the reader will find, reconciling the facts of Liu Chang's life with the official rhetoric invoked after he was accused requires a complex balancing of fact and the "spin" applied to those facts when used for condemnation or exoneration. I hope that it will become clear that the rhetorical exchanges themselves cannot be understood in isolation and must be assessed within the context of a proper reconstruction of the wider framework of events.[16]

Liu Chang's Life

Liu Chang, one of his father's secondary sons, did not become king through regular channels. In the year 120 his father, Liu Shou 壽,

15. Schaberg, *A Patterned Past*, 40–50. Schaberg defines judgment as "the statement of the case to be proved," but that definition is not helpful for cases of judicial rhetoric, such as this one, where the judgment contains a real conclusion as well as a recommendation or announcement of the punishment deemed appropriate.

16. Here I follow Schaberg, *A Patterned Past*, who, in the case of the *Zuozhuan*, demonstrates how intricately speech and historical narrative are intertwined.

king of Jibei 濟北 (r. 90–120 CE), died and was succeeded by Liu Chang's brother, Liu Deng 登, who would remain king of Jibei for the next fifteen years. Liu Shou received an exceptionally lavish funeral, attributable to the fact that he had been close to his half-brother, Emperor He (和帝, r. 88–105 CE), Empress Dowager Deng's deceased spouse.[17] The appointment, soon after his death, of Liu Shou's remaining sons as marquises was another token of the special honors the imperial court wished to bestow on the deceased.[18] Had Liu Chang not been chosen to head another kingdom, he most likely would have spent his life, like his brothers, as a marquis in close proximity to his brother's kingdom in the Mount Tai 太山 area. However, it so happened that, in 120 CE, Liu Bin 賓, the king of Lecheng (r. 111–119/20 CE) died without an heir. Liu Chang was appointed as the new king of Lecheng to restore his line (*fu li* 復立).[19]

Since we do not know Liu Chang's precise year of birth, we do not know whether he was born at the capital, where his father resided for many years even after he had been appointed king of Jibei by his half-brother Emperor He in the year 90 CE, or whether he was born at the court in Jibei, where his father was sent to live from 106 CE onward.[20] In any case, Liu Chang most likely spent most of his young life at the Jibei court in Lu city 盧城.[21]

In the year 119 CE, the Empress Dowager Deng decided to bring forty children from the households of her late husband's younger

---

17. Due to the financial hardships the empire was suffering, strict limits had been imposed on the expenditure allowed for royal funerals. For Liu Shou's funeral, however, the imperial court allowed thrice the allotted amount.

18. *HHS* 55.1806–7.

19. *HHS* 50.1673.

20. Given that Liu Shou was Emperor He's younger brother (*pace* de Crespigny, *Biographical Dictionary of Later Han to the Three Kingdoms*, 545), the earliest date for his birth would be 79 CE, the same year as Emperor He's. If Liu Shou was indeed born in 79 CE, Liu Chang could have been born, at the earliest, in 92 CE. Most likely, however, he was born years later.

21. For the little that is known about Lu city during the Han dynasty, see Qu, *Shi ji ducheng kao*, 40.

brothers, as well as thirty children of her own family, boys as well as girls,[22] to court for an education.

> And for all these children she ordered a residence opened, to teach them the classics and other writings. She personally supervised and examined them. For the little children she appointed tutors and protectors, who from dawn to dusk were in the palace. She directed [these children] gently and firmly, and she immersed them in her kindness and love.
>
> 並爲開邸第，教學經書，躬自監試。尙幼者，使置師保，朝夕入 宮，撫循詔導，恩愛甚渥。[23]

She based her action on the precedent of Emperor Ming (明帝 r. 57–75 CE), who established a similar school in the year 66 CE; but her rationale for educating these youth was that these children, bound to assume positions of leadership in the empire, should receive a strong dose of classical learning to counterbalance the life of idle luxury that they would otherwise lead by reasons of their birth.[24] By giving them a taste of life at the capital, and by her personal involvement with the school, she was surely also hoping to instill in these select students a sense of loyalty toward herself and her political goals. Moreover, given that the school was open to children of her husband's brothers as well as to children of her own family, she was also cementing, with an eye to the future, relationships between the Deng family and branches of the Liu imperial family that she privileged.

Nowhere in the sources do we find explicit mention of Liu Chang as being one of the pupils called to Empress Dowager Deng's palace

---

22. There she might have been heeding her teacher Ban Zhao's 班昭 injunction that girls should receive an education as well; see Ban Zhao's *Nü jie* 女誡, *HHS* 84.2788. On Empress Dowager Deng, see Swann, "Biography of the Empress Teng," 138–59.

23. *HHS* 10A.428; translation adapted from Swann, "Biography of the Empress Teng," 156.

24. Emperor Ming's school, meanwhile, continued to exist. Since, according to Yuan Hong's (328–396 CE) *Annals of the Later Han* (*Hou Hanji*), that school also catered to "kings, nobles, and sons and younger brothers of meritorious ministers" 諸王侯及功臣子弟, one wonders how exactly Empress Dowager Deng's new initiative dovetailed with this; *HHS* 2.113, de Crespigny, *Biographical Dictionary of Later Han to the Three Kingdoms*, 608–9, 127.

school in 119 CE. Even so, there are at least two reasons pointing to Liu Chang's possible attendance at the school. First, besides children of the Deng family, only offspring of the kings of Jibei and Hejian 河間—Liu Chang's father and uncle respectively—are explicitly named as invitees to the new school.[25] Second, Liu Chang's name is firmly coupled to that of Liu Yi 翼 (d. ca. 140 CE), who was a son of the king of Hejian, and a full nephew of Liu Chang. Both men were secondary sons, and both were appointed on the same day in the year 120 CE to restore a royal line of succession in another kingdom: Liu Chang in Lecheng; Liu Yi in Pingyuan 平原.[26] Since we are explicitly told that Liu Yi owed his appointment as king to the fact that he impressed Empress Dowager Deng with his handsome appearance during his sojourn at her school in the capital,[27] it might well be that Liu Chang also attended Empress Dowager Deng's school, and, like his cousin, earned an appointment because he had performed to her liking.

The empress dowager's decision to appoint Liu Yi and Liu Chang, both secondary sons, as kings over royal lines outside of their own bloodline was highly unusual. Throughout the Western Han and in the first century CE, royal lines frequently came to an end, either because the last king died without a successor or because the last king had been found guilty of some serious moral offense. When, at the reigning emperor's initiative, such a kingdom was revived—either almost immediately or with a hiatus of several years or even decades—the chosen king was, almost invariably, a member of the bloodline of the kingdom's founding king.[28] The two precedents for

---

25. *HHS* 10A.428.

26. *HHS* 5.231; based on the conversion tables in Wang and Li, eds., *Zhonghua tongshi da lidian*, this would coincide with June 18, 120 CE.

27. *HHS* 50.1809.

28. While this was usually a brother of the last kings, emperors sometimes also appointed the sons of an uncle or great uncle of the last king. One possible exception is Pingdi's (r. 1 BCE–6 CE) appointment of Liu Lun 劉倫 as king of Guangde 廣德 in 2 CE, as Liu Lun was from the lineage of the kingdom of Guangchuan 廣川; however, as a note in *HSBZ* 53.13a attests, the sources are extremely confused as to the final lines of descent of the kingdoms of Guangchuan and Guangde; *HS* 53.2426. Emperor Wu, on the death of one of his brothers, appointed two of his brother's sons as kings: one because he was the regular heir, the other because he

appointments such as those of Liu Yi and Liu Chang—appointments that injected them into branches of the Liu imperial family different from their own—date from Empress Dowager Deng's own reign. In 109 CE, she appointed Liu Yanping 劉延平, a secondary son of the king of Le'an 樂安 (formerly Qiansheng 千乘), as king of Qinghe 清河 (r. 109–144 CE) after the last king of Qinghe died without an heir. In 113 CE, she arranged for Liu De 劉得, another son of the king of Le'an to succeed Emperor He's own son as king of Pingyuan 平原 (r. 113–119 CE).[29] Of the four cousins appointed by Empress Dowager Deng as kings, Liu Chang was inserted into the most distant line of the imperial family: he was the only one to receive an appointment to a kingdom that was created prior to Emperor He's accession to the throne.

The empress dowager, by targeting the secondary sons of her late husband's brothers and making them heirs to royal lines that failed to produce a successor, seems to have single-handedly developed a new tool of government: she was creating a wider pool of potential heirs to the throne, all of whom she could expect to be strong allies of her family. Empress Dowager Deng had already successfully navigated two succession crises: the first at the death of her husband, Emperor He, in 105/6 CE, when his younger son, still a baby, was brought to the throne under her regency; and then again when, a few months later, the baby died, she elevated to the throne the eldest son of an elder brother of her late husband (this eldest son being Liu You 祜, also known as Emperor An 安帝 r. 106–125 CE), passing a second time over Emperor He's elder son. It is likely that, through her school, she was nurturing talents such as Liu Yi and Liu Chang either to replace Emperor An in case he should die, or to remind him that there were other good candidates for the throne with pedigrees equal to his own. Indeed, the emperor, having attained his majority, was being not-so-subtly encouraged to remain in the empress dowager's favor

---

knew he was his brother's most beloved son. For the secondary son, a new kingship was created out of the territories of another one that had been abolished due to the rebellion; *HS* 53.2433.

29. *HHS* 55.1804 and 55.1810. The founding kings of Le'an (formerly Qiansheng) and Qinghe were both sons of Zhangdi, and had been installed as kings by their brother Hedi; Liu Sheng 劉勝, Hedi's son, had been installed as king of Pingyuan just after his father's death.

and heed her commands lest he be deposed in favor of one of his newly empowered cousins.

Of the two cousins appointed in 120 CE, Liu Yi certainly received Empress Dowager Deng's primary attentions; Liu Chang was merely the reserve candidate. This is obvious from the fact that Liu Yi, not Liu Chang, was appointed to be king of Pingyuan. Pingyuan was a kingdom that had been created for the benefit of Liu Sheeng 劉勝,[30] the elder son of Emperor He, who, despite being the most obvious candidate, was passed over twice as successor, first by his younger brother, then by his cousin, Liu You 劉祜. Hence the king of Pingyuan and his heirs—whether or not they were his direct descendants—were almost automatically branded as rivals to the emperor.[31] The special status of Liu Yi is also clear from the fact that he did not have to reside in his kingdom but "was retained in the capital" 留在京師.[32] In contrast, Liu Chang was sent to live in his kingdom, even though it is possible that some time elapsed between his appointment as king and his relocation.

Liu Chang's new kingdom was located to the northwest of his father's and had already changed hands several times since the initial appointment of Liu Dang 劉黨 as Lecheng's first king (r. 72–96 CE). According to a mid-second-century survey, Lecheng was several times larger than Jibei[33] and must therefore have yielded a substantial income for its court. Given that its founding king, Liu Dang, was known

---

30. I am slightly altering the transcription of Liu Sheeng's name, as his name is written with the same character as that of Liu Sheng, king of Zhongshan, who delivered the 138 BCE speech.

31. Several attempts to depose the reigning emperor in favor of a king of Pingyuan are reported: one in 107/8 CE by Zhou Zhang 周章, who attempted to set Liu Sheeng on the throne in an attempt to take power away from the empress dowager, *HHS* 33.1157–58; after the death of the empress dowager, the Deng family was demoted on the grounds that some of its members had tried earlier to put Liu Sheeng's successor, Liu De, on the throne. Like Liu Yi, Liu De, also a descendant of a brother of Emperor He, had been injected into Liu Sheeng's line when the latter died in 113 CE without an heir. As we shall see, Liu Yi was removed from his position of king of Pingyuan at the same time as the Deng family suffered its demise after the death of the empress dowager, *HHS* 5.233, 16.616, 16.636, 78.2514.

32. *HHS* 55.1809.

33. According to de Crespigny, *Biographical Dictionary of Later Han to the Three Kingdoms*, 1197, Lecheng had 13 counties, 91,440 households, and 655,118 persons,

as a text critic and book lover, the library at the Lecheng court was probably also well stocked.[34] Liu Chang was thus suddenly thrust into a position that made him master over substantial material assets. These riches, however, came at a steep personal price. Injected into the lineage of a different branch of the Liu family, he now had to carry out ancestral sacrifices to his new family, especially to its founder, his great-great-uncle Liu Dang. Moreover, instead of being able to mourn his own father, he was obliged to don the mourning clothes and observe the mourning rites for Liu Bin, the recently deceased king of Lecheng, a man he might have only barely known, if at all. He also had to treat the latter's widow, referred to as "Great Lady" *daji* 大姬, with the respect due a mother and queen dowager. His unexpected appointment as king might also have imbued him with a conviction that he was invulnerable and would always receive protection from above.

This protection ended with the death of Empress Dowager Deng in the late spring of 121 CE.[35] Liu Chang lost his position less than a month before the first anniversary of the Empress Dowager's death. An entry in the *Annals* for that day (first day of the third month of the first year of the *jianguang* 建光 reign, i.e., May 23, 122 CE) records that "The king of Lecheng committed a crime and was made marquis of Linhu." 樂成王萇有罪，廢爲臨湖侯。[36] How closely the fates of Liu Chang and Liu Yi are intertwined is clear from the fact that Liu Yi lost his kingdom only two months after Liu Chang. Unlike Liu Chang, Liu Yi was not indicted for a crime. Liu Yi was demoted from his position as king of Pingyuan because close personal allies of Emperor An alleged that the Deng family had, at one point or other, attempted to depose Emperor An in favor of the king of Pingyuan. Hence, the Deng family fell from power at the same time as the Deng ally Liu Yi.[37]

---

whereas Jibei was comprised of 5 counties, 45,689 households, and 235,897 persons.

34. *HHS* 50.1672; unless he was not allowed to take any books with him when he was obliged to leave the capital and take up residence in his state in the year of Zhangdi's death.

35. *HHS* 5.232.

36. *HHS* 5.233.

37. There is disagreement among commentators whether this king of Pingyuan is Liu De or Liu Yi; *HHS* 5.233, 16.616, 16.636, 78.2514.

However much Liu Chang's demotion can be read against the background of power struggles at the imperial court, it is important to note that his demotion came about as a result of legal charges leveled against him, charges that possibly, but not necessarily, predate Empress Dowager Deng's death. According to Liu Chang's biography, he was indicted "[only] several months after he arrived in his kingdom" 萇到國數月。[38] Two officials initiated the charges against Liu Chang: the inspector (*cishi* 刺史) of Ji 冀 Province, the wider administrative unit that comprised Lecheng, and the kingdom of Lecheng's prime minister (*guoxiang* 國相). The exact text of the memorial they presented to indict the king is not preserved, but *Hou Hanshu* 後漢書 states that the two men argued that the king's crimes amounted to impiety (*budao* 不道), the highest crime meriting the death penalty.[39] The imperial edict, rendered in different versions in *Hou Hanshu* and *Dongguan Hanji* 東官漢記,[40] presents a long list of charges against the king. Since these charges must have been closely related to those of the original indictment, I present them here to give an idea of the kind of offenses with which Liu Chang was ac-

38. *HHS* 50.1673. There is a time lapse of almost two years between his appointment (June 18, 120 CE) and his dismissal (May 23, 122 CE). It is therefore possible that the indictment came before Empress Dowager Deng's death and was resolved only after her death; a possibility at the other extreme would be that Liu Chang was sent to Lecheng only after the death of the Empress Dowager, then indicted almost immediately afterward. What we do not know is when Liu Chang was sent to his new kingdom. If this occurred soon after his appointment, the charges against him would predate the empress dowager's death.

39. Hulsewé, *Remnants of Han Law*.

40. *HHS* 50.1673 contains the longer version of the edict, whereas a shorter excerpt of the edict is given in the reconstituted version of the *Dongguan Hanji* (*Records of the Han from the Eastern Pavilion*), based on a citation in *Taiping yulan*, *juan* 755. As the fragment from *Dongguan Hanji* has no parallel in the version of the edict found in *Hou Hanshu*, but possibly complements it, it is likely, unless the attribution in one of the two sources is wrong, that both texts cite different parts of the original edict. In other words, the versions of the edicts that we find in various received sources should not be mistaken as directly mirroring the original on which they are based, but have undergone certain literary transformations (that were, most likely, not limited to abbreviation alone). It is also possible that *Hou Hanji* renders the edict, whereas *Dongguan Hanji* draws upon the memorial of indictment. For the *Dongguan Hanji* fragment, see Liu Zhen, *Dongguan Hanji jiaozhu*, 254.

cused. In *Hou Hanshu*'s list, Liu Chang's ritual failures toward the royal couple he succeeded figure prominently:

> Even though he was aware of the great importance of the mausolea and the ancestral temples, and of the ritual requirements of his inheritance, he, nonetheless, failed to show utmost reverence or adopt a solemn and respectful attitude. On the contrary, without authority, he diminished the number of sacrificial animals, and failed to use the full set of offerings. He treated the Great Lady negligently, without heeding her instructions.
>
> 知陵廟至重，承繼有禮，不惟致敬之節，肅穆之慎，乃敢擅損犧牲，不備苾芬。慢易大姬，不震闕教。

The *Dongguan Hanji* adds more specifics to the list of Liu Chang's ritual violations vis-à-vis his adoptive family: "The king of Lecheng, while residing in the mourning hut,[41] and still wearing the clothes of mourning, entertained himself with music and chess, and refused to visit the mausolea." 樂成王居諒闇，衰服在身，彈棊為戲，不肯謁陵。The edict as rendered in *Hou Hanshu* completes the list with crimes of a different nature, involving, as the crimes of accused kings often did, women and violence toward others: "He did not follow the regulations in the manner he left and entered (his palace), and maintained depraved habits at home. He seized the wives of others, or had them offered to him as concubines or maids. He beat his officials, and acted arbitrarily and cruelly." 出入顛覆，風淫于家，娉取人妻，饋遺婢妾。毆擊吏人，專己凶暴。 If these accusations are true, it appears that Liu Chang was ill-prepared for the realities of life at a royal court where his every move was scrutinized, and where the officials appointed to supervise him, probably egged on by the hostile widow of his predecessor, were eager to find cause to indict him.

After this extensive list of Liu Chang's crimes, Emperor An's edict invokes the conventional "I cannot bear it" (*buren* 不忍) as the basis for reducing the sentence from capital punishment to something less harsh. It announced that Liu Chang would be deposed as king and made marquis of Linhu 臨湖, a fief located in the prefecture of Lujiang 廬江, in Yang 揚 Province, far to the southeast. We do not know

41. For Eastern Han mourning customs, including the use of the mourning hut, see Brown, *The Politics of Mourning in Early China*, 10–18.

how long Liu Chang lasted as marquis of his fief in the South, or if indeed he ever went to live there. If he did, he might have regarded his short brush with power with some regret: while he might have considered himself lucky to still retain both a title and a fief, he might also have preferred to live out his life as a marquis in close proximity to his living relatives, and, perhaps most important, close to his ancestral land.

The demotion of Liu Chang to marquis of Linhu disqualified him from ever becoming emperor; it did not, however, end such chances for other members of his branch of the family. When Emperor An died in 125 CE, after having deposed as heir apparent his only son Liu Bao 劉保 (the future Emperor Shun 順帝 r. 125–144 CE), his wife, née Yan 閻, chose a younger brother of Liu Chang to succeed Emperor An. However, the boy succumbed to illness after only a few months. Liu Bao succeeded as Emperor Shun to be eventually succeeded by Emperor Huan (桓帝 r. 146–168 CE), a son of Liu Yi. Thus Liu Yi, despite having lost his kingdom in 122 CE, ended up as the father of an emperor who enjoyed a long reign. The next emperor, Emperor Ling (靈帝 r. 168–189 CE) was a grandson of Liu Yi's brother.

It is indeed astonishing how, in the decades following Emperor He's death, the imperial throne, rather than being passed from father to son, shifted back and forth between descendants of Emperor He's brothers, with the powerful empress dowagers using these members of the Liu family to maintain and strengthen the family's own grasp on power.[42] Apparently having learned from Empress Lü's (呂 r. 195/187–180 BCE) example—who, in early Western Han had sought to extend the influence of the Lü family by appointing her own relatives as kings, but whose family fell from power shortly after her own death—they sought, by moving this particular group of Liu princes around, as if on a chess board, to extend their own hold on power or to promote the long-term fortunes of their native families. Empress Dowager Deng, who sowed the seeds of this marked ascendance of the families of her husband's brothers, might have done so with the long-term interests of her own family in mind. That she

42. See de Crespigny, *Biographical Dictionary of Later Han to the Three Kingdoms*, xxxiv–xxxv, for a family tree detailing the imperial inheritance of Later Han.

had carefully nurtured close ties between her own family and the families of her husband's brothers might well have cushioned the fall of the Deng family after the death of Empress Dowager Deng in 121 CE and might have provided a certain measure of protection to her legacy.[43]

Rhetorical Exchanges Related to Liu Chang's Case

I have chosen to reconstruct Liu Chang's life at some length because the rhetorical exchanges relating to his case, to the extent we can know from the preserved record, contain some unusual elements. First, they refer to the *Zhouli* 周禮 as an authoritative source that supported the policy of reducing, in the case of imperial relatives, the penalties prescribed by law. The *Zhouli*'s authority, acquired only during the last years of the Western Han dynasty, and especially due to Liu Xin's 劉歆 (46 BCE–23 CE) efforts during Wang Mang's 王莽 Xin 新 dynasty (9–25 CE),[44] provided persuaders in Eastern Han with a new tool for entering pleas on behalf of royals. Second, in the case of Liu Chang, we are in the fortunate situation of having more than one document preserved. In addition to the imperial edict previously quoted (preserved in two different sources), we also have a rare example of a plea (*yi* 議) on the king's behalf by Cen Hong 岑宏 (fl. 120), a middle-ranking advisory official (*shilang* 侍郎) attached to the Imperial Secretariat (*Shangshu* 尙書).[45] Cen Hong's plea, read in

---

43. See ibid., 1186, for a Deng family tree, showing the impact of the empress dowager's death in 121 CE, but also indicating how the family delivered another empress for the period from 159 to 165. The empress dowager's tools would have included the appointments of secondary sons as kings, but also the creation of her school, and the promotion of marriages between the families.

44. Boltz, "Chou li," 24–32.

45. The plea is part of Yuan Hong's 袁宏 (328–376 CE) *Annals of the Later Han* (*Hou Hanji*), see *Hou Hanji jiaozhu*, comp. Zhou; Li Xian's 李賢 (651–684 CE) commentary to the passage on Liu Chang in *Hou Hanshu* 50.1674 explicitly quotes Yuan Hong's text —with some variations, it adds that there is a version of the plea in the collected works of the famous statesman and literatus Huang Xiang 黃香; the plea, being Huang Xiang's, would have been memorialized (*zou* 奏) to the throne by Cen Hong and Huang Xiang together. In de Crespigny's estimation, Huang Xiang was probably dead by 110 CE, and therefore could not have been involved in Liu Chang's case; de Crespigny, *Biographical Dictionary of Later Han to the Three King-*

conjunction with the edict(s), allows us a rare glimpse into the process of imperial decision-making.[46]

Cen Hong's plea presents a neat five-part structure: two pairs of assertions, in which principle and application alternate, precede an overall conclusion or "judgment."

> (Principle) With the exception of sages, everyone makes mistakes. Hence when an heir is born to a king or a marquis, wise teachers and tutors are appointed to guide him through instruction. That is why, his sight shielded from evil, and his hearing protected from untruths, he is able to preserve his ancestral lands and fulfill his lofty and bright mandate.
>
> 非聖人，[47]不能無過，故王侯世子[48]生，爲立賢師傅以訓導之。所以[49]目不見惡，[50]耳不聞非，能保其社稷，高明令終。
>
> (Application) Chang was raised since childhood in a vassal state.[51] At home he received no instruction while crossing the courtyard;[52] while at the outside he did not have the benefit of a teacher or tutor. At the pinnacle of his youthful vigor, he suddenly received honorable rank, and after a series of small missteps, he sank into illicit behavior.
>
> 萇少長藩國，內無過庭之訓，外無師傅之道，血氣方剛，卒受榮爵，幾微生過，遂陷不義。

---

doms, 351. I will here use Yuan Hong's version. Hence, I will render the official's name as Cen Hong, not as Ling Hong 冷宏, as Li Xian writes. On the position of *shilang* ("gentleman in attendance") within the Imperial Secretariat (*Shangshu* 尙書) in Later Han, see Bielenstein, *The Bureaucracy of Han Times*, 55–57.

46. On the important role of the Secretariat and its officials in handling the imperial communication, see Giele, *Imperial Decision-Making and Communication in Early China*, 56–59, 63–66, 332.

47. Li Xian's version has 自非聖人, but the function of the *zi* 自 is difficult to understand.

48. Li Xian's version has 王太子; according to Zhou Tianyou, Li Xian makes this substitution in observance of a Tang taboo.

49. Li Xian's version has 是以.

50. Following Zhou Tianyou's substitution of *yi* 異 by *e* 惡, which he based on Li Xian's version.

51. It is important to distinguish vassal states (*fanguo* 藩國) from dependent states (*shuguo* 屬國), which were established by the Han to supervise non-Chinese people. Liu Sheng, in his 138 BCE speech, referred to himself as the head of a vassal state in the East (*dong fan* 東藩).

52. A reference to the "Ji shi" 季氏 chapter of the *Analects*; see Lau, trans., *Analects*, 16.13 and below.

(Principle) I learned of the *Zhouguan*'s[53] claims that, when deliberating about relatives, idiocy constitutes a ground for a pardon.

臣聞周官議親，惷[54]愚見赦。

(Application) Chang did not murder an innocent person. Wrongdoing was detected where there was only cause for a reprimand. He did not commit any gross, glaringly evil acts.

萇不殺無辜，以譴呵爲非，無赫赫大惡。

(Judgment) The appropriate decision is to reduce or seize his land, and to diminish his income from taxes. Thus he will be led to rectify his mistakes and start anew, reforming his heart in accordance with the Way.

可裁削奪損其租賦，令得改過自新，革心向道。

The first principle, coupled with the application, succeeds in presenting Liu Chang's faults as quite understandable, even predictable. Not born as heir (either because he was not the son of his father's queen or because he was not the eldest), Liu Chang did not receive the loving care and dedicated instruction an heir would have enjoyed almost from the moment of his birth.[55] Moreover, the plea adds how Liu Chang passed his childhood in a vassal state (*fan guo* 藩國), and therefore far from the capital and denied the opportunities for cultivation the city could offer.[56] No wonder, Cen Hong argues, that when wealth and prestige are bestowed on such a lesser-educated man suddenly, in the prime of his life, he does not know how to handle himself. Only a sage would have been able to keep his bearing in such a situation. Thus, Cen Hong implicitly criticizes the empress dowager's decision to appoint Liu Chang as king of Lecheng. In sum, the first principle-application pair shifts the narrative about Liu Chang from aggressive perpetrator of a whole host of ritual offences—as the prosecutors must have presented him—to helpless victim of a wrongheaded decision to appoint him as king of Lecheng.

53. That is, the *Zhouli*.

54. Li Xian's version has *chong* 惷 for 蠢 *chun*.

55. Kinney, *Representations of Childhood and Youth in Early China*, 53–96.

56. This seems to confirm my earlier speculation that Liu Chang was, at most, a young boy when his father was sent to live in his kingdom in 106 CE.

The second principle is a reference to the *Zhouli*, a text that, even though it was virtually unknown until late Western Han, had acquired classical status by Eastern Han times, well before Cen Hong became active in the imperial administration.[57] Cen Hong claims to have learned from the classic that "when deliberating about relatives, idiocy constitutes a ground for a pardon." With this statement, Cen Hong links two phrases from the *Zhouli* that derive from two different sections of the text—even though both are in the part on autumn, the season of punishments, and are found in relatively close proximity to one another. The first phrase, "deliberating about relatives," is found in the section that describes the duties of the vice minister of criminal affairs (*xiao sikou* 小司寇): for eight groups of people, this section stipulates, a special rule exists that requires that legal cases against members of these groups be accompanied by deliberations at court (*yi* 議).[58] These eight special rules (*ba bi* 八辟) target, besides imperial relatives, officials with a good record of service, the wise, the capable, the meritorious, the noble, the diligent, and the hospitable.[59] Hence, the phrase "deliberating about relatives" refers to the special legal status imperial relatives enjoy by right of birth and implies that cases against them should always be reviewed by the emperor in person; in fact, Cen Hong's deliberation was probably itself a part of that process.[60] The

---

57. While the text was not included in the Stone Classics of 175, several commentaries to the text were written in Eastern Han times by, *inter alia*, Liu Xin's disciple Du Zichun 杜子春, the father-son pair Zheng Xing 鄭興 and Zheng Zhong 鄭衆, Jia Kui 賈逵, and, most important, Zheng Xuan 鄭玄. See Boltz, "Chou li," 30–31; de Crespigny, *Biographical Dictionary of Later Han to the Three Kingdoms*, 1259; Biot, *Le Tcheou-li ou Rites des Tcheou*, vol. 1, 68.

58. Cen Hong's plea is also called *yi* or "deliberation." I have above used "plea" to render *yi* since his deliberation comes to Liu Chang's defense. On the meaning of *yi*, see Giele, *Imperial Decision-Making and Communication in Early China*, 186–88.

59. Shortly before this passage listing the eight special rules, there is a phrase, not explicitly alluded to by Cen Hong, that also deals with the imperial relatives, namely "clan-members of the king, when they have been found guilty of a crime, cannot be publicly executed." 凡王之同族有罪，不即市。 It could well be that Cen Hong, in his allusion to the "deliberating about imperial relatives" also implied a reference to the sentence about punishing royal relatives.

60. *Zhou li, juan* 34.3a–5a, 524–25; Biot 1851, vol. 2, 181–82; Zheng Xuan's commentary, in fact, explains this line from the *Zhou li* by referring to the practice,

second *Zhouli* phrase quoted by Cen Hong, that "idiocy constitutes a ground for a pardon," is found in the section on the supervisor of executions (*sici* 司刺), an officer in charge of capital punishment. The *sici* is required to pronounce an amnesty in cases in which the accused is a very young child, an old person, or an idiot.[61] The earliest commentary—in all likelihood predating Cen Hong—glosses "idiot" as "someone who by birth is stupid and untamable" (*sheng er chi'ai tongguang* 生而癡騃童獷), that is, someone incapable of living up to strong moral expectations. A gloss by Zheng Xuan 鄭玄 (127–200 CE) on this *Zhouli* passage about the three grounds for amnesty (minors, seniors, and idiots), explains that, according to prevailing law, juniors and seniors are considered legally incompetent, except when they have committed murder.[62]

These two quotations from *Zhouli* unmistakably point forward to the next line, the second application: "Chang did not murder an innocent person. Wrongdoing was detected where there was only cause for a reprimand. He did not commit any major, glaringly evil acts." 萇不殺無辜，以譴呵爲非，無赫赫大惡。 The target of this line is not the empress dowager's decision to appoint Liu Chang as king, but the harsh indictment of impiety leveled against the king by the two regional officials. If, as stated in the *Zhouli*, all kings should be treated with special leniency, why indict this king with impiety if he only committed a series of relatively small ritual missteps and no "glaringly evil acts"? Why accuse this king of wrongdoing (*fei* 非), if merely reprimanding (*qianhe* 譴呵) him would have been the better course of action? While the application does not explicitly call Liu Chang an "idiot," it does state that "he did not murder an innocent person." Given Zheng Xuan's gloss to the *Zhouli* passage, Cen Hong uses the application to argue that, since Liu Chang was not guilty of

---

current at his own time, that crimes committed by members of the imperial clan need to be reviewed by the emperor. (若今時宗室有罪先請是也)

61. *Zhou li*, vol. 3, 36.3a, 540; Biot, *Le Tcheou-li ou Rites des Tcheou*, vol. 2, 196.

62. "It is similar to the present regulations that stipulate that those under eight or about eighty *sui* should not stand for trial, unless when they have singlehandedly murdered someone else." 若今律令年未滿八歲八十以上非手殺人他皆不坐。 See *Zhou li*, vol. 3, 36.3a, 540. While Zheng Xuan lived after Cen Hong, the law he referred to was, most likely, also in vogue during Cen Hong's times. Note that Zheng Xuan omits idiocy from his list.

the one crime, murder, that could convert legal incompetence—on grounds of young age, old age, or idiocy—into legal competence, then the label "idiocy" referred to in the preceding principle is implicitly applicable to Liu Chang. With this line, Cen Hong offered the emperor the additional option of pardoning Liu Chang on the basis of legal incompetence. While Cen Hong knew full well that Liu Chang was not a true idiot—otherwise the empress dowager would never have appointed him—he was asking the emperor to stretch the common range of meaning of the term "idiot" from someone who, by birth, is unreceptive to moral education to someone who, due to the birth order that obtained in his family, failed to receive a good education.

Cen Hong's judgment—the final lines of his persuasion—makes perfect sense in the context of his previous argument. Since the king's missteps came about because he was so precipitously flung into too much wealth, the appropriate action would be to reduce his income. If parts of his territory were converted into districts directly governed by the central administration, his annual income would be proportionately reduced. Moreover, with his income reduced, the king, aware of having received a reprimand and no longer drowning in excessive wealth, would be able to reform and take a fresh start ("rectify his mistakes, renew himself, and reform in accordance with the Way" 改過自新，革心向道). The idiot, Cen Hong implies, can still become a sage.

The imperial edict, issued in Emperor An's name, is a carefully crafted response to Cen Hong's plea, and it is fascinating to analyze the two documents in conjunction with each other. The imperial edict consists of a judgment, bracketed by applications: the first application providing an alternative assessment of Liu Chang, the second offering an assessment of the imperial "I"s own role in the affair.

> (Application) Chang might present a human face, but is, in fact, dissolute at heart. Even though he was aware of the importance of the mausolea and the ancestral temples, and of the ritual requirements of his inheritance, he, nonetheless, failed to show utmost reverence or adopt a solemn and respectful attitude. Indeed, without authority, he diminished the number of sacrificial animals, and failed to use the full set of offerings. He treated the Great Lady negligently, without

heeding her instructions. He did not follow the regulations in the manner he left and entered (his palace), and maintained depraved habits at home. He seized the wives of others, or had them offered to him as concubines or maids. He beat his officials, and acted arbitrarily and cruelly. His transgressions and crimes are most serious, and extremely shameful.

萇有靦其面，而放逸其心。[63]知陵廟至重，承繼有禮，不惟致敬之節，肅穆之慎，乃敢擅損犧牲，不備苾芬。慢易大姬，不震閫教。出入顛覆，風淫于家，娉取人妻，饋遺婢妾。毆擊吏人，專己凶暴。愆罪莫大，甚可恥也。

(Judgment) I perused [the section on] the deliberations required in the case of the Eight Special Rules and hence cannot bear to hand him over to the judicial authorities. I hereby demote Chang from his rank and make him lord of Linhu instead.

朕覽八辟之議，不忍致之于理。其貶萇爵爲臨湖侯。

(Application) I failed to have the insight [into men's character] that would have earned me the epithet "constantly sagacious." Indeed, it came to the point that in choosing a successor I did not respect the regular rules. That because of that I failed to comfort and serve the Great Lady only adds to the eternal regret I will harbor regarding this case.

朕無『則哲』之明，致簡統失序，罔以尉承大姬，增懷永歎。」

Cen Hong's opinion ends on an optimistic note: with his territories appropriately reduced, Liu Chang will be able to "reform his heart in accordance with the Way" 革心向道. The imperial edict, in contrast, begins with a resounding negative assessment of the state of Liu Chang's heart: not a young man able to reform, but a man given to duplicity, his licentiousness masked by a veneer of human decency. While Cen Hong characterized the king's failures as misdemeanors (*guo* 過) that never amounted to gross, glaringly evil acts (*wu hehe da e* 無赫赫大惡), the edict disagrees. The imperial edict concludes that Liu Chang's "transgressions and crimes are most serious, and extremely shameful." The edict, in this first part, presents a sharply different narrative of Liu Chang, the man, and of his crimes.

In its judgment, nonetheless, the edict comes very close to following Cen Hong's recommendation. First, it acknowledges Cen Hong's

---

63. I follow Wang Niansun's (1744–1832 CE) 王念孫 gloss of *tian* 靦 as "presenting a human face" 人面之貌, see his *Dushu zazhi yubian*, 681–82.

reference to the *Zhouli* ("I perused [the section on] the deliberations required in the case of the Eight Special Rules" 朕覽八辟之議), and makes explicit the implicit conclusion Cen Hong clearly drew from that section of the *Zhouli*: Liu Chang's case should not be handled via regular judicial channels, nor should he be punished in any public way. The edict then particularizes Cen Hong's general recommendation for Liu Chang's punishment: he will be demoted from king to marquis, with a marquisate in what, in those days, still must have been the far South. Cen Hong's proposal, without calling for Liu Chang to be deposed as king of Lecheng, left open the possibility that Liu Chang would retain core parts of his kingdom as well as his title. The punishment prescribed by the edict, while severe, does not explicitly stray beyond the limits set by Cen Hong's plea. Significantly, Cen Hong's argument for leniency on the basis of idiocy is not touched upon in the edict, as, indeed, it already seems to have been refuted by the edict's opening sentence.

The judgment invokes the imperial "I" (*zhen* 朕) in its claim of "not being able to bear to hand Liu Chang over to the judicial authorities." The phrase, "I cannot bear" (*buren*), originally referred to the gut-wrenching experience of seeing a living being one cares about suffer harm; in the hands of rulers, this inability to face the prospect of seeing a loved one suffer soon became an excuse to intervene and effectively diminish the suffering to which the loved one would be exposed.[64] Emperors, throughout the Han dynasty, repeatedly invoked the "I cannot bear it" to reduce the punishment of kings requested by their officials. While some emperors truly might have had trouble witnessing the suffering of a relative—indeed, some of the kings were very closely related to the emperor, due to close family ties or because, effectively, they grew up together—it was often a tool that emperors were expected to use, and thus became routine in cases brought by officials against their royal relatives. In this case, even though Emperor An was Liu Chang's cousin, we need

64. The *locus classicus* is *Mencius* 1A.7, where the ruler with whom Mencius is in conversation "cannot bear" to see an innocent ox being led for sacrificial slaughter. He substitutes a lamb instead; Lau, trans., *Mencius*, 54–55. During Han times, emperors invoked "*buren*" over and over again to lessen the punishment requested by officials for their royal relatives.

not see the "I cannot bear it" as an expression of genuine emotion, but more as an acknowledgment that his case, as Cen Hong suggested in his reference to the *Zhouli*'s Eight Rules, should be handled differently from an ordinary legal case.

In the concluding application, the imperial "I" takes blame for what had happened. The dismissal of Liu Chang, as well as the crimes that supposedly preceded his dismissal, created a disturbance in the relations between the imperial throne and the Liu kings. It was customary for the emperor to take the blame for such disruptions. Since the issue here was one of personnel—an imperial appointment that went wrong—the edict invokes the second part of a well-known phrase from the "Gaoyao mo" 皋陶謨 chapter of the *Documents* 書, appropriate for these kinds of situations, namely "the one able to know others is constantly sagacious" 知人則哲. The imperial "I" in this case claims to have failed to exercise the kind of insight that would earn a ruler the epithet "constantly sagacious" (*zezhe* 則哲), namely, "knowing others" (*zhi ren* 知人). We find a fully contextualized version of this phrase used in an edict issued in 122 BCE when Emperor Wu took blame for the violence that had occurred in the wake of the alleged rebellion of the kings of Huainan 淮南 and Hengshan 衡山, implicitly admitting that his predecessors should never have allowed the men to become kings in the first place.[65] Here too, the implication is that Liu Chang should never have been appointed king of Lecheng. That Liu Chang's deeds had caused sorrow to the "Great Lady," the widow of the previous king of Lecheng, prompted the imperial "I" to express additional regrets. This reference strongly indicates that the widow played an active role in making sure that the regional officials brought charges against Liu Chang.

It was, however, Empress Dowager Deng who appointed Liu Chang as king of Lecheng, not Emperor An, who was in power when the edict announcing Liu Chang's demotion was issued. Why would Emperor An take blame for something that, so clearly, was not his own doing? Here it is important to recognize that the edict—like the edict that must have accompanied Liu Chang's appointment—

65. Vankeerberghen, *The Huainanzi and Liu An's Claim to Moral Authority*, 65–66.

was written in the name of a public persona, the unchanging imperial "I," not in the name of the individual who happened to be in charge of the imperial seals at the time.[66] The invocation of an imperial "I" that assumes responsibility for past mistakes enabled whoever was currently in power not only to hide the personal and transitory nature of power but also to mask the fact that this edict, perhaps more than the conclusion of a legal case, also was the opening salvo in a personal vendetta of Emperor An and his entourage against the Deng family. (Readers might recall that Empress Dowager Deng had first put Emperor An on the throne but then refused to allow him to rule for many years after he attained his majority, and that, through the appointments of Liu Yi and Liu Chang, she might have been reminding the emperor to stick to his modest role.) This is not to say that the fiction of a self-criticizing imperial "I" was intrinsically unimportant; on the contrary, it was an effective political ploy through which rulers were able to project, for the present and the future, an image of an orderly realm able to absorb small disturbances.

Linking History and Rhetoric

Hou Hanshu's biography of Liu Chang is short. Excluding its rendering of the edict, it contains a mere forty-three characters. To understand the rhetorical exchanges related to this case, I was compelled to search for clues far beyond the text of the biography itself and examine his father's position within the imperial family, Empress Dowager Deng's educational initiatives, the life of his cousin Liu Yi, and the various imperial succession crises that occurred during the first quarter of the second century. In the course of this examination, an interesting dialectic emerged between the narrative passages of the *Hou Hanshu* and the examples of rhetorical exchanges contained in it or its sister texts. Often, attempts to interpret the plea or the edict spawned new questions of the historical texts; the answers to these questions, in turn, had repercussions for the way I read the rhetorical pieces.

This dialectic gave rise to at least one seemingly irresolvable puzzle, one regarding the nature of Liu Chang's education. As I discussed

66. Giele, *Imperial Decision-Making and Communication in Early China*, 47.

earlier, the historical narrative steers one to the conclusion that Liu Chang indeed attended the palace school founded by Empress Dowager Deng in 119 CE: Liu Chang was a son of the king of Jibei, one of the two kings whose children, according to *Hou Hanshu*, were explicitly invited to attend the school; moreover, Liu Chang's trajectory in life—from his promotion as king to his demotion after the empress dowager's death—was closely linked to that of his cousin Liu Yi, whom we know attended the school. Cen Hong, however, seems to send us in the opposite direction, as his plea, especially in the first principle-application pair, was based on the supposition that Liu Chang had been denied an education. Cen Hong's statement that Liu Chang, "outside" of the Jibei court, "did not have the benefit of a teacher or tutor," seems to directly contradict the possibility that Liu Chang ever attended Empress Dowager Deng's palace school.

That Liu Chang did not go to Luoyang in 119 CE, but was promoted by Empress Dowager Deng to the kingship of Lecheng on the basis of different considerations remains a distinct possibility. Considering all possible factors in determining Liu Chang's age, Liu Chang might have been in his late twenties and thus well into adulthood when Empress Dowager Deng opened her school; if so, she might not have considered him a fit candidate. That he was an adult and therefore too old to attend the school is by no means certain. Indeed, Cen Hong's plea itself states that, during his time as king of Lecheng, Liu Chang was "at the pinnacle of his youthful vigor" (*xueqi fang gang* 血氣方剛), which suggests adolescence rather than adulthood. Also, why would the Empress Dowager have chosen to promote Liu Chang to king—a decision to which she was in no way forced by Liu Chang's birth—if there were other candidates available who had attended her school and from whom she might have expected greater loyalty and obedience?

There is another possibility. Cen Hong, alert to the interests of the emperor to whom he was directing his plea, may have knowingly misrepresented the nature of Liu Chang's education. Even though he blamed the Empress Dowager for having appointed Liu Chang as king, he might have wanted to avoid deliberately implying that Empress Dowager Deng's efforts to educate Liu Chang at her school—and perhaps by extension her educational policies as a whole—were a failure. Indeed, nothing in Cen Hong's plea registers disagreement with the empress dowager's general impulse to provide, through the establishment of her school, a higher level of education to the princes. She had justified her decision in 119 CE in the following way:

> That I invited all those children, and established an academy for them is because, truly, in our times those who inherit the position of king are of low caliber. Currently, customs are base and superficial; opportunism flourishes; the Five Classics are upheld less and less. If the children receive no moral guidance, they will, inevitably come to ruin. Hence, I wish to exalt and honor the way of the sages, so as to correct the depraved customs of our time. Does the tradition [i.e., the *Analects*] not say: "The man whose belly is full all day and who does not put his mind to some use is sure to meet with difficulties."[67] The noble families, families related to the imperial house, and the families of officials of the last few generations all wear comfortable clothes, and eat fine foods. They ride in strong carriages drawn by good horses. Being shortsighted for lack of education,[68] they no longer know whether something is right or not. These, indeed, are the causes of the current problems.
>
> 吾所以引納羣子，置之學官者，實以方今承百王之敝，時俗淺薄，巧僞滋生，五經衰缺， 不有化導，將遂陵遲，故欲褒崇聖道，以匡失俗。傳不云乎：『飽食終日，無所用心，難矣哉！』今末世貴戚食祿之家，溫衣美飯，乘堅驅良，而面牆術學，不識臧否，斯故禍敗所從來也。[69]

Cen Hong's plea echoes the empress dowager's assertion that future kings and marquises need a thorough education before they are ready to assume their positions; and like the empress dowager, Cen Hong refers to the *Analects* to illustrate his awareness that education is something arduous and therefore demands the stern engagement of teachers and fathers.[70]

---

67. Lau, trans., *Analects*, 17.22.

68. A reference to a phrase in the "Zhouguan" 周官 chapter of the *Documents* (currently among the received old text chapters), "the one who fails to study, hits a wall" 不學面牆.

69. *HHS* 10A.428–29.

70. The reference is to *Analects* 16.13, a passage in which Kongzi's son, Bo Yu 伯魚, relates to an interlocutor how, as he was hurrying across the courtyard, his father admonished him time after time to devote himself to studying. The interlocutor concluded that Kongzi "kept his son at a distance" 遠其子. It was not enough that his son mastered standard etiquette—which he showed by crossing the court-

As an official in the Secretariat, and, as such, very much in the thick of court politics, Cen Hong proffered arguments to the emperor on behalf of Liu Chang that provided the emperor with an option to find a middle ground between the harsh demands of the accusing officials and the imperative to treat his kin with appropriate leniency. The imperial edict reflects just such a compromise. The emperor accepts some of Cen Hong's arguments (particularly his argument on the basis of the *Zhouli*'s Eight Rules), while rejecting others (that Liu Chang's crimes were minor, that he was legally incompetent, and that he had not received the proper education). Driven by the adversarial dynamics of a trial, for strategic reasons, Cen Hong very likely offered as many arguments in favor of Liu Chang as possible, in the hope that at least one would prove persuasive, just as the accusing officials certainly exaggerated the seriousness of Liu Chang's crimes in their long list of charges. Cen Hong's plea, however, can also be seen as a way of helping the emperor position himself against Empress Dowager Deng and her legacy, providing justification for reversing various personnel decisions that she made—especially those involving the Deng family and its allies—without having to denounce her policies as such. Assuming that was his greater goal, Cen Hong might have felt entitled to take a certain degree of liberty with the facts. Of course, if we entertain the possibility that Cen Hong deliberately misstated the facts of his case, we substantially raise the bar when it comes to using seemingly factual information contained in any such rhetorical exchange.

It is interesting that neither Cen Hong's plea nor the imperial edict explicitly condemn the empress dowager's innovative policy of inserting secondary sons of royal lines that she favored into extinct royal lines or her overall educational policies. Indeed, Emperor An made a similar appointment only a few months after issuing the edict on Liu Chang. He revived the kingship of Lecheng, vacated by Liu Chang's demotion, in order to maintain the sacrifices to Liu Dang, Lecheng's founding king. The person chosen as the new king was another secondary royal son, Liu De 劉德, who from 122 to 151

yard in a hurried manner, a sign of respect—serious study of the classical texts was indispensable; the *Odes* and the *Rites* are specifically mentioned in the passage.

ruled over Liu Chang's former kingdom, now renamed as the kingdom of Anping 安平.[71] Liu De's brother was none other than Liu Yi.[72]

Conclusion

At the outset of this essay, I described how, according to Ban Gu, Liu Sheng's speech in 138 BCE established a new *modus operandi* between the emperor, the kings, and the officials: while the kings retained their positions as heads of hereditary kingdoms, they lost real power over their territories but were compensated for that loss by receiving expanded ritual and economic privileges. The officials had been forced to accept certain limits on their abilities to reduce the powers of the kings via legal cases, knowing that the kings would routinely receive lesser punishments than those attached to crimes for which they were convicted. The emperor held the balance between the kings and officials. It is now time now to examine whether, and to what extent, Liu Chang's case followed the *modus operandi* outlined by Ban Gu.

As far as the officials are concerned, the inspector of Ji Province and the prime minister of the kingdom of Lecheng certainly conform to the expectations raised by Ban Gu. We find two officials eager to take action against a king; and they do so in the precise way Ban Gu had described: via a memorial accusing the king of a heinous crime. Cen Hong's plea, however, forces us to make more subtle distinctions within officialdom itself. As an official coming to a king's defense, he does not fit the model of officialdom as uniformly inimical to the kings and their interests. Cen Hong's role in defense of Liu Chang certainly has to be linked to the fact that Cen Hong was a member of the Secretariat, an office often seen as representing the palace more than the government. Cen Hong was providing the emperor with arguments—besides the customary "I cannot bear it"—that could help the emperor resist his officials' demand that Liu Chang should be put to death. By overstating his defense, Cen Hong was also playing devil's advocate, allowing the emperor to stake out,

71. *HHS* 5.235, 50.1674, 55.1808.

72. Subsequent empress dowagers would also avail themselves of this tool; for examples, see *HHS* 55.1797–98 and 55.1805–6.

in his edict, a middle position between Cen Hong's and that of the emperor's outer officials.

Liu Chang's case shows that the institution of kingship endured well into later Han times and that emperors took great care to make sure that lines of inheritance continued as long as there were suitable heirs. Liu Chang's case is typical for various reasons. He was not in charge of his own fate, but a pawn in the hands of whichever power was behind the throne; his tenure at Lecheng entailed complicated ritual duties and a fair amount of economic privilege, but no powers of rulership; his every move was watched, not only by Lecheng's queen dowager, but also by regional officials ever eager to bring charges against him; when charges were in fact made, he was protected by his ties of kinship with an emperor "unable to bear" the heavy sentence proposed by the officials. Liu Chang's path to the kingship, however, was exceptional insofar as he owed his kingship to Empress Dowager Deng's new policy of appointing secondary sons of her late husband's brothers to kingdoms that had become vacant. Since Liu Chang, as a secondary son, had not become king through the regular channels of succession, his position was considerably weakened after the death of his patroness. The exceptional nature of his appointment might also explain why Emperor An did not content himself with invoking the conventional "I cannot bear it," but wanted additional assurances that leniency toward his cousin was appropriate, assurances that Cen Hong provided by citing the *Zhouli*'s Eight Rules. Liu Chang's case, indeed, is the first in which an imperial edict appeals to these rules.

The edict also conforms to the *modus operandi* outlined by Ban Gu. It strikes a balance between the harsh demands of regional officials and the demand that the emperor be lenient toward his kin. The edict nonetheless masks a balance of power that had changed radically from the period early in Emperor Wu's reign that provided the context of Ban Gu's discourse. Imperial power was now strongly, and almost permanently, contested, due to the greatly increased influence of the empress dowagers, whose power was based on their ability to control imperial succession. The edict, therefore, should also be read as one of the ways in which Emperor An, with newly acquired powers after the death of Empress Dowager Deng, sought to position himself towards her allies and her policies: willing to criticize—under the guise of apparent self-criticism—her individual appointments but not her policies as such; and willing to remove people too closely allied with the empress dowager without engaging in outright attacks on her person.

It is no coincidence that Empress Dowager Deng—as well as empress dowagers later in Eastern Han—sought to ally themselves with Liu royals and their sons. As Liu Sheng stated in his speech, due to their kinship to the emperor, the kings enjoyed a kind of immunity that the distaff families, by definition, lacked. Indeed, distaff families at the very height of their power had to be vexed by the likelihood that, like the ordinary mice and rats in Liu Sheng's speech, they could be "drowned" or "fumigated" in the not so distant future. In contrast, the Liu kings occupied a special, far more secure place, at least as long as the dynasty lasted. Empress Dowager Deng might be credited with having imbued the institution of kingship with renewed importance, as she actively created, out of the royal lines founded by her husband, a pool of trustworthy potential successors to the imperial throne. However, as her policies inevitably reduced the independent nature of the Liu kings, the empress dowager might also have deprived the institution of some of the meaning with which Liu Sheng imbued it in his 138 BCE speech, and, in fact, diminished the Liu kings' symbolic capital. Liu Chang's quick downfall seems to illustrate just that.

CHAPTER 8

Yang Xiong's 揚雄 *Final* Fayan 法言 *Chapter:*

Rhetoric to What End and for Whom?

Michael Nylan, University of California, Berkeley

My topic is the last chapter of Yang Xiong's 揚雄 (53 BCE–18 CE) *Fayan*, one of three masterworks produced by Yang late in life and the neoclassical work best known to later generations of Chinese readers. Typically, last chapters, not unlike deathbed testaments, represent the author's final summations, and readers expect such statements to be all the weightier for it. Accordingly, a long-standing tradition finds in Yang's final chapter an important criterion by which to assess Yang's moral standing within the Confucian tradition. However, any modern reader looking in the chapter, entitled "Xiao zhi" 孝至 ("Honoring the Ancestors, the Ultimate Duty"), for an obvious signpost to Yang's frame of mind will be sorely disappointed. This sense of disappointment will be underscored by further irritants and puzzles: (1) the chapter takes as its main subject an old-fashioned virtue, "filial duty," that strikes moderns living in a post-Freudian age as irrelevant at best, and reactionary at worst; (2) it is a virtue that seems to lack the rich web of associations and possible wordplays that surround some other virtue words employed by Yang, such as *ming* 明, which Yang develops in all its senses of "light" and "enlightenment"; (3) the chapter looks as if it is out of order, for filial duty, as the "base" for the higher adult virtues, should logically come first in the *Fayan*; (4) the chapter apparently rambles far beyond its stated topic to offer disparate impressions on such topics as the likelihood that good character traits will be inherited, the superior guidance offered by classical learning in comparison with rival approaches to governance, the proper priorities in good rule, and the wisdom of recent policy decisions at the Han court; and (5) near the chapter's end comes a single instance of hyperbolic praise for Wang Mang 王莽 (46 BCE–23 CE). It is those few words that have attracted the lion's share of the attention in later ages, eclipsing the contents and significance of the rest of the chapter and, indeed, the entire book.

However, it is the historian's job to inquire whether such first impressions remain valid upon closer examination. For if we historians know anything to be true, it's that "we speak in a certain manner expecting to be heard in a certain manner; and conversely, the way in which we listen to others depends on our assumptions about how they are expressing meaning and, indeed, our conceptions of what meaning is."[1] To reconstruct how Yang expected to be heard, both authorial intention and early reader reception must be assessed, however impossible those tasks seem to be at this far remove in time. This essay will argue, contra the premodern and modern moralizers, that Han deliberative rhetoric in general—and Yang's sophisticated rhetoric in particular—cannot be captured by assigning pieces, in a dichotomous way, either to the craven sycophant or the loyal remonstrant. Han rhetoricians were perfectly capable of crafting subtle arguments designed to appeal to multiple constituencies holding different views of the world, and since they operated in a world where their rhetoric had real-life consequences, the most astute among them saw to their own training. Aristotle is hardly the only classical writer to note that the most skilled rhetoricians find it useful to conflate praise and persuasion ("To praise a man is in one respect akin to urging a course of action").[2]

---

1. Kuriyama, *The Expressiveness of the Body*, 107.

2. Aristotle, *Rhetoric* 1867b37. The term "rhetoric" and variations on it (e.g., "skilled rhetorician," as here) is neutral here, referring only to an ability in crafting persuasions, which could be employed for good or bad ends. The *Analects* ascribed to Confucius excoriates glib speakers even as it praises those who know how to use speech effectively for moral ends. For a present-day expert on what rhetoric meant to the Greeks, see Boyarin, *Socrates and the Fat Rabbis*, esp. chap. 3 (which slams the usual caricature of rhetoric as equivalent to "soul-imperiling" and "dangerous" sophistry—a sloppy equation typically attributed to the *Gorgias*—as uninformed by "a century of research findings and explication to the contrary").

Yang, justly regarded as the most accomplished of the Han rhetoricians, advanced an integrated theory that went beyond proposals by Zhanguo thinkers; in a manner roughly analogous to the post-Aristotelians, he posited as vital supplement to good socialization the inculcation of habitual deliberation in light of the Classics; this therapy aimed to redirect the destructive desires of adult hearts to wiser and more constructive ends. At the same time, we should acknowledge that a court writer in the classical era, if he was to establish his authority as an author, had always to demonstrate a measure of autonomy from his patrons, for "merely to transcribe the regime's version of events would be to become a mere copyist," regardless of the author's position.[3] These observations are worth recalling when we come to review the complex rhetorical moves that Yang Xiong employs in constructing the chapters in his masterwork, the *Fayan*. In my estimation, Yang, a remarkably capable persuader, would not have devoted a careful assessment of filial duty in relation to imperial policy solely to announce or renounce his allegiance to one figure, Wang Mang.[4] Through the *Fayan*, Yang intended to direct contemporary court conversations about the all-important policy matters of war and sacrifice, even as he fashioned appeals to later generations to live up to the best traditions in Central States civilization. Therefore, this essay concerns some of the concept clusters with which Yang proposes to shape discussion about the proper direction of court policy and social cultivation.

The Focus on Filial Duty

I begin with two statements made in commentaries to chapter 13, the first by Li Gui 李軌 (fl. 317 CE), compiler of the earliest extant commentary to the *Fayan*, and the second by Wang Rongbao 汪榮寶,

---

3. Sailor, *Writing and Empire in Tacitus*, 43.

4. David Knechtges says he believes that the *Fayan* was written probably in 8 or 9 CE, but *before* Wang's takeover. Knechtges says, "The *Fa yen* was not composed all at one time, but represents Yang Hsiung's random jottings written over a decade or more." While I would query Knechtges's use of the word "random," Knechtges is undoubtedly correct in most of his assessments about the book. See Knechtges, "Fa yen," 101.

compiler of one of the latest (comp. 1911 CE).[5] Li argues that Yang's thirteenth chapter completes a hermeneutical circle, returning to the lessons about learning and cultivation that are the subject of the first chapter in the same work.[6] (Of course, every chapter in the *Fayan* ties its discussions back to the importance of classical learning.) Wang, by contrast, stresses Yang's propensity to imitate other canonical texts, especially the *Analects* ascribed to Confucius, in characterizing the highest Way as "nothing more than family feeling" (*xiaodi er yi yi* 孝弟而已矣), and "abiding in the ideas and intuitions of ancient sages" (*yu yi gui sheng ren zhi yi* 寓依歸聖人之意). In Wang's account, Yang describes the noble man's regard for the sages as kindred spirits.[7] The two famous commentators agree only that Yang is not talking about filial duty in any narrow sense (i.e., the care and feeding of parents, living and dead). Instead Yang's treatment of *xiao*, in their views, discusses the unbreakable connections between family reverence, cultivation in the polite arts, and the fulfillment of social and political obligations accomplished via fervent emulation of the sages.[8]

In the summary of the chapter's contents given in Yang's own postface to the *Fayan*, Yang ties "comforting one's parents" to "comforting the spirits" (the ancestral dead, but also Heaven, perhaps), tying both to the emperor's duty to "cheer the hearts and minds of the whole realm" (*huan xin* 歡/驩心). This linkage recalls, in turn, lines from Yang's "Sweet Springs Rhapsody," which have the emperor earning the spirits' trust by his gracious care of even the lowliest of his subjects, after which the spirits send down blessings in the form

---

5. These two commentaries are generally considered to be the most authoritative; Li, because it is in the earliest extant commentary; Wang, because his commentary is most comprehensive. See Wang Rongbao, comp., *Fayan yishu*.

6. See Wang Rongbao's compilation of Yang Xiong, *Fayan yishu*, vol. 2, 19.523. However, below the *Fayan* is usually cited by standard *juan*/para. no., as given in Han Jing's annotated edition, *Fayan zhu*. These virtues of *xiao* and fraternal love are especially associated with Shun in the excavated text "Tang Yu zhi dao" 唐虞之道 from Guodian, where Shun is portrayed as the expert on these subjects. See Zheng Jiewen, *Zhongguo Moxue tongshi*, vol. 1, 167.

7. Cf. *Fayan* 1.13. Of course, "kin" and "kindred" are cognate.

8. See Rosemont and Ames, *The Chinese Classic of Family Reverence*. Rosemont in particular has been arguing that early Chinese texts, in contrast to those of early Greece, do not articulate a "virtue ethic," but a role ethic.

of "Son after son, grandson after grandson, / Forever and always, without limit."[9] Such connections would have struck loyal members of the court in late Western Han as particularly poignant, given the absence of suitable heirs born to the Han throne. Almost certainly, then, Yang's *Fayan* does not merely, in imitation of the *Analects*, select the first two characters in the chapter for the chapter title.

As commentators, both Li and Wang were doubtless mindful that a mere four passages—the first four passages, just over one-ninth of the chapter—speak directly of the filial duties that children owe to parents, living or dead. Those first four passages reiterate stock themes in Han literature, among them that children can never repay the debt they owe their parents for conferring on them the gift of life; that children must never reckon that they can repay obligation when it suits them, since parents typically die before their children; and that to employ the ancestral sacrifices for any other purpose than to "preserve" the parents in the mind's eye is to waste cult offerings and to treat the sacred dead as mere pretexts for social events.[10] In *Fayan* 13.5, which insists that dutiful fathers usually spawn dutiful sons, the conversation shifts somewhat, to define "capable children" (*neng zi* 能子).[11] The chapter then proceeds to take up a host of topics, including the mutual obligations between family members; the use and abuse of social conventions to demonstrate one's inner commitments; the nobility of the ancient sage-kings' Ways of life; the necessity of hard work for success in any pursuit; the potential for progress in the Way that may ennoble the aged; the source of the Han imperial authority for its subjects and frontier peoples; and the proper scope and application of "forcefulness" in imperial policy-making. How do such topics build toward—or even relate to—either the ostensible topic of "filial duty" or the penultimate pronouncement in the chapter, which offers high praise for Wang Mang before a concluding encomium dedicated to the Han ruling line?

Probing the structure and contents of the chapter further, we find much of Yang's thirteenth chapter to be preoccupied with the

---

9. *HS* 87A.3534; cf. Knechtges, trans., *The* Han shu *Biography of Yang Xiong*, 24.

10. For the last point, see *Fayan* 13.4.

11. *Fayan* 13.6 cites the well-known example of a father and son noted for their punctilious service to the Han throne, Shi Fen 石奮 and Shi Jian 建.

construction of another concept cluster: the emperor's personal cultivation of the social virtues, which require his single-minded devotion to the dictates of heaven and the welfare of his people, ends in his court's implementation of successful policies, once he, in consultation with his court, has clearly defined the proper spheres and modes of activity for the Han throne. This particular connection can be said to begin with Yang's opening statement about filial duty in the chapter ("[Even] the sages could not add anything to this!"), which alludes to *Odes* and *Documents* traditions describing ideal rule,[12] and the connection ends with the chapter's closing line, which adapts a phrase from the *Odes*.[13] The initial section of the chapter argues that the Han court, if it hopes to emulate the greatness of the early sage-kings, must see its benevolent acts as inadequate repayment for its subjects' dutiful service.[14] To requite the unseen or shadowy presences that sustain us in life, as happens in the ancestral cult, defines what it means to be human for Yang, since the birds and beasts lack the imagination, the reverence, and the humility to engage in such activities.[15] Furthermore, Yang says, the man in power who acts, like heaven and earth, not for the sake of reputation, but for the sake of doing good will find his reputation secured for all time.[16]

The middle section of the chapter (13.10–13.24) conveys a single coherent portrait of the greatest sage-kings of the past: supposedly, those sage-kings were supremely mindful that their vast territories could never compare in magnitude with the debt and deference they owe the least of their loyal subjects. By persistent, incremental acts that address their subjects' needs, rather than by self-aggrandizing policies, the sages exhibited in their own persons the requisite level of perfection that was needed to elicit the admiration of the ages.[17] For their

12. Mao, no. 218; *Shangshu dazhuan*, 5.7, commenting on "Jiahe" 嘉禾 chap.; cf. *Mencius* 7A.21.

13. Mao, no. 48 ("Sang zhong" 桑中), stanza 1, in the "Yongfeng" 鄘風 section, where *tangyi* refers to a plant (dodder?), even if the Mao commentary reads the poem itself as a statement about the ruling house's failure to provide a proper moral model.

14. *Fayan* 13.2.

15. *Fayan* 13.4.

16. *Fayan* 13.8, 13.11.

17. *Fayan* 13.9.

undeniable merits, all honor and glory is due them.[18] The last ten or so units in the chapter, out of a total of thirty-four, turn to discuss the extraordinary greatness of the Han imperium (esp. 13.24–13.30), its sheer expanse over the globe and the depth of support that it commands. Section 13.31 turns to the subject of the hard work required of the emperor, if he is to keep the heart of the empire, the Central States arrayed along the Yellow River valley, in a state of good order.

> The ruler of men works hard to make the people prosper and to increase their wealth, to clarify the Way and clearly exemplify it, and to extend a sense of justice and duty to all, so as to achieve efficacy in the Lordly functions and thus accomplish the transformation of all things in heaven-and-earth. In this way, he causes the sedentary farmers[19] to laugh and feel at ease, *so that when cult is offered to the spirits, the spirits will certainly accept them*!
>
> 君人者務在殷民阜財。明道信義。致帝者之用。成天地之化。使粒食之民粲也。晏也。享于鬼神。不亦饗乎。[20]

By this argument, the emperor holds the key to effective ancestor worship, for it is his hard work on behalf of the realm that allows the vast majority of his subjects to be able to focus properly on their cult duties to the ancestral dead; without his guidance, most of the same subjects will lack not only the means but also the heart to carry out the rites. The ideal ruler's continual exertion on behalf of others is then reiterated.[21] To act with the express desire to "confer benefits"—that, we learn, is the one disposition common to the beneficent cosmos, a person's parents, and the ideal ruler of men, and it is this selfless generosity that the filial son, loyal minister, and the dutiful subject alike seek to requite through their own service in subordinate positions.[22] Note that, in contrast with other thinkers, including Xunzi, who sharply distinguished the ease and spontaneity of the heavenly order from the human Way of conscious design and

---

18. *Fayan* 13.11.

19. One is tempted to insert the phrase "of the Central Plains" here, since Yang is constructing a case against foreign wars of aggression.

20. *Fayan* 13.31 underscores and clarifies the message of *Fayan* 13.12. Italics mine.

21. E.g., *Fayan* 13.12: "The great ways in the realm are five in number, but the means to proceed along those paths is only one, what we call 'exertion.'"

22. See *Fayan* 13.2–3, 13.14.

hard work, Yang would have the emperor model himself upon heaven, in the belief that heaven advances the constant order through its slow, cumulative efforts ("Each and every day heaven advances one degree [out of 360 in a year]. That is what I call 'hard work.' By year's end, we have what we call an 'achievement,' that is, the harvest.").[23] Thus do the sun in the heavens and the emperor on earth provide the necessary light and enlightenment to those below.

Then, as if to forestall the inevitable objections by those who prefer to see the emperor as the unmoved prime mover "taking his ease while his officials toil," Yang insists that the emperor's responsibility consists of faithfully carrying out the work of the Dao, not scurrying around to micromanage a myriad bureaucratic tasks. In this remark, Yang returns to a theme enunciated earlier in the same chapter, which describes the cosmos giving birth to the people, who in turn give the ruler the authority, that he may establish a moral model for all subjects and maintain harmony in the cosmos. That means that the single-minded conformity to the sage-kings' exemplary model that is required of the "one man," the ruler, can promote all the various sorts of constructive interactions between the cosmic, social, political, and personal orders.[24]

In identifying active conformity with the Dao and Heaven (terms Yang uses interchangeably) as the proper business of the Han throne, Yang reiterates three remarkable points that are key to his vision but generally overlooked: first, that the main task of the ruler of men is to create the optimal conditions under which his subjects can flourish; second, that it is this sort of worldly activity on the part of the emperor, not prayers and incantations, that proves most pleasing to the otherworldly spirits; and third, that the emperor must never dare to "lower his sights," accepting the half-measures associated with realpolitik when he could be accepting the classical precepts, for the attainment of the Great Peace lies well within his grasp.[25] Invoking Mencius in his first point, Yang invites his readers to imagine a set of resonances tying inner to outer, visible to unseen, fashioning an individual life that will connect the ancestors in the dim past with an orderly community in the unknown future, with *xiao* devotion the

---

23. See *Fayan* 13.32, which seems to me to resonate with *Fayan* 13.16.
24. *Fayan* 13.16.
25. *Fayan* 13.9.

"ultimate" bridge between these worlds.[26] Yang makes the same point again and again in chapter 13, as in the following lines: "The realm may be truly vast, but ruling it well depends upon but one Way, so that it is manageable enough, is it not? The four seas at the ends of the earth may be truly distant, but good rule depends upon but one heart, which is near, is it not?" 天下爲大。治之在道，不亦小乎。四海爲遠。治之在心。不亦邇乎。[27]

Good rule will never be achieved, however, unless the ruler of men apprehends the distinction between shows of brute strength and the strength of will that discerns true benefit in the promotion of good rule. To Yang's way of thinking, the ideal emperor's fund of strength cannot be measured in the ordinary terms used for strong men, such as the capacity to shoulder a great bronze tripod or bear aloft a heavy battle standard:

> Someone asked me, "Strength is measured by the capacity to shoulder a great tripod or bear aloft a gorgeous battle standard. Are there likewise acts that similarly outdo others when it comes to wisdom and virtue?"
>
> "Those equal to the force of a hundred men! Compelling virtue renders the nasty and quarrelsome compliant, as Shun once did. It makes 'the myriad states accede to its rule.' And wisdom 'fathoms the true conditions in heaven-and-earth,' giving form to the unfathomable. This force surely equals that of a hundred other men!"
>
> 或曰力有扛洪鼎揭華旗。智德亦有之乎。曰百人矣。德諧頑嚚。讓萬國。知情天地，形不測。百人乎。[28]

The true strength that results from moral authority inculcates virtue in others and brings peace where there was once only violence and discord; indeed, the single goal of good rule is to instill in others that sense of security that plays such a vital role in ensuring human dignity.[29] (Earlier in the *Fayan*, Yang makes the same point—that those who impart benefit to others, via their conduct or their teachings—

26. Note, however, that Yang is usually viewed as a "skeptic" on the spirit realm, since he opposes the power of the diviners, believes the dead have no consciousness, and emphasizes this-world solutions.

27. *Fayan* 13.19.

28. *Fayan* 13.13.

29. *Fayan* 13.14.

are somehow invincible, and certainly they far outshine the tough guys who are merely physically strong.)[30] Put another way, rulers are to impart light and enlightenment to their subjects,[31] in this being like "rays of glorious light." For the ruler to achieve this state of cultivation requires unflagging attention to doing good, however, so that he may maximize the sway of his charismatic virtue.[32] Indeed, the ideal ruler's attention is so fixed on doing good that he simply has no time left to consider anything else. Even the possible existence of portents sent from heaven must come second.[33]

The ruler's duty to forge a tight circle of connections through his conferral of benefits and his determination to provide security and peace to others inevitably constrains the exercise of Han power, however, as several passages demonstrate. Chapter 13 for that reason disputes the prevailing wisdom lauding the dramatic extension of the Han territories under Emperor Wu into the far northwest and southeast. By Yang's account, this unchecked expansion; far from benefiting most Han subjects, jeopardized their economic well-being and hence their very way of life:

> As they say, "From Dragon Dunes[34] on west and from the Great Desert[35] on north is the home of the Bird Yi and the Bestial Yi. The com-

---

30. See Yang Xiong's comparison of Jing Ke 荆軻, the assassin-retainer, and Meng Ke 孟軻 (i.e., Mencius), in *Fayan* 11.4.

31. *Fayan* 13.14.

32. *Fayan* 13.15.

33. *Fayan* 13.15; cf. ibid., 12.22.

34. The phrase "As they say" is added because Jia Juanzhi's memorial advising against a southern expedition freely made comparisons between southern campaigns and those in the north and northwest, including the campaigns of 60–61 BCE following a rebellion in northeastern Qinghai. The rebellion and campaign are recounted in *HS* 69, the biography of Zhao Chongguo 趙充國 (131–57 BCE); cf. *HS* 69.2985, for a record of the total expenditures in grain, salt, and fodder used by the Han army. This passage speaks of the desert from White Dragon Dunes, in the old Western Regions or *Xiyu* 西域 (modern-day southeastern Xinjiang), to the northeast of Lop Nor (a former salt lake now dried up), on east to the Jade Gate of Gansu province. This swathe of territory would include the various polities of the Tarim Basin (i.e., the Western Regions) that lay west of these dunes. The Great Desert is the Gobi, and the groups to its north were the Xiongnu.

35. The desert stretching from the western foothills of Daxing'an 大興安 to the eastern foothills of the Tianshan 天山 Mountain range. The exact meaning of "Bird

manderies[36] bear the burden of the care and feeding of the king's troops.[37] The Han ruling house should not act in this way."
龍堆以西，大漠以北，鳥夷獸夷。郡勞王師。漢家不爲也。

The end to Zhuya[38] commandery came through Jia Juanzhi's 賈捐之[39] forcefulness.[40] Had it been otherwise, we would all have been exchanging our caps and gowns for fish scales and diving suits![41]
朱崖之絕。捐之之力也。否則介鱗易我衣裳。

An appreciation of the second passage relies upon knowledge of the story of Jia Juanzhi. In 46 BCE, Emperor Yuan (r. 48–33 BCE) was

---

Yi" (bird-Easterners) and "Bestial Yi" (beast-Easterners) is uncertain, although most assume that it is derogatory. One interpretation is "barbarians clothed in bird feathers and animal skins." See Wang Rongbao, comp., *Fayan yishu*, vol. 2, 20.554. These phrases come from the memorial of Jia Juanzhi recorded immediately below.

36. Liu Shipei 劉師培 (1884–1919 CE) reads *jun* 郡 as *qun* 群 ("many," "masses"), and Wang Niansun 王念孫 (1744–1832 CE) as *shu* 數 ("repeatedly," "constantly"), on the grounds that the "kingly" and "commandery" systems did not coexist. Wang's mistake is to ignore the continuance of many preunification terms in the mixed Han system. However, two other readings are possible. If we follow Li Gui's reading, then the line means, "To make the royal army toil in order to turn such lands into commanderies—the Han ruling house should not act in this way." And if we follow Wang Niansun, who equates 郡 = 仍 = 重 = 數, or Liu Shipei, who equates 郡 = 羣, then the line reads, "To make the royal army repeatedly toil (in military expeditions to these distant lands) is not what the Han ruling house should do." The main idea is clear, no matter which reading is chosen. The Han should not burden its people with expansionist policies.

37. What is implied: "at great expense" and "at too great a distance" from the Han court. The court has overstretched its armies and people.

38. *HS* 6.188 has Wudi setting up Zhuya and many other commanderies in the extreme south. The *HS* "Dili zhi" 地理志 tells us that Zhuya 朱[珠]崖 was located in the land corresponding to modern-day Hainan Island.

39. Jia Juanzhi was the great-grandson of the far more famous Jia Yi 賈誼 (200–167 BCE); like Jia Yi, his major contribution came while he was still relatively young. The great-grandson, to rebut the memorials of hawks urging the emperor to launch a punitive campaign against the southern rebels, offered the throne a strongly worded memorial urging withdrawal from Zhuya commandery, as recorded in *HS* 64B.2830–34.

40. Or, "The abandonment of Zhuya was Jia Juanzhi's great contribution."

41. Meaning, "We would all have become less than fully civilized," as the caps and gowns are emblems of Central States civilization. Sometimes it is said of southerners diving for pearls that they had virtually become fish. The term "fish scales" describes any seaworthy creature or object, including the special garb worn by divers for pearls or even boats. Hence, the reference to "fish scales" and "diving suits."

eager to send troops to quell a rebellion on Hainan Island, in the far south of his empire. Since the initial conquest of the island had been achieved through "the merit and moral power" (*gongde* 功德) of his predecessors, "the former emperors," Emperor Yuan felt it his filial duty to see that the island continued under Han rule.[42] Jia Juanzhi, a young candidate "awaiting appointment" to office, contradicted the imperial logic in no uncertain terms, insisting that the sage-kings of yore had amplified their power and authority through quite another method: "They ruled over all who wished to ally with them in their reputation and civilizing influence, but did not impose their ways on those who had no wish to ally with them" 欲與聲教則治之，不欲與者不彊治也。[43] To Jia's way of thinking, the only "increase" that Emperor Wu's wars of expansion brought the empire came in the form of useless exotica, increased taxes, and the numbers of corpses piled on the distant battlefields. After Emperor Yuan's chancellor, Yu Dingguo 于定國 (fl. 51–43 BCE), endorsed these objections, Emperor Yuan was finally persuaded to abandon his plan to retake Hainan Island. Zhuya commandery simply ceased to exist by imperial order. But as Jia was so impolitic as to criticize the powerful imperial favorite, Shi Xian 石顯, Jia soon—probably within the year—was condemned to public execution in the marketplace, rather than being honored as a most loyal servant of the Han.

For his contemporaries, Yang's message in the *Fayan* could hardly have been clearer, especially as he placed nearby a reference to the sedentary farming of the Central States. Foreign wars of aggression threatened to subvert the domestic order so painstakingly constructed through the efforts of the early Western Han rulers. Such wars inevitably placed undue burdens on the northern and southern frontier commanderies, whose difficult climates allowed farmers at

---

42. This revolt, which began in 48 BCE, was the third since 59 BCE; it had defied all attempts at pacification at this point. For further information, see the unpublished seminar paper "'Attractive Indeed Is the Moral Power of Han!' 漢德其可謂允懷矣: Views on Frontier Expansion, Foreign Relations, and Civilizing Influence in Late Western Han," by Yang Shaoyun, presented in my fall 2007 seminar, "Qin-Han History." I have profited much from reading his analysis, which brought several of the texts cited below to my attention, and I here register my profound debt to his work on topics relating to the outlying lands.

43. *HS* 64B.2831.

best to eke out marginal existences, when they were lucky enough to avoid being impressed into service to fight the raiding parties. Moreover, as the Han army units were made up of conscripts from all over the empire, many soldiers were living in virtual exile from their families hundreds or thousands of miles away. As if that were not enough, the lure of foreign parts and exotic products tended to upset the delicate balance between those engaged in the primary and secondary occupations.[44] Paradoxically, then, the initiatives aiming to secure dominance over the inhabitants living at the ends of the earth spelled ruin to the very way of life cherished in the heartlands of the empire.[45] The conquest of each of these places mentioned here, from the Dragon Dunes to Zhuya, had originally entailed tremendous loss of life and great hardship. And for what, Yang demands? Merely to assert power over a motley assortment of curious animals and ethnic groups,[46] since the foreign conquests do nothing to alleviate the misery of the good subjects who are called upon to risk their lives for the Han throne.

That this subject of foreign wars was continually linked with the theme of "honoring the ancestors" is easily demonstrated, for the final decision by the emperor, after consultation with his ministers, to desist from launching a punitive campaign against the rebels in Zhuya again spoke in these terms:

> Between the starvation of Our myriad subjects and the rebellion of distant barbarians that goes unpunished, which is the greater danger? [Obviously, the former!] Moreover, in these [recent] years of famine *even the ancestral shrines of the dynasty have not received their due sacrifices*—why then should We be concerned to avoid a humiliation that is not ritually proscribed?
>
> 夫萬民之饑餓，與遠蠻之不討，危孰大焉？且宗廟之祭，凶年不備，況乎辟不嫌之辱哉！[47]

---

44. Any student of Han history knows that the "primary occupation" is agriculture, while the secondary (i.e., "less essential") occupations are those of the merchants and artisans.

45. This was not a new argument. For details, see Yu, *Trade and Expansion in Han China*, passim; Chin, "Savage Exchange."

46. For the fishes and turtles, see the original memorial by Jia Juanzhi, which likens the people of the South to fishes and turtles.

47. Italics mine. See *HS* 64B.2831–35 for the entire affair, which concludes (p. 2835) with the edict.

The forgoing speeches are hardly isolated examples of the rhetorical propensity by members of the Han court to cast the duty to prosecute frontier wars in terms of filial duty, as the standard histories attest. During several court policy debates in late Western Han, groups we can loosely identify as "reformists" or "modernists" invoked similar patriotic rhetoric,[48] as Yang notes in the "historical chapters" in the *Fayan* or elsewhere in his writings.

In 36 BCE, for example, before Yang's arrival at court, the Han ministers had been sharply divided over the question of whether to reward two officials, Protector General Gan Yanshou 甘延壽 and his subordinate Chen Tang 陳湯, for an unauthorized attack on a Xiongnu leader's fortress in Sogdiana, which ended in the massacre of some fifteen hundred Xiongnu. We know, too, that later, in 28 BCE, a certain Du Qin 杜欽 advised Wang Feng 王鳳,[49] the consort clan (*waiqi* 外戚) marshal of state who monopolized state power during the first decade of Chengdi's (r. 33–7 BCE) reign, to refuse any peace overtures made by a Xiongnu king to the Han court on the grounds that

> the sage-kings divided the realm into Nine Provinces and they instituted the Five Tributary Zones. *In their concern with bringing prosperity to those within the realm, they did not pursue what lay outside it.* Now if we dispatch an envoy to convey the commands of Our emperor, sending

---

48. For the term "reformist," see Loewe, *Crisis and Conflict in Han China*, esp. chap. 5. "Reformists" Loewe characterizes in terms of their anticentralizing rhetoric, while "modernists" argued in favor of centralizing initiatives by the government, which they took to be all for the good, in that they maximized the "public interest" over "selfish" (family or individual) interests. Note, however, that the battle lines between these two groups were not always clearly drawn. On most policy matters, for example, Liu Xiang would be called a "reformer," but he backed the "modernist" line when it came to Chen Tang and Gan Yanshou.

49. Wang Feng monopolized power at the court during the years from 33–22 BCE. Although uncle to Wang Mang, Wang Feng was no particular patron of the young Wang Mang. Wang Mang, at the latter's recommendation, was appointed *huangmeng lang* 黃門郎, Courtier of the Yellow Gates, but Wang Mang was not ennobled for some six years after Wang Feng's death, even though Mang purportedly was punctilious in his treatment of his uncle during his final illness (24–22 BCE). We cannot, therefore, assume (contra several commentators) that when Yang mentions Wang Feng, he is indirectly speaking of Wang Mang. Du Qin exerted considerable influence upon Wang Feng, for Wang accepted his advice in foreign policy matters as well as when the Yellow River burst its banks in 27 BCE. For the flooding, see *HS* 97B.3974.

> along the goods of the eastern and southern groups, we will burden a whole company of officers and soldiers who will be trekking along the perilous roads. To exhaust the very men upon whom we rely simply in order to carry out an affair of no possible use to us cannot be a good strategy for the long run.
>
> 聖王分九州，制五服，務盛內，不求外。今遣使者承至尊之命，送蠻夷之賈，勞吏士之眾，涉危難之路。罷弊所恃以事無用， 非久長計也。[50]

Within a year or so, three local leaders in Zangke 牂柯 commandery, far to the southeast (present Guizhou province), had attacked one another.[51] Since the leaders ignored a Han envoy's offer to negotiate a peace, members of the Han court were uncertain how to proceed. Was it worthwhile to dispatch troops to suppress a civil war that had broken out so far away from the capital? In advising Wang Feng, Du Qin this time hedged his bets. On the one hand, Du argued that the Han realm might well consider it beneath its dignity to try to enforce a peace among such "useless" and uncivilized peoples of the far South. On the other hand, the emperor might well regard it as a solemn duty to maintain all the territories he had inherited from his predecessors, in which case the court should immediately dispatch men to execute the rebel leaders.

> If we consider this to be an utterly barren land inhabited by useless people—a land that any sage-king would not deign to trouble the Central States (*Zhongguo*) with, we ought to abolish the commandery, abandon its residents, and sever relations with its princes for all time. But if we believe that *the achievements built by generations of past emperors should never be allowed to falter or lapse*, then it would be best to nip this problem in the bud, immediately resolving it, lest harm be visited upon tens of thousands of area households [as well as army conscripts in the area], and the rebellion develop fully before we send the army in.
>
> 即以爲不毛之地，亡用之民，聖王不以勞中國，宜罷郡，放棄其民，絕其王侯勿復通。如以先帝所立累世之功不可墮壞，亦宜因其萌牙，早斷絕之，及已成形然後戰師，則萬姓被害。[52]

---

50. *HS* 96A.3886–87.

51. This set of events can probably be dated to 27 BCE. Zangke had been established as a commandery in 112 BCE, under Han Wudi.

52. *HS* 95.3843–44. Again, the italics are mine.

As skillful rhetorician, Du in both cases clothed his foreign policy suggestions in terms of the filial duty the present emperor owed to his ancestors. Apparently, however, Du Qin opposed the Xiongnu offer, since he wanted the Han to intervene in the Zangke war. In neither case did Du's urgings bring any lasting advantage to the Han ruling house, as Yang knew.[53]

Around 3 BCE, Yang Xiong himself intervened in ongoing policy discussions regarding the Xiongnu, despite noisy protestations in his *fu* 賦 and in his *Fayan* that he much preferred not to engage in any contentious matters before the court.[54] The full story is somewhat convoluted. Shortly after the boy emperor Emperor Ai's accession in 7 BCE, fifty-three court officials, including ministers and academicians, recommended that the ancestral shrine dedicated to Emperor Wu be dismantled to make way for that of Emperor Cheng (r. 33–7 BCE), in accordance with the canonical ritual prescription stipulating a maximum of five imperial shrines: four, plus that of the founding emperor. Wang Shun 王舜 and Liu Xin 劉歆, representing the strongest consort clan and the imperial clan respectively, were furious that an exception would not be made for Emperor Wu, for they believed that Emperor Wu's success in offensive wars against the Xiongnu had laid the foundation for the unparalleled level of economic prosperity and cultural supremacy enjoyed by the Han court vis-à-vis its neighbors. Emperor Ai, then a puppet of the Wang clan, hastened to reject the proposal to dismantle Emperor Wu's temple.[55] But this did not prevent Yang Xiong from portraying Emperor Wu and the chief architects of his policies in the worst possible light in his "historical chapters" of the *Fayan*, probably in the process of compilation right then.

That very same year a formal request came from the Xiongnu leader, Nangzhiyasi 囊知牙斯 (also known as Wuzhuliu Chanyu

53. Wang Feng, in response to Du's advice, replaced the prefect of Zangke with one Chen Li 陳立, a man the locals feared. Shortly after his arrival in Zangke, Chen Li summoned the king of the largest rebel group, Yelang, and beheaded him on the spot. But this failed to resolve the matter, for the father-in-law and son of the beheaded king soon revolted, in order to avenge him, and Chen Li had to fight hard to suppress them. Meanwhile the Xiongnu troubles continued. See *HS* 95.3845.

54. On the *fu*, see the works of David R. Knechtges, Paul Kroll, and Martin Kern.

55. *HS* 73.3125–27.

烏珠留單于), to pay a state visit to the Han court. Many Han court officers leveled two main objections: first, in the past, two separate visits from the Xiongnu *chanyu* had been quickly followed by the deaths of the reigning emperors, which meant the Xiongnu might have found a way to somehow put curses on the Central States rulers; and second, the badly cash-strapped Han court could not at the moment raise the necessary funds to entertain the Xiongnu in a manner likely to glorify the host and gratify the guest. The young Aidi, supremely mindful of the need to placate his imperial and maternal relatives, was inclined to deny the Xiongnu request, until he received a strongly worded memorial from Yang Xiong arguing that the peace must be secured at any price, because "the Central States [*Zhongguo*] cannot sleep peacefully at night until the northern barbarians submit." For contributing this piece of good advice, Yang was paid ten *jin* of metal (gold?)—a rather hefty reward at the time.[56] Eventually, the Han court invited the Xiongnu prince to come to the capital to attend an audience.[57] Accordingly, in 1 BCE, the Xiongnu *chanyu* paid a formal visit to the Han court, accompanied by two hundred staff and attendants, all of whom were royally entertained. The payoff for such courtesies came in 5 CE, when the same Xiongnu *chanyu* agreed to specific requests made by the Han court to abide by the terms of a treaty essentially dictated by the Han. Again, Yang's sympathies are clear, for his thirteenth chapter of the *Fayan* refers to the unparalleled power of the Xiongnu during Emperor Wu's reign, and the interstate amity prevailing in more recent times:

> Long ago, during the reigns of Han Gaozu, Wendi, and Wudi, the Xiongnu really were the strongest military force. Now they bow their heads and come as subjects of Han rule, proclaiming themselves our "Northern Defenders." This is due to the divine power of

---

56. The phrase *shi jin* 十金 (= 100,000 cash, or 100 *mu* of farmland of average grade) is the standard (legal?) phrase used to refer to the entire assets of an "average peasant farmer" throughout the Juyan documents. See Ōkushi, "Kandai no 'nakeke' no san ni kansuru kōsatsu," esp. 49. The *Yantie lun* 4.1/23/4–5 speaks of "counselors amassing 1,000 units, and *shi* (gentlemen in service, lower officers?) amassing 100 units." Yoshinami, "Kandai kōtei shihai chitsujo no keisei," 68–69, argues that 100 *jin* is one-tenth the income of a Han marquis grant given to the *guanneihou* (noble rank). Yang's reward, in that case, was considerable.

57. See *TPYL* 811.8a–8b.

> our ancestral temple, also the spirit efficacy of the altars of grain and soil. Is *that* not an experience to be savored *by us*?
>
> 昔在高文武，實爲兵主。今稽首來臣。稱爲北蕃。是爲宗廟之神，社稷之靈也。可不享。[58]

Yang was forthright in his opposition to the hawks at court, in other words, even though their numbers included his former patron Liu Xiang 劉向 (d. 8? BCE), who had once urged the emperor to reward Gan Yanshou and Chen Tang for their incursions into Xiongnu territory, and then Liu Xin and Wang Mang, probably the two most powerful men at court in Yang's later life. Yang consistently argued that the Han would command the allegiance of distant tribes and the gratitude of the spirit realm, only if the emperor first attended to the pressing needs of his own subjects.

Then, in an incident dated to 4 CE, Yang put himself for a second time on a collision course with Wang Mang, when Wang urged his great-aunt, the dowager empress Wang Zhengjun 王政君 (71 BCE–13 CE), to expand the Han territories as far as Lake Qinghai, then called the "Western Sea" (*Xihai* 西海), which was under Qiang 羌 control.

> The Grand Empress Dowager has held authority for many years. Her boundless kindness overflows, so that her harmonious *qi* fills the four corners of the earth. Every single group living in cut-off regions with strange customs admires her sense of duty. The Yuechang people through seried translators have presented a white pheasant [an auspicious sign of sagacious rule]. The Huangzhi have presented a live rhinoceros as tribute from 10,000 miles away. The king of the eastern Yi has crossed the great sea to present his country's treasures. And the Xiongnu *chanyu* has submitted to the reform of his group's institutions and abandoned the titles [signifying his independent authority].

58. *Fayan* 13.28 [adding "by us" since it is implied]. However, if one follows Sima Guang 司馬光, reading *xiang* as *hou*, the line means, "How can we not treat them generously?" In Sima Guang's view, for the throne to be cheap, when the barbarians have already submitted, is to be "penny wise and pound foolish" 愛小費而就大患乎. Cf. *TPYL* 811.8a–8b. By contrast, attempts by Wang Mang shortly after his accession to curtail the ritual prerogatives of the Xiongnu *chanyu*, aroused that nomad leader's suspicions, eventually provoking further violence. Yang Xiong intervened in Han policymaking only a few times, so far as we know.

> 太后秉統數年，恩澤洋溢，和氣四塞，絕域殊俗，靡不慕義。越裳氏重譯獻白雉，黃支自三萬里貢生犀，東夷王度大海奉國珍，匈奴單于順制作，去二名。[59]

In effect, Wang's memorial flattered Wang Zhengjun, in the hope that she would then undertake what Wang portrayed later in the memorial as something akin to the "manifest destiny" of the Han. Not only should the dowager empress see that the Han territories extend to the borders at the time of Yao, the supposed progenitor of the Liu clan; she should also venture to go even beyond those borders, so as to demonstrate the strength of her filial devotion. (Note how diametrically opposed were Wang Mang's persuasions to Yang Xiong's views in the matter.)

Wang's memorial was submitted shortly before Wang Mang solemnly assumed the new title of Duke Pacifying the Han,[60] and must have been in Yang's mind as he put the finishing touches on his two masterworks, the *Taixuan* or *Supreme Mystery* and the *Fayan*. Yang refutes Wang's arguments in the last chapter of the *Fayan* when he writes:

> The unicorn, superbly decorous, and the arrayed legions of phoenixes[61]—these are the very finest of their species! Neither fierce tigers, with their mad rampages, nor eagles and falcons, in all their predations, can ever measure up to them![62]
>
> 麟之儀儀。鳳之師師。其至矣乎。螭虎桓桓，鷹隼䎃䎃。未至也。[63]

Ferocity and violence must be forsaken, Yang says, and the unicorn, universally reckoned a symbol of perfect benevolence and compassion, and thus the proper symbol of the Han throne.

---

59. *HS* 99A.4077. The presentation of the rhinoceros is dated before 4 CE. See *HS* 28.1671; also Yu, "Han Foreign Relations," 453.

60. *HS* 99A.4076.

61. Usually the reduplicative *shishi* 師師 means "many" or "flourishing" ("resplendent"?). The subcommentary in Wang Rongbao, comp., *Fayan yishu*, vol. 2, 20.550 says of *shishi*: "It refers to the phoenixes flying; the birds who flock together number in the tens of thousands; it is like looking at an army in formation."

62. See *Fayan* 13.28–30, where the language of birds and beasts clearly refers to groups that are not from the Central States.

63. *Fayan* 13.27.

Before turning to the closing lines of chapter 13 that speak of the Han house and of Wang Mang, it may be helpful to consider four points that have arisen in connection with the foregoing review of the Chinese sources: First, Yang Xiong's mastery of recent political events was profound, and his opinions on recent events were presented in the *Fayan* in a succinct and courageous manner that leaves no doubt as to his real intentions. (In a similar vein earlier in the same philosophical masterwork, Yang's harsh assessment of Chen Tang portrayed Chen, a leader of the hawks at court, as "too hard.")[64] Second, Yang was hardly the reclusive, impoverished, or ignored poet-entertainer that he pretends to be in so many of his writings, including the "Expelling Poverty" *fu*,[65] even if Yang's penury and low status became a favorite leitmotif in later treatments of him.[66] Far from being the unfortunate object of the court's condescension, he was consulted as an expert on foreign policy, as well as on portent interpretation, two topics of signal importance to the Han court, even when his advice contradicted the opinions of the chief ministers of the time. Probably, this highly stylized construction of a demeaned self was meant to impress upon readers the extreme sacrifices that Yang had willingly made to promote classical learning.[67] Third, the evidence summarized here helps us understand why the

64. *Fayan* 9.20 contrasts Chen Tang (too hard) with a eunuch (too soft), before chiding Chen for disobedience and unprincipled opportunism.

65. Yang's "Expelling Ridicule" *fu* has his unnamed critic (the "guest") ridicule Yang in the following words: "You have never drafted a single ingenious plan or produced a single scheme, or / Offered persuasions to the ruler above, / Discoursed with ministers below." See Knechtges, trans., *The* Han shu *Biography of Yang Xiong*, 46. Ibid., 47, has Yang protesting that a "single slip" might mean the death of his entire clan.

66. As in Tao Yuanming's poem 18, of the twenty-part "Drinking Wine" series.

67. We know, for example, that Yang Xiong sought—and got—a release from his regular duties at court. The Liu Xin–Yang Xiong correspondence mentions that Chengdi had generously granted Yang three year's leave, so that he could "improve his mind," perusing documents in yet another of the imperial libraries, the so-called Stone Room (*shi shi*). See Knechtges, "The Liu Hsin/Yang Hsiung Correspondence on the *Fang yen*," 309–25, esp. 312. Cf. the assessment of the wealthy Callimachus in Cameron, *Callimachus and His Critics*, 5. Callimachus is the closest counterpart to Yang that I have found in the classical Mediterranean world, a court poet and bibliophile. For more on Yang's afterlife reception, see my *Yang Xiong and the Pleasures of Reading and Classical Learning*, and the introduction to my translation of the *Fayan* (forthcoming).

pre-Tang and Tang accounts of Yang Xiong tended to portray him as often as an exemplary praise-and-blame historian working as a latter-day Confucius in the sacred *Chunqiu* tradition as a fine poet or subtle thinker.[68] As was the case with other famous classical historians (e.g., Thucydides and Tacitus), Yang's claims to fame over the centuries chiefly rested on the belief that his assessments of past events had served as trustworthy guides in the political arena.[69] In the centuries immediately after his death Yang was equally celebrated for the elegance of his formulations outlining the perfect efficacy of cultivated ideals when applied to policy-making, as well as for his deft and pithy character assessments, whose style was later adopted by members of the *qing tan* 清談 ("pure talk") movement of the Wei-Jin (220–317 CE).[70] Fourth, the contents of Yang's thirteenth *Fayan* chapter unequivocally opposed the policies of Wang Mang and his supporters and allies. Whereas Wang's memorial to the dowager empress had ended with high praise of Wang himself as a replication of or even improvement upon the sage-king Yao,[71] Yang Xiong drew the reader's attention to what he deemed an indisputable fact: that the Han, like the sage-kings of old, had better reign principally by charismatic virtue, rather than by force:

> Han charismatic rule—how "truly cherished" it may be said to be! From south of Huangzhi and west of Daxia, in Dongti, all come with the northern Xiongnu,[72] to the Han court bringing rare items as tribute.[73] Han charismatic rule—how "truly cherished" it may be said to be! Few ages have witnessed such charismatic rule!

---

68. On this, see L'Haridon, "La recherche du modèle dans les dialogues du *Fayan* de Yang Xiong," esp. sec. 3," 187–231.

69. See, for example, Momigliano, *The Classical Foundations of Modern Historiography*; or Veyne, *Did the Greeks Believe in Their Myths*, esp. chap. 1.

70. Yang did not hesitate to regard himself as a classical master on a par with Confucius (Kongzi). In doing so, Yang did no more than Xunzi had done earlier. For Yang's claim that he is Kongzi's equal, see, e.g., *Fayan* 2.10, where, after calling Kongzi "a door" opening onto the classical past, Yang says: "Surely you do not mean to say that I myself lack what it takes to be a door?" It was not only in early China that beautiful lyrics and formalized badinage—language games—would be an acceptable vehicle by which to convey insults. See Halliwell, *Greek Laughter*, 101.

71. *HS* 96A.3886–87.

72. Here called by the perjorative term *beinu* 北奴 ("northern slaves").

73. Adding, "to the Han court," as implied by the verb "to come."

漢德其可謂允懷矣。黃支之南。大夏之西。東鞮北女。來貢其珍。漢德其可謂允懷矣。世鮮焉。[74]

Yang continues,

> The very best situation is one where the sage-ruler's charismatic virtue is so fabled as to be admired by all the faraway peoples. The next best is awesome military might, with troops engaged in punitive campaigns in every direction. What hardly rates as glorious is the many Yi wreaking havoc to the Central States by their incursions,[75] their rapacious encroachment upon the king's men, and their humiliating our domains and killing our legions.
>
> 荒荒聖德。遠人咸慕。上也。武義璜璜。兵征四方。次也。宗夷猾夏。蠢迪王人。屈國喪師。無次也。[76]

In the same chapter Yang equates the sage-kings' rule with the "great harmony" achieved by "Yao, Shun, Tang, the Shang founder, and Zhou."[77] Only the continual exercise of charismatic virtue—making peace and devising economic benefits for subordinates wherever possible—can create in the imperial person the compelling persona ascribed to the exemplary person.[78] Punitive campaigns may be called for in rare instances, but the lamentable propensity to rely habitually on such tactics marks the inferior ruler. True, the hegemons of the preimperial age engaged in such practices, but Yang's disdain for such men is evident.[79] On several grounds, as we have seen, Yang

---

74. *Fayan* 13.25. One might compare the foregoing with *Lunheng, pian* 57, "Xuan Han" 宣漢 ("Touting the Han").

75. The phrase, *manyi hua Xia* 蠻夷猾夏, is a set phrase, and Wang Rongbao, comp., *Fayan yishu*, vol. 2, 20.548–49, suggests that *zongyi* 宗夷 is a variation of *manyi*, following the "Yaodian." However, *zong* could mean *zhong* 眾 (meaning, "the many"). Adding "by their incursions," as it is implied.

76. *Fayan* 13.26. "Fabled" is literally "great." I use "fabled," since this reduplicative describes what is deep, faraway, or remote or wide-ranging, and huge.

77. *Taihe* 泰和 (*Fayan* 13.23). Yang asks about this, rather than Taiping 太平 (Great Peace), possibly because the phrase "Taiping" had become too closely associated with Gan Zhongke 甘忠可 and other figures suspected of treason against the Han throne. For further information, see Arbuckle, "Inevitable Treason," 585–97. Han Jing, comp., *Fayan zhu*, 352, n. 2, among others, identifies "Cheng" as King Cheng of Zhou, but that would be to skip a dynasty; hence my decision to take Cheng as Cheng-Tang 成湯. Zhou is not necessarily the duke of Zhou, but early Zhou rule in general.

78. *Fayan* 13.21–13.22.

79. *Fayan* 13.24.

resolutely opposed Wang's desire to push the Han territories deep into distant lands. Indeed, Yang's very mention of Yao in this connection may well have added weight to the implicit admonition against Wang, since Yao was thought to be the ultimate ancestor for the Liu clan of the Han ruling house, not the house of Wang.

Several earlier chapters of the *Fayan* show Yang repeatedly discussing the difference between those who, for careerist reasons, ape the distinguishing characteristics of the classicists (Ru 儒) in all the externals but nonetheless remain nothing more than poor imitations of the true classicists. For example, in one passage, Yang records the following exchange:

> Someone asks: "Suppose there were a man who took the surname of Kong and the sobriquet of Zhongni [like Kongzi]. Were he to enter Kongzi's door, ascend his hall, lean on his armrest, and wear his robes, could he be rightly called Confucius?"
>
> Reply: "The surface pattern would be right, but the substance would be wrong."
>
> "I dare to ask about what is substance."
>
> Reply: "A sheep in wolf's clothing will be delighted when it sees some grass, but terrified when it sees a leopard, because it will have forgotten all about the skin that it wears."[80]
>
> Reply: "The sage is as distinct as the tiger, with patterns bold and brilliant! The noble man is as distinct as a leopard, with patterns finer and elegant. The rhetorician is like the fox, its patterns dense enough to provide cover.[81] Still, a single change of the fox and it can become a leopard, and a single change of the leopard and it can become a tiger!"
>
> 或曰有人焉，(曰)[自]云姓孔，而字仲尼。入其門，升其堂，伏其几，襲其裳，則可謂仲尼乎。曰其文是也，其質非也。敢問質。曰羊質而虎皮，見草而說，見豺而戰，忘其皮之虎矣。[82]

80. Literally, a tigerskin rather than a wolf's pelt, but the translation uses the more common metaphor from English. This may be another jab at the Qin dynasty, which was often compared to a wolf or other ferocious animal. See, e.g., Jiao, *Jiaoshi Yilin*, on Hexagram Pi 否:秦爲虎狼.

81. *Yijing* Hexagram 49 (*shang*) and Image.

82. *Fayan* 2.12. Cf. *Analects* 6.15, 11.15, 11.19, and 19.23: "To wear Ru clothes; and to wear Ru caps, but not to be able to carry out the Ru Way—that is not what we mean by Ru. You are not card-carrying (canon-carrying) Ru who keep to the Way."

Those canny decisions to don Ru robes and recite Ru texts may "provide cover" for many a wolf in sheep's clothing at court—of this Yang provides abundant evidence in chapters 10–12 of the *Fayan*, which assess a range of famous historical figures, good and bad, who lived from Zhanguo through Western Han periods.[83] But the foregoing exchange ends on a surprisingly optimistic note: those equipped with classical training can become a finer sort of person, with only a "single change" (presumably after revising the object of their ultimate commitments). In chapter 13, Yang reiterates his firm belief that the proof lies in the pudding: the wisdom of a certain piece of persuasion can and must be judged by the consequences that follow from its adoption. But Yang, far more than Mencius or Xunzi, concedes the difficulties of correctly judging a person who sets out with the express intention to deceive others by a show of virtue:

> "Let us suppose a son were to subsist on beans and pulse and wear frayed clothes so that he could nourish and bring the finest clothes to his parents, and thereby seek to express his filial devotion. If others said it was all an act or put-on, what would you think?"
>
> Reply: "Let us suppose that a person assumed the robes and writings of a classicist, wearing the one while reciting the other, and this went on for three months without interruption. Who would say of the person that he is not a classicist?"[84]
>
> Someone asked me, "How is one to locate a faker then?"[85]
>
> Reply: "If a person does certain things when others are present, but stops whenever nobody is looking, he should be called a faker. In assessing others, carefully attend to the contexts in which they do or stop doing something—that's all there is to it!"

---

83. A very few late Chunqiu figures are mentioned as well, if they are very famous, including Wu Zixu (d. 485 BCE).

84. *Mencius* 6B/2 says: "If you wear the clothes of Yao, speak the words of Yao and behave the way Yao behaved, then you *are* a Yao." But cf. *Yantie lun* 5.7/36/3–5: "To wear Ru clothes; and to wear Ru caps, but not to be able to carry out the Ru Way—that is not what we mean by Ru."

85. Yu Yue defines *chu* 處 ("place," "stance") as "the place things reside in" and also "causing things to each get their proper place." Yu says that *chu* therefore refers to investigating, and he cites *Zuozhuan*, Wen 18, the *Da Dai Liji* 大戴禮記, and other Western Han texts, to prove that *chu* means *duan* 斷 ("to decide"), as here. Much of Han philosophy is based on the notion that the inner state of a human being will reveal itself, sooner or later, in the person's actions.

子有含菽緼絮而致滋美其親。將以求孝也。人曰僞。如之何。曰假儒衣書。服而讀之。三月不歸。孰曰非儒也。或曰何以處僞。曰有人則作。無人則輟之謂僞。觀人者。審其作。輟而已矣。[86]

When one remembers the pieties spouted by those in Wang Mang's circle, all of whom professed to be devout ethical followers of Kongzi, one may wonder whether such comments, sprinkled throughout the *Fayan* chapters, are not more barbed and less generic than they seem. Another passage that may be cited in this connection also comes from the *Fayan*'s chapter 13:

> Someone asked me, "Which is preferable: to start out with charismatic virtue but be without it at the end or the reverse?"
> "Which would be preferable: to be sick first and later be cured, or to be healthy first and later fall ill?"
> 或問德有始而無終，與有終而無始也，孰寧。
> 曰寧先病而後瘳乎。寧先瘳而後病乎。[87]

Wang Mang had had a promising early career, but by the time that Yang composed the *Fayan*, probably around 8 CE, according to David Knechtges, the warning flags certainly would have been up.[88] Wang was one of many who might walk the walk and talk the talk of an adherent of Kongzi, but who failed to internalize the central message of Kongzi's teachings, in Yang's view.

Yang's Concluding Remarks on the Han and Wang Mang

The preceding analysis of the contents of chapter 13 in the *Fayan* prepares us to examine two curious passages at the chapter's end. I quote them in full, since it would prove exceedingly hard to parse their language otherwise. Furthermore, the cases made for and against Yang, as loyal supporter of or villainous traitor to the Han house, have usually looked principally to the citation of these very passages.[89]

---

86. *Fayan* 13.7, which plays on 10.2.

87. *Fayan* 13.18.

88. See footnote 4 above.

89. It was this line comparing Zhougong with Wang Mang, probably more than any other single line in Yang's writing, that prompted the severe condemnation of Yang's life and writings by Zhu Xi (1130–1200 CE) and his followers, who happily imported anachronistic notions of "loyalty" into their analyses of key figures in

Since the Duke of Zhou, none have had the charismatic virtue of Wang Mang, duke of Han. By the intensity of his efforts, he surpasses E Heng.[90]

The Han was founded 210 years ago: its years seem nearly there.[91]

The Circular Moat 辟廱 [ritual center] is taken as root for it[s good rule];
Schools at the local and capital level are used to teach it;
Rites and music, to impart a grand appearance to it;
Carriages and robes,[92] to make clear standards for it;
As it restores the framework of the well-field system;[93]
The people are encouraged to serve,[94]
Splendid and great, is it not?

周公以來，未有漢公之懿也。勤勞則過於阿衡。
漢興二百一十載而中天，其庶矣乎。

辟廱以本之。
校學以教之。
禮樂以容之。

Western Han. However, I believe that Zhu Xi would have had to try to oust Yang Xiong from the pantheon of great thinkers, even had he not made this particular comment, since Yang's cosmological vision contradicted that favored by Zhu Xi. For further information about Zhu's quarrels with Yang's views, see Nylan, *The Canon of Supreme Mystery*, "Introduction." For the secondary literature on this, see Knechtges, "Yang Shyong, the *Fuh*, and Hann Rhetoric." Gong Kechang, whose *Studies on the Han Fu* might be expected to address this issue, neatly sidesteps the issue of Yang's possible support for Wang's regency or usurpation.

90. *Fayan* 13.33. E Heng [= Yi Yin] was minister to Tang the Victorious, founder of the Shang.

91. The phrase is perfectly ambiguous: it could mean it's "nearly there" [at the zenith of its power and virtue] or "to be nearly over [at its end]." The phrases that follow this suggest a positive reading, however.

92. Meaning, either "sumptuary regulations" or "imperial officers."

93. Reading xing 刑 as *xing* 型, contrary to *Fayan zhu*, 368, n. 6, which follows Wang Rongbao, comp., *Fayan yishu*, vol. 2, in retaining *xing* in the meaning of "[mutilating] punishments," despite the evidence for Wang Mang's policies on penal law. If Han and Wang Rongbao are correct, then the line should read, "It restores the proper well-field system and penal laws." Han Jing presumes that the reference here to "punishments" means that Wang Mang restored the old system of mutilating punishments. Wu Mi thought that Wang Mang had "restored" the old system of "image punishments" (by which criminals were identified by marks on their clothing, rather than their bodily mutilations).

94. See Han Jing, comp., *Fayan zhu*, 368, n. 7, for the two variants.

輿服以表之。
復其井刑，
勉人役。
唐矣夫。[95]

The translation given here is perforce tentative (as explained below), but any reader familiar with Han texts may spot a potential problem with the first paragraph: *Fayan* 13.33 baldly allows that Wang Mang is greater than Confucius himself, since Confucius lived and died during the long interval between the duke of Zhou (ca. 1050 BCE) and Wang Mang (regent 1–8 CE; emperor 9–23 CE). Equally troublesome, several lines in the second encomium are unusually ambiguous. For example, the line "its years seem nearly there" could mean either that the days of the Han mandate were numbered, or—as *all* the main commentators all take it—that the Han would soon reach the apogee of its power, if concerted efforts continued to be made on its behalf by those in its employ.[96] Presumably to Yang's way of thinking, the construction in 4 CE of two ritual centers due south of the capital, the Biyong 辟廱 (Circular Moat) and Taixue 太學 (Imperial Academy), boded well for the dynastic fortunes, regardless of who had urged their construction.[97] But is praise or condemnation the tone Yang adopts when referring to the restoration of an older system of field allocation?[98] According to the standard histories, in one of his first acts after his usurpation in 9 CE, Wang Mang called for a full restoration of the supposedly ancient well-field system, under the name "king's fields," in all its particulars, but that edict provoked such

95. *Fayan* 13.34.

96. The phrase "it's nearly there" could mean that the Han is at the zenith of its power and virtue or that "it is nearly over [at its end]." The phrases that follow this suggest a positive reading, however, as do the chief commentators. Li Gui says, for example, "How numerous and prosperous its people!" 言人民眾多富盛也, while Sima Guang (a strict disciplinarian when it came to issues of political loyalty) paraphrases the line as, "It is a nearly perfect realization of good government!" 庶者，庶幾於治也。

97. The plan to construct these two ritual centers south of the capital is ascribed to Wang Mang. See *HS* 99A.4069; Dubs and P'an, trans., *The History of the Former Han Dynasty*, vol. 3, 191.

98. Or possible, older system of punishments and field allocation (if *xing* 刑 is not read as "framework" but as "punishments").

widespread resistance that the program was abandoned within three years. Before that time, the same allusions to wells or fields gestured in the direction of less sweeping efforts to limit landholdings, put in place to foster some redistributive mechanisms and prop up the regular Han conscript service.[99] That the Han did put into law a complex scheme for land allocation correlating official rank, orders of honor, hereditary status, and meritorious service is suggested by the Zhangjiashan manuscripts of ca. 186 BCE.[100] Of this they were doubtless proud, but what scheme does Yang allude to here, that of Han or Xin? One may even wonder whether the Han or Wang's Xin dynasty was more likely to "relieve" (*mian* 免) men of corvée and conscript duty, or to "encourage" (*mian* 勉) subjects to engage in such service.

Compounding the confusion already engendered by the existence of such wildly divergent possibilities, the last line of Yang's *Fayan* is equally liable to quite contradictory constructions. The late Qing commentator Wang Rongbao, citing the *Shuowen jiezi* 說文解字 entry for *tang* 唐, reads the final line of three characters, *tang yi fu* 唐矣夫, as "How great indeed [is Han]!"[101] The modern commentator, Han Jing, however, notes that most of the early commentators explained *tang* 唐 not as a single epithet exalting the "splendid and great" achievements of the dynasty, but as a reference to Tang-Yao 堯, the sage-king whom legend portrayed as the ultimate progenitor of the Han line and wellspring of its charisma.[102] Indeed, the earliest commentary, that by Li Gui, glosses the last line as, "[The Han] has

---

99. *HS* 23.1081; *HS* 24A.1119–20. In 7 BCE, for example, the Han government tried and failed to limit landholdings and the number of slaves per household. Because of Wang Mang's first acts in 9 CE, *Fayan zhu*, 368, n. 8, assumes that the *Fayan* was written sometime between 9 and 12 CE.

100. See Loewe, "Social Distinctions, Groups, and Privileges," 296, where Loewe speaks of "a regular means of allocating land to provide a livelihood and to yield revenue for the government, a means of doing so that gave incentives for service and possibly a sense of membership of the emperor's realm, and the establishment of basic units of the population to whom these benefits were dispensed and which discharged regular duties to the government."

101. Wang Rongbao, comp., *Fayan yishu*, vol. 2, 20.565, reading *tang* 唐 as *da yan* 大言 ("great words"). Wang's *Fayan yishu* was compiled in 1911.

102. Han Jing, comp., *Fayan zhu*, 368, n. 8.

no reason to envy the age of Yao and Shun!" apparently reading the line as, "A [virtual age of] Yao and Shun [is Han], is it not?" One commentator, spinning off from Li's reading, even suggests that the early editions had *tang yu fu* 唐虞夫 in place of the current *tang yi fu* 唐矣夫, and that the current transcription reflects a misreading of the original Han clerical script.[103] Should readers therefore conclude from the final three characters (1) that the ancestral spirit of Yao is still operating to prop up the fortunes of the Han house, or (2) that the degree of hard work expended by the court and its representatives, especially in the promotion of classical learning, will decide the final fate of the Han house in the near future, or (c) that Yang approves the Han abdication in favor of Wang Mang, since a crucial transition time in the dynastic cycle is coming due? Far too much rests on how we decide to read Yang's last words in the *Fayan*, when *xiao*, filial duty, was the premier virtue claimed by successful Han rulers but not, apparently, by Wang Mang.[104]

Despite such problems in interpretation, these two encomia are routinely treated as supporting evidence in dueling assessments of Yang's intentions. Scholars have put forward no fewer than five different interpretations of this concluding passage, alleging that (1) the first passage registers heartfelt, if naïve, praise of Wang, which could be true if the *Fayan* was composed, as seems likely, *before* Wang had usurped the throne and promulgated some of the totalizing "re-

---

103. Tang Bingzheng 湯炳正, cited in Wang Rongbao, comp., *Fayan yishu*, vol. 2, 20.565.

104. For the Han ruler's endorsement of *xiao*, see Nylan, "Confucian Piety and Individualism," 1–27. Regarding Wang Mang, most Japanese scholars, noting that Wang Mang (like all the Han rulers) cites the *Xiaojing*, mistakenly conclude that Wang's suburban sacrifices were specifically redesigned to highlight his position as the supreme exemplar of filial piety in his realm. See, for example, Itano Chōhachi's *Chūgoku kodai ni okeru ningenkan no tenkai*. Were such suppositions correct, we would expect Wang's suburban sacrifices to have included a specific component devoted to ancestral worship, but this was not the case, according to the extant sources. For further information, see the (forthcoming) essay in English on this subject by Tian Tian 田天, a recent Ph.D. from Peking University (personal communication, August 2010), entitled "From the Four Directions to Chang'an: The Late Western Han Suburban Sacrifice Reform and the Evolution of the Imperial Sacrifices."

forms" that soon lost him support from many quarters; (2) this passage or part of it represents an unmarked citation of another's praise of Wang; (3) the specific wording in this first encomium, overblown yet formulaic,[105] urges Wang to continue serving the Han house, since neither E Heng and the duke of Zhou ever took the throne for themselves; (4) the extravagant praise for Wang Mang is meant to awaken Wang's conscience (cf. Aristotle's "To praise a person is to urge upon him a course of action"), or (5) the hyperbolic praise should be read sarcastically as an attack on Wang for his increasing arrogation of imperial powers. That (5) may be the best solution gains support from Yang's own unambiguous provision of a hermeneutical key to his writings: Yang insists that the more inflated his praise of a particular figure or activity, the more severe his actual condemnation ("the more I elaborated and exalted [something], the more strident my rejection of it").[106]

And there may well be yet another forceful jab imbedded in Yang's very title for chapter 13, for the *Hanshu* records a most cynical use of the prevailing rhetoric of filial piety: Wang Mang, who had managed to marry his daughter to the reigning emperor whom he served as regent, wisely let his subordinates discuss the precedents (literally, the "old regulations" 古制, 古事). Not surprisingly, the officials expressly convened to consider how best to reward Wang all said that in antiquity the Son of Heaven enfeoffed the father of the empress, who was no longer required to call himself "subject"; this elevation of the emperor's father-in-law supposedly would "honor the ancestral temple," and represent "the height of filial duty" (*xiao zhi zhi ye* 孝之至也). And while it was at it, the officials concluded, the court ought to increase Wang Mang's fief so that it would be a "full hundred *li*," the same size as the imperial domain, by some authoritative texts.[107] It is inconceivable that the precise phrase "the height of filial duty" would not be

---

105. Yang Xiong's talk of the Han at the end of *Fayan*'s chap. 13 recalls the language of Sima Xiangru in his "Letter from the Elders of Shu": "The Han flourished for 78 years, / Its virtue resplendent in the reigns of six sovereigns, / Its prestige martial and majestic. . . ."

106. *HS* 87A.3534; Knechtges, *The* Han shu *Biography of Yang Xiong*, 24.

107. *HS* 99A.4046–54.

fresh in Yang's mind, especially as some 25,600 *qing* were subsequently added to Wang's fief and justified by the term "old regulations"—all actions that would have outraged Yang's sense of propriety and concern for the poor under Han rule. Evidently, Yang redeployed the same slogan in the title of his final chapter, mocking to the last.

Earlier in chapter 13, as readers will recall, Yang had stated that the laudable peace in the Han empire was "due to the divine power of our ancestral temple, also the spirit efficacy of the altars of grain and soil." Unless we think Yang to be equally sarcastic here (and nowhere else does Yang's sarcasm extend to the spirit realm), we must take these lines to mean that Yang denies, against some naysayers, that the Han has already forfeited its mandate.[108] Still, at this remove in time, it is hard to discern Yang's precise intentions, just as it is hard to know whether Yang attempted suicide once Wang Mang became emperor simply because he feared being unjustly tortured during a treason trial investigation, or because he was fully cognizant of his guilt in harboring treasonous thoughts toward Wang.[109]

If Yang did not hesitate to lash out at the aggressive foreign policy initiatives favored by successive leaders of the Wang consort clan, from Wang Shang to Wang Mang, why resort to vague language guaranteeing plausible deniability at the end of the masterwork that he hoped would be transmitted to future generations? Conceivably, a clear-eyed assessment of the fortunes of the Han house was just too dangerous, no matter whether Yang believed that it was nearly at the apogee of its power or coming to the end of its cycle of good fortune.[110] After all, Yang had watched Gan Zhongke 甘忠可, a *Chunqiu* scholar, make a concerted attempt at the court of Chengdi (r. 33–7 BCE) to discuss such matters, and Gan was promptly condemned by Liu Xiang as a traitor, even though Gan's teachings suggested a convenient set of rituals that the Han house could use to renew its Mandate. (The instability associated with Gan's predictions was

108. For some of the famous naysayers, see Arbuckle, "Inevitable Treason."

109. *HS* 99B.4123; *HS* 87B.3584.

110. Note the language of *shu ji* 庶幾 here. See Knechtges "Uncovering the Sauce Jar,'" 229–52, for Zhu Xi's attack on the poem in praise of Wang Mang that tradition ascribes to Yang Xiong, which attack was countered by Hong Mai.

then, as it happened, exploited by the regent Wang Mang in Yang's final years.)[111] Straightforward talk could land Yang and his family in jail or even on the execution block, through the machinations of one or another court faction.[112] Still worse, from Yang's point of view, it could lead to the proscription of the very writings to which he entrusted his posthumous reputation after the death of his beloved sons.

In addition, since Yang did not believe the future to be so predictable, his own preference was to turn discussions of heaven's mysterious operations to more mundane matters.[113] At the same time, his classical training would have led Yang to hope that his admonitions would prolong the life of the dynasty he served. After all, the *Zuozhuan* was plain enough in its excoriation of the honey-tongued court advisers who, anxious to curry favor, were content to "cover over" (*gai* 蓋) a ruler's errors, "speaking only of his finer points" (*shumei* 數美). The predictable result of the continued bad behavior, his and theirs: "the spirits (*guishen* 鬼神) do not accept the offerings, so the state is made to suffer misery . . . short lives, premature deaths, bereavements, and all manner of illnesses" 鬼神不饗其國以禍之 . . . 所以夭昏孤疾者。[114] This was precisely the linkage that Yang's chapter 13 in the *Fayan* argued for. Meanwhile, several of Yang's favorite texts detailed the speed with which a ruler's decision to repent of his errors would bring Heaven's favor.[115] Accordingly Yang's thirteenth chapter in the *Fayan* advised the Han house to eschew all foreign wars, if possible, for only the heartfelt approbation of the Han subjects free to devote themselves to their own enterprises and rituals could earn the emperor his own "reward from the spirits."[116] Such

---

111. *HS* 75.3192; 99A.4094. Cf. Loewe, *Crisis and Conflict*, 278–80, and Arbuckle, "Inevitable Treason," 585–97.

112. Yang complains fairly often that he is in danger of being executed. It is hard, at this remove, to determine the degree of threat he faced, but that he took it seriously is shown by his own decision at one point to commit suicide when threatened with a judicial inquiry. See *HS* 87B.3567.

113. *Fayan* 8.13.

114. *Zuo*, Zhao 20.6 (Yang, 1416).

115. These stories were told of Lord Jing of Song 宋景公 in many Han texts that Yang cites.

116. *HS* 87B.3564; Knechtges, *The* Han shu *Biography of Yang Xiong*, 45.

advice was consistent with the grave warnings that Yang uttered in several of his *fu*. As a historian self-consciously working in the *Chunqiu* tradition, Yang refused to paper over the problems leading to misery in the state, even if he saw little purpose in protesting so loudly as to invite his own destruction, given his place at court.[117] He could meanwhile trust his "artful rankings" of historical exemplars like Jia Juanzhi to have the greatest impact.[118]

Through such judicious methods, Yang challenged the routine invocation of filial duty on behalf of swaggering empire, insisting that the Han emperors hold themselves to a higher standard derived from the portraits of good rule attributed to the sage-kings of old in the Classics.[119] Kongzi, Yao, Shun, and Yu, and the exemplary kings and regents who succeeded them all appear by turns in chapter thirteen, so that "with them one might extend the glories of their reigns to the present age."[120] If, as Yang says, "the filial child in fasting sees a way to preserve his parents,"[121] making the dead reappear before his very eyes, Yang through his dialogues seeks to make these models of good rule come alive, performing his own act of piety, even as he invites the emperor to perform his.

Conclusion

If this essay, aside from alluding to the dangers of predicting the demise of the Han fortunes, has hardly addressed one theme central to most histories of Chinese rhetoric, that of "addressing the autocrat," it is mainly for two reasons. First, Cai Yong's *Duduan* 獨斷 (comp. ca.

---

117. For Yang's identification with the supposed author of the *Zuozhuan*, see *Fayan* 10.30. According to the *Chunqiu* principles, different officers having different access to power were expected to respond differently to state crises. For further information about this complex moral calculus, see Auken, "A Formal Analysis of the 'Chuenchiou' ('Spring and Autumn Classic')," esp. chaps. 1–2; also Henry, "'Junzi yue' vs. 'Zhongni yue' in *Zuozhuan*," 125–62.

118. Yang attributed this mode of literary production to Zuo Qiuming, whom he credited with writing the *Zuo*.

119. Quotations from the Five Classics, the *Analects*, and the *Mencius*, appear in nearly every short dialogue recorded in the chapter.

120. *Fayan* 13.10.

121. *Fayan* 13.4. Yang here refers to the opening passage of the "Jiyi" 祭義 (Meaning of Sacrifice) chapter of the *Liji*.

175 CE), recently made more accessible through an excellent translation by Enno Giele, suggests that the Han court's decision-making processes were far less autocratic than consultative.[122] Second, many other primary sources for Han history allude to the actual limits placed on imperial power during Han.[123] For example, the *Hanshu*, when describing the late Western Han court under Chengdi, concurs with later romances about the Western Han, including the early sixth-century *Xijing zaji* 西京雜記, in depicting Chengdi as a ruler who feels he cannot do as he pleases, either because of the force of imperial precedents or because of the consort clans' overweening influence.[124]

The model of the autocratic ruler in China, an artifact of early Republican-era narratives, reflects the realities of late imperial China far more closely than it does those of Han.[125] No doubt rhetoric had to be suitably adjusted when its primary audience was the court making policy,[126] but that obvious fact should not cause us to forget that rhetoric like that in Yang's *Fayan* was crafted to appeal not only to the emperor and his inner circle, but also to later generations (*hou dai* 後代), who could be expected to be more impartial in their judgments about historical events.[127] If we consider the sorts of pronouncements on history and policy-making that were believed in Han to be of enduring relevance and value, we cannot but concur with David Knechtges's judicious assertion that Yang's attitude toward Wang Mang was "secondary" to Yang's "espousal of a [new]

---

122. Giele, *Imperial Decision-Making and Communication in Early China*.

123. See Nylan, "Empire in the Classical Era in China," 34–64.

124. For example, Chengdi in 32 BCE clearly is afraid to upset his uncle Wang Feng. See Liu Rulin, *Han Jin xueshu biannian*, 46. Similarly, ibid., 89, shows Chengdi loathe to initiate the sort of moves against Wang Feng that some of his best officials, including Mei Fu 梅福, call for. Hence, the fairly standard assessment, this time by Hsu Fu-kuan: "Chengdi . . . had not the force of character to oppose rule by the *waiqi* 外戚 [maternal relatives]." For more on the *Xijing zaji*, see the unpublished essay by Knechtges, "Secrets of the Western Han Court Exposed."

125. Fukui, *Kandai Jukyō no shiteki kenkyū*, chap. 1.

126. This point is made in Lloyd and Sivin, *The Way and the Word*.

127. *HS* 87B.3583 says of Yang, "He wanted to seek to compose writings and make a name in later generations."

kind of classicism, in which the classics (the *dian*) are viewed as the embodiment of all ethical principles."[128]

The entire *Fayan*—not just the thirteenth chapter—argues for the adoption of this new classicism, to which the ending of the last chapter of the *Fayan* alludes, with its talk of the ritual cult sites and the rites and music inherited from antiquity, along with the caps and robes and the institutions of learning.[129] By the standard classicism invoked in earlier eras, the classics and masterworks (*jingzi* 經子) were routinely, if sometimes perfunctorily, cited to demonstrate a given persuader's command of high cultural literacy, while lending compositions (oral and written) nice rhetorical flourishes. In the new form of classicism espoused by Yang and his most famous contemporaries, the Five Classics were to be elevated far above the various masterworks (*zhu zi* 諸子) as the most authoritative works available for consultation by all those who would solemnly deliberate upon the wisdom of policy initiatives entertained by the court.[130] Single-minded immersion in the Five Classics' pronouncements on topics that remained the burning issues of the day was of greater significance than archaic style, however pleasing.[131] Thus, in addition to the matters of sacrifice and war presented in chapter 13, Yang Xiong's *Fayan* pronounced on such vital issues as taxes, limits on landholding, the appropriate use of punishments, and the proper deference owed the ruler by all his subordinates. By the judicious wielding of public policy, ideally the Han's subjects could be, as one of the last lines of the *Fayan* put it, "encouraged . . . to serve,"[132] at which point, the more educated among them could be led to deliberate on the proper modes and ends of adult life—these being at least as important, in Yang's view, as any early socialization of the child. To this end, it was incumbent upon the court to see to it that the texts of the Five Classics, marred by multiple lacunae, interpolations, and

---

128. Knechtges, "Uncovering the Sauce Jar," 251.

129. *Fayan* 13.34.

130. Fukui, *Kandai Jukyō no shiteki kenkyū*, says that Yang and Liu Xin were the first to valorize the term "Five Classics."

131. *Fayan* 2.1.

132. *Fayan* 13.34.

misreadings, were speedily repaired using the new text critical methods that Yang and his contemporaries set about devising.[133]

That we have failed to note the monumental innovation of Yang Xiong and company is our loss as Han historians, a loss occasioned by a serious misunderstanding of the important role accorded fine rhetoric during Han by all its major thinkers. It is easy to forget that Yang was born into a culture that had no distinct concept of "philosophy," in spite of the fact that various kinds of abstract and analytic thinking had been developing for centuries before Yang. Yang was one of the first to see the advantages of constructing a systematic philosophy impervious to challenge by technical experts and rooted in that love of wisdom he ascribed to the distant past. He insisted that an ardent love of classical learning and adherence to its main precepts would promote the court's interests, even if it logically superseded them. Small wonder, then, that Yang, upon his death, was rewarded by the throne with a coveted burial spot near a Han imperial mausoleum, or that Yang was soon hailed as the most important historian and moralist of the second century of Western Han rule.[134] Small wonder, too, that an entire curriculum was organized around his masterworks at Jingzhou, the most important private academy of Eastern Han,[135] and that he became, for many, a more reliable interpreter of Confucian tradition than either Mencius or Xunzi.[136]

---

133. On these, see Nylan, *Yang Xiong and the Pleasures of Reading and Classical Learning.*

134. Yang Xiong was buried at Anling 安陵, near the imperial mausoleum of Huidi.

135. On this, see Nylan, "Legacies of the Chengdu Plain," 307–28.

136. See, e.g., the *Lunheng* for this assessment; also the writings of Han Yu. See also Pitner, "Embodied Geographies of Han Dynasty China"; also Nylan, "The Afterlife of Yang Xiong."

Works Cited

Arbuckle, Gary. "Inevitable Treason: Dong Zhongshu's Theory of Historical Cycles and Early Attempts to Invalidate the Han Mandate." *Journal of the American Oriental Society* 115, no. 4 (Oct.–Dec. 1995): 585–97.

Ariel, Yoav, trans. *Kung-Tsung-Tzu: The Kung Family Masters' Anthology: A Study and Translation of Chapters 1–10, 12–14*. Princeton: Princeton University Press, 1989.

Aristotle. *Rhetoric*. In *The Complete Works of Aristotle*, edited by Jonathan Barnes, 2152–69. Princeton: Princeton University Press, 1984.

Auken, Newell Ann. "A Formal Analysis of the 'Chuenchiou' ('Spring and Autumn Classic')." Ph.D. diss., University of Washington, 2006.

Ban Gu 班固. *Baihu tong shuzheng* 白虎通疏證. Edited by Chen Li 陳立. Beijing: Zhonghua shuju, 1994.

———. *Hanshu* 漢書. 12 vols. Beijing: Zhonghua shuju, 1997.

———. *Hanshu buzhu* 漢書補注. Annotated by Wang Xianqian 王先謙. 2 vols. Beijing: Zhonghua shuju, 1983.

Behr, Wolfgang. "Language Change in Premodern China: Notes on Its Perception and Impact on the Idea of a 'Constant Way.'" In *Historical Truth, Historical Criticism, and Ideology: Chinese Historiography and Historical Culture from a New Comparative Perspective*, edited by Helwig Schmidt-Glintzer, Achim Mittag, and Jörn Rüsen, 13–51. Leiden: Brill, 2005.

Bielenstein, Hans. *The Bureaucracy of Han Times*. Cambridge: Cambridge University Press, 1980.

Biot, Édouard, trans. *Le Tcheou-li ou Rites des Tcheou*. 2 vols. Paris: Imprimerie Nationale, 1851.

Boltz, William G. "Chou li." In *Early Chinese Texts: A Bibliographical Guide*, edited by Michael Loewe, 24–32. Berkeley: Society for the Study of Early China, 1993.

Boyarin, Daniel. *Socrates and the Fat Rabbis*. Chicago: University of Chicago Press, 2009.

Broman, Sven. "Studies on the *Chou li*." *Bulletin of the Museum of Far Eastern Antiquities* 33 (1961): 1–89.

Brown, Miranda. *The Politics of Mourning in Early China*. Albany: State University of New York Press, 2007.

Brubacher, John S., and Willis Rudy. *Higher Education in Transition*. 4th ed. New Brunswick: Transaction Publishers, 1997.

Cameron, Alan. *Callimachus and His Critics*. Princeton: Princeton University Press, 1995.

Chen Wangdao 陳望道. *Xiucixue fafan* 修辭學發凡. Shanghai: Shanghai jiaoyu chubanshe, 1932.

Chen Wei 陳偉, ed. *Liye Qin jiandu jiaoshi (di yi juan)* 里耶秦簡牘校釋（第一卷）. Wuhan: Wuhan daxue chubanshe, 2012.

Chen Yanhui 陳彥輝. *Chunqiu ciling yanjiu* 春秋辭令研究. Beijing: Zhonghua shuju, 2006.

Chen Zhihong 陳致宏. *Yuyongxue yu* Zuozhuan *waijiao ciling* 語用學與《左傳》外交辭令. Taipei: Wanjuanlou, 2000.

Chin, Tamara Da Lun. "Savage Exchange: Fighting the Foreign in the Early Han Dynasty." Ph.D. diss., University of California at Berkeley, 2005.

Chunqiu gongyangzhuan zhushu 春秋公羊傳注疏. In *Shisanjing zhushu* 十三經注疏, edited by Li Xueqin 李學勤. 3 vols. Beijing: Beijing daxue chubanshe, 1999.

Chunqiu Zuozhuan zhu 春秋左傳注. Edited by Yang Bojun 楊伯峻. 4 vols. Beijing: Zhonghua, 1990.

Cohen, Paul A. *Speaking to History: The Story of King Goujian in Twentieth-Century China*. Berkeley: University of California Press, 2009.

de Crespigny, Rafe. *Biographical Dictionary of Later Han to the Three Kingdoms*. Leiden: Brill, 2007.

Declercq, Dominik. *Writing against the State: Political Rhetorics in Third- and Fourth-Century China*. Leiden: Brill, 1998.

Dreyer, Edward L. "Zhao Chongguo: A Professional Soldier of the Former Han Dynasty." *Journal of Military History* 72, no. 3 (2008): 665–725.

Dubs, Homer, and P'an Lo-chi, trans. *The History of the Former Han Dynasty*. Vol. 3, *Imperial Annals XI and XII and the Memoir of Wang Mang*. Baltimore: Waverly Press, 1955.

Durrant, Stephen, Wai-yee Li, and David Schaberg, trans. *Zuozhuan*. Seattle: University of Washington Press, forthcoming.

Emmerich, Reinhard. "Die Rebellion der Sieben Könige, 154 v. Chr." In *Und folge nun dem, was mein Herz begehrt: Festschrift für Ulrich Unger zum 70. Geburtstag*, edited by Reinhard Emmerich and Hans Stumpfeldt, 397–497. Hamburger Sinologische Schriften, no. 8. Hamburg: Hamburger Sinologische Gesellschaft, 2002.

Fan Ye 氾曄, comp. *Hou Hanshu* 後漢書. Beijing: Zhonghua shuju, 1965.

Fayan. See Yang Xiong.

Fukui Shigemasa 福井重雅. *Kandai Jukyō no shiteki kenkyu: Jukyō no kangakuka o meguru teisetsu no saikentō* 漢代儒教の史的研究:儒教の官學化をめぐる定説の再検討. Tokyo: Kyūko Shoin, 2005.

Garrett, Mary. "Pathos Reconsidered from the Perspective of Classical Chinese Rhetorical Theories." *Quarterly Journal of Speech* 79 (1993): 19–39.

Giele, Enno. *Imperial Decision-Making and Communication in Early China: A Study of Cai Yong's* Duduan. Wiesbaden: Harrasowitz Verlag, 2006.

Goldin, Paul R. "Appeals to History in Early Chinese Philosophy and Rhetoric." *Journal of Chinese Philosophy* 35, no. 1 (2008): 79–96.

———. *Rituals of the Way: The Philosophy of Xunzi*. Chicago: Open Court, 1999.

Gong Kechang. *Studies on the Han Fu*. New Haven: American Oriental Society, 1997.

Gu Jiegang 顧頡剛. *Qin Han de fangshi yu rusheng* 秦漢的方士與儒生. Shanghai: Shanghai guji chubanshe, 1998.

Guodian Chumu zhujian 郭店楚墓竹簡. Beijing: Wenwu chubanshe, 1998.

Guoyu 國語. Compiled by Wei Zhao 韋昭. Taipei: Yiwen yinshu guan, 1974.

Guoyu jijie 國語集解. Compiled by Xu Yuangao 徐元誥 and edited by Wang Shumin 王樹民 and Shen Changyun 沈長雲. Beijing: Zhonghua shuju, 2002.

Halliwell, Stephen. *Greek Laughter: A Study of Cultural Psychology from Homer to Early Christianity*. Cambridge: Cambridge University Press, 2008.

Han Feizi jijie 韩非子集解. Edited and annotated by Wang Xianshen 王先慎. 2 vols. Beijing: Zhonghua shuju, 1998.

Han Feizi shiping 韓非子釋評. Compiled by Zhu Shouliang 朱守亮. 4 vols. Taipei: Wunan tushu chuban gongsi, 1992.

Han Feizi xinjiaozhu 韓非子新校注. Edited and annotated by Chen Qiyou 陳奇猷. 2 vols. Shanghai: Shanghai guangming shuju, 2000.

Hanshu. See Ban Gu.

Harbsmeier, Christoph. *Language and Logic*. In *Science and Civilisation in China*, edited by Joseph Needham, vol. 7.1. Cambridge: Cambridge University Press, 1998.

He Zhihua 何志華 and Zhu Guofan 朱國藩, eds. Gu Lienü zhuan *yu xian Qin liang Han dianji chongjian ziliao huibian* 《古列女傳》與先秦兩漢典籍重見資料彙編. Hong Kong: Institute of Chinese Studies, Chinese University of Hong Kong, 2004.

Henry, Eric. "'Junzi yue' vs. 'Zhongni yue' in *Zuozhuan*." *Harvard Journal of Asiatic Studies* 59, no. 1 (June 1999): 125–62.

Hou Hanshu. See Fan Ye.

Huang Jianlin 黃建霖. *Hanyu xiucige jianshang cidian* 漢語修辭格鑒賞辭典. Nanjing: Dongnan daxue chubanshe, 1995.

Huang Qingquan 黃清泉, ed. *Xinyi Lienü zhuan* 新譯列女傳. Taipei: Sanmin shuju, 1996.

Hucker, Charles O. *A Dictionary of Official Titles in Imperial China*. Stanford: Stanford University Press, 1985.

Huizinga, Johan. *The Autumn of the Middle Ages*. Trans. Rodrey J. Payton and Ulrich Mammitzsch. Chicago: University of Chicago Press, 1996.

Hulsewé, A. F. P. *Remnants of Han Law*. Leiden: Brill, 1955.

Itano Chōhachi 板野長八. *Chūgoku kodai ni okeru ningenkan no tenkai* 中國古代における人間觀の展開. Tokyo: Iwanami Shoten, 1972.

Ji Annuo 紀安諾 (Enno Giele). "Yinwan xinchutu xingzheng wenshu de xingzhi yu Handai difan xingzheng" 尹彎新出土行政文書的性質與漢代地方行政. *Dalu zazhi* 95, no. 3 (1997): 21–45.

Jiao Yanshou 焦延壽. *Jiaoshi Yilin* 焦氏易林. In *Sibu congkan* 四部叢刊. http://www.chant.org.

Jing Gong nüe 競公瘧, edited by Pu Maozuo 濮茅左. In *Shanghai bowuguan cang Zhanguo Chu zhushu* 上海博物館藏戰國楚竹書, edited by Ma Chengyuan 馬承源, 157–91. Shanghai: Guji chubanshe, vol. 6, 2007.

Johnston, Ian, trans. *The Mozi: A Complete Translation*. New York: Columbia University Press, 2010.

Jullien, François. *Detour and Access: Strategies of Meaning in China and Greece*. New York: Zone Books, 2000.

Keightley, David. "The Shang." In *Cambridge History of Ancient China*, edited by Michael Loewe and Edward Shaughnessy, 232–91. New York: Cambridge University Press, 1999.

Kern, Martin. "The 'Biography of Sima Xiangru' and the Question of *Fu* in Sima Qian's *Shiji*." *Journal of the American Oriental Society* 123, no. 2 (April–June 2003): 303–16.

———. "The Performance of Writing in Western Zhou China." In *The Poetics of Grammar and the Metaphysics of Sound and Sign*, edited by Sergio La Porta and David Shulman, 109–75. Leiden: Brill, 2007.

———. "Poetry and Religion: The Representation of 'Truth' in Early Chinese Historiography." In *Historical Truth, Historical Criticism, and Ideology*, edited by Helwig Schmidt-Glintzer et al., 53–78. Boston: Brill, 2005.

———. *The Stele Inscriptions of Ch'in Shih-huang: Text and Ritual in Early Chinese Imperial Representation*. New Haven: American Oriental Society, 2000.

———, ed. *Text and Ritual in Early China*. Seattle: University of Washington Press, 2005.

———. "Western Han Aesthetics and the Genesis of the *Fu*." *Harvard Journal of Asiatic Studies* 63, no. 2 (December 2003): 383–437.

Kinney, Anne Behnke. *Representations of Childhood and Youth in Early China*. Stanford: Stanford University Press, 2004.

Knechtges, David R. "Fa yen." In *Early Chinese Texts: A Bibliographical Guide*, edited by Michael Loewe, 100–104. Berkeley: Society for the Study of Early China, 1993.

———, trans. *The* Han shu *Biography of Yang Xiong (53 B.C.–A.D. 18)*. Tempe: Arizona State University, Center for Asian Studies, 1982.

———. "The Liu Hsin/Yang Hsiung Correspondence on the *Fang yen*." *Monumenta Serica* 33 (1977): 309–25.

———. "Riddles as Poetry: The '*Fu* chapter' of the Hsun-tzu." In *Wen-lin*, vol. 2, *Studies in the Chinese Humanities*, edited by Tse-tsung Chow, 1–32. Hong Kong: Institute of Chinese Studies, Chinese University of Hong Kong, 1989.

———. "Secrets of the Western Han Court Exposed: Anecdotes in the *Xijing zaji*." Unpublished essay.

———. "Uncovering the Sauce Jar: A Literary Interpretation of Yang Hsiung's 'Chü Ch'in mei Hsin.'" In *Ancient China: Studies in Early Civilization*, edited by David T. Roy and Tsuen-hsuin Tsien, 229–52. Hong Kong: Chinese University Press, 1978.

———. "Yang Shyong, the *Fuh*, and Hann Rhetoric." Ph.D. diss., University of Washington, 1968.

Knoblock, John, trans. *Xunzi*. Stanford: Stanford University Press, 1988.

Kominami Ichirō 小南一郎. "Tenmei to toku" 天命と德. *Tōhō gakuhō* 64 (1992): 1–59.

Kongcongzi 孔叢子. Annotated by Song Xian 宋咸. Taipei: Shangwu yinshuguan, 1971.

Kuriyama, Shigehisa. *The Expressiveness of the Body*. New York: Zone Books, 1999.

Lau, D. C., trans. *Analects*. Hong Kong: Chinese University Press, 1983.

———, trans. *Mencius*. Harmondsworth: Penguin, 1970.

Lau, D. C., et al., eds. *A Concordance to the Chunqiu fanlu* 春秋繁露逐字索引. ICS Ancient Chinese Text Concordance Series. Hong Kong: Commercial Press, 1994.

———. *A Concordance to the Huainanzi* 淮南子逐字索引. ICS Ancient Chinese Text Concordance Series. Hong Kong: Commercial Press, 1992.

Legge, James, trans. *Li Chi: Book of Rites*. Vol. 1. New York: Oxford University Press, 1885.

Levi, Jean. "L'art de la persuasion à l'époque des Royaumes Combattants (Ve–IIIe siècles av. J.C.)". *Extrême-Orient-Extrême-Occident* 14 (1992): 49–89.

Lewis, Mark E. "Warring States: Political History." In *The Cambridge History of Ancient China*, edited by Michael Loewe and Edward L. Shaughnessy, 587–650. Cambridge: Cambridge University Press, 1999.

L'Haridon, Beatrice. "La recherche du modèle dans les dialogues du *Fayan* de Yang Xiong (53 av. J.C.–18 apr. J.C.): écriture, éthique, and réflexion historique à la fin des Han occidentaux." Ph.D. thesis, Institute National des Langues and Civilisations Orientales, 2006.

Li Fang 李昉. *Taiping yulan* 太平御覽. 4 vols. Beijing: Zhonghua shuju, 1995.

Li, Wai-yee. *Enchantment and Disenchantment: Love and Illusion in Chinese Literature*. Princeton: Princeton University Press, 1993.

———. "On Becoming a Fish: Paradoxes of Immortality and Enlightenment in Chinese Literature." In *Self and Self-Transformation in the History of Religions*, edited by David Shulman and Guy Stroumsa, 29–59. Oxford: Oxford University Press, 2002.

———. *The Readability of the Past in Early Chinese Historiography*. Cambridge: Harvard University Asia Center, 2007.

Liao Boyuan 廖伯源. *Shizhe guanzhi yanbian* 使者官制演變. Taipei: Wenjin chubanshe, 2006.

Liezi jishi 列子集釋. Edited by Yang Bojun 楊伯峻. Beijing: Zhonghua shuju, 1979.

Liji zheng yi 禮記正義. In *Shisanjing zhushu* 十三經注疏, edited by Li Xueqin 李學勤, 3 vols. Beijing: Beijing daxue chubanshe, 1999.

Lin Yunming 林雲銘. "Fanli" 凡例. In *Guwen xiyi* 古文析義. Taipei: Guangwen shuju, 1984.

Lin Zhipeng 林志鵬. "Zhanguo zhushu *Bao Shuya yu Xi Peng zhi jian* yizhu" 戰國竹書《鮑叔牙與隰朋之諫》釋注. *Jianbo yanjiu* (2008): 1–18.

Ling Zhilong 凌稚隆. *Shiji pinglin* 史記評林. Taipei: Diqiu chubanshe, 1992.

Liu Rulin 劉汝霖. *Han Jin xueshu biannian* 漢晉學術編年. Shanghai: Commercial Press, 1935.

Liu Zehua 劉澤華. *Zhongguo de Wangquanzhuyi* 中國的王權主義. Shanghai: Renmin chubanshe, 2000.

Liu Zhen 劉珍. *Dongguan Hanji jiaozhu* 東觀漢記校注. Annotated by Wu Shuping 吳樹平. 2 vols. Beijing: Zhonghua, 2008.

Lloyd, G. E. R. *Adversaries and Authorities*. New York: Cambridge University Press, 1996.

Lloyd, G. E. R., and Nathan Sivin. *The Way and the Word*. New Haven: Yale University Press, 2005.

Loewe, Michael. "The Authority of the Emperors of Ch'in and Han." In *State and Law in East Asia*, edited by Dieter Eikemeier and Herbert Franke, 80–111. Wiesbaden: Otto Harrassowitz, 1981.

———. *Crisis and Conflict in Han China*. London: George Allen and Unwin, 1974.

———. "Social Distinctions, Groups, and Privileges." In *China's Early Empires: A Re-Appraisal*, edited by M. Loewe and M. Nylan, 296–307. New York: Cambridge University Press, 2010.

Lüshi chunqiu jiaoshi 呂氏春秋校釋. Compiled and annotated by Chen Qiyou 陳奇猷. Shanghai: Xuelin, 1990.

Major, John S., Sarah A. Queen, Andrew Seth Meyer, and Harold D. Roth, trans. and eds. *The Huainanzi: A Guide to the Theory and Practice of Government in Early Han China*. New York: Columbia University Press, 2010.

Maoshi zhengyi 毛詩正義. In *Shisanjing zhushu* 十三經注疏, edited by Li Xueqin 李學勤. 3 vols. Beijing: Beijing daxue chubanshe, 1999.

Martynov, Aleksandr S. "Kategoriia *de*: Sintez 'poriadka' i 'zhizni.'" In *Ot Magicheskoi Sily k Moral'nomy Imperativu: Kategoriia De v Kitajskoj Kul'ture*, edited by L. N. Borokh and A. I. Kobzev, 36–75. Moscow: Izdatel'skaia firma "Vostochnaia Literatura" RAN, 1998.

Maspéro, Henri. "La composition et la date du Tso tchouan." In *Mélanges chinois et bouddhiques*, 137–215. Brussels: Institut Belge des Hautes Études Chinoises, 1931.

Mengzi yizhu 孟子譯注. Annotated by Yang Bojun 楊伯峻. Beijing: Zhonghua shuju, 1992.

Momigliano, Arnaldo. *The Classical Foundations of Modern Historiography*. Berkeley: University of California, 1990.

Mozi jiangu 墨子閒詁. Compiled by Sun Yirang 孫詒讓. Beijing: Zhonghua shuju, 2001.

Nienhauser, William H. Jr., gen. ed. *The Grand Scribe's Records*. Vol. 1, *The Basic Annals of Pre-Han China*. Translated by Tsai-fa Cheng et al. Bloomington: Indiana University Press, 1994.

———, gen. ed. *The Grand Scribe's Records*. Vol. 7, *The Memoirs of Pre-Han China*. Translated by Tsai-fa Cheng et al. Bloomington: Indiana University Press, 1994.

———, gen. ed. *The Grand Scribe's Records*. Vol. 8, *The Memoirs of Han China*. Translated by Meghan Cai et al. Bloomington: Indiana University Press, 2008.

Nylan, Michael. "The Afterlife of Yang Xiong." Paper presented at a conference on early rhetoric, Nanyang University, Singapore, December 2010.

———. *The Canon of Supreme Mystery.* Albany: State University of New York Press, 1993.
———. "Confucian Piety and Individualism." *Journal of the American Oriental Society* 116 (Jan.–March 1996): 1–27.
———. "Empire in the Classical Era in China (323 BC–AD 316)." In *Conceiving the Empire: China and Rome Compared*, edited by Fritz-Heiner Mutschler and Achim Mittag, 34–64. Oxford: Oxford University Press, 2008.
———. *The Five "Confucian" Classics.* New Haven: Yale University Press, 2001.
———. "Legacies of the Chengdu Plain." In *Ancient Sichuan: Treasures from a Lost Civilization*, edited by Robert W. Bagley, 307–28. Seattle: Seattle Art Museum; Princeton: Princeton University Press, 2001.
———. "Mencius on Pleasure." In *Polishing the Chinese Mirror: Essays in Honor of Henry Rosement*, edited by Marthe Chandler and Ronnie Littlejohn, 1–26. New York: Global Scholarly Publications, 2008.
———. *Yang Xiong and the Pleasures of Reading and Classical Learning.* New Haven: American Oriental Society, 2011.
———, trans. *Fayan.* Seattle: University of Washington Press, forthcoming.

Ōkushi Atsuhiro 大櫛敦弘. "Kandai no 'nake-ke' no san ni kansuru kōsatsu" 漢代の中家の產に關する一考察. *Shigaku zasshi* 94, no. 7 (1985): 40–62.
Olberding, Garret. *Dubious Facts: The Evidence of Early Chinese Historiography.* Albany: State University of New York Press, 2012.
Onozawa Seiichi 小野澤精一. "Toku ron" 德論. In *Chūgoku bunka sōsho 2: Shisō gairon* 中國文化叢書 2： 思想概論, edited by Akatsuka Kiyoshi 赤塚忠 et al., 151–84. Tokyo: Taishukan shoten, 1968.

Pines, Yuri. *All the Emperor's Men: The Political Culture of Ancient China and Its Legacy.* Princeton: Princeton University Press, forthcoming.
———. *Envisioning Eternal Empire: Chinese Political Thought of the Warring States Era.* Honolulu: University of Hawai'i Press, 2009.
———. *The Everlasting Empire: Traditional Chinese Political Culture and Its Enduring Legacy.* Princeton: Princeton University Press, 2012.
———. *Foundations of Confucian Thought: Intellectual Life in the Chunqiu Period, 722–453 BCE.* Honolulu: University of Hawai'i Press, 2002.
———. "Friends or Foes: Changing Concepts of Ruler-Minister Relations and the Notion of Loyalty in Pre-Imperial China." *Monumenta Serica* 50 (2002): 35–74.
———. "The Search for Stability: Late Ch'un-ch'iu Thinkers." *Asia Major* 10 (1997): 18–31.
———. "To Rebel Is Justified? The Image of Zhouxin and the Legitimacy of Rebellion in the Chinese Political Tradition." *Oriens Extremus* 47 (2008): 1–24.
Pitner, Mark. "Embodied Geographies of Han Dynasty China: Yang Xiong and his Reception." Ph.D. diss., University of Washington, 2010.
Plaks, Andrew. "Riddle and Enigma in Chinese Civilization." In *Untying the Knot: On Riddles and Other Enigmatic Modes*, edited by Galit Hasan-Rokem and David Shulman, 227–36. Oxford: Oxford University Press, 1996.

Potter, David. *Debating in the Colonial Chartered Colleges: An Historical Survey, 1642 to 1900*. New York: Columbia University Press, 1944.

Pulleyblank, E. G. "Chinese Historical Criticism: Liu Chih-chi and Ssu-ma Kuang." In *Historians of China and Japan*, edited by W. G. Beasley and E. G. Pulleyblank, 135–66. London: School of Oriental and African Studies, 1961.

Qian Zhongshu 錢鍾書. *Guan Zhui bian* 管錐編. Beijing: Zhonghua shuju, 1979.

Qu, Yingjie 曲英杰. *Shi ji ducheng kao* 史記都城考. Beijing: Commercial Press, 2007.

Queen, Sarah. *From Chronicle to Canon*. New York: Cambridge University Press, 1996.

Rosemont, Henry, Jr., and Roger Ames. *The Chinese Classic of Family Reverence: A Philosophical Translation of the Xiaojing*. Honolulu: University of Hawai'i Press, 2009.

Sailor, Dylan. *Writing and Empire in Tacitus*. Cambridge: Cambridge University Press, 2008.

Sato, Masayuki. *The Confucian Quest for Order: The Origin and Foundation of the Political Thought of Xun Zi*. Leiden: Brill, 2003.

Schaberg, David. *A Patterned Past: Form and Thought in Early Chinese Historiography*. Cambridge: Harvard University Asia Center, 2001.

———. "Playing at Critique." In *Text and Ritual in Early China*, edited by Martin Kern, 194–225. Seattle: University of Washington Press, 2005.

———. "Remonstrance in Eastern Zhou Historiography." *Early China* 22 (1997): 133–79.

Schuessler, Axel. *ABC Etymological Dictionary of Old Chinese*. Honolulu: University of Hawai'i Press, 2007.

Shangshu dazhuan 尙書大傳. In *Sibu congkan* 四部叢刊. http://www.chant.org.

Shi ji zhuan 詩集傳. Compiled by Zhu Xi 朱熹. Nanjing: Fenghuang chubanshe, 2007.

Shijing. See *Maoshi*.

Sima Qian 司馬遷. *Shiji* 史記. 10 vols. Beijing: Zhonghua shuju, 1959.

Som, Tjan Tjoe, trans. *Po Hu Tung: The Comprehensive Discussions in the White Tiger Hall*. Vol 1. Westport: Hyperion Press,1973.

Swann, Nancy Lee. "Biography of the Empress Teng: A Translation from the Annals of the Later Han Dynasty." *Journal of the American Oriental Society* 51, no. 2 (1931): 138–59.

Taiping yulan. See Li Fang.

van Ess, Hans, "Emperor Wu of the Han and the First August Emperor of Qin in Sima Qian's *Shiji*." In Yuri Pines, Lothar von Falkenhausen, Gideon Shelach and Robin D. S. Yates, eds., *The Birth of Empire: The State of Qin Revisited*. Berkeley, University of California Press, forthcoming.

Vankeerberghen, Griet. *The Huainanzi and Liu An's Claim to Moral Authority*. Albany: State University of New York Press, 2001.

Veyne, Paul. *Did the Greeks Believe in Their Myths? An Essay on the Constitutive Imagination*. Chicago: University of Chicago Press, 1988.

Vogelsang, Kai. *Geschichte als Problem: Entstehung, Formen und Funktionen von Geschichtsschreibung im Alten China*. Lun Wen, Studien zur Geistesgeschichte und Literatur in China, no. 9. Wiesbaden: Harrassowitz, 2007.

———. "Some Notions of Historical Judgment in China and the West." In *Historical Truth, Historical Criticism, and Ideology*, edited by Helwig Schmidt-Glintzer et al., 143–69. Boston: Brill, 2005.

Waley, Arthur, trans. *The Book of Songs*. New York: Grove Press, 1996.

Walton, Charles. *Policing Public Opinion in the French Revolution: The Culture of Calumny and the Problem of Free Speech*. New York: Oxford University Press, 2008.

Wang Guowei 王國維. *Guantang jilin* 觀堂集林. Taibei: Heluo tushu chubanshe, 1975.

Wang Kefu 王可夫 and Li Min 李民, eds. *Zhonghua tongshi da lidian* 中華通史大歷典. 3 vols. Chengdu: Sichuan minzu, 1996.

Wang Niansun 王念孫. *Dushu zazhi yubian* 讀書雜志餘編. In *Xuxiu siku quanshu* 續修四庫全書, vol. 1153. Shanghai: Shanghai guji chubanshe, 2002.

Wang Zhanfu 王占福. *Gudai hanyu xiucixue* 古代漢語修辭學. Shijiazhuang: Hebei jiaoyu chubanshe, 2000.

Watson, Burton, trans. *Courtier and Commoner in Ancient China: Selections from the History of the Former Han*. New York: Columbia University Press, 1974.

———. *Records of the Grand Historian: Han Dynasty*. Vols. 1 and 2. New York: Columbia University Press, 1993.

———. *Records of the Grand Historian: Qin Dynasty*. New York: Columbia University Press, 1993.

Wei Shou 魏收, comp. *Weishu* 魏書. 8 vols. Beijing: Zhoughua shuju, 1974.

Wu, Fusheng. *Written at Imperial Command: Panegyric Poetry in Early Medieval China*. Albany: State University of New York Press, 2008.

Xiao Tong 蕭統. *Zhaoming wenxuan* 昭明文選. Zhengzhou: Zhongzhou guji chubanshe, 1990. Reprint of the 1935 Guoxue zhengli she yingyin ben.

Xijing zaji 西京雜記. Attrib. Ge Hong 葛洪 et al. Xi'an: Sanqin chubanshe, 2006.

Xing Yitian 邢義田 (Hsing I-tien). "QinHan huangdi yu 'shengren'" 秦漢皇帝與「聖人」. In Yang Liansheng 楊聯陞, Quan Hansheng 全漢昇, Liu Guangjing 劉廣京, eds., *Guoshi shilun—Tao Xisheng xiansheng jiuzhi rongqing zhushou lunwenji* 國史釋論—陶希聖先生九秩榮慶祝壽論文集, 389–406. Taibei: Shihuo chubanshe, 1988.

Xu Fuguan 徐復觀. *Liang Han sixiang shi* 兩漢思想史. 3 vols. 1975; rpt., Shanghai: East China Normal University Press, 2001.

———. "Xi Han wenxue lun lue" 西漢文學論略. In *Zhongguo wenxue lunji* 中國文學論集, 350–841. Taipei: Xuesheng shuju, 1974.

Xu Shen 許慎. *Shuowen jiezi xinding* 說文解字新訂. Edited by Zang Kehe 臧克和 and Wang Ping 王平. Beijing: Zhonghua, 2002.

Xu Zhaochang 許兆昌. *Xian Qin shiguan de zhidu yu wenhua* 先秦史官的制度與文化. Harbin: Heilongjiang renmin, 2006.

Xunzi jianshi 荀子柬釋. Compiled by Liang Qixiong 梁啓雄. Taipei: Shangwu yinshu guan, 1965.

Xunzi jijie 荀子集解. Edited and annotated by Wang Xianqian 王先謙. 2 vols. Beijing: Zhonghua shuju, 1988.

Yang Ximei 楊希枚. *Xian Qin wenhua shi lunji* 先秦文化史論集. Beijing: Zhongguo shehui kexue chuban she, 1995.

Yang Xiong 揚雄. *Fayan yishu* 法言義疏. Compiled by Wang Rongbao 汪榮寶. 2 vols. Beijing: Zhonghua shuju, 1987.

———. *Fayan zhu* 法言注. Annotated by Han Jing 韓敬. Beijing: Zhonghua shuju, 1992.

Yantie lun zhu zi suoyin 鹽鐵論逐字索引. Compiled by He Zhihua. Xianggang: Shangwu yinshuguan, 1994.

Yanzi chunqiu yizhu 晏子春秋譯注. Annotated by Chen Tao 陳濤. Tianjin: Guji chubanshe, 1996.

Yoshinami Takeshi 好並隆司. "Kandai kōtei shihai chitsujo no keisei" 漢代皇帝支配の形成. *Tōyōshi kenkyū* 35, no. 2 (Sept. 1976): 39–70.

Yu Ying-shih. "Han Foreign Relations." In *The Cambridge History of China*, vol. 1: *The Ch'in and Han Empires, 221 B.C.–A.D. 220*, edited by Denis Twitchett and Michael Loewe, 377–462. Cambridge: Cambridge University Press, 1986.

———. *Trade and Expansion in Han China*. Berkeley: University of California Press, 1967.

Yuan Hong 袁宏. *Hou Han ji jiaozhu* 後漢紀校注. Compiled by Zhou Tianyou 周天游. Tianjin: Tianjin guji, 1987.

Zhanguo ce zhushi 戰國策注釋. Compiled by Liu Xiang 劉向 and annotated by He Jianzhang 何建章. Beijing: Zhonghua shuju, 1991.

Zhang Fentian 張分田. *Zhongguo diwang guannian—shehui pubian yishi zhong de 'zun jun—zui jun' wenhua fanshi* 中國帝王觀念—社會普遍意識中的"尊君—罪君"文化範式. Beijing: Zhongguo renmin daxue chubanshe, 2004.

Zhang Suqing 張素卿 (Chang Su-ching). "'*Guoyu*' de 'yu': neirong yu xingshi—cong pingxi 'Ji Gong jian Mu Wang zheng Quan Rong' chufa"《國語》的「語」：內容與形式——從評析「祭公諫穆王征犬戎」出發. In *Zhongguo gudian wenxue yanjiu* 中國古典文學研究 1 (June 1999): 1–22.

Zhang Yiren 張以仁 (Chang Yi-ren). "Cong *Guoyu* yu *Zuozhuan* benzhi shang de chayi shilun houren dui *Guoyu* de piping" 從國語與左傳本質上的差異試論後人對國語的批評. In *Chunqiu shilun ji* 春秋史論集, 105–82. Taipei: Lianjing chuban shiye gongsi 聯經出版事業公司, 1990.

Zheng Jiewen 鄭杰文. *Zhongguo Moxue tongshi* 中國墨學通史. 2 vols. Beijing: Renmin chubanshe, 2006.

Zheng Liangshu 鄭良樹. "Lun *Yanzi chunqiu* de pianxie ji chengshu guocheng" 論《晏子春秋》的篇寫及成書過程. *Guanzi xuekan* 管子學刊 1 (2000): 25–33 and 2 (2000): 33–62.

Zheng Shaozong 鄭紹宗. *Mancheng Hanmu* 滿城漢墓. Beijing: Wenwu, 2003.

Zhou li 周禮. In *Shisanjing zhushu* 十三經注疏. 3 vols. Taipei: Yiwen, 1981.

Zhouli zhengyi 周禮正義. Annotated by Sun Yirang 孫詒讓. 14 vols. Beijing: Zhonghua shuju, 1987.

Zhu Dongrun 朱東潤. *Shiji kaosuo* 史記考索. Shanghai: Huadong shifan daxue, 1996.

Index

Harvard East Asian Monographs
(*out-of-print)

*1. Liang Fang-chung, *The Single-Whip Method of Taxation in China*
*2. Harold C. Hinton, *The Grain Tribute System of China, 1845–1911*
3. Ellsworth C. Carlson, *The Kaiping Mines, 1877–1912*
*4. Chao Kuo-chün, *Agrarian Policies of Mainland China: A Documentary Study, 1949–1956*
*5. Edgar Snow, *Random Notes on Red China, 1936–1945*
*6. Edwin George Beal, Jr., *The Origin of Likin, 1835–1864*
7. Chao Kuo-chün, *Economic Planning and Organization in Mainland China: A Documentary Study, 1949–1957*
*8. John K. Fairbank, *Ching Documents: An Introductory Syllabus*
*9. Helen Yin and Yi-chang Yin, *Economic Statistics of Mainland China, 1949–1957*
10. Wolfgang Franke, *The Reform and Abolition of the Traditional Chinese Examination System*
11. Albert Feuerwerker and S. Cheng, *Chinese Communist Studies of Modern Chinese History*
12. C. John Stanley, *Late Ching Finance: Hu Kuang-yung as an Innovator*
13. S. M. Meng, *The Tsungli Yamen: Its Organization and Functions*
*14. Ssu-yü Teng, *Historiography of the Taiping Rebellion*
15. Chun-Jo Liu, *Controversies in Modern Chinese Intellectual History: An Analytic Bibliography of Periodical Articles, Mainly of the May Fourth and Post-May Fourth Era*
*16. Edward J. M. Rhoads, *The Chinese Red Army, 1927–1963: An Annotated Bibliography*
*17. Andrew J. Nathan, *A History of the China International Famine Relief Commission*
*18. Frank H. H. King (ed.) and Prescott Clarke, *A Research Guide to China-Coast Newspapers, 1822–1911*
*19. Ellis Joffe, *Party and Army: Professionalism and Political Control in the Chinese Officer Corps, 1949–1964*
*20. Toshio G. Tsukahira, *Feudal Control in Tokugawa Japan: The Sankin Kōtai System*
*21. Kwang-Ching Liu, ed., *American Missionaries in China: Papers from Harvard Seminars*
*22. George Moseley, *A Sino-Soviet Cultural Frontier: The Ili Kazakh Autonomous Chou*

23. Carl F. Nathan, *Plague Prevention and Politics in Manchuria, 1910–1931*
*24. Adrian Arthur Bennett, *John Fryer: The Introduction of Western Science and Technology into Nineteenth-Century China*
*25. Donald J. Friedman, *The Road from Isolation: The Campaign of the American Committee for Non-Participation in Japanese Aggression, 1938–1941*
*26. Edward LeFevour, *Western Enterprise in Late Ching China: A Selective Survey of Jardine, Matheson and Company's Operations, 1842–1895*
27. Charles Neuhauser, *Third World Politics: China and the Afro-Asian People's Solidarity Organization, 1957–1967*
*28. Kungtu C. Sun, assisted by Ralph W. Huenemann, *The Economic Development of Manchuria in the First Half of the Twentieth Century*
*29. Shahid Javed Burki, *A Study of Chinese Communes, 1965*
30. John Carter Vincent, *The Extraterritorial System in China: Final Phase*
31. Madeleine Chi, *China Diplomacy, 1914–1918*
*32. Clifton Jackson Phillips, *Protestant America and the Pagan World: The First Half Century of the American Board of Commissioners for Foreign Missions, 1810–1860*
*33. James Pusey, *Wu Han: Attacking the Present Through the Past*
*34. Ying-wan Cheng, *Postal Communication in China and Its Modernization, 1860–1896*
35. Tuvia Blumenthal, *Saving in Postwar Japan*
36. Peter Frost, *The Bakumatsu Currency Crisis*
37. Stephen C. Lockwood, *Augustine Heard and Company, 1858–1862*
38. Robert R. Campbell, *James Duncan Campbell: A Memoir by His Son*
39. Jerome Alan Cohen, ed., *The Dynamics of China's Foreign Relations*
40. V. V. Vishnyakova-Akimova, *Two Years in Revolutionary China, 1925–1927*, trans. Steven L. Levine
41. Meron Medzini, *French Policy in Japan During the Closing Years of the Tokugawa Regime*
42. Ezra Vogel, Margie Sargent, Vivienne B. Shue, Thomas Jay Mathews, and Deborah S. Davis, *The Cultural Revolution in the Provinces*
43. Sidney A. Forsythe, *An American Missionary Community in China, 1895–1905*
*44. Benjamin I. Schwartz, ed., *Reflections on the May Fourth Movement.: A Symposium*
*45. Ching Young Choe, *The Rule of the Taewŏngun, 1864–1873: Restoration in Yi Korea*
46. W. P. J. Hall, *A Bibliographical Guide to Japanese Research on the Chinese Economy, 1958–1970*
47. Jack J. Gerson, *Horatio Nelson Lay and Sino-British Relations, 1854–1864*
48. Paul Richard Bohr, *Famine and the Missionary: Timothy Richard as Relief Administrator and Advocate of National Reform*
49. Endymion Wilkinson, *The History of Imperial China: A Research Guide*
50. Britten Dean, *China and Great Britain: The Diplomacy of Commercial Relations, 1860–1864*
51. Ellsworth C. Carlson, *The Foochow Missionaries, 1847–1880*
52. Yeh-chien Wang, *An Estimate of the Land-Tax Collection in China, 1753 and 1908*
53. Richard M. Pfeffer, *Understanding Business Contracts in China, 1949–1963*

*54. Han-sheng Chuan and Richard Kraus, *Mid-Ching Rice Markets and Trade: An Essay in Price History*
55. Ranbir Vohra, *Lao She and the Chinese Revolution*
56. Liang-lin Hsiao, *China's Foreign Trade Statistics, 1864–1949*
*57. Lee-hsia Hsu Ting, *Government Control of the Press in Modern China, 1900–1949*
*58. Edward W. Wagner, *The Literati Purges: Political Conflict in Early Yi Korea*
*59. Joungwon A. Kim, *Divided Korea: The Politics of Development, 1945–1972*
60. Noriko Kamachi, John K. Fairbank, and Chūzō Ichiko, *Japanese Studies of Modern China Since 1953: A Bibliographical Guide to Historical and Social-Science Research on the Nineteenth and Twentieth Centuries, Supplementary Volume for 1953–1969*
61. Donald A. Gibbs and Yun-chen Li, *A Bibliography of Studies and Translations of Modern Chinese Literature, 1918–1942*
62. Robert H. Silin, *Leadership and Values: The Organization of Large-Scale Taiwanese Enterprises*
63. David Pong, *A Critical Guide to the Kwangtung Provincial Archives Deposited at the Public Record Office of London*
*64. Fred W. Drake, *China Charts the World: Hsu Chi-yü and His Geography of 1848*
*65. William A. Brown and Urgrunge Onon, translators and annotators, *History of the Mongolian People's Republic*
66. Edward L. Farmer, *Early Ming Government: The Evolution of Dual Capitals*
*67. Ralph C. Croizier, *Koxinga and Chinese Nationalism: History, Myth, and the Hero*
*68. William J. Tyler, tr., *The Psychological World of Natsume Sōseki,* by Doi Takeo
69. Eric Widmer, *The Russian Ecclesiastical Mission in Peking During the Eighteenth Century*
*70. Charlton M. Lewis, *Prologue to the Chinese Revolution: The Transformation of Ideas and Institutions in Hunan Province, 1891–1907*
71. Preston Torbert, *The Ching Imperial Household Department: A Study of Its Organization and Principal Functions, 1662–1796*
72. Paul A. Cohen and John E. Schrecker, eds., *Reform in Nineteenth-Century China*
73. Jon Sigurdson, *Rural Industrialism in China*
74. Kang Chao, *The Development of Cotton Textile Production in China*
75. Valentin Rabe, *The Home Base of American China Missions, 1880–1920*
*76. Sarasin Viraphol, *Tribute and Profit: Sino-Siamese Trade, 1652–1853*
77. Ch'i-ch'ing Hsiao, *The Military Establishment of the Yuan Dynasty*
78. Meishi Tsai, *Contemporary Chinese Novels and Short Stories, 1949–1974: An Annotated Bibliography*
*79. Wellington K. K. Chan, *Merchants, Mandarins and Modern Enterprise in Late Ching China*
80. Endymion Wilkinson, *Landlord and Labor in Late Imperial China: Case Studies from Shandong by Jing Su and Luo Lun*
*81. Barry Keenan, *The Dewey Experiment in China: Educational Reform and Political Power in the Early Republic*
*82. George A. Hayden, *Crime and Punishment in Medieval Chinese Drama: Three Judge Pao Plays*

*83. Sang-Chul Suh, *Growth and Structural Changes in the Korean Economy, 1910–1940*
84. J. W. Dower, *Empire and Aftermath: Yoshida Shigeru and the Japanese Experience, 1878–1954*
85. Martin Collcutt, *Five Mountains: The Rinzai Zen Monastic Institution in Medieval Japan*
86. Kwang Suk Kim and Michael Roemer, *Growth and Structural Transformation*
87. Anne O. Krueger, *The Developmental Role of the Foreign Sector and Aid*
*88. Edwin S. Mills and Byung-Nak Song, *Urbanization and Urban Problems*
89. Sung Hwan Ban, Pal Yong Moon, and Dwight H. Perkins, *Rural Development*
*90. Noel F. McGinn, Donald R. Snodgrass, Yung Bong Kim, Shin-Bok Kim, and Quee-Young Kim, *Education and Development in Korea*
*91. Leroy P. Jones and Il SaKong, *Government, Business, and Entrepreneurship in Economic Development: The Korean Case*
92. Edward S. Mason, Dwight H. Perkins, Kwang Suk Kim, David C. Cole, Mahn Je Kim et al., *The Economic and Social Modernization of the Republic of Korea*
93. Robert Repetto, Tai Hwan Kwon, Son-Ung Kim, Dae Young Kim, John E. Sloboda, and Peter J. Donaldson, *Economic Development, Population Policy, and Demographic Transition in the Republic of Korea*
94. Parks M. Coble, Jr., *The Shanghai Capitalists and the Nationalist Government, 1927–1937*
95. Noriko Kamachi, *Reform in China: Huang Tsun-hsien and the Japanese Model*
96. Richard Wich, *Sino-Soviet Crisis Politics: A Study of Political Change and Communication*
97. Lillian M. Li, *China's Silk Trade: Traditional Industry in the Modern World, 1842–1937*
98. R. David Arkush, *Fei Xiaotong and Sociology in Revolutionary China*
*99. Kenneth Alan Grossberg, *Japan's Renaissance: The Politics of the Muromachi Bakufu*
100. James Reeve Pusey, *China and Charles Darwin*
101. Hoyt Cleveland Tillman, *Utilitarian Confucianism: Chen Liang's Challenge to Chu Hsi*
102. Thomas A. Stanley, *Ōsugi Sakae, Anarchist in Taishō Japan: The Creativity of the Ego*
103. Jonathan K. Ocko, *Bureaucratic Reform in Provincial China: Ting Jih-ch'ang in Restoration Kiangsu, 1867–1870*
104. James Reed, *The Missionary Mind and American East Asia Policy, 1911–1915*
105. Neil L. Waters, *Japan's Local Pragmatists: The Transition from Bakumatsu to Meiji in the Kawasaki Region*
106. David C. Cole and Yung Chul Park, *Financial Development in Korea, 1945–1978*
107. Roy Bahl, Chuk Kyo Kim, and Chong Kee Park, *Public Finances During the Korean Modernization Process*
108. William D. Wray, *Mitsubishi and the N.Y.K, 1870–1914: Business Strategy in the Japanese Shipping Industry*
109. Ralph William Huenemann, *The Dragon and the Iron Horse: The Economics of Railroads in China, 1876–1937*
*110. Benjamin A. Elman, *From Philosophy to Philology: Intellectual and Social Aspects of Change in Late Imperial China*

111. Jane Kate Leonard, *Wei Yüan and China's Rediscovery of the Maritime World*
112. Luke S. K. Kwong, *A Mosaic of the Hundred Days:. Personalities, Politics, and Ideas of 1898*
*113. John E. Wills, Jr., *Embassies and Illusions: Dutch and Portuguese Envoys to K'ang-hsi, 1666–1687*
114. Joshua A. Fogel, *Politics and Sinology: The Case of Naitō Konan (1866–1934)*
*115. Jeffrey C. Kinkley, ed., *After Mao: Chinese Literature and Society, 1978–1981*
116. C. Andrew Gerstle, *Circles of Fantasy: Convention in the Plays of Chikamatsu*
117. Andrew Gordon, *The Evolution of Labor Relations in Japan: Heavy Industry, 1853–1955*
*118. Daniel K. Gardner, *Chu Hsi and the "Ta Hsueh": Neo-Confucian Reflection on the Confucian Canon*
119. Christine Guth Kanda, *Shinzō: Hachiman Imagery and Its Development*
*120. Robert Borgen, *Sugawara no Michizane and the Early Heian Court*
121. Chang-tai Hung, *Going to the People: Chinese Intellectual and Folk Literature, 1918–1937*
*122. Michael A. Cusumano, *The Japanese Automobile Industry: Technology and Management at Nissan and Toyota*
123. Richard von Glahn, *The Country of Streams and Grottoes: Expansion, Settlement, and the Civilizing of the Sichuan Frontier in Song Times*
124. Steven D. Carter, *The Road to Komatsubara: A Classical Reading of the Renga Hyakuin*
125. Katherine F. Bruner, John K. Fairbank, and Richard T. Smith, *Entering China's Service: Robert Hart's Journals, 1854–1863*
126. Bob Tadashi Wakabayashi, *Anti-Foreignism and Western Learning in Early-Modern Japan: The "New Theses" of 1825*
127. Atsuko Hirai, *Individualism and Socialism: The Life and Thought of Kawai Eijirō (1891–1944)*
128. Ellen Widmer, *The Margins of Utopia: "Shui-hu hou-chuan" and the Literature of Ming Loyalism*
129. R. Kent Guy, *The Emperor's Four Treasuries: Scholars and the State in the Late Chien-lung Era*
130. Peter C. Perdue, *Exhausting the Earth: State and Peasant in Hunan, 1500–1850*
131. Susan Chan Egan, *A Latterday Confucian: Reminiscences of William Hung (1893–1980)*
132. James T. C. Liu, *China Turning Inward: Intellectual-Political Changes in the Early Twelfth Century*
*133. Paul A. Cohen, *Between Tradition and Modernity: Wang T'ao and Reform in Late Ching China*
134. Kate Wildman Nakai, *Shogunal Politics: Arai Hakuseki and the Premises of Tokugawa Rule*
*135. Parks M. Coble, *Facing Japan: Chinese Politics and Japanese Imperialism, 1931–1937*
*136. Jon L. Saari, *Legacies of Childhood: Growing Up Chinese in a Time of Crisis, 1890–1920*
137. Susan Downing Videen, *Tales of Heichū*

138. Heinz Morioka and Miyoko Sasaki, *Rakugo: The Popular Narrative Art of Japan*
139. Joshua A. Fogel, *Nakae Ushikichi in China: The Mourning of Spirit*
140. Alexander Barton Woodside, *Vietnam and the Chinese Model: A Comparative Study of Vietnamese and Chinese Government in the First Half of the Nineteenth Century*
*141. George Elison, *Deus Destroyed: The Image of Christianity in Early Modern Japan*
142. William D. Wray, ed., *Managing Industrial Enterprise: Cases from Japan's Prewar Experience*
*143. T'ung-tsu Ch'ü, *Local Government in China Under the Ching*
144. Marie Anchordoguy, *Computers, Inc.: Japan's Challenge to IBM*
145. Barbara Molony, *Technology and Investment: The Prewar Japanese Chemical Industry*
146. Mary Elizabeth Berry, *Hideyoshi*
147. Laura E. Hein, *Fueling Growth: The Energy Revolution and Economic Policy in Postwar Japan*
148. Wen-hsin Yeh, *The Alienated Academy: Culture and Politics in Republican China, 1919–1937*
149. Dru C. Gladney, *Muslim Chinese: Ethnic Nationalism in the People's Republic*
150. Merle Goldman and Paul A. Cohen, eds., *Ideas Across Cultures: Essays on Chinese Thought in Honor of Benjamin L Schwartz*
151. James M. Polachek, *The Inner Opium War*
152. Gail Lee Bernstein, *Japanese Marxist: A Portrait of Kawakami Hajime, 1879–1946*
*153. Lloyd E. Eastman, *The Abortive Revolution: China Under Nationalist Rule, 1927–1937*
154. Mark Mason, *American Multinationals and Japan: The Political Economy of Japanese Capital Controls, 1899–1980*
155. Richard J. Smith, John K. Fairbank, and Katherine F. Bruner, *Robert Hart and China's Early Modernization: His Journals, 1863–1866*
156. George J. Tanabe, Jr., *Myōe the Dreamkeeper: Fantasy and Knowledge in Kamakura Buddhism*
157. William Wayne Farris, *Heavenly Warriors: The Evolution of Japan's Military, 500–1300*
158. Yu-ming Shaw, *An American Missionary in China: John Leighton Stuart and Chinese-American Relations*
159. James B. Palais, *Politics and Policy in Traditional Korea*
*160. Douglas Reynolds, *China, 1898–1912: The Xinzheng Revolution and Japan*
161. Roger R. Thompson, *China's Local Councils in the Age of Constitutional Reform, 1898–1911*
162. William Johnston, *The Modern Epidemic: History of Tuberculosis in Japan*
163. Constantine Nomikos Vaporis, *Breaking Barriers: Travel and the State in Early Modern Japan*
164. Irmela Hijiya-Kirschnereit, *Rituals of Self-Revelation: Shishōsetsu as Literary Genre and Socio-Cultural Phenomenon*
165. James C. Baxter, *The Meiji Unification Through the Lens of Ishikawa Prefecture*
166. Thomas R. H. Havens, *Architects of Affluence: The Tsutsumi Family and the Seibu-Saison Enterprises in Twentieth-Century Japan*

167. Anthony Hood Chambers, *The Secret Window: Ideal Worlds in Tanizaki's Fiction*
168. Steven J. Ericson, *The Sound of the Whistle: Railroads and the State in Meiji Japan*
169. Andrew Edmund Goble, *Kenmu: Go-Daigo's Revolution*
170. Denise Potrzeba Lett, *In Pursuit of Status: The Making of South Korea's "New" Urban Middle Class*
171. Mimi Hall Yiengpruksawan, *Hiraizumi: Buddhist Art and Regional Politics in Twelfth-Century Japan*
172. Charles Shirō Inouye, *The Similitude of Blossoms: A Critical Biography of Izumi Kyōka (1873–1939), Japanese Novelist and Playwright*
173. Aviad E. Raz, *Riding the Black Ship: Japan and Tokyo Disneyland*
174. Deborah J. Milly, *Poverty, Equality, and Growth: The Politics of Economic Need in Postwar Japan*
175. See Heng Teow, *Japan's Cultural Policy Toward China, 1918–1931: A Comparative Perspective*
176. Michael A. Fuller, *An Introduction to Literary Chinese*
177. Frederick R. Dickinson, *War and National Reinvention: Japan in the Great War, 1914–1919*
178. John Solt, *Shredding the Tapestry of Meaning: The Poetry and Poetics of Kitasono Katue (1902–1978)*
179. Edward Pratt, *Japan's Protoindustrial Elite: The Economic Foundations of the Gōnō*
180. Atsuko Sakaki, *Recontextualizing Texts: Narrative Performance in Modern Japanese Fiction*
181. Soon-Won Park, *Colonial Industrialization and Labor in Korea: The Onoda Cement Factory*
182. JaHyun Kim Haboush and Martina Deuchler, *Culture and the State in Late Chosŏn Korea*
183. John W. Chaffee, *Branches of Heaven: A History of the Imperial Clan of Sung China*
184. Gi-Wook Shin and Michael Robinson, eds., *Colonial Modernity in Korea*
185. Nam-lin Hur, *Prayer and Play in Late Tokugawa Japan: Asakusa Sensōji and Edo Society*
186. Kristin Stapleton, *Civilizing Chengdu: Chinese Urban Reform, 1895–1937*
187. Hyung Il Pai, *Constructing "Korean" Origins: A Critical Review of Archaeology, Historiography, and Racial Myth in Korean State-Formation Theories*
188. Brian D. Ruppert, *Jewel in the Ashes: Buddha Relics and Power in Early Medieval Japan*
189. Susan Daruvala, *Zhou Zuoren and an Alternative Chinese Response to Modernity*
*190. James Z. Lee, *The Political Economy of a Frontier: Southwest China, 1250–1850*
191. Kerry Smith, *A Time of Crisis: Japan, the Great Depression, and Rural Revitalization*
192. Michael Lewis, *Becoming Apart: National Power and Local Politics in Toyama, 1868–1945*
193. William C. Kirby, Man-houng Lin, James Chin Shih, and David A. Pietz, eds., *State and Economy in Republican China: A Handbook for Scholars*
194. Timothy S. George, *Minamata: Pollution and the Struggle for Democracy in Postwar Japan*

195. Billy K. L. So, *Prosperity, Region, and Institutions in Maritime China: The South Fukien Pattern, 946–1368*
196. Yoshihisa Tak Matsusaka, *The Making of Japanese Manchuria, 1904–1932*
197. Maram Epstein, *Competing Discourses: Orthodoxy, Authenticity, and Engendered Meanings in Late Imperial Chinese Fiction*
198. Curtis J. Milhaupt, J. Mark Ramseyer, and Michael K. Young, eds. and comps., *Japanese Law in Context: Readings in Society, the Economy, and Politics*
199. Haruo Iguchi, *Unfinished Business: Ayukawa Yoshisuke and U.S.-Japan Relations, 1937–1952*
200. Scott Pearce, Audrey Spiro, and Patricia Ebrey, *Culture and Power in the Reconstitution of the Chinese Realm, 200–600*
201. Terry Kawashima, *Writing Margins: The Textual Construction of Gender in Heian and Kamakura Japan*
202. Martin W. Huang, *Desire and Fictional Narrative in Late Imperial China*
203. Robert S. Ross and Jiang Changbin, eds., *Re-examining the Cold War: U.S.-China Diplomacy, 1954–1973*
204. Guanhua Wang, *In Search of Justice: The 1905–1906 Chinese Anti-American Boycott*
205. David Schaberg, *A Patterned Past: Form and Thought in Early Chinese Historiography*
206. Christine Yano, *Tears of Longing: Nostalgia and the Nation in Japanese Popular Song*
207. Milena Doleželová-Velingerová and Oldřich Král, with Graham Sanders, eds., *The Appropriation of Cultural Capital: China's May Fourth Project*
208. Robert N. Huey, *The Making of 'Shinkokinshū'*
209. Lee Butler, *Emperor and Aristocracy in Japan, 1467–1680: Resilience and Renewal*
210. Suzanne Ogden, *Inklings of Democracy in China*
211. Kenneth J. Ruoff, *The People's Emperor: Democracy and the Japanese Monarchy, 1945–1995*
212. Haun Saussy, *Great Walls of Discourse and Other Adventures in Cultural China*
213. Aviad E. Raz, *Emotions at Work: Normative Control, Organizations, and Culture in Japan and America*
214. Rebecca E. Karl and Peter Zarrow, eds., *Rethinking the 1898 Reform Period: Political and Cultural Change in Late Qing China*
215. Kevin O'Rourke, *The Book of Korean Shijo*
216. Ezra F. Vogel, ed., *The Golden Age of the U.S.-China-Japan Triangle, 1972–1989*
217. Thomas A. Wilson, ed., *On Sacred Grounds: Culture, Society, Politics, and the Formation of the Cult of Confucius*
218. Donald S. Sutton, *Steps of Perfection: Exorcistic Performers and Chinese Religion in Twentieth-Century Taiwan*
219. Daqing Yang, *Technology of Empire: Telecommunications and Japanese Expansionism in Asia, 1883–1945*
220. Qianshen Bai, *Fu Shan's World: The Transformation of Chinese Calligraphy in the Seventeenth Century*
221. Paul Jakov Smith and Richard von Glahn, eds., *The Song-Yuan-Ming Transition in Chinese History*

222. Rania Huntington, *Alien Kind: Foxes and Late Imperial Chinese Narrative*
223. Jordan Sand, *House and Home in Modern Japan: Architecture, Domestic Space, and Bourgeois Culture, 1880–1930*
224. Karl Gerth, *China Made: Consumer Culture and the Creation of the Nation*
225. Xiaoshan Yang, *Metamorphosis of the Private Sphere: Gardens and Objects in Tang-Song Poetry*
226. Barbara Mittler, *A Newspaper for China? Power, Identity, and Change in Shanghai's News Media, 1872–1912*
227. Joyce A. Madancy, *The Troublesome Legacy of Commissioner Lin: The Opium Trade and Opium Suppression in Fujian Province, 1820s to 1920s*
228. John Makeham, *Transmitters and Creators: Chinese Commentators and Commentaries on the Analects*
229. Elisabeth Köll, *From Cotton Mill to Business Empire: The Emergence of Regional Enterprises in Modern China*
230. Emma Teng, *Taiwan's Imagined Geography: Chinese Colonial Travel Writing and Pictures, 1683–1895*
231. Wilt Idema and Beata Grant, *The Red Brush: Writing Women of Imperial China*
232. Eric C. Rath, *The Ethos of Noh: Actors and Their Art*
233. Elizabeth Remick, *Building Local States: China During the Republican and Post-Mao Eras*
234. Lynn Struve, ed., *The Qing Formation in World-Historical Time*
235. D. Max Moerman, *Localizing Paradise: Kumano Pilgrimage and the Religious Landscape of Premodern Japan*
236. Antonia Finnane, *Speaking of Yangzhou: A Chinese City, 1550–1850*
237. Brian Platt, *Burning and Building: Schooling and State Formation in Japan, 1750–1890*
238. Gail Bernstein, Andrew Gordon, and Kate Wildman Nakai, eds., *Public Spheres, Private Lives in Modern Japan, 1600–1950: Essays in Honor of Albert Craig*
239. Wu Hung and Katherine R. Tsiang, *Body and Face in Chinese Visual Culture*
240. Stephen Dodd, *Writing Home: Representations of the Native Place in Modern Japanese Literature*
241. David Anthony Bello, *Opium and the Limits of Empire: Drug Prohibition in the Chinese Interior, 1729–1850*
242. Hosea Hirata, *Discourses of Seduction: History, Evil, Desire, and Modern Japanese Literature*
243. Kyung Moon Hwang, *Beyond Birth: Social Status in the Emergence of Modern Korea*
244. Brian R. Dott, *Identity Reflections: Pilgrimages to Mount Tai in Late Imperial China*
245. Mark McNally, *Proving the Way: Conflict and Practice in the History of Japanese Nativism*
246. Yongping Wu, *A Political Explanation of Economic Growth: State Survival, Bureaucratic Politics, and Private Enterprises in the Making of Taiwan's Economy, 1950–1985*
247. Kyu Hyun Kim, *The Age of Visions and Arguments: Parliamentarianism and the National Public Sphere in Early Meiji Japan*

248. Zvi Ben-Dor Benite, *The Dao of Muhammad: A Cultural History of Muslims in Late Imperial China*
249. David Der-wei Wang and Shang Wei, eds., *Dynastic Crisis and Cultural Innovation: From the Late Ming to the Late Qing and Beyond*
250. Wilt L. Idema, Wai-yee Li, and Ellen Widmer, eds., *Trauma and Transcendence in Early Qing Literature*
251. Barbara Molony and Kathleen Uno, eds., *Gendering Modern Japanese History*
252. Hiroshi Aoyagi, *Islands of Eight Million Smiles: Idol Performance and Symbolic Production in Contemporary Japan*
253. Wai-yee Li, *The Readability of the Past in Early Chinese Historiography*
254. William C. Kirby, Robert S. Ross, and Gong Li, eds., *Normalization of U.S.-China Relations: An International History*
255. Ellen Gardner Nakamura, *Practical Pursuits: Takano Chōei, Takahashi Keisaku, and Western Medicine in Nineteenth-Century Japan*
256. Jonathan W. Best, *A History of the Early Korean Kingdom of Paekche, together with an annotated translation of* The Paekche Annals *of the* Samguk sagi
257. Liang Pan, *The United Nations in Japan's Foreign and Security Policymaking, 1945–1992: National Security, Party Politics, and International Status*
258. Richard Belsky, *Localities at the Center: Native Place, Space, and Power in Late Imperial Beijing*
259. Zwia Lipkin, *"Useless to the State": "Social Problems" and Social Engineering in Nationalist Nanjing, 1927–1937*
260. William O. Gardner, *Advertising Tower: Japanese Modernism and Modernity in the 1920s*
261. Stephen Owen, *The Making of Early Chinese Classical Poetry*
262. Martin J. Powers, *Pattern and Person: Ornament, Society, and Self in Classical China*
263. Anna M. Shields, *Crafting a Collection: The Cultural Contexts and Poetic Practice of the* Huajian ji 花間集 (*Collection from Among the Flowers*)
264. Stephen Owen, *The Late Tang: Chinese Poetry of the Mid-Ninth Century (827–860)*
265. Sara L. Friedman, *Intimate Politics: Marriage, the Market, and State Power in Southeastern China*
266. Patricia Buckley Ebrey and Maggie Bickford, *Emperor Huizong and Late Northern Song China: The Politics of Culture and the Culture of Politics*
267. Sophie Volpp, *Worldly Stage: Theatricality in Seventeenth-Century China*
268. Ellen Widmer, *The Beauty and the Book: Women and Fiction in Nineteenth-Century China*
269. Steven B. Miles, *The Sea of Learning: Mobility and Identity in Nineteenth-Century Guangzhou*
270. Lin Man-houng, *China Upside Down: Currency, Society, and Ideologies, 1808–1856*
271. Ronald Egan, *The Problem of Beauty: Aesthetic Thought and Pursuits in Northern Song Dynasty China*
272. Mark Halperin, *Out of the Cloister: Literati Perspectives on Buddhism in Sung China, 960–1279*

Harvard East Asian Monographs

273. Helen Dunstan, *State or Merchant? Political Economy and Political Process in 1740s China*
274. Sabina Knight, *The Heart of Time: Moral Agency in Twentieth-Century Chinese Fiction*
275. Timothy J. Van Compernolle, *The Uses of Memory: The Critique of Modernity in the Fiction of Higuchi Ichiyō*
276. Paul Rouzer, *A New Practical Primer of Literary Chinese*
277. Jonathan Zwicker, *Practices of the Sentimental Imagination: Melodrama, the Novel, and the Social Imaginary in Nineteenth-Century Japan*
278. Franziska Seraphim, *War Memory and Social Politics in Japan, 1945–2005*
279. Adam L. Kern, *Manga from the Floating World: Comicbook Culture and the* Kibyōshi *of Edo Japan*
280. Cynthia J. Brokaw, *Commerce in Culture: The Sibao Book Trade in the Qing and Republican Periods*
281. Eugene Y. Park, *Between Dreams and Reality: The Military Examination in Late Chosŏn Korea, 1600–1894*
282. Nam-lin Hur, *Death and Social Order in Tokugawa Japan: Buddhism, Anti-Christianity, and the* Danka *System*
283. Patricia M. Thornton, *Disciplining the State: Virtue, Violence, and State-Making in Modern China*
284. Vincent Goossaert, *The Taoists of Peking, 1800–1949: A Social History of Urban Clerics*
285. Peter Nickerson, *Taoism, Bureaucracy, and Popular Religion in Early Medieval China*
286. Charo B. D'Etcheverry, *Love After* The Tale of Genji*: Rewriting the World of the Shining Prince*
287. Michael G. Chang, *A Court on Horseback: Imperial Touring & the Construction of Qing Rule, 1680–1785*
288. Carol Richmond Tsang, *War and Faith:* Ikkō Ikki *in Late Muromachi Japan*
289. Hilde De Weerdt, *Competition over Content: Negotiating Standards for the Civil Service Examinations in Imperial China (1127–1279)*
290. Eve Zimmerman, *Out of the Alleyway: Nakagami Kenji and the Poetics of Outcaste Fiction*
291. Robert Culp, *Articulating Citizenship: Civic Education and Student Politics in Southeastern China, 1912–1940*
292. Richard J. Smethurst, *From Foot Soldier to Finance Minister: Takahashi Korekiyo, Japan's Keynes*
293. John E. Herman, *Amid the Clouds and Mist: China's Colonization of Guizhou, 1200–1700*
294. Tomoko Shiroyama, *China During the Great Depression: Market, State, and the World Economy, 1929–1937*
295. Kirk W. Larsen, *Tradition, Treaties and Trade: Qing Imperialism and Chosŏn Korea, 1850–1910*
296. Gregory Golley, *When Our Eyes No Longer See: Realism, Science, and Ecology in Japanese Literary Modernism*

297. Barbara Ambros, *Emplacing a Pilgrimage: The Ōyama Cult and Regional Religion in Early Modern Japan*
298. Rebecca Suter, *The Japanization of Modernity: Murakami Haruki between Japan and the United States*
299. Yuma Totani, *The Tokyo War Crimes Trial: The Pursuit of Justice in the Wake of World War II*
300. Linda Isako Angst, *In a Dark Time: Memory, Community, and Gendered Nationalism in Postwar Okinawa*
301. David M. Robinson, ed., *Culture, Courtiers, and Competition: The Ming Court (1368–1644)*
302. Calvin Chen, *Some Assembly Required: Work, Community, and Politics in China's Rural Enterprises*
303. Sem Vermeersch, *The Power of the Buddhas: The Politics of Buddhism During the Koryŏ Dynasty* (918–1392)
304. Tina Lu, *Accidental Incest, Filial Cannibalism, and Other Peculiar Encounters in Late Imperial Chinese Literature*
305. Chang Woei Ong, *Men of Letters Within the Passes: Guanzhong Literati in Chinese History, 907–1911*
306. Wendy Swartz, *Reading Tao Yuanming: Shifting Paradigms of Historical Reception (427–1900)*
307. Peter K. Bol, *Neo-Confucianism in History*
308. Carlos Rojas, *The Naked Gaze: Reflections on Chinese Modernity*
309. Kelly H. Chong, *Deliverance and Submission: Evangelical Women and the Negotiation of Patriarchy in South Korea*
310. Rachel DiNitto, *Uchida Hyakken: A Critique of Modernity and Militarism in Prewar Japan*
311. Jeffrey Snyder-Reinke, *Dry Spells: State Rainmaking and Local Governance in Late Imperial China*
312. Jay Dautcher, *Down a Narrow Road: Identity and Masculinity in a Uyghur Community in Xinjiang China*
313. Xun Liu, *Daoist Modern: Innovation, Lay Practice, and the Community of Inner Alchemy in Republican Shanghai*
314. Jacob Eyferth, *Eating Rice from Bamboo Roots: The Social History of a Community of Handicraft Papermakers in Rural Sichuan, 1920–2000*
315. David Johnson, *Spectacle and Sacrifice: The Ritual Foundations of Village Life in North China*
316. James Robson, *Power of Place: The Religious Landscape of the Southern Sacred Peak (Nanyue 南嶽) in Medieval China*
317. Lori Watt, *When Empire Comes Home: Repatriation and Reintegration in Postwar Japan*
318. James Dorsey, *Critical Aesthetics: Kobayashi Hideo, Modernity, and Wartime Japan*
319. Christopher Bolton, *Sublime Voices: The Fictional Science and Scientific Fiction of Abe Kōbō*
320. Si-yen Fei, *Negotiating Urban Space: Urbanization and Late Ming Nanjing*

321. Christopher Gerteis, *Gender Struggles: Wage-Earning Women and Male-Dominated Unions in Postwar Japan*
322. Rebecca Nedostup, *Superstitious Regimes: Religion and the Politics of Chinese Modernity*
323. Lucien Bianco, *Wretched Rebels: Rural Disturbances on the Eve of the Chinese Revolution*
324. Cathryn H. Clayton, *Sovereignty at the Edge: Macau and the Question of Chineseness*
325. Micah S. Muscolino, *Fishing Wars and Environmental Change in Late Imperial and Modern China*
326. Robert I. Hellyer, *Defining Engagement: Japan and Global Contexts, 1750–1868*
327. Robert Ashmore, *The Transport of Reading: Text and Understanding in the World of Tao Qian (365–427)*
328. Mark A. Jones, *Children as Treasures: Childhood and the Middle Class in Early Twentieth Century Japan*
329. Miryam Sas, *Experimental Arts in Postwar Japan: Moments of Encounter, Engagement, and Imagined Return*
330. H. Mack Horton, *Traversing the Frontier: The* Man'yōshū *Account of a Japanese Mission to Silla in 736–737*
331. Dennis J. Frost, *Seeing Stars: Sports Celebrity, Identity, and Body Culture in Modern Japan*
332. Marnie S. Anderson, *A Place in Public: Women's Rights in Meiji Japan*
333. Peter Mauch, *Sailor Diplomat: Nomura Kichisaburō and the Japanese-American War*
334. Ethan Isaac Segal, *Coins, Trade, and the State: Economic Growth in Early Medieval Japan*
335. David B. Lurie, *Realms of Literacy: Early Japan and the History of Writing*
336. Lillian Lan-ying Tseng, *Picturing Heaven in Early China*
337. Jun Uchida, *Brokers of Empire: Japanese Settler Colonialism in Korea, 1876–1945*
338. Patricia L. Maclachlan, *The People's Post Office: The History and Politics of the Japanese Postal System, 1871–2010*
339. Michael Schiltz, *The Money Doctors from Japan: Finance, Imperialism, and the Building of the Yen Bloc, 1895–1937*
340. Daqing Yang, Jie Liu, Hiroshi Mitani, and Andrew Gordon, eds., *Toward a History Beyond Borders: Contentious Issues in Sino-Japanese Relations*
341. Sonia Ryang, *Reading North Korea: An Ethnological Inquiry*
342. Susan Huang, *Picturing the True Form: Daoist Visual Culture in Traditional China*
343. Barbara Mittler, *A Continuous Revolution: Making Sense of Cultural Revolution Culture*
344. Hwansoo Ilmee Kim, *Empire of the Dharma: Korean and Japanese Buddhism, 1877–1912*
345. Satoru Saito, *Detective Fiction and the Rise of the Japanese Novel, 1880–1930*
346. Jung-Sun N. Han, *An Imperial Path to Modernity: Yoshino Sakuzō and a New Liberal Order in East Asia, 1905–1937*
347. Atsuko Hirai, *Government by Mourning: Death and Political Integration in Japan, 1603–1912*
348. Darryl E. Flaherty, *Public Law, Private Practice: Politics, Profit, and the Legal Profession in Nineteenth-Century Japan*

349. Jeffrey Paul Bayliss, *On the Margins of Empire: Buraku and Korean Identity in Prewar and Wartime Japan*
350. Barry Eichengreen, Dwight H. Perkins, and Kwanho Shin, *From Miracle to Maturity: The Growth of the Korean Economy*
351. Michel Mohr, *Buddhism, Unitarianism, and the Meiji Competition for Universality*
352. J. Keith Vincent, *Two-Timing Modernity: Homosocial Narrative in Modern Japanese Fiction*
353. Suzanne G. O'Brien, *Customizing Daily Life: Representing and Reforming Customs in Nineteenth-Century Japan*
354. Chong-Bum An and Barry Bosworth, *Income Inequality in Korea: An Analysis of Trends, Causes, and Answers*
355. Jamie L. Newhard, *Knowing the Amorous Man: A History of Scholarship on* Tales of Ise
356. Sho Konishi, *Anarchist Modernity: Cooperatism and Japanese-Russian Intellectual Relations in Modern Japan*
357. Christopher P. Hanscom, *The Real Modern: Literary Modernism and the Crisis of Representation in Colonial Korea*
358. Michael Wert, *Meiji Restoration Losers: Memory and Tokugawa Supporters in Modern Japan*
359. Garret P. S. Olberding, ed., *Facing the Monarch: Modes of Advice in the Early Chinese Court*